HISTORICAL DREADNOUGHTS

HISTORICAL DREADNOUGHTS

*Arthur Marder, Stephen Roskill and
Battles for Naval History*

Barry Gough

PUBLISHING

Copyright © Barry Gough 2010

First published in Great Britain in 2010 by
Seaforth Publishing,
Pen & Sword Books Ltd,
47 Church Street
Barnsley S70 2AS

www.seaforthpublishing.com

British Library Cataloguing in Publication Data
A catalogue record for this book is available from the British Library

ISBN 978 1 84832 077 2

All rights reserved. No part of this publication may be reproduced or transmitted in any form
or by any means, electronic or mechanical, including photocopying, recording,
or any information storage and retrieval system, without prior permission in writing
of both the copyright owner and the above publisher.

The right of Barry Gough to be identified as the author of this work has been asserted
by him in accordance with the Copyright, Designs and Patents Act 1988.

Designed and typeset by M.A.T.S., Leigh-on-Sea, Essex
Printed and bound in Great Britain by CPI Antony Rowe, Great Britain

Contents

List of Illustrations		vii
Preface		ix
Principal Persons		xv

Part One: Historians in the Making

1	Marder: Examining Britannia's Anatomy	3
2	Roskill: Guns Ashore and Afloat	40
3	Marder's Admirable Admirals: Richmond and Fisher	68
4	Marder: The Ali Baba of Historical Studies	101
5	Roskill and the Politics of Official History	134
6	Marder Ascendant: Swaying Palms, Instant University, and Dreaming Spires	172

Part Two: Collision Courses

7	The Fight for Hankey's Secrets	195
8	Historians at War: Quarrels over Churchill and Admirals	216
9	Roskill: Refighting Jutland	252

Part Three: Closings

10	Rising Sun and California Sunset: Marder's Farewell to History	279
11	Roskill at Churchill College: The Laurels and the Legacy	297
Epilogue	Our Historical Dreadnoughts	316
Notes		322
Bibliography		338
Index		355

Also by the same author

The Royal Navy and the Northwest Coast
To the Pacific and Arctic with Beechey
The Northwest Coast: British Navigation, Trade and Discoveries
Gunboat Frontier
HMCS HAIDA: Battle Ensign Flying
Fighting Sail on Lake Huron and Georgian Bay
Fortune's a River: Collision of Empires in Northwest America

LIST OF ILLUSTRATIONS
(*between pages 206 and 207*)

1. Marder's influences
William L. Langer, Harvard historian and deputy director of the CIA. *Photo Fabian Bacharach*
Admiral Sir Herbert Richmond. Portrait by Wilfred Gabriel de Glehn. *By courtesy of the Masters, Fellows and Scholars of Downing College, Cambridge*
Peter Gretton, when in command of the destroyer *Wolverine*.
Peter Kemp. *Photo Daniel Forster*

2. Go to the sources
Discussing Admiralty documents access: Vice Admiral Sir Geoffrey Barnard, Vice Admiral Sir Peter Gretton, and Marder, 1960. *By courtesy of the Marder family*
Marder beneath the great guns of Admiral Tōgō's *Mikasa*, triumphant at Tsushima. *By courtesy of the Marder family*

3. When naval history made news
Admiral Lord Fisher writing a fiery letter while a naval rating on fire rescue detail stands by. *By courtesy of the* Evening Standard
Marder photographed in Hyde Park on the eve of the Jutland 50th anniversary. *By courtesy of the* Evening Standard
Marder en route to the BBC Studios reads reviews of his *Jutland and After*, 31 May 1966. *By courtesy of the Marder family*

4. Success opens doors
Marder at his desk at the University of California, Irvine, 1975. *By courtesy of the Marder family*
At the Admiralty 1979: First Sea Lord Admiral Sir Terence Lewin (later Baron Lewin of Greenwich) with, left, Lady Lewin and, right, Jan and Arthur Marder. *By courtesy of the Marder family*
Admiral of the Fleet the Earl Mountbatten of Burma with Marder, at Broadlands, 1979. *By courtesy of the Marder family*

5. **The young naval officer**
Stephen Roskill, about 1920, in naval uniform. *By courtesy of Nicholas Roskill*
Elizabeth and Stephen Roskill on the occasion of their wedding, 12 August 1930. The dalmatian was Elizabeth's, the spaniel Stephen's. *By courtesy of Nicholas Roskill*

6. **Naval command**
Captain Stephen Roskill, RN, when in command HMNZS *Leander*. *By courtesy of Nicholas Roskill*
A pre-war view of the cruiser HMS *Leander*, without camouflage and carrying a seaplane. She was loaned to the Royal New Zealand Navy in 1941. *By courtesy of Nicholas Roskill*

7. **Controversial admirals, controversial books**
Dustjacket of Roskill's *Churchill and the Admirals*.
Dustjacket of Marder's *From the Dreadnought to Scapa Flow, Volume III: Jutland and After*.
Admiral Sir David Beatty, when Commander-in-Chief, Grand Fleet, 1916-19. Portrait by Sir Arthur Cope. *National Maritime Museum BHC2537*
Admiral of the Fleet Sir Dudley Pound. Portrait by Captain A. D. Wales-Smith. *National Maritime Museum BHC2960*

8. **Academic honours**
The Roskill brothers on the occasion of the Encaenia, and the awarding of an honorary doctorate to Stephen, 25 June 1980. Left to right: Ashton, Stephen, Oliver and Eustace. *By courtesy of Nicholas Roskill*
Captain Stephen Roskill, RN, Life Fellow of Churchill College, Cambridge. By Michael Noakes. Portrait from the Roskill Library. *By courtesy of the artist and the Master, Fellows and Scholars of Churchill College*

The English admirals are not those who built up the power of their country. If England has had Rodney, Hawke and Nelson, we have had Duquesne, Tourville and Suffren. It is that impersonal being that is called the English Admiralty; it is that which has prepared all the elements of British greatness; it is that which has known how to create homogeneous fleets, to arm them, equip them, enlist crews for them (God knows at the price of what sacrifices), and to place at their head the most capable men. Its severity has often been excessive; but, with admirals for its support.

Commander René Davelny,
The Genius of Naval Warfare (1909).

Preface

IN the course of modern history, Britain's Royal Navy has been a powerful instrument with an illustrious reputation. As an arbiter in world affairs, a guardian of seaborne trade, and a shield for the British Isles and the British Empire, the Navy – the Senior Service of Britain's Armed Forces – played a prominent role in the history of the world from the sixteenth century on, from the years of Queen Elizabeth I to the present. However, in the seven decades beginning with 1880, it faced its severest trials and tribulations. Britain's paramount position was then beset by forces largely beyond the control of the nation and empire. New foreign rivals appeared on the world stage with aggressive intent. Two great wars were to prove the supreme test of the fleet and the nation.

Two remarkable historians of great stature took up the task of writing the history of the Royal Navy in these turbulent and trying years. They did so at a time when few if any serious historical studies had been undertaken of the modern Navy. This book is their story.

The present work began as one thing – a biography of Professor Arthur Marder – and ended up as something quite different, both in scope and in design: a sort of double life, as it were, of Marder and of his famous sparring partner, Captain Stephen Roskill, Royal Navy. As the course of my research made clear, Marder and Roskill were then, as they are now here in the telling and retelling, as different in personality and character as could be imagined. Beyond this, their abiding quest for pre-eminence in the field, and the grave animosity that developed between them following an initial quarrel – over the use of the diaries of 'the man of secrets', Lord Hankey – made for a historians' battle the like of which has seldom been seen and recorded (the battle between Sir Geoffrey Elton and J.H. Hexter, likewise acknowledged experts on Tudor English history, and that between Hugh Trevor-Roper and A.J.P. Taylor are two that come to mind). Marder without Roskill, or perhaps the opposite, would have been like Hamlet without the Ghost.

Marder and Roskill died within two years of one another. The first was from academia, the other from the Service. One was American, the other

English. The former, first in the field, was abundantly successful in the historical profession and academic life before the other entered the lists. Of the two, Marder was the more *analytical* and Roskill was the more *strategic* in thinking. Marder was pointillist in style, layering on well-sorted evidence and building up his case; Roskill was magisterial but had a slight tendency to get off track. Doubtless the personality, character, disposition, and health of a historian shape his ability to write on a subject. In Marder and Roskill, their unique characteristics profoundly affected their work. Each in his own way made substantial contributions to the annals of history. We are the better for the rich tapestry to which they both contributed magnificent strands.

In the end, Roskill, who was in effect an 'official historian' and an exemplary practitioner in that branch of historical inquiry, found hard to bear the encroachments, both persistent and unrelenting, of his celebrated precursor. As correspondence between them and interviews with those who knew either of them (or even both) now makes clear, a great, swelling drama was being acted out between them. Roskill engaged a large supporting cast. Marder refused to counter with such an act. This dialectic, aspects of which appeared most notably in the *Times Literary Supplement*, can now be revealed more fully from materials in their private papers, which make evident that their public spat – remembered to this day by naval historians and others – had deep, private dimensions.

At the time, some observers bemoaned the disputatious nature of the quarrel, and some have thought that history would have been better served if the two had patched up their differences. But nothing could be done to change the direction that they took, so strong-willed was each of the players. The record also shows the paucity of the argument that, had they not had this quarrel, there would have been a better sharing of historical materials. Almost to the end, the pair responded to each other's needs for evidence and exchanged documents on loan. A public war did not prohibit scholarly exchange. The fight may appear unseemly, but, in fact, it had important historical legacies: it obliged each of the contenders to do further research to find, present and demonstrate documentary support for his arguments.

From the outset, I have worked diligently to maintain an impartial view. We need, I contend, more great historians such as Marder and Roskill, to say nothing of audiences willing to read good history. Had these two persons never met and quarrelled, their legacies would be profound and enduring in any event. Their vast and vital corpus of work, detailed in the Bibliography at the end of this book, adds spice as well as true historical and personal interest to an unusual episode in the history of the modern world and of the Royal Navy in particular. Biographies of historians can make for compelling reading, as John Clive's *Macaulay* and David Cannadine's *G.M. Trevelyan* make clear; and how historians pursue their calling as detectives of the past tells us much about the way in which human beings deal with that past and portray it to the present.

Neither Marder nor Roskill were known to me personally, though I was introduced to each on at least one occasion. This was in the late 1960s, when both were in their prime. I recollect Marder as impeccably, even nattily, dressed, when I had occasion to hear his August 1966 post-lunch address to the American Historical Association in Portland, Oregon. The subject was 'That Hamilton Woman: Clio and Emma Reconciled', and he spoke with the same self-assurance that was evident in his writings. I remember Roskill best from a 1968 council meeting of the Navy Records Society (NRS) at the old Public Record Office in Chancery Lane, London. His deafness seemed so restricting that it quite hindered any council dealings of the day, though he carried heavy executive responsibilities nonetheless. At the time, he was dealing with the demanding and difficult issue of getting what became known as the 'Harper Narrative' published by the Navy Records Society and fending off critics of the project, notably the 2nd Earl Beatty, son of the famous admiral.

In gathering materials for this book I have accumulated many debts. My first is to Professor Samuel Clyde McCulloch and his wife, Sally. Our friendship predates this book by decades but grew in depth in the mid-1990s when, in conversation, I enquired of Sam what papers Marder had left at University of California, Irvine (UCI, as it is commonly called), where they had been colleagues. 'Come to the university and see,' he replied, knowing as he did so that a huge, untouched treasure trove awaited me. That took me to the splendid UCI, in Orange County. Five visits later – invariably coordinated (I confess) to escape the chilliest weeks of the Canadian winter – I completed the survey of the Marder Papers, thirty-five file boxes in all. Throughout the demands of documentary research, Sam and Sally provided counsel and filled in all the details about the personalities of the great 'instant university' (the term is Sam's and he used it in his recent history of UCI).

My research was begun not too soon, for already persons who knew Marder had passed away. All the same, I was just in time to probe the memories of surviving informants. I was enriched by discussions with two of Marder's friends, John S. Galbraith, historian of the British Empire, and Henry Cord Meyer, historian of Germany and of air ships and founding chairman of the Department of History at UCI. Both have died since this work was commenced. Meyer knew Marder from wartime days in the Office of Strategic Services (OSS). I also benefited from discussions with Marder's colleagues Spencer Olin, Keith Nelson, Alan Lawson, and Richard Hufbauer, and with a teaching assistant of those times, Kenneth Hagan, the naval scholar. From Marder's PhD students at UCI, I have learned much. Gerry Jordan lent me his Marder file. John Horsfield provided encouragement. So did Mark Jacobsen. I am grateful to them for their comments on sections of the text. At UCI Libraries, Jackie M. Dooley, Steve MacLeod and Andrew Jones, of Special Collections and University Archives, guided me through the research. At the University of California, San Diego, Mandeville Special Collections, Lynda Claassen, eased my research in John S. Galbraith fonds.

In Honolulu and at the University of Hawaii, where Marder was on faculty before his move to California, I queried the lawyer who acted in the damages case of his incinerated documents, Axel Ornelles, and spoke with colleagues, students, and friends of Marder, notably George Akida, Cedric Cowing, Daniel Kwok, and John Stephan. My quest there, and at UCI as well, led me to so many near contemporaries that I felt much like an anthropologist among historians. Perhaps I should not have been surprised, but when I made my inquiries in Honolulu in 2007 personal memories of Marder's time were still vivid among those who had known him there.

Many of the great fighting seamen of the recent past made their appearance in the letters I sifted through: admirals all — Bruce Fraser, William Chalmers, Ernle Chatfield, Frederic Dreyer, William James, William Jameson, and Louis Mountbatten, to name a few. Their correspondence to Marder was rich, frank, and full — and it peppers this narrative. Marder's files led me to Captain Anthony B. Sainsbury, who in 1961 had visited Marder in California and later received him in London. Subsequent correspondence with Sainsbury led me to the second half of the project. From the late Alan Pearsall, formerly of the National Maritime Museum, who was a great help and inspiration to me, I learned that Sainsbury used to speak to Roskill like an uncle, and I know that Sainsbury also treated Marder with avuncular consideration. Thus, I owe much to Sainsbury's insistence that both historians be given their due, and I hope that at the end of the day the whole edifice balances. Certainly, that has been my intent.

In London, Greenwich, Oxford, and Cambridge, I have worked in a number of public and private collections. I am grateful to the National Maritime Museum for a Caird Fellowship that allowed me to search the Beatty, Fraser, Gretton and other papers. Lawrence Phillips has been of immeasurable help, and words cannot be found to express my deep gratitude for his guidance, especially in darkest days. Patricia Methven and the Liddell Hart Centre for Military Archives at King's College, London, opened the G.S. Graham files. Mrs Mary Graham provided additional correspondence and reminiscences of Graham's friendship with Marder. Noble Frankland, Jock Gardner, the late John Grenville, Richard Harding, Peter Hore, Roger Knight, Andrew Lambert, Hugh Murphy, Ian Nish, the late Mary Z. Pain, Nicholas Rodger, and Roderick Suddaby are among the many who have helped. I owe to the late Admiral Sir Arthur Hezlett his personal reflections about the Bikini Atoll atomic trials.

At Churchill College, Cambridge, where Roskill was a fellow, Dr Piers Brendon and Allen Packwood, successive keepers of the Churchill Archives Centre, guided my research. Correlli Barnett, Marion Stewart, and Michael Hoskin are among others who helped. My experience researching at Churchill College differed from that in Irvine. For, whereas Marder was only a distant memory in Irvine and his huge archive there (with a rich library of naval history, including microfilms) largely unused – I was the first to have consulted them – Roskill reigns supreme at Churchill: the research room is named in his memory, his books line the walls, his documents are neatly calendared, a portrait of him is prominently displayed, an exhibition of his life has been held, and a biennial lecture is given in his honour. His reputation grows with the years. Roskill is regarded as one of the college's founding fathers. He provided the energy and commitment to build an archive of statecraft and military art. I thank the Master and Fellows of Churchill College for twice electing me an archives by-fellow.

This work could not have been completed without the aid of many others. I wish to thank especially Robin Brodhurst, David Cannadine, Andrew Cook, John Ehrman, Sir Michael Howard, Roger Louis, and Zara Steiner. For additional assistance on Marder research, I thank Robert W. Smith of the University of Oregon, Frank K. Lorenz of Hamilton College, the late 2nd Lord Chatfield of Victoria, British Columbia, Anthony Simmonds of Greenwich, England, and several of Marder's former students, including J.W. Cahill. Of special value to my work on Marder's early life were his friends or Harvard acquaintances Josephine Massell, Martha Paisner, Miriam Emden, and Helen Rutstein Baker. Suzanne Sigman and Samantha Harrington unearthed early Boston school records and Michelle Gachette brought to my attention a number of items at the Harvard University Archives. Jenny Duke, former editor at UCI, Anna Sander of Balliol College, and Alice Millea of Oxford University Press Archives provided historical gems. In addition to those mentioned, I wish to thank Dean Allard, Christoper Bell, Sadao Asada, Kenneth Cozens, Roger Dingman, Rob Davison, Nicholas d'Ombrain, Jan Drent, Penney Edwards, James Goldrick, William Glover, Vice Admiral Mike Gretton, Michael Hadley, Paul G. Halpern, Kenneth Hansen, John Hattendorf, Judy Hough, Wilfred Lund, Chris Madsen, Richard Mayne, Marc

Milner, the late Richard Ollard, the late Tom Pocock, David Ramsay, Eugene Rasor, Dean Ruffilli, Roger Sarty, Donald Schurman, Matthew Seligmann, Jon Sumida, Tim Travers, and Michael J. Whitby. Lee-Anne Stack provided photographic help.

To the families I extend my thanks, more particularly to Arthur's children Tod Marder, Toni Kaplan, and Kevin Marder, his grandson Gregory Kaplan, his sister-in-law Bobbie Marder, and still others with more distant connections, as well as Nicholas Roskill, son of Stephen, and Julian Roskill. I have benefited from their advice and counsel. Nicholas Roskill had his father's 1975 text recounting the dispute with Marder 'released' from its secrecy embargo so that I could use it here. For this generous act, and for comments on sections of the text read in draft, I am grateful. Likewise, I am thankful to him for the freedom that he has granted me in interpreting the life of his father. Wherever possible I have selected photographs from the respective family albums, and thanks are due for permission to publish them here.

To aid the reader I have provided a list of Principal Persons in alphabetical order. In the Bibliography, the books and articles of Marder and Roskill are listed in chronological order. The first portion of the book treats the parallel lives, beginning with Marder, moving on to Roskill as 'official historian', and concluding with Marder's relocation to the University of Hawaii. The second section begins with the genesis of the quarrel and moves successively through the disputatious arguments over Churchill and the admirals, much of it set out in the *Times Literary Supplement*, where the letters exchanged by the duelling historians are tribute to what editor Bernard Levin dismissed too lightly as 'academic bitchiness'. The third and final section portrays Marder and Roskill in their final years, and ends with an appraisal of their contributions to historical writing. I have not included Stephen Roskill's differences with David Irving over the disaster of the Russian Convoy PQ.17, an essentially legal matter lying outside the bounds of this work.

I thank my wife, Marilyn, for her support. To my editor, Curtis Fahey, I extend my gratitude for his aid in sharpening the arguments presented here and for much else. This work owes so much to Rob Gardiner and his team, my publishing partners in this enterprise.

In closing, I might say that I leave this subject with regret, for the literary trail has been an exciting and compelling one. I alone am responsible for any errors, whether of fact or interpretation, that remain.

BARRY GOUGH
VICTORIA, BRITISH COLUMBIA

Principal Persons

The 3rd Earl Beatty: who mistakenly grants Roskill copyright clearance to use his grandfather's papers and unwittingly creates a nightmare scenario.

Sir Norman Brook (Lord Normanbrook): secretary to the Cabinet Office, who mediates between Winston Churchill and Roskill in a clash of historical judgements over Roskill's *War at Sea*.

Professor Sir James Butler: historian and fellow of Trinity College, Cambridge, who, as editor of the Official War Histories of the Second World War, steers Roskill's typescripts through the crooked corridors of power.

Sir Winston Spencer Churchill: statesman and historian, who haunts the margins of Roskill's 'official history' and seeks to curb his judgements, with some success.

Sir John Cockcroft: atomic-secrets specialist, first master of Churchill College, who welcomes Roskill to an academic fold peopled by scientists.

Alvin Coox: historian of Japanese military affairs, who speeds Marder's research for his last book, on the Royal Navy and the Imperial Japanese Navy.

Captain John Creswell, Royal Navy (retired): historian of naval tactics who proposes a book, 'Control of Sea Communications', that eventually becomes Roskill's *War at Sea*; avuncular in manner, he steps forward (though always behind the scenes) to become a main prop for Marder.

Geoffrey Cumberlege: publisher of Oxford University Press, who snatches Marder from the disappointed Jonathan Cape.

John Ehrman: noted historian and fellow 'official historian' who befriends Roskill at the Cabinet Office and in his last, agonizing days.

Vice Admiral Sir Peter Gretton: former escort commander and noted historian on naval matters, including Churchill and the Royal Navy; provides sympathetic aid and counsel to Marder when his texts are incinerated.

Nina, Dowager Duchess of Hamilton: intimate friend of the late Admiral Lord Fisher and guardian of his letters, who opens the vaults of literary gold to Marder.

Lieutenant Commander Peter Kemp, Royal Navy (retired): submariner, editorial staff of *The Times*, and in Naval Intelligence Division during the Second World War; later head of the Naval Historical Branch and Naval Librarian in the Ministry of Defence; high profile arch-Marderite who guides his research and vets his manuscripts.

Sherman Kent: Yale historian of France, who forces Marder's exit from Research & Analysis, a precursor of the CIA.

Stephen King-Hall: naval officer, writer, and future MP, who introduces Roskill to analytical research.

William Langer: dean of international historians, Marder's Harvard mentor, who takes him into Research & Analysis.

Sir Basil Liddell Hart: noted military historian and strategist, who engages Roskill in discussion about the trials of 'official history' and shapes Marder's thinking about the Dardanelles and about Churchill as war leader.

Samuel Clyde McCulloch: historian and academic administrator, who hires Marder in California on advice from fellow historian John S. Galbraith, then backs his rising star against campus turmoil.

Arthur J. Marder: internationally famous historian, known especially but not exclusively for his five-volume history of the Royal Navy in the First World War.

Henry Cord Meyer: historian and friend of Marder, who strangely foresees Marder's work on Admiral 'Jacky' Fisher and also on the Imperial Japanese Navy.

Henry Allen Moe: head of the John Simon Guggenheim Foundation in New York, guardian angel of academic philanthropy, who secretly proposes Marder for an Oxford professorship.

Earl Mountbatten of Burma: admiral of the fleet, who parries unsuccessfully Roskill's challenge regarding his powers as supreme commander, South East Asia; devoted aide to Marder.

Richard Ollard: judicious editor at the publisher William Collins, historian himself, and stout defender of Roskill against the trustees of the 2nd Lord Beatty, though critical of Roskill's account of his relationship with Marder.

Admiral Sir Herbert Richmond: historian of statesmen and sea power, who grants Marder his wish to examine his explosive, behind-the-scenes diaries.

PRINCIPAL PERSONS

Kenneth Rose: biographer, man of letters and journalist, astute bystander to personal quarrels, and newspaper commentator on the Marder-Roskill dispute.

Stephen Roskill: naval officer and historian of the Royal Navy, celebrated worldwide as the official historian of the navy in the Second World War.

Captain Anthony B. Sainsbury: historian, trustee of the *Naval Review*, judicious reviewer, who befriends Marder and Roskill in like fashion and attempts mediation between the quarrelling duo.

Sir Eric Seal: principal secretary to the first lord of the Admiralty, Churchill, who later seeks to expose the shortcomings of Roskill's work and lives long enough to alert Marder to the same.

A.J.P. Taylor: stormy petrel of British historians, broadcaster and journalist, a literary king-maker who rhapsodizes about Marder in reviews and on the BBC.

Part One

Historians in the Making

Chapter 1

Marder: Examining Britannia's Anatomy

LEGEND has it that an American scholar, having just arrived in England moments before, burst into the Students' Room of the British Museum Library, panting in exhaustion. He pleaded to the attendant that his order for materials be given exceptional, overwhelming priority. 'I haven't a moment to lose!' he gasped. 'I've only got four months!'[1] That scholar was Arthur Marder, and the date probably 1959, when he was writing his history of the Royal Navy from 1904 to 1919. This was a typical entry of Marder to a public research institution, and the story would have been as true for him if he were a postgraduate student or a senior scholar writing the last of his books. Speed was of the essence with Marder, to which was combined assiduousness in tracking down documents and discernment about the subject on which he was working. In due course he earned the august title, as the *Times Literary Supplement* (*TLS*) said, of 'founding-father of modern naval history'. On this score, Marder himself was more self-effacing. When queried on the matter by a writer from the London *Evening Standard*, he replied, 'I am America's greatest expert on Lady Hamilton. I'm even going to read a paper about her at a luncheon, proving that she is not nearly as black as she has been painted.'[2] Marder, true to form, might have talked flippantly about Nelson's famous love Emma but he would then turn the conversation in complete earnest to the Battle of Jutland, or some such. What always amused reporters, critics, and rivals was that Marder did his work from non-English and very American bases – Boston, Hawaii, or California. The road to the study of the Battle of Jutland in the First World War, and of many years before and after, was a long one for Marder, by no means easy. In fact, it was dictated by the whims of fate.

Sir John Keegan, the military historian, once questioned why Britain's two greatest naval historians had been American. He placed the name of Arthur Marder beside that of Admiral Alfred Thayer Mahan.[3] Indeed, it is a curious fact that the first great modern professional historian of the Royal Navy should have come from Boston, a cradle of the American Revolution, and from a poor immigrant family.

Marder was singular in appearance.[4] He was built on a powerful frame, though he was neither tall nor corpulent. The hair on his head thinned quickly towards middle age. He wore a four-o'clock shadow. He had horn-rimmed glasses, later replaced by those heavy black frames with wide arms common in the 'beat' generation. His well-spaced dark eyes gave away little emotion; in fact, he had the appearance of being extraordinarily serious and wore a frown all the time. He had a noble head, and there was something of a Roman senator in his profile, set off by a magisterial nose and firm jaw. Debonair and well turned out, he was precise and exact in appearance and form. One observer who in the mid-1970s took note of Marder's manner was struck by his similarity to Thomas Babington Macaulay, the historian, namely: he was never at a loss for words; he brooked no distractions and focused on research; he did not shy away from trenchancy in personal expression; and he had a formidable capacity for work and a dauntingly capacious memory. He was of ready wit and abundant humour. He carried an undoubted air of authenticity; self-assurance was his highest trait.[5] Competitive in academic matters, he would state his disagreements quickly, and early in his university career he was known to have stormed out of a room in protest, only to be brought back by a junior colleague who convinced him that if he wanted to change the issue at hand he would have to return. This was a Marder tactic, of enduring memory even in his last university post.

Jacob Arthur Marder, for so he was named before he entered Harvard, when Arthur replaced Jacob as preferred first name, was born in Boston on 8 March 1910, the son of Russian Jewish immigrants from what is now Grodno, Belarus, Maxwell J. Marder and Ida (née Greenstein). Arthur was the oldest of five children; he had one brother and three sisters. In early years the family lived in west Boston near Bunker Hill but later moved to a three-storey house, 103 Ellington Street, in the respectable but low-rent borough of Dorchester. The family was hard-pressed for cash. Max Marder, who loved baseball as much as opera, was a tailor and businessman. He ran a suit and coat business with a partner, B. Horn. Max was conscious of the value of education and particularly of reading to a young person's success. Each payday he gave Arthur a book. Arthur developed a passion for history, embracing the subject at a young age with a dedication hardly to be appreciated. He became engrossed in the prospect of a career as a college teacher. Like many another first-generation American, he was devoted to personal advancement by means of hard work.

Marder grew up in a conservative and orthodox Jewish household. He attended Boston public schools and entered, in his seventh year of schooling, the English High School, the oldest high school in the United States (founded 1821) and one known for its double capacity of excellent academic preparation and of superb technical training. Marder, in the academic stream of studies, excelled in English and history as well as Latin, French, and mathematics, taking top prizes – the Lawrence in each of English and history, and the highest prize, the Washington and Franklin medal, for overall academic excellence – and earning strong support for university entrance. His target was Harvard in nearby Cambridge, Massachusetts. Arthur Marder demonstrated an early love of learning coupled with application for high achievement. He told a Honolulu reporter, Charles Parmiter, in 1956 that at the age of thirteen he knew that he was going to teach college history. He was not only a high performer: even before entering university, he showed immense scholarly ability to organize and analyse material and showed generosity to fellow students in developing what are termed study habits. In fact, one such student, beholden to Arthur for helping her get through courses in high school, took him as her date to her graduation dance.

In the fall of 1927 Marder entered the undergraduate Harvard College without scholarship, and so if there existed a quota on the admission of Jews he came within it. Edwin O. Reischauer, the historian of Japan who was there at the same time, later wrote that Harvard was still an aristocratic and parochially New England institution, largely centred on the undergraduate college which was populated largely by 'preppies'. 'A few bright New York Jews and Middle Westerners were tolerated, but not really welcomed.'[6] Marder was certainly not among the Boston and New England bluebloods or so-called Brahmins that made up Harvard's elite or that of its female college, Radcliffe. Rather, as a Jew of hard-pressed immigrant parents, he was an outsider, dependent on his own abilities for successful progression. There was no time for the characteristic off-hours rowdiness of the undergrads. In his case, merit had to rule, and merit could be achieved by brilliance attached to hard work. Otherwise preoccupied with work and study, he took part in no campus clubs of prominence, not even the Menorah.

The stock market crash in 1929 threatened his higher education, but Harvard provided aid from the Price Greenfleaf Fund. The next year, on merit, he won the Rebecca A. Perkins scholarship. Important in his education was Harvard's Widener Library, famed repository of books, journals, and newspapers, and there, with a small carrel for his own use, Marder had the run of the rich holdings. Outside the classroom, Marder had summer and perhaps occasional Saturday employment in a confectionery, Sunday's Candies, run by an owner who was dedicated to seeing young persons of promise such as Marder get ahead. He also found employment in the US Postal Service. In

1931 he graduated BA cum laude, that is, for distinction in one subject, in his case history. He entered the Graduate School of Arts and Sciences the next term, while still living at home. The Depression kept him out of Harvard in 1932–33, but he returned for completion of an MA in history in 1934 and a PhD in the same field two years later.

Harvard was then (and arguably still is) one of the world's pre-eminent history schools, some would say the most prominent. The department was a galaxy of great historians. Seven future presidents of the American Historical Association held appointments. Dominant in the field of modern European affairs and international relations was the rising star William Leonard Langer, later Coolidge Professor of History, who was then pioneering the relationships between foreign policy and naval and military affairs in his great works *Alliances and Alignments* (1931, 2nd ed. 1950) and *Diplomacy of Imperialism* (1935, 2nd ed. 1950). Son of an immigrant family and Boston-born like Marder, Langer shared the view widespread among immigrants and their children that the United States was a land of freedom and opportunity. Formidable in appearance and well respected by colleagues and administrators, he had been in France with the US Army chemical-warfare unit during the late war. A man of discerning temperament and independent mindset (he was a Unitarian), and a Republican with conservative tendencies, he had been educated according to the principles of Leopold von Ranke. This school of history demanded the collection of all known sources and documents and then the rigorous appraisal of these in the course of developing a narrative replete with analysis. Langer had an extraordinary capacity, one of his last students, Brian Loring Villa, says, to pull revelations out of mundane-appearing documents: 'At squeezing lemons he was the best I have ever seen.'[7] His residence was the venue for his senior seminars, where Marder and others would present the fruits of their labour and face the most challenging cross-examination from the master. When one student, in answer to Langer's question as to where the Italian sources were for a particular topic that demanded their use, said that he did not read that language, Langer replied sharply, 'Well, have you ever tried?'

Marder held Langer in highest regard. In 1969 he paid his mentor this tribute on the occasion of Langer's retirement:

> Some of your contemporaries may have sired a more distinguished group of historians, though I wouldn't be prepared to concede this without a stiff argument. But I dare say that none of them has been responsible for launching the careers of a more devoted and appreciative band of teachers and scholars. The reasons are . . . clear enough.

Your lectures in Continental European and Near Eastern history were ... models of lucidity, organization, and content. And they were delivered in such a compelling way — dynamism spiced with a unique sense of humour and cadence — as to become occasions eagerly looked forward to. My own teaching style has unquestionably benefited tremendously from those years in your classroom.

No less stimulating was, and is, your example as a scholar, as through your guidance ... in seminar and your writing of those classic works of historical scholarship. I would like again to acknowledge my profound indebtedness to you for steering me into the then virginal field of naval history of the non-'drum-and-trumpet' sort, where I have been so happy all these years.

Finally, Bill, every one of us, [I] damn well know, is exceedingly grateful for your continuing interest in us — as individuals and as fellow professionals. Surely, few senior historians have committed perjury so often (and so successfully) on behalf of their disciples![8]

Langer played a key role in the shaping of Marder's career. In answer to inquiries from inquisitive or puzzled Englishmen, such as a registrar of the University of London, a writer in the *Naval Review*, and Lord Mountbatten of Burma, Marder explained the origins of his historical interests in a brief autobiographical sketch that he would use for various speeches and honorary occasions:

> ... my immersion in British naval history goes back to a perfectly chance event on a lovely day in May 1930. I was then a junior at Harvard. On this day I found myself rushing down the stairs of the Widener Library in a pell-mell dash to keep a luncheon appointment. Not looking where I was heading, I ploughed into a considerably older person who was proceeding up the stairs, nearly knocking him off his feet. To my utter dismay, I realized that the enraged gentleman was none other than one of my professors, William Langer, the distinguished historian, one of the deans of modern European diplomatic history. Quickly recognizing me as one of his own, he recovered his composure to ask what topic I had chosen for my senior 'distinction thesis' (required of all students seeking a bachelor's degree with honours in a discipline). My reply was, 'Some facet of the influence of the German generals on pre-war [that is, pre-1914] German foreign policy.' But Langer dissuaded me: it was too diffuse and difficult a subject for a 50–100 page undergraduate thesis and was more suitable for a PhD dissertation. Well,

then, what would he recommend? He thought a moment. 'Suggest you do your thesis on the Haldane Mission. The relevant British Foreign Office documents have been published recently, which would give you a chance to throw some fresh light on the subject. Besides, there are challenging possibilities in studying the relationships between foreign policy and naval policy.'

Marder knew that the secretary of state for war's famed mission to Berlin early in 1912 was the last serious attempt of the two governments to do something about the intensified Anglo-German rivalry in naval armaments. 'I was hazy on the details and not at all certain I would find the topic as interesting as my original one. But I agreed to give it a try.' 'By that autumn', Marder recollected, 'I had found *my* mission – to study the Royal Navy in all its ramifications from the pre-dreadnought era (the quarter-century prior to 1905) through the First World War and its immediate aftermath. My "Haldane Mission" was written in 1930–31. Subsequently, when I was a graduate student of his, Langer made sure that I would not stray too far from my new love. I did British naval seminar papers and my PhD dissertation under his direction. And so I was launched into, quite literally, uncharted seas.'[9]

Marder liked to stress how this story, though nothing remarkable, illustrated how decisive 'fate' can be in human affairs. Had it not been for that chance encounter on the library steps, he wrote, probably he would have dedicated himself to a lifetime's study of the kaiser's generals – 'a fascinating subject, yet a thoroughly uncongenial one'. He added that it had been otherwise with his subject of choice, 'which has been pure joy, in part because of the friendships I have made in the Service'. And 'fate' was indeed kind. 'Nature abhors a vacuum', Marder explained to *The Times*, which had expressed wonder that an American should have written so well on the subject of the Royal Navy in his five-volume *From the Dreadnought to Scapa Flow*, 'and there was this fat subject waiting to be picked up'.[10]

When asked, as he repeatedly was, why he had not chosen instead to write on the United States Navy, he answered that others had already studied it, and, in any event, he did not find American admirals particularly interesting. By that he meant that Samuel Eliot Morison's fifteen-volume history of US naval operations in the Second World War was well under way, and that indeed the study of American naval history was well travelled. Morison, though Harvard educated and employed, was distant from Marder, and he came from the Brahmin Bostonians so far removed from Marder's roots. There is no known connection of a scholarly sort, save for Morison's distant association with Roskill when the latter was 'official historian'.

Interviewing Marder in 1971, A.J.P. Taylor, the historian and critic whose rhapsodizing of Marder was significant in the latter's rise to fame, noted that it was a very curious fact that the German generals, when once put to the test of war, were no good 'and yet everybody writes books about them'. Why, asked Taylor, did nobody think about 'writing about the chaps who won, till you did in America?' Marder replied: 'I've been asked a million times: "Surely our own people are doing this, why are you mucking about with it?" And I've had to say that there was nobody really interested in modern naval history. Herbert Richmond was in his last years and he wasn't really doing it in any case, Roskill hadn't begun his career as a naval historian: there just wasn't anybody in the Navy or in the academic world concerned with it, and nature, as you well know, Alan, abhors a vacuum.'[11]

Taylor wondered, too, if Marder's success at gaining access to materials that were denied to others was the result of his American nationality, his personal charm, the fact that he had come so far for his archival materials and that, in any case, since he had come from so far away, there really was no harm in letting him know all the secrets. 'It was my charm,' replied Marder. Glibly he recounted his meeting with Dr G.P. Gooch, the prominent English historian, and telling the great man that he hoped to get at the Admiralty papers, adding, 'I understand that nobody has got to see them for the post war period, could you help me in some way?' 'My dear young man', Gooch said wearily, 'I have tried and they have refused to do anything for me, so I think your cause is a hopeless one.' Marder, not to be dissuaded, showed a flash of opportunism that was his hallmark. 'I went back to my hotel room and decided I really had little to lose, so I wrote to the Secretary of the Admiralty. The Munich crisis was beginning to come to the boil and I, an absolute unknown, had the nerve to write these busy people. I wanted to know if they could let me see the records from 1880 to 1905 – which eventually went into *The Anatomy of British Sea Power*, published in 1940 – and I'd appreciate a reply at their earliest convenience because I expected to leave for America early in September.' He made his request the second week in August. He continued:

> What they should have done was to have said: see here, we simply have never shown these documents to anybody and who are you, we don't give them to our own people, so good day. But they didn't do that: they made some reference to the fact that these documents were not available but they went on to say: and besides you tell us in your letter that you have to get back to America in a few weeks and it would take longer than that to get these records up [from safekeeping]. I was saddened

when I read it but when I reread it I saw an opening. I wrote back immediately to say that there had been a misunderstanding: I didn't have to go back early in September, I could stay until Christmas, so please don't be in a hurry. Afterwards I got it from an important Admiralty personage, who saw all the papers on this business, that the authorities were hoisted on their own petard because I'd really cut them out, and instead of falling back on the real reason which they had touched on in their letter, that the documents were out of bounds, they felt that as gentlemen they had to do something for me. They wrote to say: since you're staying around, perhaps we can do something for you – would you provide us with a list of topics on which you want information? Well, I was practically in. I gave them 20 topics, making sure that I missed nothing of importance.

The secretary, librarians, and archivists of the Admiralty were not only kind and considerate to the young American scholar: they gave him, when the rules permitted, access to certain files hitherto unused – on the condition that he would not cite them specifically. Invariably it was the Admiralty librarian as opposed to the head of the Records Office who would plead Marder's case for getting access. That he was working on an academic thesis may have eased his passage, and when the book was published the Admiralty took no steps to stand in his way. Marder stuck by the commandment of the Admiralty, stating in one telling footnote: 'The Admiralty archival material will not be cited in reference footnotes in this work.' Such initial favour did not mean subsequent success in getting access to other documents. It was one step at a time.[12] But Marder took care not to blot his copybook: on the first occasion he kept the commandment, and noted it in print. Afterwards, though, on repeated application, the Admiralty caved in reluctantly and never speedily to Marder's pleadings for access. They were anxious never to show favouritism to a foreigner when a British scholar could not get access. They also worried about secrecy being compromised.[13]

Nothing ever came easily with Marder in relation to the Admiralty, zealous guardian of its archives and secrets. In one case, discussed in chapter 4, a battle royal ensued about Marder's use of documents in print, the matter being the sensitive court-martial of Rear Admiral (later Admiral Sir) Ernest Troubridge in regard to the failure to engage the German battlecruiser *Goeben* in 1914. These and other documents were materials of the first importance, containing immense secrets hitherto unknown to the public. The Board of Admiralty, like MI5 or the CIA in our times, was chary of exposing itself to ridicule or correction. It often had to defend itself in Parliament and in the press. Because Marder, as a contemporary historian searching the recent past in the age in which a freedom-of-information act was unheard of, always found himself butting up against access restrictions – for the '50-year rule' of access then applied – his determination to get at the sources was unfaltering. He was tenacious (and some thought unbearable) in his demand for access to sources. Not least, Marder had a sense of timing: if he could not get access, he would work on the 'open' documents, then await the opening of the 'closed'. He did this with his first book, and with his last. He went after sources and sometimes, by twists of fate in later years, they came to him.

Marder first travelled to England in 1935–36, his last year at Harvard, on the basis of a Archibald Cary Coolidge fellowship, intended for study abroad. Apart from his stay in England, he joined other students in roaming the battlements and cathedrals of France, Holland, and Germany, and he even made a vain attempt to interview the ex-kaiser, Wilhelm II, in exile in Holland. But he spent most of the year in England completing work on his dissertation, which was called 'English Navalism in the Nineties'. This was later incorporated in *The Anatomy of British Sea Power*. He visited Newcastle-on-Tyne, the naval yards at Chatham, and other places of shipbuilding, learning first hand certain aspects of the relationship between government and the armament industries. He met some of the leading naval writers of the times, including H.W. Wilson and Spenser Wilkinson (both in their senior years: the sole surviving agitators of the 1890s), and he interviewed a number of prominent admirals including Sir Reginald Bacon, the naval biographer. Inquiries took him to the Navy League and the labour unions. In London, incidentally, he was able to witness the funerals of the famous admirals of the fleet who had been at Jutland and later became first sea lords, John Jellicoe and David Beatty. 'The memory of the seriously ailing Beatty walking in the funeral procession of his one-time chief is one I shall never forget,' he recollected. He followed, too, the Ethiopian crisis, when Mussolini's Italy extended its empire in east Africa unopposed by the British, an event that led him to wonder about the degree to which naval considerations affected, and handicapped, the makers of British foreign policy during the crisis.[14] Try as he might, Marder could not get access to Admiralty papers then under wraps; his application to the secretary of the Admiralty, Sir Oswyn Murray, was held up in red tape or bureaucratic resistance, the Admiralty seeking the opinion of the Foreign Office on certain shared matters. Marder was stalled for the moment, but he had material sufficient to complete his thesis.

Throughout his travels and research inquiries, Marder kept Langer informed of his progress. Langer was pleased to hear of these advances, and on one occasion he gave the young student this salutary reminder: 'There is only one thing that you must be very careful about, and that is the matter of length. If you will allow me to say so, I think you have a tendency to be prolix . . . You must try hard to discipline yourself . . . Otherwise, you will continue to weaken your own work.'[15] Those words echo down the years, and they are an indication, but not the sole reason, of why it took Marder five volumes rather than one to complete what is generally regarded as his greatest work, *From the Dreadnought to Scapa Flow*.

Returning to Harvard in the fall of 1936, Marder became research assistant to Dr Donald Cope McKay, the historian of France, and for that term worked on various projects. By January 1937, he was across the continent in Eugene, Oregon, as an assistant professor of history at the premier university of that state, the University of Oregon. He arrived with high hopes. His teaching duties were various, and he was supposed to be there for two academic years. But covert anti-Semitism compelled his exit; his contract was not renewed despite student acclaim for his work. The chairman of the department told him within three weeks of his arrival, 'Had I known you were a Jew I would never have hired you.'[16] In those days, state laws did not exclude the hiring of Jews in universities, though, as in the case of at least one distinguished Californian Jew, Abraham Nasatir, access to Berkeley was marred by racist attitudes and a transfer followed to a college in San Diego. Marder, in later years, treated it all matter-of-factly, as well he could in more comfortable times. But the event was another blow to his sense of what he could achieve professionally. His temporary professorship expired at Oregon in June 1938.

Marder rushed back to Harvard, where he was a known commodity and admired: he was named a research associate of the Bureau of International Research of Harvard University and Radcliffe College. The title seems august, even pretentious, but it covered Langer's work and that of his colleagues interested in international security. At the bureau, Marder found constant guidance and inspiration from Langer, McKay, and Michael Karpovich – 'my Harvard Godfathers' – and eventually dedicated *Anatomy* to them. Bureau grants enabled him to return to London on research, for the balance of 1938. It was on this occasion that Marder first got access to Admiralty papers. These included some Sir John Fisher papers (denied two years previous on grounds that they might not be available for decades) and Director of Naval Intelligence files. Papers of the 5th Earl Spencer, first lord of the Admiralty in the 1890s, came to him through private hands. He now came to realize that it was papers of first lords of the Admiralty (political heads) and first sea lords (professional heads) that would become his means of analysing and portraying British naval policy, warts and all: Earl Spencer's papers, and some of Sir John Fisher's, pointed the way, and Marder imagined that he might be able to follow the trail right up through Winston Churchill's years (his first) at the Admiralty. In short, Marder's second trip to Britain on research had yielded a bountiful crop. He now knew how to gain access to papers in private hands and how, or so he thought from first experience, to approach the Admiralty with a reasonable chance of success. He had enlarged his earlier network of admirals and navalists. Not least, he had extended his connections with librarians and archivists. The Admiralty officials could see that Marder's successful entry might lead other scholars to try similarly – and, were they denied, charges of favouritism could ensue. As Marder told Langer, 'the Lords Commissioners of the Admiralty have hinted that the news of the exception they have made had better not be broadcast'.[17]

When Marder returned to Harvard, early in 1939, he 'plunged into the writing of the opus of the century', as he jested in his entry in the Harvard class of 1931 yearbook. The approach of war in Europe affected Marder's research and made him increasingly conscious of how he held England dear. He had been attracted to Thomas Hardy and to the novelist's views of provincial town and country life, and his own travels outside London had enriched his appreciation of English ways. Back at Harvard, and in letters to his girlfriend, Martha Kaplan of Providence (addressed magically with such titles as the Crown Princess Martha, Miss Martha Magnesium, and Miss Marushka Kaplanovich), Marder warned of Hitler's threats to the United Kingdom and of Russian actions: 'Stalin has something up his sleeve'. The looming crisis dominated talk in the famed Harvard Quad; conversations discussed it from every angle, diplomatic, economic, and military. Soon Hitler waged war on Poland, and Marder's mind turned to the safety of his English friends, one of whom had foretold that England would be changed irrevocably by the war. Marder followed the war closely, especially this fateful opening campaign. But, with characteristic whimsy, he likened his pursuit of Martha to a battlefield scenario: 'In the siege of Providence the heavy artillery will be what I possess in the way of character and personality . . . teaching ability will be as effective in this campaign as the Polish cavalry outside Warsaw.' In time, Marder's approaches, 'my brazen flirtations', he called them, offended Martha, for he was simultaneously chasing one of Martha's close friends, Norma. By early 1940, in one of his letters written from 'H.M.S. Toasted English Muffin, somewhere at sea', he capitulated: the siege of Providence had been lifted.

His letters show rare insight into his work habits. Sometimes he reports the navy at anchor, with little to show for his work, and other times he reports steady progress, having got the Royal Navy through the Mediterranean crisis of 1898. Then it was on to the final eight chapters, all constructed from raw material and masses of notes. He kept up a torrid pace and by February all the difficult chapters were finished, the book nearing completion. He aimed to get everything finished by June, with publication on Trafalgar Day, 1940. 'More and more I am coming around to my assistant's opinion that I have, if not a literary masterpiece, an outstanding historical work, one that is bound to command attention . . . Let's hope so.' Among the principal chapters was that on the Navy's relationship to the armament industry. Marder's Navy adviser, Admiral Sir Douglas Nicholson, objected to inclusion of that chapter on grounds that Marder was 'raking up old quarrels, etc.' 'Anytime I say something uncomplimentary about the navy (e.g. its inefficient condition in the 1880s), the admiral sees red! All in all a most interesting letter valuable for the psychology of an English Admiral (and a high Tory at that!). There were a few constructive suggestions which were to the point.'

Meanwhile, Marder continued his energetic, disciplined search for a mate (Martha and Norma were succeeded by, among others, a woman in Seattle as the object of pursuit). His actions bordered on the duplicitous, but he objected to being charged with playing a 'sham' game of love. No trifler, he took such matters with seriousness. His letters to Martha described a whirlwind social calendar of football games, opera, and concerts, mixed with romantic reflection on the English landscape, poetry, travel, art history, and film. (He was then teaching a pioneering course in Russian history through film.) Yet success in love eluded him.

During that same summer of problematic courting, Marder found himself in the oddest of academic circumstances. The head of the European division of the History Department of the University of North Dakota, Clarence Perkins, solicited from Langer names of prospective candidates to fill a position. The previous holder of the appointment was moving on to a possibly more agreeable spot. Could Langer help? Yes, he replied, and proposed Marder, whom he suggested was not a student of the very highest calibre but in some respects had decidedly more than average ability. 'This is notably the case in all matters requiring original investigation where he shows himself indefatigable in the search for materials.' He was attractive and fluent in speech and had extensive training in the United States and abroad. Perkins looked warmly on the letter of recommendation and, before he decided to appoint Marder, asked Langer why the candidate was willing to venture to Fargo for such a low salary of $1,650 per annum. An odd question, surely, but Langer gave a frank answer: Marder was hungry and needed work, which was true. Perkins also asked Langer about Marder's political views and sympathies. Langer told Perkins that he could not answer for Marder's inner life but that, from all that he knew of Marder over a long period of years, he had never heard him say anything that would indicate either Communist or Nazi sympathies. 'I am morally certain that you need fear nothing on this score.' Langer's responses satisfied Perkins. Marder was duly appointed pending legal confirmation. Excited about the prospects, the jubilant Marder even sent an article to the *Journal of Modern History*, subsequently published, in which he prematurely gave his institutional affiliation as University of North Dakota.[18]

Marder's appointment lasted a week. Perkins sent two letters to Langer dated 10 June 1940: the first in which he said Marder was appointed, the second reporting that more information had been received about Marder and that this definitely precluded his appointment by the state's Board of Higher Education. What that additional information is will never be known: neither History Department nor Board of Higher Education files give a hint. It must be recalled that United States isolationism was the prevailing political opinion in those days and also that North Dakota was a conservative, agrarian state backing isolationist positions. Marder, in contrast, was a committed internationalist. It could also be that Marder was a member of some political organization or club or that he was aiding Jewish refugees. Or perhaps Perkins found out from Oregon that Marder was a Jew. In any event, Langer got hot under the collar when he received Perkins's second letter, which took him to task for not telling the entire truth about Marder and, as Langer put it, gave the impression that he 'knew from the outset of the factor which now makes his appointment impossible.' Langer told Perkins that this insinuation was wholly gratuitous, especially since Perkins would not reveal the particulars. 'I gave you all the information about Marder that I had and answered your questions to the best of my ability. Naturally I am not acquainted with the private lives of all my students, neither can I answer for what they may have done here or there . . . I have never misrepresented a student knowingly to anyone, and I have not done so in this case. Frankly, I am simply flabbergasted by your letter, particularly by the imputation of lack of integrity on my part.' The only clue Perkins gave Langer of the reason for the turn-down was his statement that, although he had not the slightest doubt of Marder's research and teaching ability, the young scholar would 'unquestionably . . . be successful, but NOT HERE'. In other words, the political world of North Dakota could not support a man of Marder's origins, views, or activities. Another door had slammed shut against Marder, and the only record of this strange affair is to be found in Langer's files.[19] But Langer never failed Marder; in fact, his professional devotion to him only increased with the years.

Despite social distractions and academic-appointment reverses, the text for his book was completed on schedule and sent to Alfred A. Knopf, the prominent New York publisher with whom Langer had personal connections.[20] *Anatomy of British Sea Power*, when delivered to the publisher, bearing a preface dated Cambridge, Massachusetts, July 1940, was massive – in print, it would number six hundred pages. Knopf groaned about the length; Langer assured him that it was all first-rate material. In addition, the timing for this book was remarkably astute though unintended, for Marder did not have a future war in mind when he commenced research on it. In the early 1940s a great struggle between forces of darkness were being worked out in Europe. As in 1588, England's survival was again at stake as country after country fell under the Nazi yoke, leaving the eyes of the world again turned to English shores and their surrounding seas. Before long, proofs were available, and a copy was sent across the Atlantic to win the hoped-for support of a prominent British house, Putnam. The latter requested the advice of Commander Gordon Steele (winner of the Victoria Cross for valour in the Royal Navy's engagement with the Red Russian Navy at Kronstadt in 1919), who promptly replied that an English version would be a great success and of interest to the general public as well as 'the large naval circle of the present day'. The book was likely to become the standard text for all naval educational establishments and was likely to appear in all libraries of Royal Navy ships. It was, he said, a complete and accurate record of the period it covered. What impressed Steele was the considerable trouble that Marder had gone to compile the work: 'He sets his subject out in an unbiased bold style, with reserved personal opinions and sound comments, thereby forming a very valuable addition to naval literature.' Steele thought British readers would like a different title than *Anatomy*, an unfortunate one, he said, when applied to naval history. To this he added: 'The term "navalist" is a good one, when one gets used to it, but a footnote to explain it as used in the same sense as "militarist" in the Army, would soften what readers well regard as an Americanism.' He also pointed out that terms such as Royal Navy and Admiralty should be spelt with capitals. Such points, when corrected, would make for a good book, he predicted, and thus closed his unqualified recommendation for acceptance.[21] As to titles, Steele suggested 'The Vital Years of British Sea Power', or 'British Naval Policy, 1880–1905', or 'The Construction of British Sea Power, Being a Naval Historical Record', with same dates. In the end, the second was chosen for the English edition.

The London edition appeared in September 1941, but, since it had been printed in the United States, Putnam had to import copies under licence and, consequently, the numbers available were few, in the low hundreds. Marder was advised by the chairman of Putnam that 'there appears to be no question that we shall sell out our stock. Whether then we can get a licence to import further copies is by no means certain.' But, should sales not be up to expectations, the chairman fell back on that old reliable: the reviews were superb. He closed his letter with 'congratulations on the splendid reception that your book has had in England, which is perhaps more notable than you realise, as there is often a prejudice here against American books on essentially British subjects.'[22]

Marder's *Anatomy of British Sea Power* offered an immense tour of the horizon of British naval influence. In the age of Pax Britannica, the Navy sailed all oceans and most of their watery annexes. British power extended globally, though such influence was neither ubiquitous nor of paramount effect and imperial overstretch brought immense burdens to the British state. Marder's research thus took him through documents concerning the state of affairs on the shores of east Asia, the Cape of Good Hope and other coasts of Africa, the Caribbean as a cockpit of empires, and, above all, the Mediterranean, that parade ground of British naval might. British actions were predicated on an informed response to French, German, Russian, Japanese, and American rivalries (sometimes in combination); and, in an era when continental European powers were extending their influence offshore, the Royal Navy was a counter to blue-water rivals and, often, inshore competitors alike. Marder's knowledge of these affairs acquired global proportions, though necessarily viewed from the perspective of Whitehall and Westminster, the financial interests of the city of London, and naval and armaments constructors. His familiarity with foreign languages (except, at this stage, Japanese) extended his scholarly reach.

All this, too, was preparation for pioneering teaching work in world, or global, history. Not a narrow subject, and rather the reverse, British naval history opened up international perspectives. As Marder saw it, British naval history was something on which the sun never set; only the history of the navies of the British dominions escaped him, possibly because he saw them as ancillary to his larger tale. His book disclosed the naval rivalries of the age attendant on the collapse of the Chinese empire and the rise of German and Russian influence there. How Asian affairs effected a European revolution in naval rivalries was a radical departure in history; this was the Marder touch. He offered a sharp, new perspective on international affairs and history, long before the quest of the kaiser and Grossadmiral Alfred von Tirpitz to secure Germany its own place in the sun based on a calculated theory of risk management. The key year was 1893, when the British set about rebuilding their fleet so as to maintain a clear check on a combination of the next two naval powers, France and Russia. The famed innovative battleship *Dreadnought*, with its superior guns, armour, and speed, was the logical extension of the British search for enhanced naval security, and Marder's account of it formed the natural conclusion to his mammoth book.

Marder always cited the book as *Anatomy of British Sea Power*, and reviewers in Britain had little problem with that, though the medical and possibly pathological allusions made for interesting dissection. The receptions accorded to the book make for fascinating reading nowadays, and it must be remembered that, at the time the book came into print, the United States was not yet in the war. When the London edition came out, a few months later, British defence rested critically on sea power.

Academic journals, invariably slow to comment on books, judged the work on its scholarly merits. It was in the press, however, that the most telling responses appeared. In the *New Republic* (31 March 1941) Dr Alfred Vagts of Princeton, influential military historian of German sea power, reported the work to be an anatomy of the *choler* rather than the subsequent *melancholy* of British sea power. The era Marder had described was one abounding in panics, and the reviewer wondered whether the nation acquired thereby such immunity to scares that in the 1930s it could look with equanimity on the obvious dangers to its security along the Rhine and in Spain. Vagts wanted more on Anglo-American naval cooperation, a differentiation among the various causes of the naval scares, and, above all, the laying of a finger definitely on the focal infection of Anglo-German relations. He was looking for traditional questions: '*Who* rather than *what* was the British navy at the time? Where did its officers come from? Were the avenues still kept open for the Nelsons? Or were the days of naval genius over in England as elsewhere and had the officers altogether become engineers or bureaucrats with the German [Grossadmiral] Tirpitz as the supreme type of naval official, politician and organizer in his day?'

In all, it was a thoughtful review, but it got Marder's goat. From his office in Widener Library at Harvard, he answered Vagts' dissection of his *Anatomy*, particularly the reviewer's disappointment at the absence of certain elements not supposed to be there in the first place. Marder replied that he never intended to write a history of Anglo-German relations. As to the social background of naval officers, 'Mr Vagts . . . can't understand my failure to ride his hobbyhorse with him. The fact is that I have written on the *whys* and *wherefores* of the British navy, not on the *whos*,' and he pointed out that the English naval historian Michael Lewis had recently published his book *England's Sea-Officers*. But Marder was tetchy, even ungracious – he could not leave any point of criticism alone, as this sentence of his, in his reply of 5 May 1941, makes clear: 'Mr Vagts, relenting, is generous enough to describe my treatment of the origins of the dreadnought as "good, if not definitive".

Since, as explained in the volume, I have examined every pertinent source on the subject, including all the hitherto inaccessible records of Sir John Fisher, the father of the dreadnought policy, I am curious to know what Mr Vagts could add to my account.' The arrogance shows, or was it just academic pride? Vagts had wanted a more philosophical treatment, to which Marder replied that he was writing history — and, correctly, that the field was practically unexplored: 'I have been content to show how and why the Royal Navy and British naval policy developed as they did. The book, I maintain, remains what it set out to be: "a reasonably complete study" of British naval policy in the pre-dreadnought era.'

Vagts had the last word, as a reviewer should: 'As there will be many who share Dr Marder's concept of history', he replied, 'perhaps a word of explanation is due.' Vagts thought the 'who' also to be the 'why' of history — personnel of armed forces often explain policies, even down to the choice of arms. The study of personnel is sometimes better than the studying of documents, he said. Vagts showed the wisdom of his years when he queried: 'Is Dr Marder, who claims to have 'examined every pertinent source', oblivious of the basic historiographical principle that what is not in the documents may still be in the world? Or does Dr Marder think that the modern mass army, the *levée en masse*, might just as well have appeared in the frozen autocracy of old Austria as in the socio-economic conditions of France during the Revolution? To my way of thinking, military and naval developments of all countries bear the marks of their backgrounds.' And then the telling last line, one of broad vision, which may or may not have stopped Marder in his tracks: 'No doubt Dr Marder has done exactly what he set out to do . . . my hope was merely to stimulate him and other able students — a few of whom now turn to military and naval history — to a broader and more ambitious formulation of their historical problems.' Marder had received an invaluable lesson from Vagts, and in the years to come he was never to forget the role of personality and character in the making of history.

Other American journals showed interest and expressed a variety of opinions. The *Christian Science Monitor* (23 November 1940), granting high praise, cut to the quick: 'Accelerated naval construction created huge industrial enterprises that grew fat on what they fed on. When the world was progressing peaceably, business was bad . . . everyone wanted ships: capital because it wanted dividends; labour, because it wanted wages. Thus when a French militarist wrote a thesis on how to invade England by flat boats, financial prosperity in England went up with the national temperature.' Rampant imperialism provided a potent additive. Thus, Marder's history was 'really only Exhibit A in a lesson on the pitfalls of nationalistic ambition which people everywhere are just beginning to take to heart.' The Philadelphia *Inquirer* (11 December 1940) remarked that, because the United States 'apparently will inherit the supremacy at sea wrested by England from Spain so long ago and for so long defended by the British against the challenge of the Dutch, the French and the Germans', the implications and problems of sea power, new to Americans, 'the great land-exploiters of the world', were of great moment. A precursor to Paul Kennedy's argument in *The Rise and Fall of Great Powers* (1988), Marder's book compared the British problems of the 1880–1905 era to the American problems recently inherited: 'These problems comprised insular security, imperial protection, pressure by the armament industries, irresponsible political opportunism, and the stubborn stupidity of men encased in tradition. Each has its parallel in our country and in our time, right now, here, today, this minute.'

In Britain, where such matters as Marder had written about remained largely unknown from the naval angle, blunt and full comments came from well-informed sources. Admiral Sir Herbert Richmond, Britain's prominent naval historian, writing in the *Spectator* (26 September 1941), proclaimed *Anatomy* to be a most valuable and informing work, replete with lessons for all time. 'The story that Mr Marder unfolds is that of the danger – the very real danger, as we can see today – to which Great Britain is exposed, of the struggles of those who pointed out the danger of the technical problems both of personnel and material, that had to be solved.' Then as now, Richmond said, the two issues were invasion and stoppage of trade. Soldiers might argue for a stronger army if naval defence were frail and Admiral Fisher might worry that starvation was the key worry if the navy were beaten in war. Protection of shipping required the building of cruisers; coordination between naval and military forces rendered difficult the finding of solutions. The only matter with which Richmond took issue was Marder's terminology: 'Though it is clear that the author appreciates the fact that sea-power is the foundation-stone of British security he is curiously derogatory in the epithets he employs in regard to the movements made during those years to revive public interest, overcome apathy and maintain the navy. Those statesmen, pressmen, and seamen who opened the eyes of the public to their danger he calls variously navalists, sensational agitators and panic-mongers.' Richmond thought 'scares', 'bogeys', and 'panics', some of which led to 'hysterical shrieks', unsuitable terminology and usage in such a fine book. Otherwise it was 'an exhaustive and highly informing volume'.

These themes were taken up by the Birmingham *Mail* (16 September 1941), with particular note of the battle waged behind the scenes between the Army and the Navy. In *Time and Tide*, the noted critic D.P. Capper said that, whereas some readers might think that Marder's book was poorly timed in its appearance ('Could any book be more ludicrously inopportune than one which examines the details of our domestic politics and naval controversies in the days before Germany became a rival at sea?'), the fact was that, conversely, this book was 'one of those rare monumental works by American authors which, born to be great, triumph over their moment of birth. It would be hard to find a text more carefully documented . . . one could wish at times that the author had allowed himself a little more elbow-room from his authorities.' Capper noted the escalating tensions of the era — the competitive naval building — and the fact that scarcely a year passed without some great power casting a threatening shadow over British waters. In 1896, to take one year, France, Russia, Germany, Turkey, and the United States posed hostile positions of one sort or another. The Two-Power Standard — according to which the Royal Navy had to match the combined fleets of any two rival naval powers — was the natural outcome, 'but it is particularly interesting to note the effect of party politics on naval expansion, and of naval expansion upon party politics.'

A reviewer in the Glasgow *Herald* pointed out laconically (14 October 1941) that it had fallen to an American to write a book of fundamental importance on the first great crisis of modern British sea power. Marder, the reviewer thought, had overplayed his hand with respect to the shrieks and groans of the alarmists: he was perhaps unappreciative of the British public's natural alarm when threats to its naval primacy occurred. Britain's security and influence in Europe were due to its insular position, which led to the view that 'there was no help unless the sure shield of the Navy was held between the island and the great military Powers of the Continent.' The great French historian Jules Michelet had said, in explanation of the fundamentals of British policy, that England was an island. 'And the man in the street', stressed the reviewer, 'without any very deep thought, was resolved that, cost what it might, the island was going to remain one. Doubtless this made him the victim of fools and knaves, but in the last 10 years the absence of this automatic reaction that has proved our moral and intellectual progress over our fathers has been purchased at a very considerable price, which is not being paid.' Worth noting too, in the reviewer's opinion, was that historical inquiry into British naval policy for the pre-1880s had revealed similar variants of hysteria: navalist hyperbole was a fact of life, and it grew in intensity with demands of press and Parliament, factors that Marder had been the first to explore.[23]

It was in the *Naval Review*, a privately published journal whose circulation was restricted to naval officers, that the fullest analysis of Marder's book appeared, and for good reason.[24] That journal, which Richmond's energies had been so effective in developing just before the First World War, was dedicated to open but unattributable discussion on all manner of naval and defence matters. Aimed at encouraging commentary on subjects relating to the efficiency of the Navy (in peace or war), the *Naval Review* offered a forum, a place of comment and disputation, that the hidebound Navy so desperately needed, said Richmond and his cohorts.

Marder's book came to 'H.W.R.' – Richmond himself – for review. That critic pointed out that very few studies had ever addressed Marder's topic – but ought to have. The *Cambridge Modern History*, or histories of British foreign policy, even collections of British foreign-policy documents such as 'Gooch and Temperley',[25] failed to throw light on the widespread, significant problems arising out of, and influencing, British naval policy. 'And it is not a subject with which naval officers should be ignorant.' History no longer ends at Waterloo, Richmond chided, for the nineteenth century could be seen as furnishing the key to the problems the British were dealing with in 1941. 'If the people of this country had been a little better acquainted with the criminal record of modern Germany – the Germany of the last seventy or so years – it is at least possible that so much nonsense about the 'wicked' Versailles Treaty would not have been written, or so much weakness shown to her while she was breaking that Treaty and rearming herself for another attempt on the liberties of the world. Nor, it may also be surmised, should we, in the persons of our statesmen, have played ducks and drakes with the Navy and allowed a Government of very ignorant men to emasculate the Service on which our safety so pre-eminently rests.' Richmond regretted that such a supremely important topic should have been addressed by a foreigner. It was galling to think that the story was written by a Harvard University research scholar and that it was financed by an American university. He criticized Marder for seemingly treating the hysteria of the navalists with disdain, but he balanced this with appreciation of Marder's assessment of the administrators, one might even say saviours, of the Navy, including the first sea lord, Sir Frederick Richards, whose name Marder had rescued from the scrapheap of history. Considering the perilous position of 1941, when British statesmen had squandered away Britain's predominance by naval treaties and peace arrangements of no benefit to the premier maritime nation, Richmond found in Marder's book a lesson for all time. 'The need for preventing these well-meaning but dangerous citizens from once more destroying the defences of the country will again arise, and a thorough acquaintance with the past will be of service as a warning and a guide resisting these efforts.'

To this he added, quoting *The Times* of December 1894: 'We do not accuse our rulers of lack of patriotism, but the traditions of a reckless, heedless, and in the end ruinous economy are still potent . . . in our public offices . . . the strength of the navy is never adequately maintained unless the country insists on its rulers doing their duty.'

Marder had examined public opinion in regard to the Navy and to national security, and that was to his credit. He was critical of at least one other scholar, E.L. (Sir Llewellyn) Woodward, a fellow of All Souls, who in *Great Britain and the German Navy* (1935) had treated public opinion 'very superficially'. Langer had taught Marder and others to research the newspapers and the learned journals of the time, and that the young scholar had done. In so doing, he found too many warnings lightly turned aside. Writing in an era when 'navalism' was still regarded as a disease, and a cause of the Great War – it had been one of President Woodrow Wilson's fundamental causes – Marder was not about to be taken in by the axiom that if you will have peace you should prepare for war (*Si vis pacem para bellum*), so beloved of Admiral Fisher. He steered away from such rhetoric, and his American position gave him advantageous detachment.

As Marder saw it, and he repeated this time and again, his job as a historian was to tell the story, to let the facts speak for themselves. 'Not being a "naval expert", my sole aim has been to give the facts, or, as a certain Talleyrand once said: "Je ne blâme ni n'approve: je raconte."' Later, true to form, Marder would restate this credo:

> I bring no theories of history to my research and writing, nor do I arrive at any startling conclusions. I am essentially a narrative historian. I want to tell a story and to tell it well, and with a liberal infusion of the personal, the human, component, for at bottom, to quote Sir Lewis Namier: 'The subject matter of history is human affairs, men in action, things which have happened and how they happened.' The world is indeed more a stage than a laboratory. One aspect of this outlook is my conviction that the writing of history must include a sense of how events appeared to the participants, bereft of the knowledge possessed by historians and others writing long afterwards. The story that I shall tell [in *Old Friends, New Enemies*, about the Royal Navy and the Imperial Japanese Navy (IJN)] is, basically, a tragic one, with man's limitations all too prominently displayed, such as his moral cowardice at times and his short-sighted thinking. Yet it will also show man at his sublime best, for there are many instances of courage, moral as well as physical, of far-sightedness, and of an extraordinary spirit of self-sacrifice.[26]

'To look at yesterday with the eyes of yesterday, that is the historian's real task,' Marder often told a close associate, the naval librarian and editor Lieutenant Commander Peter Kemp.[27] That is why he often used memoirs and reminiscences, as problematic as they might be as sources. Captain A.B. Sainsbury, reviewing the 1964 reprint of *Anatomy*,[28] made the exaggerated charge that Marder had relied heavily on reminiscences and memoirs at the expense of contemporary records. The danger here was that 'old men forget', as Duff Cooper said. Marder quoted extensively from the old admirals, who, from their splendid rural retreats, portrayed the world as a far simpler place than indeed it was, and one in which 'war with a capital W' was never considered. It served Marder well to portray the Navy as a comfortable yacht club, content with ruling the waves; but by contrast, as he demonstrated, many in the Service as well as in Parliament and the press constantly urged the improvement of the Navy. When the ultimate test came, as it did in 1914, all doubts about effectiveness and readiness were set aside.

In fact, the memoirs Marder examined revealed little. Naval memoirs were not full of complaints about lords of admiralty and politicians. Rather, the choice of words was invariably guarded, and those admired in the Service were praised while those not admired were omitted from the discussion. This tells us something about navies and the Royal Navy in particular: 'Fear God. Honour the King.' was the Royal Navy's motto. While personalities were admired, even encouraged (or tolerated) within the Service, the larger obligation was to the crown and the state. The individual officer answered to his superiors but he held a royal commission. In such circumstances, he zealously kept his secrets. And the ties that bound were not only those of commission, duty, honour, and the traditions of the Service; British naval captains and admirals were also linked by class, and indeed, taken together, they formed one of the distinct and significant segments, one might almost say castes, of society.[29]

The voice of the lower deck, *The Fleet* (October 1941), adored Marder's reference to undue attention being given to spit and polish. Referring to the poor gunnery of the Navy in the period, the reviewer mentioned the action of Lionel Yexley (the founder and first editor of *The Fleet*) in exposing the scandal of 'spit and polish' taking precedence over target firing: 'From time to time we would fire at a target about 500 yards from the ship – usually a cask with a red flag on it. If it wasn't convenient to finish the rest of the ammunition it would sometimes be thrown over the side, and got rid of that way.' It was the Cinderella of all drills. One writer said that on the battleship *Alexandra* only one and a half hours a week were spent on gun drill, and the men were not encouraged to hit the target because it caused delay: the blast of smoke and gunfire sullied and blackened the paintwork and so was regarded as a nuisance. 'Enamel paint, shining brass work and an air of spick-and-span smartness became the criteria by which ships were judged.'

We need not concern ourselves with the many other reviews, invariably favourable,[30] except to say that the leading American academic journals – the *Journal of Modern History* and the *American Historical Review* – provided thorough analysis. The era in question had now been given deeper meaning. Naval history had acquired new dimensions within international scholarship. The Princeton consortium on military affairs and strategy headed by Edward Mead Earle embraced Marder's interpretation and cited it extensively in Margaret Tuttle Sprout's discussion of Mahan as a maker of modern strategy.[31] Meanwhile, Knopf had nominated Marder's book to the American Historical Association. Marder won the prestigious George Louis Beer Prize, much coveted in the historical profession in recognition of outstanding writing in European international history. It gave him a new, elite status in American academe, from which better employment might be expected to be forthcoming. At the American Historical Association's 1941 Chicago meeting, Marder was on stage with Alan Westcott, professor at the US Naval Academy, and Theodore Ropp, expert on the French Navy. Earle was the fixer in all of this, and Marder, who read a paper reappraising Admiral Sir John Fisher, now was more firmly placed among military and naval historians, though still without his desired permanent faculty employment.

At Harvard and its Bureau of International Research, Marder had short-term employment in 'American Defense, Harvard Group', which operated out of Widener Library Room 94 under one of his Harvard godfathers, Donald C. McKay. Marder crafted papers, or backgrounders, for release to the press, providing commentary on existing international affairs and particularly difficulties facing Britain. First was 'The Struggle for Power in the Mediterranean', released on 12 January 1941, which commented on possible Axis dominance of the Mediterranean and the attendant loss to British interests. The British might have the Italians on the run, and hold all the trumps in the Mediterranean by virtue of sea and air power, but the crisis continued. With Germany pressing into Bulgaria, a prelude to wide action in the Balkans, British gains might be nullified. To parry a blow from this new quarter, Britain must be given renewed strength from 'the arsenal of democracy'. 'America can speed up cargo-shipbuilding. She can make arrangements to take over British shipping routes in the Pacific. The administration may find it practicable to release further over-age destroyers to Britain. And finally, and most important, there is always the possibility of Atlantic convoy by American naval vessels.'

A second Marder paper, 'Naval Balance of Power', was released on 14 September and a third, 'Battle of the Atlantic', on 2 March 1942. 'These highways — the Atlantic and Pacific Oceans in the case of American defense — can be denied an invader primarily through superior sea power. Conversely, were either ocean to fall into Axis control, it would offer little or no assurance of security. For a victorious hostile fleet, in command of either or both oceans, could seize advanced bases within the Western Hemisphere and from these launch a direct invasion or establish an economic blockade. The vital question, then, is this: "Do we have sufficient sea power to cope with the armada of our potential enemies?"' Marder was laying out the cause for intervention. He directed his message to Americans, for, as he said, to assure the control of the oceans the Royal Navy had to be kept afloat and fighting and the totalitarian menace swept from the seas.

On 11 July 1941, nearly half a year before Japan attacked Pearl Harbor, the United States government established the office of Coordinator of Information (COI). The name was short-lived. A precursor of both the Office of Strategic Services (OSS) and the CIA, it reported to President Franklin Delano Roosevelt. The brains behind this was Colonel William (Wild Bill) Donovan, crusader in the business of intelligence warfare, who had the president's ear. The mission, Donovan said, was 'to impose our will upon the enemy'. In its early days, the system that developed was quixotic and irregular — prone to unsystematic regulation and analysis of findings — and in Donovan's hands the material that the president considered was that which Donovan insisted that he see. The COI had two facets: finding politically and strategically important factual evidence and holding the same in reserve for later use, and applying all kinds of factual data to worldwide American journalism and propaganda activities, notably press and radio. When war broke out for the United States (7 December 1941, with the Japanese attack on Pearl Harbor), these two approaches in one organization were incompatible: one was bent on secrecy, the other on fullest publicity. In consequence, in the summer of 1942, a reorganization of the firm resulted in a refocused OSS, with publicity activities put into a new organization, the Office of War Information (OWI).

In the process of these changes, a remarkable intelligence community was assembled, and in this Marder, who was brought into it by Langer, played a novel part. His appearance in the drama of intelligence history is a cameo one, a bit like Alfred Hitchcock's appearance in one of his films. When Marder joined the firm, it was called the Coordinator of Information. Not yet a full CIA, it nonetheless combined functions of familiar British intelligence organizations: Special Intelligence Service (also known as MI6), Special Operations Executive, Political Warfare Executive, and the Foreign

Office Research Department.[32] One of the branches was Research and Analysis. R&A, so-called, became known as 'the campus' and was, to many an onlooker, a refuge for a large bevy of men with thick-lensed glasses who spent a lot of time with books. It was, said McGeorge Bundy of the Ford Foundation, 'a remarkable institution, half cops-and-robbers and half faculty meeting'.[33] Its main purpose was to provide militarily useful data. Its scholars, previously trained in academe, had the skills required for extracting from recondite sources all such extant details that operational branches of the OSS or the Armed Forces might require. It was, in brief, research in the service of war. 'Proof of effectiveness' was another matter, but those employed in gathering data, putting it on three-by-five-inch index cards, and sometimes making summary reports had straightforward if somewhat tedious tasks. In Britain, intelligence estimates and appreciations on specific topics, such as German submarine construction, as well as Admiralty handbooks, largely geographical, were the sort of thing compiled. In the United States, it was much the same, though individual essays, or briefs, took the place of huge compendia. At R&A, an early job was to produce Joint Army Navy Intelligence Studies, or JANIS.

R&A fell under control of Dr James Phinney Baxter III, president of Williams College, in Massachusetts, and the pioneering historian of naval technology, having written *The Introduction of the Ironclad Warship* (Harvard University Press, 1933). A ten-person Board of Analysts, chaired by Baxter and composed of a military officer, a naval officer, and eight other specialists from various fields of international affairs and social sciences, had direction of the research agendas. Some one hundred researchers, in various staff divisions and subunits, were organized in topical or geographical specializations, such as French history or psychology or geography. R&A's original directives called for concentrated research on the intentions of Japan, the situation in Iberia and North Africa, and the exposed rear of the United States, South America. Factual research was thus undertaken, with little room left for interpretive comment.[34] All evaluation was to be done 'higher up', which meant Donovan and his coterie of advisers.

Donovan and Baxter recruited Langer as chief of the Special Information Division. Langer devised the initial bureaucratic organisation of R&A in terms of then current intelligence needs and awareness. He hired Marder, Henry Cord Meyer, and a number of other experts, many from various Ivy League and prominent state universities — but all bona fide scholars and experts in their fields. The talents gathered together in Washington on COI business reads like a 'who's who' of American academe, and particularly the historical profession. Among many luminaries of later years were Conyers

Read, Walter Dorn, John K. Fairbank, Gordon Craig, Felix Gilbert, and the later philosopher and theorist Herbert Marcuse. At least thirty prominent historians – and dozens more – helped shape 'intelligence'.[35]

Not always were the assignments suitable for the personnel. Meyer, for one, recruited to the Mediterranean Section as an expert who knew about German thrusts towards the Near East in the First World War, found himself examining West African communications. Gordon Craig, historian of Germany, likewise found himself assigned to West African matters. Of Marder, one author has written: 'We hope that ... the great expert on the British navy was amused to find himself in charge of Mediterranean (water).' Marder, who arrived in September 1941, found himself under Dr Sherman Kent. Kent, a Yale historian of note and an expert on France, was a hard-working theorist of history, then completing the classic *Writing History*, published that year. First to write, as he did after the war, a systematic analysis on the nature of strategic intelligence, Kent was young and tenacious, and he took easily to the demands of the bureaucratic obligations of R&A.

Kent's Mediterranean Section was the first put to the test, for military intelligence knew that the invasion of North Africa was at hand and authoritative local data was needed for Operation Torch. Langer imposed Marder on Kent, and that suited Kent well. Indeed, Kent, in his initial pep talk with Meyer, who joined later that same September (the thirty-seventh new employee of COI), said that Marder was in effect 'gift of the gods', for he knew all about the whole Mediterranean, a prime locus of concern. One of Marder's tasks was to supply quick facts and background information on whatever the journalists required, and every day or so some query might be received. To such sudden interventions in the normal course of office routines Marder would respond, giving particulars on the basis of naval intelligence in the public realm about British warships and bases.

By the time Marder had completed initial assignments on the Mediterranean, especially naval ones, the situation in the Mediterranean had rapidly evaporated. Questions of command of the sea had given way to those of littoral warfare. For a while he did diligent work on topography of Algeria and Morocco, besides some private work for Langer. Meanwhile, Conyers Read of the University of Pennsylvania had been brought in to do 'British Empire' and that left Marder with no prospects there. Marder chafed under the prescribed requirements of JANIS, feeling like a whale stranded on a beach. Nothing was done about the Mediterranean except to transfer it to Read's British Empire Section (which also included Italy, the Balkans, and Iberia), while North Africa commanded the spotlight in Marder's division. The assumed logic about the Mediterranean as a strategic basin was breaking down into subsections. All that remained was northwest Africa. By the end of June, Marder was, so to speak, out of a job; and by the summer of 1942 the plan for Torch, the Anglo-American invasion of North Africa, was ready.

In the circumstances, Marder found that all his hard-earned expertise on the Royal Navy was of no use to the war effort. He found it distressing and irritating. He tried to get out of R&A, and as early as February 1942 he made some overtures to the Board of Economic Warfare, the State Department, and the Department of the Navy. Meanwhile, relations between Kent and Marder deteriorated. Marder found himself toiling in isolation from others, and he liked it that way. He worked in air-conditioned comfort (rare in those days) on the third floor of the new Jefferson Building. He was just steps away from the Library of Congress annex, with all its tempting books at his potential command. He compensated for loss of influence on Mediterranean affairs by using sizeable chunks of office time to further his own British naval research. He did some lightweight work, and it caught up with him.

In the spring of 1942 Meyer was standing in Kent's outer secretarial office when he heard the latter boom out, 'That God-damn Marder! He's writing a joint army-navy intelligence study on the Azores or Canary Islands and he's talking about sugar cane!' Truth to tell, Marder was laundering and embellishing the subject, talking about 'as the sun sets, the weary peasants of Madeira depart for their hearths, leaving the stalks behind in the field to fertilize next year's crop . . . etc.' 'Where does he think sugar cane comes from?' shouted Kent in derision. Marder resigned before being sacked; the reason: failure to adjust to bureau requirements.

Marder's work was not up to the mark (for, as Meyer puts it, 'a sailor did not always take a keen interest in locomotives'), and his supervisor (Meyer himself) found it 'skimpy'. All the glowing prospects set before Marder by Langer about the role of sea power in the war were gone.

The career of 'Arthur Marder, Research Analyst' was over. Marder's friend Meyer tried to put a friendly face on the course of events by hosting a farewell luncheon for him in mid-June 1942. The location was the Dodge Hotel, with all of Marder's section present, including Kent. Meyer arranged for the baked popovers that Marder loved. And that was not all. To highlight the event he penned a skit, actually a book review of an alleged tome that Marder had not yet written but that Meyer, with amazing prescience, assumed or hoped might one day come from Marder's pen. Meyer read this to the group and headed it: 'Hirohito's Hotfoot – The Saga of the Nipponese Navy by Arthur J. Marder':

That famous sea-dog, Admiral Lord Fisher, once brilliantly wrote:
'There are four things for a Big Life:
1. A great Inspiration
2. A great Cause
3. A great Battle
4. A great Victory

Having got those four things, then you can preach the gospel and rest and build an altar to repose.'

How well does the life of Lord Fisher's Boswell reflect these prescient words! For behind this book lie all these things. Here is a brilliant successor to *The Anatomy of British Sea Power*.[36]

Meyer told how, mysteriously, Marder had been drawn to the Japanese odyssey. 'It is devoutly to be hoped that Dr. Marder will some day be the Xenophon to write this American *Anabasis*.' Marder, imagined Meyer, had written a great tour de force, with himself as a participant or agent in the action. 'Perhaps the highest of many high points in the entire book is the dramatic description of that final battle in which the naval power of Japan met — as Dr Marder so well puts it — its Waterloo. The explosions, the crashes, the bubbling cries — no, this reviewer has not read so stirring a narrative since Edward Gibbon's description of the Council of Nicaea.' Meyer wanted more on docks and slipways, and some slight changes of style: 'One would perhaps not appear ungrateful in desiring that instead of describing the battle cruiser *Nokomi* as "that fanged greyhound of the deep" the author had given its draft, net tonnage, gross tonnage, displacement tonnage, capacity, cargo tonnage, and cover charge; or that he had given the fire-power of the gunboat *Sukiyaki* rather than calling it a "snub-nosed carrier of destruction".' He closed his wonderful spoof with this: 'In its broad scope this volume will remain a classic in the field. Any scholar who intends to invade the field of Nipponese studies must consult this work — and its author. To conclude, again, with the words of Admiral Lord Fisher: "I have culled the garland of flowers / Mine is the string that binds them."'

Again Marder found himself out on the street, and in search of work. He packed up from his rooms in North East Washington, near Mount Rainier, Maryland, and drove north to Boston.

Once out of the COI, he turned to learning Japanese and thence to the study of Japan and East Asian affairs. This would allow him, once qualified with rare linguistic ability, a re-entry to war work, as he called it. Once again, his mentor Langer and his other professors at Harvard, notably Donald McKay and the brilliant student of Japanese history, Edwin Reischauer, gave him a new lease on life. Through their aid he won a six-month, renewable Rockefeller Foundation Fellowship to study Japanese at Harvard. There he made steady progress in learning the language: after a year's intensive study, he had mastered 1,780 characters and acquired a vocabulary of nearly 5,000 words and the ability to read articles in naval periodicals. He had in mind qualifying for 'a certain post' in the US Navy Department, or in some sort of other work in military intelligence. However, an odd set of circumstances – his advancing age, poor eyesight, failure of a medical examination that disclosed sinus trouble – then intervened. A nasty operation corrected the sinus problem and that qualified him for possible appointment in the Navy if he could be admitted. But a suddenly presented offer of employment in the naval historical branch of the Office of Naval Intelligence (ONI) in Washington had to be set aside when a freeze was placed on that department. Yet again Marder faced difficulties with stoic courage. 'So ends the saga', he wrote to Langer, putting the best face on it. 'My high hopes of last June have been blasted sky high, but I have two things I didn't have year ago – two things they can't take away – a swell foundation in Japanese and a firmer grip on Far Eastern and especially Far East.'[37]

In 1943 Marder cast his net wider and, in a bold move, applied for entry as an officer in the Royal Navy with a view to working in naval intelligence or historical work. Perhaps this is not as odd as it seems. Many Americans were serving in the British and Canadian Forces, so Marder's prospects were not impossible. Marder asked the Alfred A. Knopf press representative in the United Kingdom, Raymond Postgate, to make special approaches to naval persons of his acquaintance. Postgate, taking up the challenge, thought that Marder's knowledge of Japanese did not grow on every tree, as he put it to the officers in charge. The secretary of the Admiralty duly replied that Marder's nationality was no bar, but, although the offer to serve in the Royal Navy was appreciated, there were practical difficulties in the way. First, there was the matter of his ill health (Marder had reported serious sinus infections), which would make Marder unfit for service in the Far East despite his admittedly useful Japanese-language skills. Second, no openings then existed in the Naval Intelligence Division. Third, the work in the Historical Section (said Alfred C. Dewar, of that unit) required naval experience and technical knowledge which civilian historians unfortunately did not possess. Though Marder challenged these points, especially that about his sinus (now abated by operation), the final word from the Admiralty to Marder was that 'no suitable vacancies have arisen in which your qualifications could be utilized.' To this was added the suggestion that it would be preferable for Marder to offer his services to the US Navy (USN) once more, particularly as he was now fit for service and a resident in the United States. But the dossier on Marder also shows that the director of naval intelligence, Admiral C. Nicols, was worried that the appointment of Marder would savour something of poaching. The Special Branch of the Royal Naval Volunteer Reserve, too, had a look at his application, but in the end Marder faced a closed door. His hope – 'my keen desire' – to enter the British Navy ended in disappointment. The matter had gone all the way to the top: the first lord of the Admiralty, who had given no support to the candidacy, had the final say.[38] Marder made an attempt to join the Royal Canadian Navy, thinking his talents might there be used. Again the door was barred.[39]

Then, all of a sudden, Marder found employment. The War Department, which knew of Marder's competence in Japanese, had an Army Specialized Training Program (ASTP) at Hamilton College, in Clinton, upstate New York. On 9 July 1943 he received a telegram from the dean, inviting him to take up an appointment for three months, extendable to twelve, at a favourable salary of $3,600. He accepted the position effective the 12th, the start-up date of a unit of soldier-trainees who began thirty-six weeks of 'area-language' training in French and German and related strategic matters. The War Department had indicated the importance of Marder's work, and Marder used this in appealing to the Draft Board for a deferment, failing which he would become a General Enlistment, commonly known as a GI. The affairs of the world were swirling around Marder, who in any event was prone to sudden shifts of occupation and focus. Conscription, or the draft, hung over his head, with possible induction into the Army or a commission in the Navy.

President W.H. Cowley of Hamilton College was pleased with Marder's appointment, but the US Army had Marder on their draft list, and he was scheduled to be called up. Cowley intervened and the deferment was granted after some earth-shattering episodes. 'I think I understand your situation,' Cowley replied to one urgent letter from Marder. 'You are on the military treadmill, and you must do what you must do. I do hope, however, that if you are neither inducted into the Army nor given a Naval commission you will not make any commitments about your future plans until we have had an opportunity to talk.' Marder went to Rome, New York, that day for a physical examination. He apparently met all the needs for Uncle Sam, and in the course of that term he made a brief appearance in the Armed Forces, presumably the Navy. 'Dynamic is the word for Dr Marder,' wrote the editor of the *ASTP Hamiltonian* for 1944. 'In the middle of one term he left us to join the fighting forces of the United States, but several days later he returned to become an armchair strategist par excellence. He knows all the towns in

Russia by their first names, how to say "seats" in Japanese, and is generally considered to be a well-spring of incidental historical information.'[40]

But, by 1 April 1944, when the ASTP programme closed, Marder had begun another assignment. An offer of an associate professorship at the University of Hawaii had come his way, with effect from the 'fall term', an incongruous designation in the tropics. How Marder got this assignment is shrouded in mystery; no paper trail can be traced. Was he sent there for intelligence purposes because of his Japanese abilities? Possibly. But, again, Marder's preoccupation was with modern European, Russian history and the new field of world history. Given that so much survives about Marder's other appointments and misadventures, his deployment to the Central Pacific seems strange, even fantastical.

On his departure from Hamilton College, Marder received a glowing tribute from President Cowley: 'It was grand to have you with us. You did a beautiful job, and all of us are full of gratitude to you.' Cowley had formed an excellent opinion of Marder, as this testimonial reveals: 'He has been an indefatigable worker in an assignment which required the re-thinking of European problems and the re-casting of methods of procedure and lines of approach. He has shown considerable mental flexibility in that assignment.' Marder had carried a huge load in lectures and tutorials. 'He has sought to drive facts into a frame work of organization', observed Cowley, 'opinions have been subordinated to facts.' The same could be said of his writing. 'He has been a hard taskmaster by his insistence on facts.' Enthusiasm dominated Marder's days at Hamilton. Cowley found him 'loaded with enthusiasm', which was not without consequences: 'His enthusiasm takes the expression of a flood of ideas which sometimes leads to impatience of their slow execution by others. *Frequently he is persistent when concession would make for smoother relationships*' (emphasis added). Cowley closed his testimonial with this comment: 'At the same time his desire to be friendly and his proclivity to regard acquaintances as close friends gives the first impression of forwardness, but Dr Marder grows on people and during his stay at Hamilton has made many enthusiastic and intimate friends.'

When he had control of events, Marder was a master of time management, and thus, with a view to arriving in Honolulu in time for his teaching assignments, he taught a summer session at the University of New Mexico, not the last occasion he would squeeze in a summer assignment between other duties.[41] Marder arrived in Honolulu by Matson Steamship lines, to be greeted at dockside, as was the custom of the History Department in those days, by his new colleagues. Marder had entered a war zone, and the Honolulu piers and city airport huts wore battle-grey paint.

Martial law and curfews were in effect, and the Federal Bureau of Investigation (FBI) was on the hunt for enemy agents and saboteurs. The irony of his arrival in Hawaii could not have escaped him. Here, with the war in the Pacific not yet over, history had scant relevance and that of the British Navy even less so. Harvard, his old haven of refuge, lay half a world away. All his family were on 'the mainland'. Los Angeles was linked by expensive flying clipper flights or a seven-day boat voyage. Out-of-territory travel was authorized but not at territorial or university expense. The 'Paradise of the Pacific', so called, was a world of contrasts, an American melting pot. Honolulu was a small city and mammoth hotels had not yet sprung up at Waikiki, and Marder liked it that way. Being in advance of urbanization suited him. The Hawaiian chain, remarked Mark Twain, was 'the loveliest fleet of islands that lies anchored in any ocean.' Out in the solitude of the vast Pacific, Marder had found a home, one apparently remote from the workaday world. For him it was just the opposite.

The History Department was a cluster of generalists, and not many of them were publishing scholars with ambitious agendas. The university had been founded in 1907 as an agricultural college, and over time it had matured into an Arts and Sciences Faculty with a Faculty of Education and a few additional skeleton departments in agricultural and technical fields. Marder was welcomed as the Department of History's new talent but was given no special privileges. He carried his share of the burdens. The department was chaired by Charles Hunter, who had no inclination for publishing himself but lionized Marder as its star, much to the annoyance of John Albert White, author of *The Siberian Intervention*, published by Princeton University Press in 1950. White had joined the faculty in 1947 as a Chinese specialist, and, like Marder, he had advanced competency in Japanese. Although White had first-hand knowledge of Russian history as a publishing historian, Hunter favoured Marder. In fact, it was Marder who was always being quoted in the local press when it came time for comments on Stalin's death, Russian activities in space (such as Sputnik's launch), or the Hungarian Revolution. Still, Marder and White were great friends as well as rivals, and, in any case, Marder's self-assurance needed no help from Hunter. On one occasion, White burst into Marder's office bearing a splendid review of one of his books. 'Ah, yes', Marder is reported to have exclaimed, easing back in his chair with pride, his hands folded behind his head, 'they speak of genius.' Marder's regular 'Professor's Notebook' column in the Honolulu *Star-Bulletin* spread his name wide and far in the islands.

With the end of hostilities and the passage of the GI Bill, the university readied itself for an influx of students. The hundred or so faculty, including

A. Grove Day, who devoted himself to the literature of Hawaii, and who arrived with Marder, were necessarily generalists. The pace of research production reflected the easy lifestyle of the tradewind island, though the Hawaiian historian Ralph Kuykendall was busy chronicling the history of the archipelago. Promising students such as George Akita, Gavin Daws, and James Connors were students of Marder's or otherwise knew him, and all of them became members of the department in later years.

Despite periodic seismic shifts in Marder's employment, he began to formulate ideas concerning a possible history of Japan's sea power, including one much along the lines of *Anatomy*. The thought was engaging: two great island empires, both relying on the sea for communication and power, for defence, and for security, presented a splendid possibility for comparative study, as awkward and trying as that might be. Furthermore, OSS expectations were that, in the post-war world, 'area studies' — that is, principally non-North American and non-European fields of inquiry — would be emphasized in universities and in matters of world security.

Marder sought, customarily, to be in the forefront. What were Japanese concepts of sea power? Was the Navy subordinate to the Army, and why? But where should he start given the long history of Japan? In the spring of 1944 he began collecting data, principally printed documents, on early Japanese naval history. He was the first non-Japanese scholar to do so for the early period. His findings were published as 'From Jimmu Tenno to Perry: Sea Power in Early Japanese History, 660 B.C.–A.D. 1853' in the prestigious *American Historical Review* (*AHR*) for October 1945.

For those interested in the subject, nothing could have been a more timely publication, especially considering the state of international politics. Readers must have wondered why this masterful precis of pre-imperial Japanese naval history had not been available before Pearl Harbor. Marder showed that, in the early days of 'a semi-hermit nation', the Japanese Navy was a purely defensive force. When Kublai Khan and the Mongols invaded in 1274, Japan lay at their mercy, and only in consequence of great storms were Khan's fast-strike campaigns ruined and Japan saved. The Japanese called this divine blessing 'divine wind', *kamikaze*. Providence favoured the Japanese in times of national emergency. By 1281, pressing on with amphibious operations, the Japanese crushed the Mongols. The message seemed clear enough: 'You must choose the place of battle outside the Country,' observed the Japanese historian and strategist Ogasawara in 1906. On another occasion, yet another lesson was learned: it was Japan's Napoleon, Hideyoshi, who made the fundamental error of subordinating the fleet to the army for the attempted subjugation of Korea in 1592. The Japanese learned that, without adequate military means on the sea, the Koreans could control Japanese lines of communication and supply and thereby bottle up whatever naval assets the Japanese had. When the Chinese came to help the Koreans in 1598, Japan's aspirations during a restless, belligerent period of its history were curtailed absolutely – and so were Japan's naval abilities during this 'dark age'. By the time Commodore Matthew Perry of the US Navy arrived in 1853 to open Japanese ports to American trade, the Japanese already understood the fundamentals of maritime strategy as follows: 1) use of the fleet was vital as an instrument of aggressive imperialism; 2) control of the surrounding seas was essential; and 3) careful preparations were needed in peacetime.

Marder was fastidious in drawing conclusions, though he was not timid in his judgements. Reviewing the then recent historical literature on the subject, Marder noted Alexander Kiralfy's observation that the Japanese Navy was always subordinate to the Army and thus defensively minded. By contrast, Stefan Possony, ignoring ancient Japanese naval history, concluded that the Navy 'must be deemed as an essentially offensive force'. Marder said that both were partially right: 'Strategically, the pre-Menjii fleet was regarded mainly as a means of transporting and protecting expeditionary forces. Tactically, it was at times used cautiously, particularly in Hideyoshi's Korean campaigns; but, when properly led, as at Dan-no-ura, it was permeated with the offensive spirit.'

For various reasons, Marder did not pursue his language study of Japanese or the subject of the Imperial Japanese Navy when the war ended. As soon as he could, he returned to the subject of the Royal Navy, to complete an agenda of publishing that would ultimately require no less than eleven volumes. Further study of Japan's sea history, and of the language, would have to await the appropriate time for the always opportunistic American scholar. Meanwhile, in his 1945 *AHR* article, he had elucidated the maxims of Japanese military strategy. These are summarized in five lessons gleaned from medieval writings as brightly illuminated for the modern era by Marder:

1. Win first and fight afterwards [which from the text appears to mean: thorough preparations and prosecution of the war lead to certain victory].
2. Do [it] to the enemy before he does [it] to you [that is, be a victor, not a victim].
3. Make the enemy move for you.
4. Fight like a high-strung bow [that is, fight violently and instantaneously like the discharge of an arrow from a high-strung bow].
5. Fight aggressively, not passively.

By the time this analysis of early Japanese naval history reached print, Marder was in his second year at Hawaii. Students there knew him as a stylish, singularly well-informed, and erudite but amusing lecturer on world and Russian history. They remembered his throwing candies to them in class – to the delight of the young females from the plantations. All the same, he was formidable, particularly in his special courses on historical methods or European history; these classes, taught à la Langer, were chosen only by males. Some found him aggressive in style. They knew him less well, or probably not at all, as becoming recognized as something else – the ranking authority on the Royal Navy of the dreadnought era.

Marder was considered by his students as something of an eccentric, and they liked that in him; in fact, he bolstered his own reputation in that regard from time to time. He drew attention to himself the year after his arrival by managing to lose himself and a female companion, a nurse, for three days while on an intended one-hour hiking expedition in Koolaus, in the upper Manoa valley. An extensive search – by police, National Guard, and helicopters – had to be made for the pair. The local press complained that, for this rescue search, considerable expenses were being run up just at the time that money was needed for the war effort. The story spread: the New York *Times* reported the famous British naval historian as missing. In the end, the nurse strode out of the wilderness but an exhausted Arthur appeared on a stretcher, flanked by rescuers. The misadventure became legendary, and Charles Hunter, department chair, delighted in recounting it. So did his envious colleagues. 'It's got so I can't even mention mountains or climbing in my lectures, or the kids break up in laughter,' was the way Marder described the general response. The university Senate, in a fit of collegial zest, even enjoined Marder not to make excursions beyond a certain distance from the city.[42]

But all's well that ends well. Honolulu was socially agreeable, and Marder took to Chinese cooking, taking courses in that subject and being the sole man in a class of two dozen women. He did so well in the kitchen line that he was asked to write the preface for the about-to-be published Mary Sia treatise on Chinese cookery. He also studied hula dancing, and one of his colleagues remembers that Marder had only two certificates on his office walls: one was from the Chinese cooking school, the other, of the hula dancing course. Everything considered, these were enjoyable, fulfilling years. A freedom to do his work and to develop his career ended his cramped existence of the early 1940s, with the war in Washington and elsewhere swirling around him. Hawaii offered many professorial opportunities.

It was to be a source of wonder, as A.J.P. Taylor often mused, that the energetic Marder could do his work on the Royal Navy from Hawaii – of all places! Marder had a long career there, one that gave him much happiness. Yet the problems of office politics would continue, and in due course he would tire of Hawaii and Honolulu, for the centre of United States academic life was on the mainland and Honolulu was becoming more urbanized. Harvard could not have been far distant from his thoughts but a professorship there lay beyond reach. Naval history, and British naval history at that, lay out of bounds, a specialized field confined almost wholly to the US Naval Academy in Annapolis and the US Naval War College at Newport, Rhode Island.

Marder received great support from the University of Hawaii, where his achievements were well recognized: he was made professor in 1951 and senior professor in 1958. During 1949–50 he was a visiting professor at Harvard (*vice*-Langer, as he put it) working on new projects — Richmond and Fisher — and during these same years he travelled extensively to London and elsewhere, his work funded by a grant from the Guggenheim Foundation of New York. His agenda was ambitious and beyond anything previously considered by a British naval historian. His time in England was always precious, and he travelled great distances to get to his sources. At home and abroad, he was perpetual motion, showing a characteristic restlessness that matched his energy.

We have yet another glimpse of him from his archives — a guest sermon he gave at Temple Emanu-El, Honolulu, on 25 June 1954, entitled 'Theodor Herzl: A Study in Practical Idealism'. It was a testament to a certain kind of 'history-maker': one who has the ability to dream great dreams and to realize them, in whole or part. Herzl, the architect of Zionism, was like Jefferson to Marder's way of thinking: both a great leader and a practical man of affairs, besides being a prophet and dreamer. It was Herzl who said: 'If you will it, it will be no fairy tale.' Indeed, it was not. Marder's Judaism, interest in Zionism, and Herzl never commanded any attention from those who knew him personally. One of his friends wrote of this: 'He indubitably had a special stance on his own that did not belong to the public domain.'[43] Colleagues in Hawaii were surprised when this author told them of Marder's background. By the time he arrived there, his Jewish orthodoxy had diminished if not disappeared, left behind by his academic pursuits, government work, and liberal experiences. He never left the faith but rigid conformity to Judaism had vanished. And the influence of his family background in such new circumstances, so far distant from the old Boston, was lessening. Marder had been reinvented by history.

For many years, Marder had been immensely lonely and unable to find a suitable mate. In one of his summer visits to California, however, a fellow classmate from Harvard and his wife introduced him to the Stanford University graduate Jan North Altman, a widow with two children, Tod and Toni (later Kaplan). Jan, a Jew by birth who had become an adherent of Christian Science during her husband's illness, was the daughter of Robert North, a vaudevillian and Hollywood producer. In 1955 Arthur and Jan were married in the same Los Angeles garden where they had met.[44] Marder did not join Christian Science, but that was one of the few things he and Jan did not share. He said that, in taking his name, Jan and her children would be regarded fully as a family and the children as his own. Not long after, they had a child by this union, a son whom they named Kevin. They lived at 4921 Kolohala Street in the newer suburb of Waialae-Kahala, not far from the University of Hawaii's main campus. Arthur devoted two days a week to his writing, he told the journalist Charles Parmiter, in a typical description of his regimental discipline as a historian. Jan was active in the League of Women Voters of Honolulu. Although he and Jan were now collecting research materials on frequent visits to Europe and 'the mainland', he still found time to garden. 'My wife considers this a dubious success,' he told the reporter, in his customary style. 'It keeps me from attending to other chores.'

Marder's Hawaiian years were those of growth as a professional teacher and historian. The university was a place to develop his own interests and skills as a teacher. Easy it would have been to languish in this easy clime free from customary academic pressures of the mainland United States. A scholar less well disciplined than he could have succumbed to pleasures of surf and sand. To keep on the straight and narrow: that was the challenge. Fighting his own restlessness, and with a permanent Ivy League or other major university post beyond grasp, Marder had to become self-contained, as it were, and to follow his own star. With continuing problems in London facing him – access to documents was a persistent problem in these years – Marder marked time with reading memoirs and histories of the Royal Navy of the Jacky Fisher era. Time spent on such reconnaissance was not wasted on Marder, so that when doors were at last opened he was ready for the documents, and their treasures, which he anticipated would unlock the secrets of a world known only to a few.

Chapter 2

Roskill: Guns Ashore and Afloat

STEPHEN WENTWORTH ROSKILL was a child of the Edwardian epoch. The palmy days of the Victorians and their empire were fast passing into a new, harsher reality of domestic uncertainty, one made more urgent by foreign challenges to Britain's trade, credit, and seaborne prowess. In the home islands a long century of peace – and pride in Britannia's unrivalled status – was quickly coming to a close, the fear of falling a constant subject of discussion among the chattering classes. Stephen Roskill was cut from an entirely different cloth to Marder. In his character and deportment, there was a strong strain of judicial and legal certitude based on principle. This derived specifically from his father. There was also a hint of England eternal and of advanced liberalism. This came to him directly from his mother.

Roskill was lean and tall and swarthy of complexion, and had about him a singular air of professional elegance. He deported himself very much as a captain of the Royal Navy, that is, one sure of his rank and station. He had a long nose and slightly protruding lips and a very determined but small chin. The litheness of his movement, for he walked on the balls of his feet, and the quietness of his approach (he would place his hand on your arm quietly and with gentleness) were matched by a soft voice that issued words in a consecutive, quiet, neat, and attractive flow. At meetings of the Navy Records Society he kept control but by no means needed to shout, and he dominated the organization in this manner for a long time. The New Zealand sailors who got to know and respect him when he was executive officer of HMNZS *Leander* called him 'the black mamba', in reference to the snake that appeared suddenly and, in Roskill's case, would sum up a faulty situation and take immediate charge. He had a good, kindly smile that enhanced the lines of his cheeks and a fine but not thick head of hair parted decisively and on the left side. He was an animated conversationalist like Marder but he was almost a complete opposite of the American outsider in many respects, including nationality, class, and professional training. If Marder was Athens, Roskill was Sparta.

He was born in London on 1 August 1903, son of John Henry Roskill, King's Counsel, and Sybil Mary Dilke, daughter of Ashton Wentworth Dilke, one of the members of Parliament for Newcastle-on-Tyne. 'I was, as I told you', he wrote to Dr Zara Steiner, the historian and wife of his colleague George Steiner at Churchill College, 'half Jewish (on my father's side) and half a scion of a very ancient and not undistinguished English family the Dilkes – who come down in direct line from Thomas Wentworth, Earl of Strafford whose head Charles I chopped off after a discreditable piece of Royal chicanery.'[1]

Stephen was the second of four brothers, the oldest being Ashton (later Sir Ashton) Wentworth Roskill, born in 1902, who had a distinguished career in law and government, and the younger sons being Oliver Wentworth Roskill, born in 1906, and Eustace Wentworth Roskill, later Eustace, Lord Roskill, born in 1911. Oliver was educated at Oundle School and Lincoln College, Oxford, while Eustace went to Winchester and Exeter College, Oxford. Oliver, an industrial consultant in a wide variety of areas and projects, served in intelligence for the British government during the Second World War, then going on to a second career in industrial-development projects in Iran, Pakistan, and Malta. Eustace, called to the bar, Middle Temple, worked at the ministries of Shipping and War Transport from 1939 to 1945 and became a judge of the High Court of Justice, Queen's Bench Division, and eventually lord of appeal in ordinary in the House of Lords and a baron.[2] Eustace and Ashton achieved the respectability in the law to which their father 'had so earnestly aspired' and failed to attain.

John Henry Roskill, Stephen's father, was the son of Gustavus Roskill and Theresa Windmuller. Gustav was a German Jew and had arrived in Manchester in the 1840s to start an import-export textile business focused on the Far East. G. Roskill and Company, later Roskill Samson and Company, seems to have done well. Upon his death, Gustavus was buried in a Unitarian cemetery. 'When the infamous Nuremberg Laws were passed in 1935 our German cousins flocked over here to get copies of Gustavus' burial certificate and that is how they, though almost certainly 100% Jewish, escaped the impact of those laws.'[3] John was educated at Owens College, the precursor of Manchester University, and Corpus Christi, Oxford. In London he read for the bar and was installed in chambers with H. H. Asquith, the rising politician. An uncontrollable temper, however, eventually destroyed a flourishing practice. Through his connections with Asquith, he became recorder for Burnley, a post he retained from 1907 to 1909. Later, from 1909 to 1937, he held the modest judgeship of Salford Hundred Court of Record. He stood twice for Parliament and was unsuccessful. He loathed Lloyd George and held him responsible for the decay of the Liberal Party.[4]

To his great chagrin, John Roskill never got a High Court Judgeship, the heart of his ambition, and was never elected a bencher of his inn, the Inner Temple. Of his father, Stephen wrote that although his father's family were German Jews 'he tried hard to live that down and was in truth a bit of an anti-Semite himself.' He had republican sympathies, declined to attend the coronation of George V, and died a lonely, wealthy, and embittered man in 1940, predeceased by his wife, who had died in their residence, by accidental fire, in 1930. 'I now think', Stephen recalled in the late 1970s, 'that the frustration of his own hopes and ambitions, largely due to his own fault, made him over-ambitious on our behalf . . . I well remember how he once put in his oar in with the Admiralty about an appointment for me, without consulting me and with the most embarrassing results. At any rate on one of my last visits to him he eyed my gold braid and brass hat with very evident pride.'[5]

Stephen's mother was connected to the Liberal Party through her father, who, besides his parliamentary activities, was proprietor of the *Weekly Despatch* newspaper. Sybil Mary Dilke was a niece of Sir Charles Dilke, the gifted statesman, and at the same time a niece of Mrs Virginia Mary Crawford, wife of Donald Crawford, MP. The sensational divorce case of the high Victorian era – *Crawford & Crawford v. Dilke* – went through two trials and revealed, among other philandering by Dilke, an incidence of a three-in-the-bed sexual activity. Dilke was exposed and his career ruined.[6] (Stephen quipped that he and his brothers were in the singular position of being great-nephews to both respondent and co-respondent.) Sybil was elegant – tall, stately, and beautiful. All the Dilkes were agnostics but she became an Anglican by choice at age eighteen, and the change may have been related to the sensational divorce case. A devout Anglican, she took a greater interest than most mothers of her class in the upbringing of children, and she would send Stephen books for his self-edification, believing passionately, and correctly, that the Navy attached little importance to the intellectual improvement of its officers.[7]

Stephen's devotion to his mother knew no bounds and in later years he wondered why she had married John Roskill. 'Why she, a most beautiful girl of "good family", should have accepted him when he made a second proposal of marriage remains a mystery,' he noted. Sybil had been passionately devoted to Charles Trevelyan, later Sir Charles Trevelyan, future Labour minister of education; yet it was clear to Stephen why the Trevelyans, among Northumberland's most influential families, should not want to be mixed up with a Dilke. Sybil met John Roskill in social and political circles in London and accepted him, so to speak, on the rebound.

From the outset they lived at 33A Montagu Square, Marylebone, a ground-floor residence that Stephen described as 'a large and rather gloomy house', which much describes it today. The boys grew up in a cultivated and politically sensitive family and circle of some means. Stephen said that it was a thoroughly conventional Edwardian household. From the whirl of chambers, church, and judicial circuit, the country beckoned, and when Stephen was very young his parents purchased Heatherfield, on a lovely spot off Newtown Common at Newbury in Berkshire. Stephen thought it an ugly villa, but he found the countryside idyllic and on his pony, Silver, the joy of his life, ranged far through woods and over down lands. A Londoner had now acquired a deep affection for country life. And he learned for future use a few tricks from his father about buying up land and cottages, enlarging his holdings, and managing property.

Stephen was drawn at an early age to enter the world of hard knocks: the Royal Navy. His parents did not encourage him to think about a naval career; in fact, nothing in his parents' make-up would necessarily encourage it. Even so, this was the high noon of empire, and the Royal Navy, in the years leading up to the Great War, called all to its support. Like many another lad of his class, Stephen was given *Boy's Own* and even *Jane's Fighting Ships* as presents. As a day boy at Mr Egerton's School at 13 Somerset Street, behind Selfridges department store, he seems to have been swept up in the imperial and naval enthusiasms of the headmaster, who, as Stephen later recalled, was relentless in promoting the Empire and the Navy in particular. Stephen later wrote that it seemed odd for his Liberal parents to place him in a school run by 'a Tory of Tories'. There, Stephen won several prizes, including a signed copy of Henry Newbolt's *Drake's Drum*. The boys were marched to Hyde Park and drilled to the patriotic songs of the age. 'Edgy's rampant, flag-waving patriotism' was to wear thin as the war proceeded, Stephen noted.

At age eight, Stephen 'fell in love with all things naval', and this continued for the next five years at his boarding school, Horris Hall, near Newbury, until he was old enough for a Royal Navy cadetship. Roskill was a product of English preparatory schools as much as the Navy. He remembers his time at Horris Hall School as one of homesickness exacerbated by being bullied, knocked about, jeered at, and selected to be 'squished' by bigger boys. Yet, despite all of this, he became head boy.[8] 'It was my first, though by no means my last, lesson in the use – and misuse – of power', he later jested. In July 1917 he got a resounding send-off from his classmates. His parents had hoped that he would go to Winchester, and the headmaster was of the opinion that he would get there on scholarship. However, they did not stand in the way of his desire to be in the Navy, and thus, on 1 August 1917, age fourteen, he passed into the Royal Naval College at Osborne, Isle of Wight.[9]

The civilian masters, or tutors, at Osborne could be kind and helpful, but this was not true in Roskill's case. On one occasion, he said, the master A.P. Boissier

> entertained us at his house by playing a gramophone. But it was an incident on the playing field which really aroused my hatred for him. He and his wife were watching a game of football, and the woman remarked to her husband, 'Roskill plays quite well.' 'Yes,' he replied within the hearing of cadets on the touchline. 'But I don't like him. He is a Jew boy' (which was less than a half truth). This remark was of course repeated with glee in the dormitory that evening. It was my first, though not my last taste of the anti-Semitism which was so marked a feature of the British upper class then, and for many years later. I still find it hard to forgive A.P. Boissier for making the remark. Later he became Headmaster of Harrow School, and I was not surprised to learn that he had been anything but a success in that capacity.[10]

At age fifteen, Roskill moved on to the senior college, Dartmouth. There, the spit and polish promoted by his uniformed instructors were in sharp distinction to the care that the civilian masters, including two of the historians, Michael Lewis and Guy Pocock, showed in the mental development of their charges, Roskill was wont to say. Thanks to the latter, he began to read widely and this, writes Correlli Barnett, who knew him well, was to make him a 'critical and innovative naval officer, and later still an outstanding historian'. Equally important is the fact that the strict discipline and ceremony of the naval colleges left indelible marks: 'Stephen remained to the end of his life punctilious over the performance of his professional work and his social duty.'[11]

In later life, Roskill, who much resembled his reformist mother in her protective, progressive nature, stated his entire opposition to the system of the thirteen-year-old cadet entry. His unhappiness at Osborne, and his less than enthusiastic remembrance of Dartmouth, led to his later complaints. Brutality there undoubtedly was, and he did not do particularly well at sports, though he did represent Dartmouth at rackets. He wrote subsequently that anti-Semitism in the Navy was a force against him, and in consequence of this he devoted his time and energy not to the rugby and cricket pitches but to college journalism. He also referred to 'the rabid anti-Semitism to which I was subjected as a cadet and later', being 'half Jewish (on my father's side).' To Zara Steiner, he quipped: 'If anyone thinks only Germany was subject to such evil emotions they haven't a clue to the attitudes of the English upper class.'[12] Yet such anti-Semitism as did exist failed to stop Stephen Roskill from successful performance as a naval cadet. He emerged with a first-class leaving certificate and an Admiralty prize for French.

A latent sidelight on Roskill's views on naval education and training was provided in 1981, when he remarked in his biography of Earl Beatty that the system of training naval cadets in earlier days 'now seems extraordinarily ill-conceived', adding that 'though it is true that some boys came through it with little apparent harm, and ultimately became fine officers who rose high in the service, others were undoubtedly ruined by it and either left the navy totally disgruntled at the first opportunity or served on with increasing dislike of the life which they had chosen, or which had been chosen for them by parents, to become thoroughly bad officers.' In particular, he stated that pushing cadets into a pre-conceived and rigid application by harsh, even inhuman, disciplinary measures (some enforced by boys only a few months older than their victims) served to stifle originality. Roskill keenly pointed out that this was a contributing factor to British failings at sea during two world wars.[13] In 1921 Roskill passed out of Dartmouth with a first-class certificate and then cruised to the Mediterranean in the old coal-burning battleship *Temeraire*. Then made midshipman, he was appointed to HMS *Durban*, a light cruiser 'resplendent in tropical white paint', commanded by Captain Basil Washington and bound for the China station. The *Durban* was a happy, smart ship, and Washington a gentleman. The voyage took them to all the great imperial ports of call that, as Admiral Jacky Fisher had put it, 'locked up the world' to the Navy and the Empire. Roskill found Shanghai to be the Paris of the Far East and Wei-Hai-Wei a sort of British insular golf and country club. But 'showing the flag' was an imperial preoccupation in those days. At one point, the *Durban* escorted the battle cruiser *Renown*, carrying the Prince of Wales and his young sub-lieutenant, Louis Mountbatten, on the royal tour of Far Eastern ports. The *Renown* visited Japan, dodging a typhoon at Kobe and an earthquake at Yokohama, and Roskill in the accompanying cruiser had his first taste of Japan.

The Prince of Wales had begun this tour amid worries over the security of Britain's Far Eastern empire. The Anglo-Japanese alliance had been abrogated by the British, acting in response to fears in Washington and Ottawa of Japan's military rise in the Pacific. Japan was in the early stages of estrangement from the West, prompted in part by the 1922 Naval Treaty of Washington, which imposed limitations on Japan's naval ambitions. The country's naval might was growing and highly visible to the British visitors. 'Next to our own service I have never seen such fine ships,' Mounbatten noted in his diary. 'Any one of them could have taken us on, on equal terms

. . . I received the impression that here was a power to be reckoned with in a way in which no one who has not been here and seen for himself can possibly conceive . . . I was glad that we were in as fine a looking ship as the *Renown* and only wished that the *Hood* could have been escorting us instead of the tiny *Durban*.'[14]

In the *Durban* with Roskill was an intelligent torpedo officer with a keen political sense, Stephen King-Hall. Roskill and he were drawn together. The Far East was 'changing damned quickly', as the prescient King-Hall, sometime naval intelligence officer and MP, put it. He wrote about it in several books, notably *Western Civilization and the Far East* and *The China of Today*. Roskill came under King-Hall's wings and was bound to share his mentor's view that the 'immemorial and never changing East' was undergoing a revolution. 'The last people who could see what was going on around them and the revolution brewing up under their noses were the Taipans and the "old China birds",' wrote King-Hall bluntly in his memoir *My Naval Life, 1906–1929*.[15] Intended as a wake-up call, this book exposed the extent to which Japan was in the hands of militants determined to conquer Asia. (It had no popularity in Shanghai, said its author.) From a Mr Young of the *Kobe Chronicle*, King-Hall had obtained an insider's view of the Japanese political situation, and with the help of Roskill he sifted through seven years of printed debates of the Diet. King-Hall records that he worked on these translations and documents in the steamy chart house from 10 p.m. to 1 a.m. night after night, and we can picture Roskill toiling beside the great man, as a ready aide. From this research King-Hall obtained a real insight, he says, into Japanese politics and particularly of the political importance of the Shinto religion, with its distinctive views on the ideal relationship between local communities and the state.

The *Durban's* voyage thus gave Roskill his first chance to do analytical research, besides exposing him for the first time to the study of Japanese politics. Japan was then smarting under various diplomatic realignments or adjustments, including the abrogation of the Anglo-Japanese alliance, the 5:5:3 ratio in capital ships which left the Japanese fleet inferior to those of Britain and the United States, and the institution of the 'Open Door' principles espoused by the United States. 'Our empire has lost everything and gained nothing', complained the prominent journalist and Diet member Mochihizuki Kotaro, 'and only the expense of building warships is spared.'[16]

These experiences, and this enlarged world, were not lost on Roskill. In the 1920s his professional competence developed considerably. After he called on his captain to take his leave, he was given a summary of a report on his performance; such documents were popularly known as 'flimsies' because of the thin paper on which they were produced. Two of his read: 'of a dreamy artistic temperament. Has brains which he will probably use more when fully grown'; and 'keen . . . gifted . . . a very good officer and shipmate . . . a good leader'.[17]

In June 1925, after a promotion course at Royal Naval College, Greenwich, and now a sublieutenant, Roskill joined the sloop *Wistaria* on the North America and West Indies station, one of the oldest parade grounds for showing the flag. All the key ports of the Caribbean, the eastern United States, Canada, and Newfoundland were visited. He was officially commended in the report of A.B. Cunningham, flag captain to the Commander-in-Chief, for his conduct in the Caribbean hurricane of 1926, when he rendered meritorious service. In heavy seas he swam with a rescuing hawser to a warship adrift and in danger of running aground. For a time he was flag lieutenant to the governor of Newfoundland, Sir William Allardyce, and during his time there he studied the local politics and economy. Supplied with a constant stream of reading matter sent by his parents, Roskill, now in his early twenties, developed an intellectual bent. He was inclined to reflect that such widening horizons kept him in the Service in the 1920s.

In 1925 he made his debut as a published writer, contributing a piece on the coal industry of Cape Breton, Nova Scotia, to the Manchester *Guardian*. That same year he became a member of the *Naval Review*, the beginning of a life-long association, using various pen names, Diogenes and Argus among others. From December 1926 to March 1927, he was in Freiburg-im-Breisgau, Germany, to study the language, and he made a report on the state of that country's politics. This time and, indeed, subsequent service in four capital ships – the battleships *Ramillies*, *Royal Sovereign*, and *Warspite* and the carrier *Eagle* – were highlights of any young officer's ambition in that age of interwar parsimony and limitation in naval construction. Gunnery was the naval officer's god. Battleships, with their big firepower and heavy armoured protection, dominated the thinking of the Admiralty and the Navy: the historian Sir Basil Liddell-Hart quipped that a battleship was to an admiral what a cathedral was to a bishop, and right this was for those times.

Gaining the gunnery specialization was an important milestone in an ambitious officer's career. Officers and ratings (non-commissioned personnel) trained in the famous gunnery school, HMS *Excellent*, at Whale Island, Portsmouth, were inculcated not only in technical knowledge but also in the Navy's standards of drill and discipline. Roskill did the specialist 'Long Course' in 1928–29 and remained as an instructor for a further year. Now aged twenty-six, he was employed in gunnery-specialist positions of increasing responsibility at sea and afloat over the next twelve years. He left

Whale Island for the *Royal Sovereign* as 2nd gunnery officer. This was followed by a further position ashore in the gunnery school at Chatham. He found his next appointment not so agreeable: gunnery officer in the carrier *Eagle* in January 1933. 'I wasn't too pleased to be appointed to the *Eagle*', he recalled years later, 'not so much because she was bound for China as because carriers were notorious difficult ships to run successfully – especially for the Gunnery Officer, whose weapons had to take second place to aircraft.' Gradually, Roskill came to accept that his new assignment was not a product of maliciousness on the part of the Admiralty, for 'this was the time when the Adm[iralt]y was, albeit reluctantly, coming to recognize that the carrier had a big future.' He adds, immodestly, 'Thus they were sending to them officers whom they thought pretty highly of instead of the elderly duds who had been sent to them in the 1920s.'

Once again he found himself in the Far East, a place he regarded as undergoing momentous change and, in terms of British security, undoubtedly deteriorating. Japan, in particular, offered fewer of the warm welcomes to the British and the Royal Navy that nine years before had been so commonplace. The Japanese, he recollected, 'were in such a nasty frame of mind that incidents multiplied and it [the visit] was definitely not a success.'[18] China, though even then dark clouds covered the land, offered something more pleasing. What Roskill saw there was very much Westernized China, the British entrepôts of Shanghai and Hong Kong.

With him for a time was his wife, Elizabeth Charlotte Van den Bergh, whom he had married 12 August 1930 in London. She was a Jewess of Dutch parentage. Her father, Henry, 'the margarine king', who manufactured Blueband margarine, was a keen businessman. He was also a philanthropist who dreaded publicity and who slipped out of his Kensington Palace Gardens mansion to do good by stealth in the poorest quarters of London.[19] Stephen and Elizabeth met when she was travelling in Austria, where Roskill was on a skiing holiday with friends. They forged a great partnership. They were not very rich; indeed, a large part of Stephen's life was spent in considerable financial anxiety. Elizabeth converted to Christianity. She became a practising, devout Anglican, very much like Stephen. A junior officer's pay could not allow for the extensive touring that Elizabeth was to undertake in order to follow her man to distant ports of call in the Mediterranean, Indian Ocean, and South China seas, and for this purpose it is likely that she used her small allowance from her father.

In Hong Kong, Roskill relished a developing friendship with Stephen Balfour, a brilliant linguist who introduced him to many Chinese students and a Chinese dining club. With a touch of nostalgia, Roskill remembered that 'I managed to introduce E[lizabeth] into that delightful Anglo-Chinese society which really did flourish during our Colonial era,' adding: 'We were blissfully happy – not of course dreaming that we had witnessed the twilight of the white man's dominance in these parts.'[20]

Stephen and Elizabeth spent Christmas in Singapore, and then all too soon came time for Elizabeth to return to England. The Ethiopian crisis was developing, and the *Eagle* was ordered to Malta to reinforce the Mediterranean fleet. 'Three carriers had been assembled for the first time', Roskill remembered, 'and we exercised hard the new weapon of seaborne air power; but it wasn't needed – just yet.' The *Eagle* was ordered home to Plymouth.

There, in the late spring of 1935, Roskill found waiting a letter appointing him to HMS *Excellent* as instructor for the long-gunnery course qualifiers. This duty, he quipped, was 'I suppose the plumiest job the Branch could give a junior Lieutenant-Commander.'[21] Time there also gave him opportunity to polish up what he confessed later was rather rusty theoretical knowledge about gunnery. Besides, the chance existed to keep apprised on innovation in weapons design, for members of the course, and their instructor, made visits to chief armament manufacturers. Thus, Roskill's redeployment from the placid and small world of the *Eagle* to that of the *Excellent* gave him a new lease on life as a gunnery expert.

His time in the *Excellent* affected him adversely in one important way. In his summary record of service and disability, compiled in 1948, he noted that it was during the intensive periods of firing while on the long gunnery course at HMS *Excellent*, from November 1927 to June 1929, that the first noticeable damage to his hearing was done. 'It seems, in retrospect, remarkable that no warning regarding the danger of gun-deafness was given in the Gunnery School and no encouragement, let alone compulsion, was given to the wearing of protective devices.' By early 1932, and now gunnery officer of the 5th Destroyer Flotilla, 'gun-deafness was becoming apparent and appreciable'. He consulted specialists on hearing in London and was told that, for his form of nerve deafness, nothing could be done, an opinion confirmed repeatedly from naval as well as civilian aurists. Still, his work in gunnery continued, and by November 1936 his deafness was well known to his pupils. 'In consequence of my own experience I rigidly enforced orders for my pupils to wear ear defenders whenever firings were in progress. It is noteworthy that *none* of my pupils suffered then or later from gun-deafness.'[22] Little in subsequent naval service gave him relief from gunnery practice or weapons experiments. In his case as a gunnery specialist, deafness was an occupational hazard.

The domestic side of Stephen's life provided a counterpoint to the vicissitudes of his naval service. Elizabeth and he seem to have been blissfully happy, and in due course they were to have seven children, four sons and three daughters. Much attracted to the English countryside, they rented various properties, including a house in Porchester owned by Commander, later Admiral Sir Geoffrey Barnard. There, the Swiss housekeeper, Louise, and the English gardener, Pratt, became devoted to an ever-increasing family. In 1936 Stephen and Elizabeth began an extensive, wearying search for something permanent. Stephen was prepared to commute thirty miles each way, even though he started work at 8 a.m. in Portsmouth. He also wanted to be within reach of a good train service to London, realizing that he was bound to find himself at the Admiralty sooner or later.

They chanced upon a period house (mainly dating to 1699 but with some parts Elizabethan) in northeast Hampshire on twelve acres with a cottage, bought at auction for £2,700. Thus, they became owners of Blounce, South Warnborough, Hants. The hired man made a lovely garden out of a desert. Unspoilt country surrounded the house and buildings, an idyllic setting for a young family engaged in country pursuits. 'When the war came it became a true oasis of peace and beauty, to which my thoughts and longings were always directed,' he recollected. Two cottages were built, more land acquired, and more livestock. The establishment grew. Elizabeth and Stephen acquired horses, and for the children ponies. A groom was hired and another gardener plus butler, cook, and kitchen maid. The payroll mounted. Roskill denies any 'Upstairs Downstairs' class division but he does say that the butler, Smith, an excellent servant, was 'like many of his type a terrible snob. If we had a dinner party he would announce "Lord and Lady Splurge" fortissimo; "Sir George and Lady Snooks" forte; and "Mr and Mrs Bumble" pianissimo! He enjoyed nothing so much as putting out for me full dress uniform with decorations, or the Hunt Club evening dress; and if I wasn't going to change he always showed his disapproval by saying "Only a lounge suit, Sir." Great while it lasted; but it soon became apparent that a day of reckoning was approaching.' Indeed, the establishment had to be reduced drastically and financial expenditures put on a short leash: Smith was let go.

In November 1936 Roskill was appointed to the Queen Elizabeth class battleship *Warspite*, and thus began a love affair with a vessel that culminated in Roskill's 1957 biography of what he termed 'the smartest and most successful ship in the fleet'. That assignment, he noted privately, was 'the best the navy could offer me; but I had no illusions that it was bound to be a difficult one.'[23] *Warspite*, now over twenty years old, was the first of her class to undergo complete modernization, and when he first saw the vessel she was an enormous rusty hulk in Portsmouth dockyard, with an immense cavity in the middle where all the machinery had been. She was being fully re-equipped with Admiralty-type boilers, lighter machinery, and geared turbines made by Parsons. Savings in weight made it possible to modernize her armament. Modifications to turrets increased gun elevation from twenty to thirty degrees, which, combined with a new projectile, extended the range of the big guns to 32,000 yards (16 nautical miles). The anti-aircraft armament was also strengthened. Finally, *Warspite*'s appearance was transformed by her new tower bridge and trunked single funnel in place of her original two.

The *Warspite* was needed in the Mediterranean as soon as possible, for it was designated the flagship for Admiral Sir Dudley Pound. Any and all delays in the dockyard work and any poor performance by the ship itself in trials and manoeuvres (and there were many) infuriated Pound. The Admiral needed two efficient battleships on station.

Meanwhile, in Portsmouth, Roskill scorned the shoddy work of the dockyard and the delays that ensued – all evidenced when the sea trials revealed that a great deal was not in proper order. Extensive trials of the new armament were held, 'which certainly did my hearing no good'.[24] Roskill dug in his heels on what he regarded as critical matters about the armament's effectiveness and readiness. At the completion conference, he refused to sign off on the dockyard's work, and his hard-headed stance on this led to 'a flaming row', with all sorts of threats being levelled by dockyard officers that they would block his promotion. 'I stood firm – and won,' he later commented. One wonders what consequences flowed from this episode. Perhaps there were none at all. What is revealed is his penchant for standing on principle, which led him to acquire numerous enemies as he rose through appointments and promotions.

The *Warspite*'s crew grew anxious about when their ship would sail. She was Chatham-based; accordingly, the men had to take long and expensive train journeys every time they went home. Roskill observes that the executive officer, Commander D.H. Everett, sparked a minor mutiny by his callous and indifferent actions. Admiral Sir Max Horton was called to investigate this episode of 30 June 1937, and his report resulted in several officers being reappointed elsewhere. Roskill escaped this, and his comments on the affair reflect his sympathetic support of the men. Still, Roskill's observations were not without fault, and, as H.P. Willmott says, they may have been diluted in their intensity in order to avoid direct criticism of Dudley Pound and his protégés. The Admiralty ordered Roskill to act as first lieutenant as well as gunnery officer, but the dual position was to no career advantage and he was frozen in his then current rank, lieutenant commander. This was a trade-off, he believed, and fair enough in the circumstances.[25]

The *Warspite* sailed for the Mediterranean and arrived in Malta on 14 January 1938. Admiral Pound, irritated at the attendant delay, went on board his new flagship on 6 February and took out his anger in a sharply worded address to the ship's company. One of his staff officers recorded: 'They had come, Pound told them, with a bad name and he would not stand for indiscipline in his fleet, and he even mentioned [the mutiny at] Invergordon. It was an unhappy speech that misjudged the fine spirits of officers and men, who were proud of their great ship and had spared no effort to make her worthy of wearing his flag and to win his approbation on arrival.'[26] Roskill was witness to this event. The animus he developed to Pound's high-handed and insensitive behaviour was bound to shape his thinking when he came to write about Pound as first sea lord.

As for Roskill, to be in charge of the guns of a super-dreadnought in an age when battleship mentality still ruled was a precious obligation. The *Warspite* was the first reconstructed 15in gun battleship and its new and varied armament called for a quite exceptionally heavy programme of trials and firings. In Malta harbour, the commanding officer, Captain Victor Crutchley, VC, remarked to Roskill while the two strolled the quarterdeck: 'After all, this ship exists only to carry those eight big guns.' Those words stuck Roskill forcibly. 'I glanced up at the burnished muzzles and the shining, crested tampions of the great guns above us, and knew quite well that Crutchley had left half his remark unspoken. "And", he might have added, "it is your job to see that their complicated machinery (of which I knew nothing) works perfectly, and that the five hundred or so officers and men who man and control them are every one of them masters of their craft."'

'That then [Roskill observed] was the purpose towards which we worked for more than two years, and then just before war came, I was called to other duties, and had to turn "my" big guns over to other hands. But I knew by that time that the tool we had fashioned would not fail when the test came; for *Warspite* was the finest ship in which I ever served. I never saw her again after I left her, for the war took me to waters far distant from those in which she covered herself with glory; but I have never forgotten her and never shall.'[27]

Roskill's time in the great battleship was not without unfortunate incidents. Once, a junior midshipman at one of the multiple pom-poms, an anti-aircraft weapon, opened fire on his own account – a stream of shells landed on an army range ashore. Roskill served in the *Warspite* until December 1938, the last two months as its commander. Gaining the rank of commander was a critical hurdle since it was the first rank for which promotion was by competitive selection rather than time in rank. Roskill achieved this milestone in December 1938 at the age of thirty-five and was appointed to the Admiralty to serve in a gunnery position – what he called 'the Anti-Aircraft Desk' – in the Training and Staff Duties Division. On his 'flimsy' Captain Crutchley commented that Roskill had performed 'to my entire satisfaction both as gunnery and executive officer', a fine compliment.[28]

In his new appointment ashore, Roskill won few friends. The less than happy memory of the *Warspite* experience lingered in many minds; he was seen as an agent of change, a source of trouble. As Gunnery Officer of the *Warspite,* he had pioneered a new means of fire control from a protected location beneath the armour instead of a position high aloft exposed to spray and smoke. Once on the Admiralty staff, he 'again made himself unpopular', says Barnett, 'by insisting on the Admiralty buying Swiss Oerlikon 20mm guns in preference to an inferior British design, by opposing Professor Frederick Lindemann's pet idea of replacing anti-aircraft guns with rockets, and later by demanding that each big-gun turret in a battleship should have its own fire-control radar, a demand which led one of his seniors to pronounce: "Roskill, you're mad."'[29] In regard to the adoption on the eve of the war of the Oerlikon gun, he was doubtless a keen initiator and a strong proponent. That weapon was critical to the defence of merchant shipping under the Red Ensign and to the protection of warships from enemy air power.

One night in 1940, when Roskill was duty commander in the Admiralty, a German bomb found its mark. Roskill's office was destroyed. He suffered slight injuries, though none that affected his hearing. On another occasion, he went north to Scapa Flow to check some gunnery problems on the new *Prince of Wales.* After that he went to the battle cruiser *Hood,* where he did some gunnery checks on the vessel (all was well). He was invited to stay aboard overnight, since it was getting late. He declined because of pending work in London, so he took the boat ashore and the night train south. The two warships sailed that night for the Denmark Strait and their rendezvous with the *Bismarck* and *Prinz Eugen.* Roskill later realized what a close call this was, for there were only three survivors when the *Hood* blew up in the action.[30]

Roskill left the Admiralty in 1941 an embittered man. His efforts had come to a close, leaving his reformist zeal checked and his reputation not exactly in tatters but not emblazoned on the list of those highlighted for advancement. In his own words, he 'left behind . . . a legacy of mistrust, and even dislike, among some senior officers.' John Ehrman, who subsequently worked with him in the Cabinet Office, states that this impression may have been exaggerated.[31] If that is true, perhaps we have an indication of Roskill's sense of victimization and aggrandizement. He carried his hurts with him, rather righteously. 'The urgency of war', reflected Ehrman in attempting to explain this murky phase of Roskill's life in the Navy, 'may have lent an edge to an intellect and temper by now impatient of folly . . . for if Roskill's temperament remained artistic it had long ceased to be dreamy: he was a determined, vigorous man, with high standards and clear-cut opinions, and most reluctant to admit defeat. When he was appointed at very short notice as Executive Officer to a cruiser in the Pacific, he accordingly concluded that he was being sent out of the way.'[32]

In September 1941 Roskill was posted to the New Zealand Navy as executive officer of HMNZS *Leander*, a cruiser with 6in guns. He clearly knew that his career had suffered a setback: 'The Adm[iralt]y . . . constantly appointed officers who had blotted their copybooks or had proved "difficult" to distant stations — to get them out of the way; and . . . I certainly did make some enemies while on staff.'[33] The captain of the *Leander* was Robert Bevan, RN. He was proof of Roskill's assertion that the unpopular (Churchill thought him negligent) were dispatched from the Admiralty to other, remote duties. Bevan, serving in the Admiralty, had mishandled a signal from the naval attaché in Madrid on 10 September 1940, a critical point in the lead-up to a British-Free French operation, called Menace, intended to capture Dakar in Vichy-French controlled French West Africa (a subject of Marder's later research). That signal had announced that a French squadron was to pass through the Gibraltar Straits (it escaped unmolested).[34] Bevan refused to wake up Pound, who was then first sea lord at the Admiralty, though the matter was urgent. Churchill, then Pound's superior as first lord, was furious and Bevan was sent packing.

The Royal New Zealand Navy, as it became in 1941, was heavily dependent on the Royal Navy for its ships, officers, and senior ratings. As of 1939, it consisted of two modern light cruisers of the *Leander* class, one minesweeping trawler, and one oil-supply ship, altogether a more limited sphere of opportunity than Roskill had been accustomed to. The *Leander* was sister ship of the famous *Achilles* that had earned a distinguished reputation in the engagement with the pocket battleship *Graf Spee* in the Battle of the River Plate in 1939.[35]

Leander was not a happy ship, recalled Roskill. He found her in a filthy state, a sure sign of bad discipline aboard. The running of the ship, in the absence of its commander (who had been posted away), had fallen to her navigator and first lieutenant, Charles Vereker, and Roskill soon learned that the source of the trouble was the first lieutenant's disloyalty to his captain,

Bevan, when the latter was away from his ship. With help from Chief Petty Officer George Lawes, Roskill restored discipline, and in doing so he received most heartfelt thanks from Bevan upon his return. As Bevan put it: 'You stepped into as difficult a job as can be imagined and cleaned it up most admirably: I hate to think of what the ship would have been like if the previous regime had gone on longer . . . that the transformation was mainly your handiwork is beyond dispute.'[36]

For a time, the cruiser's duty was to act as an escort, the customary fare, and the work in the South Pacific was hot and tedious. Such protracted duties were felt keenly by the ship's company, but, as it turned out, the ship's mission soon changed: it was assigned to replace the US cruiser *Helena*, sunk by Japanese 'long lance' torpedoes in the Battle of Kula Gulf on 6 July 1943. As part of Task Force 18, a Solomon Islands-based unit, under Rear Admiral Walden L. Ainsworth, USN, the *Leander* was on the fringe of things, quite unintegrated with the force, says Roskill. There was much on the minds of the Americans at the time, with the recent loss of the *Helena* to be avenged. The *Leander* – now under the command of Captain C. Aubrey L. Mansergh (later the distinguished editor of the *Naval Review*) – was slower (28 knots) than the American ships and had a wider turning radius. 'She is a handsome ship', wrote an eyewitness, the American historian Samuel E. Morison, in his battle notes, 'disguised by a tall foremast unspoiled by radar grid. Her bronze-skinned men (the New Zealand Navy fights shirtless and in shorts) are in marked contrast to the American blue jackets, who wear long-legged dungarees for protection from burns, and blue-dyed caps so as to attract no strafing bullets. "Pug" [Ainsworth] gives *Leander* a hearty welcome, and she blinks back, "Hope to help you avenge the loss of *Helena* and *Strong*."'[37]

Every night during the Solomons campaign, the Japanese threatened to send ships south through the narrow waters of the Solomons known to American observers as 'the Slot'. The Americans called this fearsome enemy unit the 'Tokyo Express' and their aim was to prevent it from delivering reinforcements to Guadalcanal or to bombard Henderson Field. Early on, the Japanese had been masters of these night battles, and when the *Leander* came into action American tactics had still not been perfected. The Allies were at a disadvantage.[38]

At 5 p.m. on 12 July, the *Leander* sailed from Tulagi as part of Ainsworth's Task Group 36.1. The previous night's passage up 'the Slot' had been uneventful but the sorties from Tulagi were never routine. 'Once more upon the waters! Yet once more!' was the Byronic quotation that came to Morison's mind when orders arrived from the fleet commander Admiral 'Bull' Halsey to sortie once again.

The intent of this fifteenth sortie was to intercept the Tokyo Express, which was expected to depart Rabaul, run down the Slot, and land troops at Vila, at Kolombangara, in the Solomon Islands. That night the light cruiser *Jintsu*, flagship of Rear Admiral Shunji Izaki, and five destroyers were covering four destroyer-transports carrying 1,200 soldiers and supplies destined for Kolombangara. That same evening, Ainsworth's task group passed Guadalcanal Island and Savo Island to port and then took Santa Isabel Island close to starboard (so as not to be silhouetted against the bright moon). By midnight, course was shifted from northwest to west, at 28 knots. The task group assumed a line-ahead formation, with five destroyers in the van, then the heavy cruiser *Honolulu* leading the *Leander* and the heavy cruiser *St Louis*, followed by destroyers. The sea was calm, the sky clear.

The two formations approached on opposite courses, closing at a mile a minute, unknown to one another. Then a searching Black Cat US Navy plane gave early warning. A minute before one o'clock, the Japanese ships appeared as blips on Ainsworth's radar screens, bearing down at 30 knots. Ainsworth sent lead destroyers to release torpedoes. The *Leander* and the other destroyers also fired torpedoes; *Jintsu* exposed a searchlight on the leading American destroyers and thus became a target. The *Leander*'s guns opened at 11,000 yards. Between 0112 hours and 0130 hours, its gun crews fired 160 rounds of 6in shells. By this time, it was intensely dark, the moon hidden behind dense rain clouds. Altogether the three cruisers, the others being the *Honolulu* and the *St Louis*, threw 2,630 rounds at the *Jintsu*, which sank at 0145 hours.

By inter-ship communication, Ainsworth ordered a turn of 180 degrees to port so as to avoid a Japanese torpedo attack. The *Leander* and the following destroyers missed this executive order, however, and were obliged to manoeuvre radically to avoid collision. Morison notes that the *Leander*'s main radio aerial had been shot out by Japanese fire and that, further, the *Honolulu*'s voice radio was not functioning. The cruisers were left to follow the flagship irregularly through gun smoke.

All of a sudden, the cruisers of the task force found themselves bunched together, as Roskill put it. The *Leander*, which had turned wide, caught a 24in 'Long Lance' starboard amidships, leaving it with a thirty-foot hole in the hull. Soon the forward boiler room was flooded, all power was lost, and 3,000 tons of water poured in. Twenty-eight men were killed and the ship put out of the battle. Roskill himself was 'a good deal knocked about', with a leg injury. He had been nearly swept overboard. For some hours, he directed the work of damage-control parties until incapacitated by his wounds. US destroyers *Radford* and *Jenkins*, detached by Ainsworth to stand by the *Leander*, rendered vital assistance. Morison, an observer to these events, noted the massive fire and explosions on Japanese and Allied ships alike, and in consequence of this encounter the enemy lost the *Jintsu*.[39] The episode became known as the Battle of Kolombangara.

How the officers and men of the *Leander* saved the sorely stricken ship is one of the classic tales of successful damage control. That they succeeded is an example of courage, discipline, training, and, above all, teamwork. Stories of individual leadership and heroism are legion. Of Roskill, Mansergh wrote in his report: 'The high standard of organization and training shown by all hands was largely due to his initiative and leadership.' Drills, lectures, and demonstrations had made the ship's company 'damage control conscious'. 'Well, it was just what we had been told it would be like,' was the general reaction. Power was restored in the ship and a speed of 12 knots was reached.

The crippled cruiser limped south to Tulagi and made port, where temporary repairs were effected and the wounded cared for. It then steamed to Auckland. Surveyors determined that the damage was so extensive that the vessel should make the long passage to Boston for repairs. Meanwhile, Roskill spent a week in hospital; back pain later developed and medical examination revealed spinal damage (these details figured materially in his later pension awards). Yet he was soon well enough to be given command of the *Leander* for the voyage to Boston. He was promoted to acting captain for this passage to the American dockyard, and so it was with pride that he could list in his *Who's Who* entry: 'Commander and Captain, HMNZS *Leander*'. On 21 March 1944 he was awarded the Distinguished Service Cross for what was described as 'outstanding courage, skill and enterprise in charge of Damage Control' during the Battle of Kolombangara. The events of this phase of the Pacific war were crucial to Allied success and they marked the opening of the offensive phase of that campaign. But this was the end of Roskill's combat experience. As for the *Leander*, it underwent repairs for two years and thus saw no further action during the war.

Through subsequent years, Roskill kept contact with the ship's company. To Commander R. T. Jackson of the Royal New Zealand Navy, he wrote in 1979, 'I shall always look back on my three years as Commander and Captain of the ship as one of the most worthwhile experiences of my naval life; for she was a very fine ship with a fine band of officers and men. It has touched me that many of them have come to visit me when in the old country, and to talk over old times; for it has made me realise that the bond of comradeship which was refined and burnished in the furnace of war still holds good. I earnestly hope that it may always be so, and that the young generation of the RNZN may perhaps learn something from those of us who went before them and, perhaps[,] gave them some hints on the art of the sailor. [At the reunion dinner] I should like to be remembered to all those who served with me.' Roskill always remembered 13 July 1943 as the anniversary of the *Leander* episode and did so 'with a mixture of pride in the ship and its company and a sorrow at the loss of so many of our shipmates.'[40]

In Boston, Roskill began his long and close acquaintance with Americans on American soil. On 12 May 1944 he joined the British Admiralty delegation in Washington, of which in due course he became chief officer (Administration and Weapons). No doubt he realized that dealing with the Americans would not be all clear sailing, but the extent of the problems he had to confront likely surprised even him. The troubles began when he found that, contrary to the Lend-Lease agreement between the two countries, the US Navy Department flatly refused to release a large quantity of manufacturing information the British required under another agreement, that involving patent interchange. Vickers Armstrong wanted particulars on gun mounts and certain small engines; a British fuse manufacturer, details on American rugged tubes and batteries. In his report, Roskill recounted the many difficulties, the many particulars of which need not concern us. But it was clear to Roskill that the relations between the US Navy's Board of Ordnance and the British Admiralty delegation stiffened progressively as the sea war in the Pacific became more and more an American affair and, not least, as Britain made interminable alterations and additions to its equipment requests. He wrote: 'They [the Americans] were determined to subordinate our needs to their own. Moreover there was the undoubted desire among a certain circle in the Navy Department to reserve to their own Service the entire credit for defeating the Japanese Navy and to treat the European and Mediterranean theatres as secondary to the Pacific.'[41]

Roskill was not alone in his appreciation of the limits to Anglo-American cooperation. Admiral James W.A. Waller headed the British Admiralty delegation and his American counterpart, Admiral Joseph M. Reeves, though retired, was one of the persons with whom he had to liaise under the arrangements established between Churchill and Roosevelt. The main purpose was implementation of such joint naval arrangements as the respective governments had agreed on. Cooperation and patience were called for on both sides and by all engaged in this unusual Allied enterprise. The secretary of the navy, Frank Knox, was answerable to the president to make sure the arrangements were effected without difficulty. At the Combined Munitions Assignment Board, Reeves, well connected to the White House as a naval aviation pioneer and former chief of naval operations, was a stickler for protocol. He was senior to Waller by rank and years; besides, he was as sharp as a tack as well as alert to any charges that the Americans were not serving British interests in the war effort. Waller met regularly with Reeves to oil the diplomatic naval machine. Yet friction was bound to occur. The defence of warships against enemy attack from the air preoccupied Roskill's thinking, for on all seas the Royal Navy continued to face innovations devised by the enemy as well as contending with existing disadvantages. This was the situation as of 4 July 1944 when Roskill went to see Reeves. He had been there the previous day, when all had gone nicely. But on the 4th he breached protocol and upset the American admiral considerably. Later that day, Reeves wrote to Waller: 'I found Captain Roskill not only inadequately informed upon the subject under consideration, but apparently unable to conduct the discussion in an appropriate and dignified manner.' He added, 'Should you find it desirable for any reason to send a representative to discuss a subject orally, I shall appreciate your sending someone who is aware of the customary conventional and courteous manner of doing it.'[42]

The argument between Roskill and Reeves was over a gun director – a device for controlling the aim of a gun mounting (in this case 40mm Bofors anti-aircraft weapons) from a remote position.[43] This director was an updated version of the one designed by Charles Draper at Massachusetts Institute of Technology and mass-produced by Eastman Kodak in Rochester, New York. Roskill naturally sought to obtain the quantity agreed upon but found to his alarm and dismay that the US Navy had suddenly requisitioned the lion's share. His conversation with Reeves does not survive in recorded form, but that of Reeves with Waller does, in US naval archives. Roskill placed upon Reeves the personal responsibility for the unfair treatment the British had received. 'His attitude certainly was not the attitude that I have been accustomed to in any officer of any rank in our service, and his manner was not; and his criticisms of me were most severe,' complained Reeves.

Waller first talked the matter over with Roskill, who said that, yes, Reeves seemed 'a little bit clipped'. Yet Roskill expressed surprise at Reeves's allegations, and so Waller went to see Reeves on 14 July to defend his man. Reeves repeated to Waller that he had never been spoken to as Roskill had to him. It was a matter of protocol breached. He was offended. Waller, coming to Roskill's rescue, pointed out that other American admirals, Walden Ainsworth and Robert Ghormley, had formed the highest opinion of Roskill. Indeed, Roskill's competence in armaments had been the reason the Admiralty had selected him for the post in the first place. Reeves could not be assuaged or deflected. So strongly had Roskill effected his mission, Reeves told Waller, that he wondered if higher-ups had directed a new course of action in Anglo-American naval relations. Was Roskill the instrument of this? No, replied

Waller. When Waller suggested that the British were at a disadvantage in relation to their more powerful American counterparts – he mistakenly used the David and Goliath parallel – Reeves grew even more furious. Here was a prospect that Central Casting would have loved. At the end of the day, the matter was resolved to mutual satisfaction, with Reeves at least aware of the necessity of playing by the rules, though he never admitted responsibility in this case. At Waller's request, he retracted his own letter, for Waller had told Reeves that as long as it existed in British hands Roskill could call for a court-martial to clear his name. Reeves therefore obliged. How Waller dealt with Roskill is not known, except to say that he kept quiet about it and did not inform the Admiralty. Roskill may have learned an important lesson and thereafter exercised greater caution in his actions in Washington. He says that he took the matter as high up as he could, with an intriguing result:

> At one of the Mission's weekly staff meetings soon after my row with Reeves I suggested that I should fly home to tell the Admiralty the plain truth about what they could and could not expect us to do; and the Admiral [Waller] immediately supported the idea. So back I came [to London] by air, told the Supply Departments how things stood, and asked to see Admiral Sir Andrew Cunningham [first sea lord]. When I explained our difficulties he said, 'Roskill, we'd get on better if you'd shoot Ernie King [admiral, US chief of naval operations]! to which I replied 'Is that an order, Sir, or merely a suggestion?' Whereupon he turned me out of his office – with a twinkle in his eye.[44]

Roskill's duties in the United States subsequently involved much work in experimental gunnery, including rockets, and firing at numerous ranges and on board American warships. He had considerable success in his relations with the Bureau of Ordnance and the Bureau of Ships, owing to the fact, as he explained, that he had the technical knowledge to meet the American high-powered specialists on something like equal terms. As he put it, the word went around the bureaus that 'here's a goddam Limey who knows something about ordnance engineering and who talks the same language as we do.' Roskill says that he could get what he wanted from the Americans, including the gyro sights which had been promised but whose delivery Admiral Ernie King had stopped: Roskill, at considerable risk to his counterpart's job security, put them aboard one of the British escort carriers at Norfolk and sent them to Britain.[45] Roskill became good at his work. Accordingly, he rose to become chief of staff (Administration and Weapons) to the head of the British Admiralty delegation, and he remained there until 1946.

At the end of Roskill's appointment, President Roosevelt named him an officer in the United States Legion of Merit.[46] Ehrman says that he was not a born diplomat but he liked Americans and had been impressed with what he saw in the Pacific. 'He was dealing with technical problems suited to his experience and imagination; and – always of importance to him – [was] respected and liked by his immediate superiors.' Barnett, by contrast, recollects that Roskill's posting to Washington was not a happy one, and the reason for this was the anti-British attitude of US Admiral King and his personal staff. At his memorial service, in Cambridge, it would be said that Roskill exhibited frankness and openness in Washington, and this did not make him the best diplomat in the world.[47] Whatever the truth of these matters, major and minor, it is clear that Roskill carried off rather nicely the latter portion of his Washington assignment. Many an officer of the Royal Navy could find relations with American counterparts amiable in public but might speak privately in less satisfactory terms. At the official level, Roskill carried the day, and his Legion of Merit would not have been awarded had he not coupled diplomatic ability with his distinguished record at sea at the Battle of Kolombangara.

Of these days, Roskill later recounted – and his private correspondence shows his darker side – that he was never as unhappy as during his first months in Washington. The weather was hot and sticky – oppressively so despite his experience in the South Seas – but he was also miserable because 'with victory coming in sight Lend-Lease was in its death throes and the US navy people under King were being perfectly beastly to us.' Yet he also acknowledged that the chief of the Bureau of Ordnance, Admiral G.F. Hussey, and his deputy, Rear Admiral Willard F. Kitts, became his first friends in the American capital. Both provided great hospitality then as in his 'later life' as official historian. Roskill seems to have had much freedom in Washington, for his superior, Waller, preferred fox-hunting in Virginia. Roskill remarks of Waller: 'He was completely useless to me.' Given such freedom as presented itself, Roskill could go about, as he claimed, transforming the British Admiralty mission 'without telling the people at home'. He did this by shifting 'the whole staff on to co-operating with the US Navy in technical developments'.[48] Roskill was taking risks, but such ventures as he undertook were not opposed, and this led to his next assignment. Waller, for his part, never betrayed Roskill and he shielded him from criticism: in fact, in official reports he classified him as 'an outstanding officer'.

Roskill had just returned to Blounce when he got a phone call to attend at the Admiralty on urgent business. He did so. Would he go back to the South

Pacific, this time on a quite different venture? The nature of the assignment was outlined and the ramifications for British sea power were literally explosive. On 1 April 1946 the deputy first sea lord, Sir Charles Kennedy Purvis, appointed Captain Roskill as senior observer to the British delegation assigned to the atomic tests at Bikini Atoll in the Marshall Islands, in the mid-Pacific, 4,500 miles west of San Francisco.[49] Bikini was to be the setting for many US atomic tests between 1946 and 1958, including the first nuclear weapons. On the occasion in question, Operation Crossroads, as it was called, was intended to determine what effects atomic-bomb explosions would have on warships (surface and submarine), equipment, and material and, more generally, give an indication of the survivability of warships in the event of nuclear war. From a scientific point of view, technical experiments were also planned on nuclear-weapon explosion phenomena and radiation contamination. The results could only be imagined. Military planners with a view to the future wondered how naval tactics as used in the Second World War would be effected by the new weapon: Ought surface units to be dispersed or were fleets still possible? How would the bomb change the relative merits of navies and air forces, and would naval combatant forces even be redundant if long-range bombers could drop the new lethal weapon? 'Why should we have a navy at all?' asked Carl A. Spaatz, leader of US Army Air Forces during the war. 'The Russians have little or no navy, the Japanese Navy has been sunk, the Germans never did have much of a navy. The only reason for us to have a Navy is because someone else has a navy and we certainly do not need to waste money on that.'[50] The atoll's native population was evacuated, and the potential bomb site, a tropical paradise, was soon to change character – its shores a tangle of rusting machinery and cables, decaying houses, and concrete bunkers, its lagoon a graveyard of vessels of war.

Roskill was later to write, in his notes to Zara Steiner, that he accepted the Admiralty's invitation provided he could choose his own team and that he would go out under the auspices of the chiefs of staff, not the Admiralty, since it was to be an inter-service affair. This is only partially true. The first sea lord called for one submarine officer, a torpedo officer, a senior naval constructor, and a commander in the Engineering Branch. The submariner selected was Arthur Hezlet (later Vice Admiral Sir Arthur Hezlet), who told me that 'Captain Roskill assumed command and made it perfectly clear he was the boss, even though there were seniors there, including the Senior Naval Constructor.' The British were treated with the greatest suspicion by the Americans, Hezlet said, and this was where Roskill came in handy: 'He was extremely first class in getting the Americans on side.' Discussions among team members were hard work, but Roskill was invaluable in picking out the key Americans and determining what should be looked for in the results from the scientific experiments.[51]

The observation party assembled at the British naval mission in Washington, and there they used the Arlington Hotel as headquarters. One of the members carelessly left a confidential British document – London's instructions to Roskill – in a desk. Somehow, that desk was removed to the US Navy Department, where its contents were found and sent, unopened, to London. The matter was hugely embarrassing. Roskill reported the loss of the document, as he was bound to do, but already the matter had reached the permanent secretary of the Admiralty, Sir John Lang, who reported to Roskill their lordships' displeasure at his administrative carelessness. That document had been under his charge.

The British team was off to a bad start, even before embarking on their immense journey. They crossed to San Francisco by special train and then sailed via Honolulu to Bikini, at the time an idyllic atoll in the South Pacific. Roskill had taken on board a well-stocked liquor cabinet, a useful contingency given US regulations against Armed Forces personnel drinking on official premises or aboard ship. That rule did not apply to British personnel. Roskill became an agreeable host and an expert in fluid diplomacy. At Bikini they were greeted by a mass of out-of-date US, German, and Japanese warships all anchored in a formation devised by Admiral William Blandy, commander of the US inter-service organization called Joint Task Force One.

Roskill quickly learned of the mission's goals. A terrible new weapon had been developed, one that would revolutionize foreign policy and military strategy and tactics. He knew that atomic bomb 'Little Boy' had been dropped on Hiroshima on 6 August 1945 and 'Fat Man' on Nagasaki three days later, leading to the total surrender of imperial Japan on the 14th. Much had still to be learned about flash, atomic waste, debris, and particularly damage that could be caused with such weapons on the surface, below surface, or from the air. Strategic implications were enormous, tactical aspects more so. Accordingly, the Americans planned tests for each of these. They had Roskill's team on the scene almost out of courtesy, for they had no intention of sharing many secrets. In fact, they placed the British team in the same location as the pack of journalists. But Roskill elbowed his way in and lodged a complaint: he got the British observers a more advantageous position.

On 1 July 1946 Roskill and the British party were aboard the US naval auxiliary *Blue Ridge* twenty-three miles distant from the first explosion, one caused by a bomb named Able dropped from a B-29. The bomb created an air-burst detonation about five hundred feet above the water. The party did not see the blinding flash since they were under instructions to stand with their backs to it. There was a colossal explosion, said Hezlet. They then spent a fortnight examining the large number of ships, noting the damage. In fact, the US Air Force (USAF) had missed its target – the old battleship *Nevada* painted bright orange to assist the bomber crew to find their aim point – and the British observer team chuckled at this, for the USAF had boasted they could put the bomb in a biscuit barrel. In the event, the heavy cruiser *Sakawa*, two destroyers, and a pair of attack transports were sunk but most of the ships stayed afloat. Something more dramatic had been expected.

On 26 July the second bomb, 'Baker', suspended one hundred feet beneath the target vessels, was detonated. Observers were much closer this time, distant eleven miles. This blast sank eight vessels including the battleships *Arkansas* and *Nagato* and the carrier *Saratoga* as well as two submarines. Baker generated a wave and spray of radioactive water and debris. As Robert Ballard writes, military researchers (and this would include Roskill and company) were flying blind when it came to risks of radiation.[52] The third bomb, 'Charlie', was called off. Blandy had all he needed. The observers had no doubts about the potential lethal power of underwater explosions and their remarkable implications for naval war, particularly the prospects of exploding devices under keels of vessels.

Roskill knew of the media circus about the explosions, and wisely he decided that it would be best to write up the report in San Francisco, away from the whirl of the moment. The party flew to Honolulu and then sailed for San Francisco in extremely heavy weather. In a fine hotel, for six weeks, the team drafted and redrafted the text. Hezlet says that the constructors and engineers would have preferred to do their own reports but Roskill insisted that the report was to be one document. Hezlet decided on the shape or form of the document because it was he who had to determine the effects of atomic explosions under various categories: A – vessels sunk, B – disabled, C – seriously damaged, and so on. The object was to assess damage according to scale. Different scenarios were imagined. What, for instance, could a single bomb do to a convoy, or harbour, or an amphibious operation?

Hezlett and A.V. Hill, an expert in measurements, were key players in the writing of the technical material. When asked if Roskill wrote the report, Hezlet replied that, no, he did not. 'He altered it with considerable style but did not change anything materially. He accepted it.' Thus, this report, which indicated that submarine warfare was the war of the future, consisted of a series of segments, one by each of the specialists.

The British report, which Roskill liked to think of as his own, was brief yet comprehensive.[53] The American report as compiled was enormous, with too much detail to be of use. The Americans were found later to be using the

British report because it was the only one that covered the event and did so in good style – and the implications for future warfare were spelled out with distinct clarity. All the documents collected by the British team were shipped home in the Cunard liner *Franconia*, stashed in cabins with secure bolts. Roskill called this 'my Top Secret load'. When the liner docked at Liverpool, Roskill and the treasures were escorted off by Royal Marines guard to the surprise of the passengers. Then, at the Lime Street station he boarded the train and was locked into a first class compartment under guard. In London, an armoured car awaited him and drove him to the Foreign Office, for the Americans had insisted that these papers be delivered there and not to any other department. When the Foreign Office said that they knew nothing about it and refused the deposit, Roskill wisely had them placed in a secure room in the Admiralty's heavily fortified Citadel.

On the party's return to London, says Hezlet, the members all resumed their respective duties. There was a period when Roskill gave lectures on the effects and implications of the Bikini trials, his presentation being accompanied by a film, provided by Admiral Blandy, showing the explosions. Hezlet went along as interlocutor, aiding the largely deaf speaker at question time. What surprised Hezlet was that he was never asked any question when, five of six years later, the British set up their own trials. In 1978 Roskill went in search of the copy of the Bikini report that he had given to the British chiefs of staff and, to his dismay, could not find it. But by dint of perseverance a copy was eventually located – not in the Admiralty records but in the papers of the Air Historical Branch, a curious twist to a story of British observers, atomic blasts, naval tonnage, and a tropical lagoon now heavily contaminated.

Roskill's last years in the Service were made difficult by recurrent pain from war injuries and by increasing deafness (a handicap that led him to become proficient at lip-reading). Yet they were also years of recognition and advancement. Fresh from his success at the Bikini atomic trials as head of the British team, Roskill found his reputation with the Admiralty enhanced. In a new era of Anglo-American naval cooperation, with the Cold War entering its initial stages, Roskill, with his experience in Washington on military procurement matters and knowledge of the impact of atomic weapons on naval warfare, was a new-found, valued asset at the Admiralty. The upper hierarchy of the Service now looked on this 'former rusticated delinquent whom the Navy had succeeded in keeping as far away from Whitehall' as a commodity in demand. In London, in tandem with his new position as deputy director of naval intelligence, he served as British naval liaison officer to the US naval team headquartered in Grosvenor Square. When, in 1949, this tour of duty came to an end, he received a letter of congratulations and thanks from Admiral R.L. Conolly, commander-in-chief US Naval Forces Eastern Atlantic and Mediterranean.

It was his pen that led to his appointment to the naval intelligence staff. The director of naval intelligence, Rear Admiral Edward Parry, Roskill's commander in *Eagle* days, complained about the quality of the members of his division and their inability to prepare a memo with suggestions. Would Roskill help? He needed well-written papers about current problems produced. Roskill obliged, and within hours Parry came back to Roskill with the invitation to join his office as one of his two deputies, subject to agreement of the naval secretary to the first lord of the Admiralty. Roskill agreed and the appointment was confirmed. 'I had nothing else in prospect,' Roskill later wrote. He worked in this happy job, while simultaneously carrying out his liaison duties, for two years. In this position he would have known about the vast Anglo-American microfilming project, under way nearby, which involved the copying of German naval documents that British units had clutched from the jaws of fate at Tambach Castle, Bavaria, in May 1945. And, although not in the inner circle of those knowing the Ultra secret (the decrypting and decoding of German military intelligence by the British at Bletchley Park), he would have been alert to its existence and importance. He had a genial director to work for. 'But all the time there lurked in my mind the undeniable fact that unless I could get another sea command the Navy held no future for me beyond compulsory retirement on reaching the top of the Captain's list.'[54] He needed an appointment to command a ship so as to be considered later for promotion to rear admiral. No such opportunity arose in this era of naval cutbacks of ships in commission.

As early as December 1947, Roskill had known that his days in the Royal Navy were limited. All the same, he had a strong desire to be invalided out of the Navy rather than to wait a few years more and then be thrown out without regard to a disability which was entirely attributable to his service. On 11 January 1949 a medical survey was taken of Roskill. He was found unfit for further naval service. A seagoing appointment was not possible. Accordingly, their lordships found it necessary to place him on the retired list of the Royal Navy, effective 8 May 1949.

The finality of this to Roskill may be imagined, though he had a glimmer of what would transpire. From Sir John Lang, permanent secretary of the Admiralty, he received a letter of commendation touched with regret. Segments of this follow:

> My Lords desire me to take this opportunity to convey to you an expression of their appreciation of your services during a long and

successful career . . . through which you have shown yourself an outstanding officer.

In June, 1944, whilst serving on the staff of the British Admiralty Delegation, Washington, you were promoted to Captain and continued in this appointment . . . until 1946, when you were appointed as Senior British Naval Observer at the trials of the atomic bomb carried out by the United States. My Lords are gratified to know that your relations with the Americans were at all times most successful and much which has been achieved between our two countries in the field of weapon technique can be accredited to the excellent sprit of collaboration brought about by our personal efforts. Your outstanding work in this connection has been fully continued in your final appointment as Deputy Director of Naval Intelligence (Organization) and British Naval Liaison Officer with the United States Forces, in which capacity you carried out your duties with the same decisive leadership, competence and success which have marked your whole career.

I am also to inform you that it was a source of satisfaction to My Lords that your distinguished service was recognized by the President of the United States by the award of the Degree of Officer in the Legion of Merit.

Finally, I am to express my Lords' great regret that your valuable services to the Navy, and a career which could have been expected to carry you to the highest ranks, have been prematurely terminated through the injuries which you received in peace and war during the course of your duties.[55]

The glowing praise of their lordships' letter was tempered by the sharp reality that the curtain had been drawn on a significant phase of Roskill's life. He retreated to Blounce and the pleasures and duties of house and country property. In the circumstances, it would have been easy to play country squire. But riding to the hounds, though delightful, was not enough. He continued to write for the *Naval Review*, his anonymous articles on 'Science and the Service' being of particular significance. His Bikini report was, strangely, his ticket to a new career. Those who knew him in the Service regarded him as the atomic naval secrets man, and his ability to liaise with the Americans, and keep them onside, so to speak, was of additional credit and value. The ability of his pen was known and recognized. And so, by a curious twist of fate, he would soon be vaulted back into government employment and even greater prominence, this time as 'official naval historian'.

Chapter 3

Marder's Admirable Admirals: Richmond and Fisher

Dust was still settling on war-torn Britain when Marder made his long-awaited return to London, in early 1946. From the swaying palms of Honolulu to the fog-bound streets of the imperial capital was a goodly distance in space and mentality. The war and the unavailability of key Admiralty documents had delayed his urgent plans — made six years before — to undertake research for a sequel to his acclaimed *Anatomy*. He now had in mind an examination of the years from 1904 to 1919, which he dubbed, or enshrined as, the Fisher Era. For the projected book he even had a working title: The Dynamics of British Sea Power. He intended to make up for lost time. He came to London with the zeal and energy that was characteristically his, a marvel to all who had the pleasure of his acquaintance or friendship but of which he could have no control as to its influence or effect. And from this time dates the legend, often repeated, that Marder burst into the British Museum Library and thrust a fistful of completed request slips into the hands of a surprised keeper who was told, with a sense of urgency more suitable to a fire brigade answering a call, that he needed the items pronto: 'I've just arrived in London and have not a moment to lose.'

Marder had ready access to the holdings of the British Library, including such manuscripts as were not in the 'restricted' category. Try as he might, however, he could not get to the golden lode, the Admiralty files that had been so advantageous in the writing of his *Anatomy of Naval Power*. Such success as that book had achieved, Marder stated, was largely due to the exceptional opportunities he had to ransack the Admiralty archives. Now the immediate difficulty stared him in the face: without such renewed access, any knowledge of those inner workings of the Admiralty could only be a matter of speculation. Too many historians had written naval histories without the inside story. But *Anatomy* had set a new standard, one that Marder intended to maintain. He thus hoped to repeat his 1938 coup and breach the wall of Admiralty documentary defence.

In 1946 he applied to the secretary of the Admiralty along the same lines as before. He wanted access to the records of the pre-1914 decade and of the First World War period, nothing more. Though his letter of application was dated thirty-eight years after the end of the Great War, he received a frosty answer, and indeed he got nowhere then or in subsequent appeals for the next ten years. The documents were sealed – for departmental and cabinet use only. Each year he sent virtually the same letter to Whitehall and received the same brusque and negative reply. 'Many English scholars had complained of the Admiralty's favouritism – and to a foreigner at that. The Admiralty were not going to stick their necks out again,' he recounted. Under such unpromising circumstances, and while marking time, Marder embarked on two other projects – studies of Britain's foremost admirals of the modern era, Admiral of the Fleet Lord Fisher and Admiral Sir Herbert Richmond. In fact, by the time Marder arrived in London in 1946, he had already written a fulsome article on Fisher, published in the *US Naval Institute Proceedings* for 1942, and was no stranger to the machinations and intrigues of that unlikely holder of Britannia's trident. Marder also had his eye on Winston Churchill as a historical subject of naval administration and operations, and he would publish his first work on this subject – 'Churchill as First Lord of the Admiralty' – in 1953, in the same journal. He also was studying the art of leadership, examining Nelson's career with a view to determining traits that recur most often in careers of outstanding naval and military officers. His findings were later published in the *Naval Review* in 1961. In other words, Marder was casting his net far and wide, but still he could not land the big fish, those Admiralty papers.

In any event, the return-to-London academic term of 1946, with leave granted from the University of Hawaii and funding provided by the prestigious John Simon Guggenheim Foundation of New York, his first purely research term since 1940, initiated annual visits, some lasting weeks, others a month or more. For the next fifteen years, until he sent to his publisher the script of the first volume of *From Dreadnought to Scapa Flow*, he kept up a steady correspondence with those who would help him. Reading his list of acknowledgements in the prefaces of his volumes reads like a Who's Who of living admirals and other officers agreeably aiding Marder and his research. While the Admiralty's records department kept its doors tight shut against him, he exchanged letters with the likes of Captain A.C. Dewar (retired), who made their own private collections of materials available to him. Thus, Marder's Churchill article would be based on unpublished Jellicoe and Fisher papers and profited greatly from Dewar's information.[1]

But that was not all, for aid was now coming from wider quarters and unexpected places. His reputation as a great historian preceded him and, in 1946, opened new avenues — the first to be exploited by any historian — to a non-government world. Some were based on deferred acceptances of invitations to visit or call, each one leading to others. Journeys into deepest countryside to view hitherto unexploited private diaries or to interview retired admirals and captains or their next of kin, trips to Oxford to examine Asquith's manuscripts, and calls to defence institutes or military and naval establishments all extended his connections, with fruitful gain. During this time, Marder first visited Admiral Lord Fisher's heir and commenced the gathering and editing of correspondence later published as *Fear God and Dread Nought*, in three volumes (1952–59). During this time, too, he became friends with then Rear Admiral Peter Gretton, a life-long supporter and a historian in his own right, who provided aid from his post at the Imperial Defence College; Gretton later went to University College, Oxford, where his support and guidance never flagged. Almost without exception, Marder's friends and professional associates gave unstinting and loyal support.

It was on one such expedition of inquiry that Marder found himself face to face with a powerful figure, Admiral Sir Herbert William Richmond.[2] With clear but shrewd blue eyes looking out from a lined and thoughtful face in which humanity and kindness were perhaps the dominant traits, as one visitor (Stephen Roskill) described a likeness of the man, Richmond then held the revered mastership of his Cambridge college, Downing.[3] Richmond had been Vere Harmsworth Professor of Imperial and Naval History from 1934 to 1936, and the only naval officer to hold that chair, or, for that matter, be head of college. Richmond bulked large as Britain's leading naval historian, a prolific writer, and a veteran commentator on naval, defence, and strategic affairs. His first historical work had been completed before the First World War, *The Navy in the War of 1739–48*, although delayed in publication, by war, until 1920. Richmond's connections with Cambridge were deep, and his grandfather and father were noted artists. He was not as dismissive of others as legend has it; rather, he moved easily with the great and the good of which he was a member by class and social bearing. Even so, in earlier years he had a tendency to be, as observed, his own worst enemy, and his abundant criticism of others' actions or inadequacies had made itself known in the Service. Though once an intimate of Jacky Fisher, the two had parted ways, with Richmond for a time largely relegated to assignments that did not tread on the old sea lord's parade ground.

Within the Service, Richmond had a reputation as a heretic and troublemaker. He had been a leading force in establishing a 'Corresponding

Society for the Propagation of Sea-Military Knowledge'. 'We are going to have a try to stir up interest in what Kempenfelt called the 'sublime' parts of our work – strategy, tactics, principles ... what I hope to develop is the mental habit of reasoning things out, getting at the bottom of things, evolving principles & spreading interest in the higher side of our work' (Diary, 27 October 1912). That society produced for private circulation the *Naval Review*, first published in February 1913. Richmond's intent was to improve officer education and advance the study of naval policy and organization, and he recognized his actions as a revolt 'against the naval tradition that only senior officers need be concerned with such sacrosanct subjects as tactics, strategy and other aspects of the higher conduct of War'. To this he added, 'I wonder what the authorities will say when it reaches their ears!'[4] In May 1915 the Admiralty objected to the journal's discussion of the ill-starred Battle of Coronel. The previous November, the German Vice Admiral Maximilian Graf von Spee and the East Asiatic Squadron had caught an inferior British force under Rear Admiral Sir Christopher Cradock off of Coronel, on the Chilean coast. The crushing German victory had left many unanswered questions about the composition of the British force that had sailed to its doom. These and other matters were discussed in the *Naval Review*. In July the first sea lord, Admiral Sir Henry Jackson, decided that publication should be suspended on grounds that the journal's printed statements could be detrimental to British interests if the enemy knew them. Nowadays the Young Turks, as they became known, led by Richmond, K.G.B. Dewar, and William Henderson, are applauded, or at least understood, in naval historical circles; but in their time they spelled trouble or at least caused unease, and publication of the *Review* did not resume until 1919. The well-intended criticism as led by Richmond, designed to awaken the Royal Navy to its past (and the lessons of maritime strategy), was regarded in certain circles as dangerous to the Service and to the country. Dewar, for instance, found that independent thinking harmed his advancement, while Richmond, for his part, although one of the best sea officers of his time, was regarded as, to quote Prime Minister David Lloyd George, 'a paper man'.[5] This meant that, despite high-level urgings, Richmond failed to be appointed to a cabinet advisory post on naval affairs during the war. And, even though he had some senior commands, including flag captain of HMS *Dreadnought*, and some positions of prominence in the Admiralty Operations Division, Richmond did not advance commensurate to his talents and his comparative youth. In 1931, when holding the rank of admiral, he was dismissed from the Admiralty for public views attacking the then received policy on battleships.

All these details would have been familiar to Marder. Similarly, he would have been aware, that morning that he attended on the old admiral, that he might be facing the unexpected: historical ferret that Marder was, he would be on the alert for any insight into the main features of policy that directed the course of British naval warfare of the Fisher era.

At the outset of his visit to Richmond, Marder could not have known that, beginning in 1909 and running right through to 1920, Richmond had kept a diary, or, more correctly, a record of impressions. The diary included personal comments on British naval affairs and his observations on how the Admiralty conducted its war at sea. In particular, it directed hard-hitting jabs at Churchill, the first lord of the Admiralty, and Fisher, the first sea lord. The former he chastised for his lack of strategic knowledge; the latter for his tendency (which we now know not to have been the full measure of the man) to be a materialist, concentrating on the instruments of naval war. The diary contained extensive commentary on the Admiralty's lack of strategic knowledge and of war plans. To Richmond's way of thinking, the war at sea was conducted largely under the heading of muddling through. Richmond, we surmise, had no plans to publish his diary. He had taken no steps to publish it. But would he have minded if someone wished to publish it posthumously? Probably not, for it is this author's opinion that Richmond would have welcomed someone advertising his insights and strictures. After all, he was a self-admitted heretic in naval affairs. His earlier observations on a poorly run and executed naval war would be a good reminder to later generations.

What happened next is recorded by Marder: 'Having manoeuvred a warm invitation, I found myself one March morning, at the Master's Lodge, Downing College, Cambridge. There followed five or six of the most interesting hours I have ever spent.' Richmond's geniality and interest in Marder put the younger scholar completely at ease. 'We talked shop mostly − of my fumbling naval research and of his *Statesmen and Sea Power*, which he hoped to complete if his heart behaved (his appearance belied his 74 years and precarious health); and about all naval aspects of the recent war, the status of naval historical scholarship, and the 'Fisher era' in the Royal Navy.'[6]

The two top living historians of the Royal Navy were now in the same room. Marder judged Richmond as, with A.T. Mahan and Julian Corbett, one of the three outstanding naval historians of the twentieth century. He had all the assets of a great historian, according to Marder, including a succinct and lucid style, a profound grasp of his subject, and a brilliant ability to analyse situations and to deduce from them fundamental principles. Richmond knew a good deal about Marder, too. He held him in high professional regard. He had reviewed *Anatomy* at length in the *Naval Review*, devoting fuller attention to the book than any other reviewer or publication. Richmond had also placed a flattering review of it in the *Spectator*. In fact, because Marder had told his readers more about the Navy's history in the 1880–1905 period than they had ever known, the veteran had many fine points and observations to make that day, and those to a fellow historian of note who understood these matters completely, implicitly. Richmond was then, with the help of his daughter, readying an expanded version of his 1943 Ford Lectures delivered at Oxford for the Clarendon Press. That book, *Statesmen and Sea Power*, published in 1946, became a classic exposition of the uses of sea power by the Royal Navy over a period of five hundred years. 'The air enthusiasts aren't going to like it,' he told Marder.[7] Working historian that he was (he had been nurtured by Corbett, the most influential naval historian and strategist of his age), he took an interest in Marder's agenda. Still demonstrating insatiable energy despite six years of poor health, Richmond conversed with the young American in an engaging way. Marder was about to chance on a gold mine.

Marder takes up the story:

> At one point my eye accidentally fell on a section of the book shelves, where some seven or eight 8 by 12½ inch volumes labelled 'Diary' were resting innocently. To my query as to the nature of these diaries, he replied modesty that they were just odd jottings and reflections he had made in the years 1909–1920. 'There's nothing much in them.' My curiosity stimulated, I received permission to examine one of the volumes. The contents quickened my pulse: candid and penetrating comments on events, trends, people and policies in the Royal Navy, conversations with the makers of naval policy, and copies of his official papers and private correspondence, altogether a veritable El Dorado of unpublished primary source material on the Navy in one of the most critical periods in its history. The Admiral was certain that I would not find much in these volumes for my sea-power work, but agreed that I should cart them off to London for a more leisurely examination. Subsequent study confirmed my first impression of the immense historical importance of the material.[8]

Marder had visited Richmond none too soon, for on 15 December 1946 came news of Richmond's death, in college, of heart failure. Many fine things were said about him. 'His charm and his affability – no-one could have been easier for anyone to speak to – showed how well he knew how to encourage young men' formed part of the tribute to Richmond by a Cambridge don, who added that 'as the Head of his House, he believed in a "band of brothers" and proved what the infection of such a belief can be. He was impatient of quiddities and taradiddles, but was too good a fighter as his professional and scholarly record shows, to decry honest controversy decently conducted.'[9] The great historian G.M. Trevelyan, the only English historian to shun Marder (I suspect because of Marder's book on Richmond), in giving the eulogy following a private service in college, summed up Richmond's achievement: 'In all relations of life he was as nearly perfect as it is given to man to be, and those who were nearest to him knew best what he was. When goodness and beauty of character, greatly superior to what we ordinary men can show, are united to great and well-disciplined powers of mind, we see to what height in the hierarchy of being a brother man can arise.'[10]

Marder was deeply touched by the loss of his new historian associate, Richmond. On learning of his passing, Marder asked Lady Richmond for permission to study the diaries in a more detailed way with a view to publishing them. His intention was twofold: to contribute a valuable piece of British naval history as such, and to pay tribute to and provide a memorial of an admiral 'who was as great a man as he was a seaman, teacher and naval historian.' No biographical portraits of Richmond had yet been published and no autobiographical account either. Lady Richmond gave permission. She, too, had kept a diary of some of those same years and knew all about her husband's ruminations and outbursts. 'When he was courting me', she recalled to Marder, 'the chief thing I remember about our conversations was his outlining with fervour his plans for a Naval General Staff.'[11] She must have been aware, too, of her late husband's admiration of and trust in Marder's abilities, else she would not have permitted publication, and no members of the immediate family made objection. For biographical information, Marder searched far and wide. William H.L. Richmond, a son, prepared notes for him, and two brothers of the admiral supplied appraisals of Richmond's character and personality. Marder also gathered data on Richmond from various obituaries and appreciations, and he found Rear Admiral H.G. Thursfield, a contemporary of Richmond and naval correspondent of *The Times*, helpful in several ways. Some twenty-five naval officers contributed anecdotes or appreciations of Richmond. Marder drew heavily on published accounts and records and at the same time extended his search through Foreign Office, War Office, and Admiralty libraries. In the last of these, his friend H.H. Ellmers of the Admiralty Record Office helped Marder tie up loose ends. All these insights went into the biographical sketch Marder included in the book. As for the text proper, Marder selected those sections of the diary he thought suitable for publication, since, given limitations of space, the whole was impossible; and to these apt selections he added some memoranda and personal correspondence. The memoranda he might already have seen in the Admiralty papers but the diary and personal correspondence were all new, revelatory — and explosive. Yet Marder himself never saw publication as opening a bottle of a genie, or, for that matter, a can of worms. 'I wonder if we shall live to see a true history of the war published!' Richmond had noted in his diary on 4 December 1916. Marder took this to mean: 'The material which follows supplies much of the raw material for that "true history" which has yet to be written. Although he never considered publishing his diaries — in fact, nothing was further from his mind — they may be regarded as his legacy to the Navy and the country. At the same time they serve as a mirror to a brilliant mind.'

Portrait of an Admiral: The Life and Papers of Sir Herbert Richmond was a sizeable tome, at 407 pages. Marder dated his preface May 1950, but the volume did not appear until April 1952, published by Jonathan Cape in London and Harvard University Press in Cambridge, Massachusetts. It contains a one-chapter, eleven-thousand-word biography of Richmond — Marder titled it 'A Biographical Essay' — based mainly on family papers and recollections, also snippets of how others saw Richmond. Marder portrayed Richmond as one of the ablest men who ever served in the Navy, an outstanding officer, teacher, and historian. Of the last two there could be no doubt. It was the first — that he was a particularly outstanding officer, the finest of his time — that brought forth a swarm of criticism, for not only was Marder partisan in saying that Richmond stood above the rest in quality, he was guilty in putting his subject, gilded, on a plinth. Richmond had long been a target in certain circles. Thus, publication of this book inadvertently made Marder a target. It was an early example of frank biography. To some who read it, the entries in Richmond's diaries selected for the book gave the impression that Richmond had sat down in the evening to record the events of the day, dipped his pen in vitriol, and, so to speak, let off steam.

On the one hand, Marder showed Richmond as a man of charm, intelligence, and character, 'in a measure denied to a handful of mortals inhabiting this planet at one time' (says the dust jacket). Marder considered that 'the true history of the English naval aspects of the First World War has not hitherto appeared in print, and that Richmond's diaries give the kind of detail missing from the official history'. On the other hand, the old guard did not appreciate Marder's redemption of Richmond. To those who regarded Richmond as a danger within, a poor team player, a provocateur, a spiteful critic, or even all of the above, Marder's own largely innocent attempt to provide an insider's view could only spell trouble. Richmond pulled no punches, gave hard facts. 'He was in a position to know a great deal and made the most of it.' He made 'many pithy comments' on Britain's civil and military leaders, 'and they do not always coincide with recorded history'. And again: 'In a word the book contains a sort of inner, behind-the-scenes history of the Royal Navy in what was perhaps its most critical period.'

Marder now had his first volume of Fisher papers on the stocks and was moving it quickly through the press. This constituted a most demanding time in his life, one of juggling balls in the air and of travelling back and forth between Honolulu, Harvard, and London. It was also a time of urgent reappraisal of British naval history. Controversy persisted about the performance of the British against the German fleet at Jutland in 1916, a case of victory denied to a British nation expecting another Trafalgar and annihilation of the enemy. Then there was the Dardanelles disaster, when Churchill and Fisher had embarked on a 'by ships alone' strategy to knock the Turks out of the war. 'Damn the Dardanelles!' Fisher had ranted, 'they will be our grave,' and they were. Who was responsible for such planning, such oversights? The pointing of fingers continued. W.S. Chalmers' authorized biography of Admiral of the Fleet Earl Beatty (one of the antagonists in the refighting of Jutland) appeared at just the time as Marder's *Richmond*, and the jury was still out on how the Royal Navy had stumbled so badly in the First World War. Meanwhile, Roskill was labouring away at his first volume of *War at Sea*, ever mindful of perils that Sir Julian Corbett, Richmond's historical mentor, had faced as official historian. The large number of books on British naval activities in the Second World War did not lessen the need for more dealing with the First, of which Richmond's diaries and papers as selected by Marder were wholly engaged. The Richmond book was bound to draw fire.

It was in such circumstances as these that *Portrait of an Admiral* was widely reviewed in leading British newspapers and journals. Marder, back in his air-conditioned office in distant Honolulu, received copies of these reviews via a London press-cuttings service, forwarded from his publisher Jonathan Cape that spring and summer of 1952. None of the reviews can be said to be brief; all of them, in fact, were generous examinations of the book at least in length. The first review to reach Marder was from the London *News Chronicle* (28 April). The caption blazed out the thread of approach: '1914 Churchill's Order: "Foolery," Says the Admiral.' That leader put up the dialectic between Richmond and Winston Churchill, which is how the *Chronicle* wanted to portray the story. The writer, Vernon Brown, pitched his review as Richmond's attacks on Churchill's activities as first lord of the Admiralty, before following on with snippets, or extracts, from Richmond criticizing Fisher. Then as now, Churchill always made good copy, as journalists knew, and Brown's gathering up of all Richmond's juicy jabs at Churchill was typical of other reviews that Marder's books garnered in the daily press. The *Yorkshire Post* (9 May) noted wryly that, given Richmond's diaries, it would astonish an American reader that Britain ever had the wit or the guts to have a Navy at all. The problem, as Richmond had commented upon time and again, was an absence of fighting spirit. Edward Crossley, who did the review, noted that it would delight the irreverent to read that Churchill was insane and that Fisher was narrow-minded and stupid. Equally enlivening was Richmond's portrayal of some at the Admiralty as 'the cabbage-headed people' and those in Whitehall as 'the fat heads'. 'All this is legitimate,' wrote Crossley, who added: 'If we do not have men in the Navy who are thinking on independent lines that are the fruit of careful study there is no hope for the Service. But in this diary the opinions on people are too often extreme . . . His diaries make lively reading and will fascinate everyone interested in naval affairs, but they are one man's opinions, private when written. Men with far greater practical experience than he ever had of the handling of fleets in battle and of the policies of the nation have written in peace far more temperately of those with whom they could not agree in war.' Fair comment, all of it.

The general lines of critique were being laid down. Mark Arnold-Foster, in the Manchester *Guardian*'s Books of the Day (15 July), got to the heart of the matter as to why this sort of book had never appeared before. With tight prose he explained the heretofore wall of silence about what went on in the Admiralty during the First World War. He reminded readers that the Navy preferred to keep its secrets to itself: 'Those who serve in it are trained from the day they join until long after they have retired to exercise discretion. To their credit, they say as little about the Navy's merits as they say about its failures. It is a fine tradition, loyally observed, but it has some unfortunate results.' The tradition, he said, postponed criticism, and mistakes did not become apparent until after death or retirement of the senior officers who made them. Lessons, which could have been learned, become redundant, and the conduct of sea warfare continues to depend on trial, error, and out-of-date doctrines. Arnold-Foster coupled Marder's *Richmond* with Stephen King-Hall's *My Naval Life*, published at the same time. 'Both officers agree that the first error of all was an error of training, a failure to think about war first and gun drill and paintwork afterwards. This resulted in a navy commanded by 'amateurs' and a lack of any coherent doctrine. 'No one', wrote Admiral Richmond in retrospect in 1919, 'had clear and agreed-upon views as to how war would be conducted. This applied to both strategy and tactics; it was the direct outcome of the educational system.' King-Hall expressed it more briskly when he said that Fisher's dreadnought policy produced an enormous collection of ships, each succeeding class bigger, more expensive, but the colossal output of floating war potential was not accompanied by any output of thought as to how it would be used. This, too, was Richmond's theme. Says Arnold-Foster: 'Each passage [of the diaries] illuminates, with appalling clarity, the intellectual weaknesses of the British naval staff. Many of them, perhaps unfortunately, betray their author's impatience with his more stupid superiors. But they constitute a rich source of historical materials.'

Leading weeklies played upon these same points. The admiral-historian William James, who had served with Richmond, obtained the assignment for the *Spectator* (9 May). Drawing on his own knowledge as an insider, he explained that many senior officers greeted the transformation of the Victorian Navy into the majestic fleet of 1914 with residual resistance against, or at best grudging support of, the small cadre of officers led by Richmond who 'saw that this battle-power would not be exploited unless officers studied war and unless there was a trained naval staff'. In an era when strategy and tactics were regarded as the business of admirals and not of junior officers, Richmond was seen as an unpractical visionary. James thought Richmond one of the finest commanders and seamen of his time who drew the best from his ship's company; those who liked to portray Richmond more as a professor than a naval officer, James added, frequently forgot these characteristics.

In later correspondence with Marder, James was to rank Richmond above all other officers of his time, thus confirming Marder's own published appreciation: 'It is strange', wrote James on 28 September 1961, 'how many of these clever fellows who had such sound ideas about staff and training for war were not much good at the ordinary work of a naval officer – organizing and managing a ship's company, drawing loyal, wholehearted service from their officers and men when in command of ships. Richmond was the exception. A first rate Commander and a Captain for whom officers and men would do their best. It is, I suppose, rare to find all the qualities in one man.'[12]

In his review James held that Richmond's tragedy lay in the fact that he served so frequently under officers who derided his efforts to direct naval thought in new directions. Not until Beatty met Richmond did the latter's chances of working at the Admiralty improve. 'He has brains, has studied, and will, I hope be a great help to me,' wrote the first sea lord, who added: 'He is of an independent character, and will always say what he thinks, which is one of the reasons I could not get him here before.' That was in 1918, when

Richmond was appointed director of Training and Staff Duties. As James points out, once in his new billet Richmond – and the new Plans Division – was treated with scant respect. He had no powers in decision making, and his policy proposals foundered during their voyage from basket to basket. The principal officers at the Admiralty were all subject to Richmond's attacks on paper. James notes how this translated into day-to-day behaviour: 'His severe strictures on so many Admirals will be unwelcome to those who esteemed them, and the rapidity with which he changed his estimate of their abilities after disagreement is evidence that intolerance sometimes marred his judgement. Constant frustration fans intolerance, but those who served under some of the Admirals whom he impugns will not be surprised that, gifted as he was with vision and burning with zeal, he found them exasperatingly unimaginative and resentful of advice.'

Next came an unsigned review in the *Economist* (21 June), which contended that the evidence presented sufficient reason for a full study of Richmond's life and work. But, tellingly, the same evidence did not justify Marder's conclusion that Richmond was 'perhaps the ablest officer of his generation'. 'Nor is acceptance of the diaries as a self-portrait entirely fair to Richmond. For he used them as a safety-valve for the anger and frustration he felt over the many rebuffs he received.' The reviewer stated that Richmond had great powers of exposition. He was an officer deeply imbued with knowledge of past wars. He had immense professional competence. But his diaries 'also reveal a sensitive, hypercritical man, extremely stubborn in his views and arguments and unable to accept even honest disagreement.' The tragedy, Marder had explained, was that this ability, clear thinking, and prophetic foresight were so little used. The Admiralty was surely not to blame, as Marder had implied, said the reviewer, who went on to say that Richmond went about his work in a way 'calculated to frustrate his purposes and to make enemies for himself'. More moderation might have allowed him to accomplish more of his objects. 'However much of a philosopher Richmond was in his historical studies and in his writing and research work he was, as a naval officer, ambitious and it was the failure of his ambitions that brought him distressing, even undignified, disillusionment and bitterness. It is therefore good to know that, in the autumn of his life, he found fulfilment and a just appreciation of his work and stature in the University of Cambridge.'

Many other reviews followed these general trends. Roskill reviewed the book for the *Naval Review*. In support of Marder, Roskill said it was fair to admit that Richmond was often ahead of his time 'and that many excellent seeds were sown by him on barren ground'. Theodore Ropp, a Harvard man and authority on the French Navy, said that Richmond resembled the US

Navy's Admiral W.S. Sims in outspokenness and brilliance. John B. Heffernan, of the Department of Naval History in Washington (and Admiral Samuel Eliot Morison's aide in the preparation of the US Navy's history of operations in the Second World War), said that Richmond's prominence after 1919 did not justify Marder's conclusion that a great career was ruined by zeal and outspokenness. He also objected to Marder's tendency to assume that Richmond's opinions, as recorded in the diaries, were correct beyond question, when many contrary views were held. Burke Wilkinson, author of books on naval warfare, took an opposite tack. He found *Portrait of an Admiral* an appropriate explanation of why Richmond was 'marooned in posts which made too little of his gifts'. Richmond was a rebel: 'Cross the historical sense of a Mahan with the dedication of a Billy Mitchell, add a pungency of phrase that was all his own and you have an idea of the man who emerges from this book.' With all its comments on Jutland, the Dardanelles, cruisers, destroyers, mines, and the scuttling of the German fleet at Scapa Flow, the book, said Wilkinson, 'is a trove for the student of naval history'. And Wilkinson thought that, in his last mellow years, Richmond must have looked back on those earlier days, when he was hot for certainties, and laughed at the juxtaposition: 'For, from this rich and rewarding volume, it is the sweetness of the character of the man, the lack of bitterness for all the brilliant bitter controversy, that stays longest with us.'

All of these reviews must have resonated with Marder, and so far there could be no reason for complaint or objection about the book's reception. He did not spoil for a fight, but, as his published responses to Alfred Vagts's spiking of his *Anatomy* in 1941 had shown, he would surely not back away when once aggrieved or outraged.[13] Nor did he when the *TLS*, or, as it was then called, the Literary Supplement of *The Times*, published its review of *Portrait of an Admiral* on 30 May under the heading 'Naval Service'. When Marder read it he could only guess who the reviewer was. His files do not betray any hunch. Best bet is Admiral Thursfield, already mentioned, who had helped him with some of the research particulars. Thursfield, a powerful naval analyst and commentator, and a prominent figure in *Brassey's Naval Annual*, went right for the jugular. In a long critique (that said not one nice thing about the book), the reviewer laid out his points. He did not think the diary extracts sufficient justification for the subtitle *The Life and Papers*. Further, he contended that Richmond would never have allowed his intimate thoughts recorded at the time, hot from the mint of his powerful intellect, to be used without any consideration of the larger context. Marder had a thing or two to learn about the historian's craft: 'So professional a historian as the occupant of a university chair in that art cannot be suspected of having yielded to the temptation to pick out passages in Richmond's diaries which, by reason of outspoken criticism of the behaviour or abilities of prominent persons, make the most piquant reading. Yet that is the impression which the book may well convey to the reader who knew Richmond's real stature.' Then the reviewer tightened the screw. He thought Marder's portrait one-sided. The reviewer was eulogistic about Richmond, but he carped at the misleading nature of Marder's selection: he cited and compared Richmond's description of Sir William May in 1910 as an 'ignorant obscurantist' with his appreciative memoir of the same great sea captain on his death in 1934. He concluded: 'The future historian of the naval side of the 1914–18 war cannot afford to ignore Professor Marder's volume, if only for the insight it affords into the actual conduct of the higher direction of it as recorded at the time – even if only in private expressions of extreme exasperation – by one who saw only too clearly many of its glaring shortcomings.' He added, however, that the historian of the future ought to consult the diaries themselves rather than Marder's selections from them and also Richmond's published works and lectures.

'I would be grateful for the privilege of replying to the grossly unfair review,' Marder wrote to the editor of *The Times* on 29 July 1952.[14] In typical numerical fashion, he detailed his complaints:

1. Richmond left nothing else behind, or 'more accurately, I saw nothing else, and when, on two occasions, I sounded out the Admiral's heirs about the existence of other material, I was actually given to understand there was nothing else of value.'
2. 'It was not my purpose to write a full-scale biography, if only because of the extreme paucity of the material.' He had given the various topics adequate treatment: 'My main purpose, after all, was to present the edited papers.'
3. 'How then explain that he attached no strings to my use of the papers?' was Marder's response to the charge that Richmond would never have allowed his diaries to be used, exclusively, as the basis for an appreciation of the man or the Navy at that time.
4. 'This is a canard!' wrote Marder about the snub 'so professional a historian as the occupant of a university chair.' 'I make it perfectly clear in my preface that everything I regarded as having historical value was included. There was no attempt, conscious or unconscious, to pick the material for its spiciness alone! The reviewer might have taken the trouble to check with the original before making such a baseless insinuation.'

5. Yes, there were lots more to the man than suggested by his papers, as indicated in the biographical introduction.
6. 'I think', replied Marder to the matter of May, that 'the historian will prefer Richmond's opinions of 1909–11 on Admiral May, based as they were on first-hand observation and concrete fact, to the obituary notice of 1934.'
7. 'Three general observations: to judge from the length of the review, the book is not one to be dismissed lightly. Secondly, the reviewer is more royalist than the King. I thought I was Sir Herbert Richmond's most ardent admirer! Thirdly, there appear to be Englishmen who do not relish having British naval history written by foreigners. They do not feel that outsiders can have the proper sympathy and understanding. Perhaps so but I would suggest that perspective and detachment are pretty good substitutes. There may even be those who would rate such assets much higher. P.S. I love the Royal Navy – its history and traditions.'

The editor of the *TLS*, Arthur Crook, replied on 12 August thanking Marder for his letter, which had been passed on to the reviewer for comment. Crook included the reviewer's points in his letter while maintaining the reviewer's anonymity.[15] The reviewer sent the following, under this general remark: 'It is only fair to Professor Marder to let him know that the reviewer knew Richmond well for over half a century, and was thus fully acquainted with his habit of mind. So far, therefore, as there is a difference of view in that sphere between the author and reviewer, the balance of authority probably rests with the latter.' Then, after following Marder's order of battle for three points, the reviewer struck out on his own, though continuing to attack him on professional historical grounds. We follow the line of reasoning:

1. 'Professor Marder does not challenge my stricture that the sub title 'Life and Papers' is hardly justified by the use of papers covering no more than eleven years of a long life; he merely says that they were the only papers he saw! That hardly seems to me to be the attitude of a conscientious historian.'
2. 'This [the shortness of biographical treatment] hardly calls for an answer. My statement is endorsed by every one of Richmond's relations and intimates. I do not know for what purpose Richmond allowed Professor Marder access to his diaries, but I am quite sure it was not for the purpose of a book about himself. He never saw the book himself, for he was dead before it was written.'

3. 'I adhere to the view that the book conveys the impression I stated [of selecting certain passages only], but Professor Marder will note that I prefaced that remark with a disclaimer of any suspicion that he had actually yielded to the temptation mentioned.'
4. 'I cannot accept Professor Marder's view that a portrait drawn while the writer, as I put it, was "suffering under a sense of frustration, or while unhappy and tired by long and unprofitable argument with obstinate or stupid brother officers" is more accurate than one based on mature consideration. Moreover, it is just not true that Richmond "mellowed" with age, as those who were privileged with his intimacy knew very well. Throughout his life, as I wrote, "no man was less hasty than he in the judgements he expressed in his published works"; and that is why I protested against the hasty jottings of his private diaries being presented on his whole mind. At the same time, I would whole-heartedly endorse the view that there was a serious dearth of talent in the upper ranks of the R.N. in the period 1907–1920.'

The reviewer had the advantage of an insider's intimacy with the subject. That sure-handed thrust was more than one-upmanship: it was 'in Service', something that Marder could not replicate irrespective of how hard he tried. That having been said, the reviewer showed no charity or appreciation of Marder's work, only the musings of a fellow officer turned writer who thought Richmond had been betrayed. He was unwise, and unfair, to charge that Marder's portrait was 'one-sided', for the general thrust of scholarship since has not changed his views appreciably. In any event, Marder made no response to the reviewer, and no evidence survives that gives an indication of his further considerations and feelings on the matter. The *TLS* did not publish his response, or the reviewer's counter-attack. Marder's complaints were kept quiet. Under such circumstances, Marder abandoned further objections to the review, but he cannot have been any the happier for being told that 'his attitude as a conscientious historian' was inadequate. Priding himself on thoroughness of research and on the specific definition of task, Marder could not but have taken umbrage at the reviewer's strictures. He was touchy about being an outsider to the Navy, particularly as a foreigner (by which he meant American), and he betrays this in his letter to the editor. At the same time, he is clear that perspective and detachment can be even more valuable than proper sympathy for and understanding of the Service. This, in fact, was his strong suit. He did not change his technique, and by the time his Fisher letters and papers were published his star was rising fast. Even so, he would have licked his wounds from the *TLS* encounter, in print and in correspondence, and continued his inquiries. The *TLS* was to treat him more appreciatively on future occasions, but, then again, it had no longer to deal with the thorny problem of Richmond and his blatantly frank views made inside the Admiralty in years of peril. It was not until Marder's difficulties with Stephen Roskill that the *TLS* began printing his rejoinders.

Subsequent historians have not left Marder's treatment of the diaries alone (though they seem not to have consulted the various reviews, or have not given evidence of having done so). Donald Schurman, in *The Education of a Navy*, says that Richmond's finding of fault in others and penchant to disturb the status quo kept him opposed to his brother officers. Barry Hunt, Richmond's biographer, states that Richmond was a heretic to be watched with great care. His difficult temperament made him unpopular with fellow officers, and he was fussy, given to exaggeration, and inclined to refuse postings offered. The Australian naval officer Mac Hoban calls him a 'ratbag' but points out that original thought, tolerance, and cooperation, not uniformity, are Richmond's telling legacy. He loved his country and the Navy, and he served them both well.[16]

In 1963 Roskill wrote a retrospective on Richmond for the *Naval Review*'s golden jubilee issue. It was a chance to get in shots at Marder. Roskill set out to show a difference of interpretation between the published diaries and the Admiralty records of those days. Richmond's official correspondence revealed moderation in expression and clear-sightedness, not the intolerant and uncompromising opinions expressed in the private record. Roskill also said that Richmond had an uncomfortable habit of being proven right by events, and, as an example, he cited Richmond's suggestion that the Dardanelles theatre be shifted to Palestine. According to Roskill, Churchill first dismissed Richmond for 'criticising an operation which had already been approved' but later – on the basis of third-hand evidence – changed his mind. On one occasion, Richmond and Churchill met informally and Richmond recounted the reason for his dismissal. In Roskill's telling, Churchill, with magnanimity, replied, 'You were quite right, Richmond, and I was wrong.' For Roskill, these were musings, part of his interwoven narrative of various fragments. As to the publication of Marder's book, Roskill wrote: 'In common with many others who knew and admired Richmond, his Cambridge associates unanimously regret the publication of extracts from his diary.'

Others took the same view. Thursfield said that Marder's publication of Richmond's diaries was unfortunate: the Navy did not like its laundry being washed in public. Besides, there seems to have been a difference between the public and the private Richmond. Hunt, who may have conversed with

Roskill on this point, put it similarly. He admitted that Richmond's pre-1914 correspondence showed him to be not 'very level headed', but he added that many of his memoranda demonstrated wisdom and moderation. Like Roskill, Hunt thought that Marder's selection gave a wrong impression of Richmond.[17] It is hard to know whose interests are being served here. Certainly, the criticisms do not further the cause of finding out about Richmond's private thoughts about naval administration and strategy during the First World War. That subject seemed to have frightened everyone except Marder and, in recent years, Daniel Baugh, Barry Hunt, and James Goldrick.

The 1970s flowering of the study of maritime strategy and the examination of the greats of naval history who discussed the topic — Mahan, Vice Admiral Philip Colomb, Corbett, and others — naturally led to a new look at Richmond's books. Although Richmond never wrote a treatise on maritime strategy, from his works all sorts of lessons and examples can be gleaned, not least about amphibious operations, the value of smaller, heavily-gunned ships, and blockade. In the wake of the Mahan centenary in 1990, the US Naval War College in Newport, Rhode Island, sponsored a 'Mahan is Not Enough Conference', in which the works of Corbett and Richmond were featured. Baugh drew the opening assignment to review Richmond in historical context, and he leaned heavily on *Portrait of an Admiral* for fact and interpretation. The most startling aspect he discovered in reviewing the book against the diaries was that Marder had not included the discussion, already mentioned, about Lloyd George's intimation that Richmond was 'a paper man' and therefore, despite pleading from Commander Joseph Kenworthy (later Baron Strabolgi), was not brought in as a naval adviser to the cabinet. Inclusion of that encounter would have made a choice addition to Marder's appreciation of Richmond's unappreciated value. If in fact Marder knew about it, and we can surmise that he did, the explanation for exclusion lies in his own statement: 'Much has been left out in this work, but practically everything I regard as having historical value has been included. Except for a scattering of epithets that might have given needless offence to a few persons, there have been no "judicious omissions".'[18] The omission could have been made on editorial advice and perhaps there were legal implications.

At the same conference, Hunt reported that Admiral Sir Frederic Dreyer had been outraged by the publication of Marder's Richmond. On the basis of the *TLS* review of 1952, Dreyer had now realized 'what appalling stuff Marder had handed out. Richmond had largely a bogus reputation.' So incensed was Dreyer at *Portrait of an Admiral* — it showed Richmond for what he was, said Dreyer, namely, a disloyal cad (besides being clever, unbalanced, and conceited) — that he wrote a book of his own as a form of rebuttal: *The*

Sea Heritage: A Study of Maritime Warfare (1955).[19] Another scholar, the Royal Australian Navy officer and naval historian James Goldrick, judiciously placed Richmond where he rightly belonged, as a moving force in the formation of the Naval Society, and showed that he was by no means alone in his quest to educate the officers in their knowledge about history, strategy, and tactics. Drawing heavily on Marder's book, he matched it equally with documentation from many collections. In the end, this reaffirmed the general appreciation of Richmond begun forty years previous by Marder.[20]

Today, it is hard to imagine the study of the Royal Navy in the First World War without resort to *Portrait of an Admiral*, which has taken its place among the most engaging behind-the-scenes accounts of naval policy making and of the views of those directing affairs at the Admiralty. It was ahead of its time, the first oar in the water, so to speak. Those who study training and education in navies similarly use Richmond's text as a firm basis for discussion.[21] Ultimately, *Portrait of an Admiral* may be Marder's longest-lived book if not his most influential one. It began with good fortune and happenchance, and the opportunity was not lost on the American.

As of the date of the publication of *Portrait of an Admiral*, Marder had yet to get access to those precious Admiralty files that would allow him to unlock the secrets of naval direction. For that reason he shifted to Fisher as a subject, and by the time his Richmond book appeared his first Fisher volume was not far behind – and that is another chapter in the story of how persistence paid off and how life was never easy for the American naval historian in a British world wrapped in the White Ensign. Even his Fisher studies tended to dredge up old problems and, much like the Richmond diaries, made Marder a subject of admiration matched with suspicion. Getting on the inside of the anatomy did not come without a good deal of bloodshed.

Marder's publisher, Jonathan Cape – in the wake of the success of the Richmond book – had encouraged Marder to undertake the project of editing for publication the letters of the celebrated, volcanic admiral, the 'stormy petrel' Lord Fisher of Kilverstone. Needing little encouragement, Marder happily launched forth on this new venture. He could not have known that the project would consume fully a decade, and he did not break the back of it until 1955. The volumes, three in all, were published in 1952, 1956, and 1958 as *Fear God and Dread Nought: The Correspondence of Admiral of the Fleet Lord Fisher of Kilverstone*.

Currently, Fisher is a household name among those familiar with the history of the modern Navy in the dreadnought era, especially those who read biography, most notably Jan Morris's inviting *Fisher's Face*. But at the time Marder began his research into the correspondence of this unlikely and unusual admiral, the career and political intrigues of the first sea lord were more narrowly known, even forgotten. A fossilized perspective had arisen, partly as a result of Fisher's self-portrait in his *Memories* and *Records* and partly because Admiral Sir Reginald Bacon's official biography had awarded him too much undeserved credit. Bacon's book, published in 1929, nine years after the old admiral's death, had characterized Jacky Fisher as probably the most remarkable Englishman of the century, which was possibly true, and the greatest sea officer since Nelson, 'who never made a mistake so far as the Navy was concerned', which was patently false.[22] Reviews of Bacon had been poignant and unreservedly sharp to the point of hostility. They had also been lengthy, for shadows cast by the Fisher era on the Royal Navy had been long and dark. When Winston Churchill read Bacon's portrait of Fisher, he wrote a stormy review of it in the press, and this got a new lease on life when it appeared in the second edition of *Great Contemporaries* (1932). Churchill had had no intention of dredging up details of the Dardanelles campaign, but Bacon's book forced his hand. Now it was time to point the finger at Jacky Fisher. However, the story did not die with Churchill. Nor has it ever died. The story of the titans at the Admiralty – Fisher and his political boss Churchill – is of enduring attraction.

Marder did not take Bacon's line of uncritical acceptance. On the other hand, he was clearly enchanted by his subject and gave Fisher a sympathetic treatment by a fresh appraisal. In fact, from the first article that he wrote on Fisher, in the *United States Naval Institute Proceedings* in March 1942, which carried the title 'Admiral Sir John Fisher: A Reappraisal', originally submitted in 1941 in the Institute's prize-essay contest, right down to his last exploration of the matter, the entry on Fisher in Peter Kemp's *Oxford Companion to Ships and the Sea* (first published 1976), he maintained that Fisher was the principal architect of that British command of the sea that, more than any other factor, won the First World War. But Marder's edition of Fisher correspondence exposed the full measure of the first sea lord, warts and all, making him even more conniving and devious than had ever been appreciated – and, surprisingly, more likeable.

The research trail that led to the publication of the Fisher trilogy was a long and fascinating one. As long as the mother lode of Admiralty papers lay beyond his grasp, Marder could usefully spend his time trawling through various other collections, chiefly in private hands. And he travelled where angels feared to tread, charmingly opening doors for himself among the glittering peerage and less well-to-do gentry, retired admirals and captains, their widows, and other kin or friends.

In 1946 Marder ventured north from London to Lennoxlove, Haddington,

East Lothian, to call on Nina, Duchess of Hamilton ('a Most Gracious Lady', he was to style her in his dedication to her memory when the first volume appeared in print). The dowager duchess, age sixty-eight, the long-time confidant of Fisher (he called her the 'Beneficent One'), had offered to put at Marder's disposal some Fisher papers that she kept in store. While married to the 13th Duke of Hamilton, she had been Fisher's lover, and his passionate letters to her were one of the reasons she kept them under her care. She loved the Navy, and her bonds with it were strong. Her late husband had been a sometime lieutenant in the Royal Navy and came from three generations of naval officers; one of her grandfathers had been a rear admiral. Fisher had been a close friend of the duke and duchess, more particularly the latter, and he spent much time in Scotland with Nina or in their house at 19 St James's Square, London. Eventually, Marder was to see over one thousand Fisher letters, all packed away in a score or more of dusty trunks, a good sample of some six thousand Fisher letters that Ruddock Mackay was to catalogue there and elsewhere in the late 1960s.[23] Always, however, more Fisher papers turned up. Those Marder saw in 1946 did not include certain other papers held by the dowager duchess, and these she had intended to send to Marder shortly before her death in December 1951. At the kind invitation of her son, the 14th Duke of Hamilton, in 1955, Marder was to see these in Scotland in time to include a selection in the third and final volume. And other collections of documents were to be seen – of particular note, some Fisher papers at Kilverstone Hall, near Thetford, where Jacky Fisher, when he became Baron Fisher of Kilverstone, had what might be called his country seat. By advance correspondence, Marder had been promised access to these private holdings.

In his 1955 travels in search of Fisher, using London as his headquarters, Marder kept up a torrid pace. True to his promise, as he put it graphically in a grant application, he would

> ransack the Admiralty Library, any Admiralty Record Office material that might be placed at my disposal, the Jellicoe and other papers in the British Museum, and the pertinent papers at the National Maritime Museum, Greenwich (the Madden, Noel, Kelly, etc., etc., Papers). I would also wish to consult with certain naval officers and other individuals having specialized knowledge of the Royal Navy in this century: Lord Hankey, Rear Admiral H.G. Thursfield, Professor Michael Lewis, etc., etc. I would then go to Calne, Wilts, to examine the Lansdowne Papers, visit Cornwall to examine the McKenna Papers; the Esher Papers, near Oxford; the Asquith Papers at Balliol College, Oxford; certain Fisher Papers at Newcastle (with the family of the Admiral's

Naval Assistant); then up to Scotland: the Duke of Hamilton's estate.[24]

All of this was true. The itinerary, the furious stops along the way, with hardly time for tea or gossip, though eating sandwiches on the job, resembled a whirl, a strange wind sweeping through country gardens and terraces, vaults and muniments rooms, attics and annexes. But that was Marder's style – the above brutally demanding schedule was all to be completed in three months.

Fisher had been a profuse letter writer all his life, and Marder's selection of these letters went a long way towards revealing the real character and personality of the man. In the first volume, subtitled *The Making of an Admiral* and embracing the 1854–1904 period, Marder traced Fisher's development from the time when, as the 'friendless, forlorn, penniless' small midshipman who joined the *Victory*, he was sent to the China station. Fisher's letters reeked of grammatical oddities and unusual punctuation. Everything he wrote bore a stamp of breathless directness; his style had an enduring freshness to it. As a naval cadet, a mere boy, he was totally uninhibited. His letters show this tendency, and how he won the affection of successive captains. At age eighteen, he had a baptism of fire in the disastrous attempt to storm some enemy forts during the China War – this 'dreadful, horrible work'. In 1870 his career took a new turn, as an energetic reformer and weapons enthusiast. He foresaw that underwater weapons would revolutionize naval warfare and imagined clearly what the Whitehead torpedo would do to an unprepared surface ship of war. He got the *Vernon* started as a torpedo school, separate from the gunnery establishment *Excellent*. He was appointed captain of the *Inflexible* in 1881 and, upon the end of the commission, reverted, with renewed energy, to modernizing weapons and weapons training as director of naval ordnance. He had a brief spell as admiral superintendent, Portsmouth, and then was appointed to the Board of Admiralty as controller in 1892. He had a number of clashes with politicians, when the sea lords, supported by Lord Spencer, the first lord, threatened to resign unless the new construction programme was adopted. With Spencer's aid, Fisher survived. Command of the North America and West Indies station followed, and then that of the Mediterranean. Fisher's star was in the ascendant, but his rise depended solely on political power and sufferance. The Earl of Selborne was next to bring Fisher along, and his letter of invitation to Fisher asking him to take the appointment as second lord, with no promise of ever becoming first lord, makes clear that Fisher was to confine himself to assigned duties and to keep clear of wider obligations that might trample on other lords' obligations.

In Fisher's 'prelude to power' we see him responsible for the opening of

Osborne and Dartmouth colleges, also for a new system of officer entry and training. Then followed his work on the Esher committee for the reform of the War Office, during which time a valuable relationship developed between himself and Reginald Brett, Lord Esher. Esher was not really a party politician but worked for the good of the country, as he saw it, and because he loved dabbling in everyone's business. Esher served as Fisher's guide, protector, and minder, time and again saving him from numerous slips and falls when others would have let him hang himself. Other allies were King Edward and, for a time and to a lesser extent, the Prince of Wales, both of whom gave Fisher their confidence and friendship.

Strategic, financial, and technical questions predominated in Fisher's thinking: men were everything and material nothing, he said. But others saw him as a big-gun man, mainly because of his style, when, in fact, the sort of naval warfare of the future that he imagined was of a different sort – of the lethal torpedo and its countermeasure, the destroyer and destroyer flotilla. Remembering Palmerston, he filled his letters with aphorisms. For example, Fisher said the Army was a mere projectile of the Navy and was, besides, a service that gobbled up far too much money that could better be spent on ships and sailors. (Palmerston similarly, more delicately, tended to regard the British Army, though small, as a sword in the hand of the fleet.[25]) Fisher's vituperations against those standing in the way of making the Navy the most efficient fighting force in the world were legion. He liked to prophesy about events that would come to pass fifty years later. He foresaw amalgamation of the naval and military strength into one fighting machine. He saw that violence in war needed to be left untrammelled and those who thought otherwise were fools. His integrity, his love of the Service, and his devotion to his country made for a powerful combination. There was only one Fisher.

On being appointed first sea lord in 1904, he found himself, surprisingly, having to bargain with the government over his salary: 'The King told [Earl] Selborne [first lord of the Admiralty] *straight* I would save them millions, and they haggled at giving me a few hundreds . . . The Prime Minister, the Chancellor of the Exchequer, and the First Lord of the Admiralty, all swearing eternal friendship to me and see me d___ed before they give me a shilling! And bring me up from the plumb of the Service at Portsmouth to penal servitude at the Admiralty to suit their convenience! On half pay and double the work!' As Esher put it soothingly, concerning the politicians: 'All these people are really ciphers. Remember, not more than a dozen people in England count for anything (a large estimate) and you happen to be one of them.'[26]

Shortly after the publication of volume 1 (1952), Marder got a lovely letter of thanks from Fisher's son:

> Allow me to congratulate you on your brilliant character sketch of my father, when he was 1st Sea Lord. I think it wonderful how you have drawn such an accurate picture of him, without ever having seen him.
>
> No doubt he made things very much more difficult for himself by the brusque way he dealt with all those not in the 'Fish Pond'. But that, no doubt, was his nature; intensified by the life of conflict he led from his earliest days; always brushing away cobwebs, and forcing new ideas on what *was* a very conservative Service.[27]

A second letter followed: 'Hearty congratulations on . . . the very favourable reviews of it by our leading newspapers. I think the present volume will interest the general public more than Vol. II will do; because Vol. I is not so controversial. The same was the case with Adm. Bacon's "Life". I hope you will receive an adequate reward for all the trouble you have taken in selecting the letters to be published.'[28]

Making of an Admiral gathered fine reviews and much private correspondence. Among the letters Marder received was one from a young James (Jan) Morris, then contemplating a biographical study of the admiral, which would eventually appear in 1995 as *Fisher's Face*. As of late 1952, Morris was in the imperial and foreign department of *The Times* and had got the then Lord Fisher's blessing. He had thought it best to see if Marder intended a similar book himself, hence the inquiry. 'I should hate to trespass upon any territory which you intend to occupy, so if you have a biography of the Admiral in mind or preparation perhaps you would be kind enough to warn me off,' wrote Morris, who added that he thought that such a work would not clash with the admirable edition of Fisher correspondence and would supply a need that did not disappear with Bacon's book. A second letter from Morris laid out the scheme more exactly, saying that the work would be addressed to a general rather than a specialist readership. No definitive judgement of professional activities was intended, though reforms and innovations, and what transpired accordingly, would be dealt with incidental to the story of his life. Morris intended to begin immediately, adding that he hoped his decision was not a trespass on Marder's territory, that he could have forgiveness in advance if he pestered Marder for advice or information, and that he hoped the book might stimulate an interest in more scholarly, technical studies.[29] This was a masterly letter from a skilled writer and brilliant biographer, whose sketch of Fisher, *Fisher's Face* (1995), was well worth waiting for. A friendship developed between Morris and Marder, with the former visiting the historian in Honolulu on one occasion.

Reviews of Marder's first Fisher volume were, as Fisher's son said, glowing. They showed none of the rancour, crabbing, jealousy, and backbiting of the reception given the Richmond diaries. Perhaps reviewers were relieved that Marder was not going to expose further weaknesses in the Royal Navy. Marder's Richmond had been too close to the mark, too visceral: Richmond was, so to speak, too inside, too undercover. Fisher, by contrast, was entertaining and, though abidingly controversial, invariably delightful from a literary angle. He had always been at the storm centre of controversy – a publisher's delight – but the volume also showed him as 'one of the most intelligent, honest, brave, single-minded persons in all our history'. Whether he was the greatest sailor since Nelson, in the sense of seaman-warrior, remained open to question. He held certain views on strategy and tactics uniquely his own, and he never commanded a great fleet in a great action. Possibly he might have combined all the best qualities of a Beatty with those of a Jellicoe if it had come to that, and he might even, had he been given the chance, been another Nelson. The mind boggles at the thought, but as a young naval officer he had devoured all the books about Nelson that he could lay his hands on and he adored a portrait of Lady Hamilton.[30]

Marder showed Fisher at his ebullient best. Just as Fisher charmed by the gaiety of his conversation and the furiousness of his dancing, so did he entertain by his letters. His voice seems to speak from his correspondence. To a 'Very Important Person' who had asked him to come in and help clean up the War Office, he spouted: 'I am absolutely certain we can make a good job of the War Office! But a drastic change is imperative. We must be ruthless, relentless, and remorseless, and there must be no mincing matters, and the Committee's resolutions must be swallowed whole, not leaving out any single one of the ingredients of the pill! Or the patient won't be cured. Yours in violent haste, J.A. Fisher. This letter is sacredly private, but of course show to Mr Balfour if you desire.'

On another occasion, the admiral had written to a former first lord of the Admiralty from Malta:

Dear Lord Spencer.

. . . There is a great deal in what [Admiral Lord Charles] Beresford [Fisher's Second-in-Command and later antagonist] urges, but he exaggerates so much that his good ideas become deformities and are unpractical, and his want of taste and his uncontrolled desire for notoriety alienates his brother officers! He promised me faithfully (for we have always been great friends) that he would be circumspect and judicious in what he was going to say in public. He has been neither! and has forced me against my will to disavow him on some points of importance because he could do so much good for the Navy with the public, for there is no doubt the 'oi polloi' believe in him and listen to him like no one else![31]

In fact, Fisher's revelation about Beresford's uncontrolled desire for notoriety was on the mark, though 'Charley B', an Anglo-Irishman, thought he was serving the country and the Navy. Yet Jacky Fisher's opponents accused him of the same fault. It may be, as a reviewer noted, the common accusation made by the mediocre against the geniuses, and by the half-hearted against the keen, or by those who want to get their names in the paper when they themselves cannot do so. Fisher was single-minded, and his name will be in the papers of the future, and in books too. He always retained the enthusiasm of youth.

If the letters showed Fisher's single-mindedness, they also revealed his shameless patronage and above all his ruthlessness in furthering the Navy's cause. His patronage his enemies called favouritism. So as to oblige a friend of the first lord's private secretary, Fisher sent a young lieutenant who was 'in a scrape' to a foreign station at twelve hours' notice. In doing this, Fisher 'committed a most flagrant injustice to another lieutenant who I had to take out of the ship so as to make the vacancy'. 'I would do the same again,' says Fisher in a postscript. His reforms were vital and necessary, preparing the Navy for a conflict which only Fisher and (as he admits) the kaiser had at first envisaged. By the end of the last ten years covered in this book, Fisher had changed from rebel to ruler, and the ruler's judgement came to be questioned by the generation of the First World War. 'Even so', wrote Mark Arnold-Foster in the Manchester *Guardian*, 'Fisher's half-century of glorious revolt made it possible for his younger critics to criticise at all. His own blunt, rude, vigorous account of his first fifty years in the Navy reads like an anarchist's diary. He must have been the world's worst sufferer of fools and one of the most impatient, outspoken, mutinous, loyal admirals that the Royal Navy has ever, to its lasting benefit, endured.'[32]

There were flattering comments, too, about Marder. There was only one Fisher; there was only one Marder. The astonishing Fisher would have kept the Navy talking for a century, but Marder had shown many hidden, unsuspected merits in the admiral, including kindliness as well as an amazing capacity for intrigue. Gathering these letters together was a continuation, said the Glasgow *Herald*, of 'the discharge of the pious duties he [Marder] has undertaken towards British admirals by beginning the publication of his letters. Many have been already printed in this or that publication as well as in the memoirs and the biography, but it is very satisfactory to have now this first instalment of the collected letters, for no other documents show Fisher so startlingly clearly.' Marder was given high praise by the *Herald* for his editorial skills – 'scrupulous, discreet, and able to help the reader with proper identification notes and connecting narratives'.[33] *The Times* reviewer, hard-headed and exacting almost to a fault, called for all of Fisher's papers to be published, not just a selection, and (unrealistically) could not see why Marder did not do what Sir Harry Nicolas had done in editing the letters of Nelson. The reviewer was Thursfield, likely the very same critic who had objected to the over-severity of Marder's pruning. He wrote:

> The editor assures his readers that complete objectivity has been his criterion in the use of the blue pencil, and those who trust his judgement implicitly will doubtless be satisfied with that assurance. But since it is he who has decided on the absence of interest or importance in what he has suppressed, it is inevitably Professor Marder's estimate of Fisher's character that emerges from what has escaped the editor's scissors, rather than a portrait that another might draw from the full material. Moreover, the letters themselves are such good reading, so vivid, so expressive of a vibrant and flamboyant personality, that the reader could well welcome many more than those that his editor has allowed to see the light of print. Fisher himself wrote 'Reiteration is the secret of conviction', and he should surely have been allowed by his editor to display his observance of that maxim, unless it was to be made to appear but one more picturesque phrase thrown out for effect on the spur of the moment.[34]

Other publications and reviewers did not share this ice-crusted view. There was, too, an eager public awaiting the next instalment, for the book had foreshadowed 'the force of character that was to sweep the Admiralty clean of dust, and that was to create the *Dreadnought*, and was to forge the arm with which England and Jellicoe could win the 1914 war.'[35]

In distant Hawaii, attending to other professorial duties and urgently seeking foundation monies to advance his research and fund another visit to the United Kingdom, Marder had reason to be satisfied. This time, unlike with his previous two books, no need existed to take issue with any of the reviews. Now it was time to tie up a thousand loose ends in the manuscript of the second volume and to try to uncover a few letters of importance he knew were extant. He needed, too, to interview a few surviving associates of Fisher.[36]

'VOLUME TWO IS A WINNER WILL WRITE YOU ABOUT THE REVIEWS WILL VISIT YOU DECEMBER.' So cabled Peter Gretton to Marder, who scribbled happily on the telegram: 'Captain Peter W. Gretton, R.N. – one of the ablest officers in H.M Navy'.[37] This volume of Fisher's voluminous correspondence was even more fascinating than the first – and, in fact, contained more contentious letters. It carried the subtitle *The Years of Power 1904–1914*.

The volume divided itself easily into two phases: 1904–10, when Fisher was first sea lord and at the height of his influence, and 1910–14, when he was out of office but still wielded great influence over naval, and wider, affairs by way of his close friendship with Reginald McKenna, his old political boss at the Admiralty. This was an age of indiscretion in high places, and Marder had the pick of juicy letters from and to Esher and McKenna's successor at the Admiralty, Winston Churchill. For instance, Esher sent Fisher all the most secret news. The admiral then passed this on to Mrs McKenna under the heading 'Now for some secrets'. Moreover, Fisher leaked his innermost thoughts to journalists such as Arnold White, W.T. Stead, and, for a time, J.L. Garvin. Such behaviour was as reprehensible as the stuff he received, of course. Fisher lacked restraint, and this likely encouraged others. Fortunately for Marder, the letters offered prime material and, for the working student of history today, are of immense value. Fisher would often tell recipients of his letters to burn them, and he did likewise with all but a dozen letters he received from Edward VII. But 'BURN THIS!!!' was an injunction to be ignored.[38] Fisher himself added that the great advantage of letter writing as opposed to conversation is that 'the written word remains'.

Marder's second Fisher volume attracted glowing comments about its firm editorial judgement, apt notes of explanation, short biographies of persons who wrote or received letters, splendid small introductions, transitions, and bridges, illustrations, and index. Marder, if anyone had doubted it, was now an editor of pre-eminent status. Readers saw this book as biography, the letters becoming the true life, as it were. The reviewer for the *Times Literary Supplement* for this second volume (likely James Morris), who had replaced his frosty predecessor, had opposite views on Marder and his work: 'It takes a good editor to give coherence to this mass of ebullience.' He continued:

Professor Marder succeeds triumphantly. Never a misquotation goes uncorrected (and Fisher nearly always got his quotations wrong); not a minor figure of the Edwardian scene goes unidentified. Occasionally, indeed, there are facts in these endnotes of supremely limited interest (the precise measurements, for example, of Herkomer's portrait of Fisher): but in general one can for once accept with gratitude that insistence on detailed cross-reference that sometimes belabours American scholarship. There is nothing heavy about Professor Marder's approach – indeed, the very fact that a Professor at the University of Hawaii should be editing Fisher's letters adds a spice of piquancy to the proceedings. His explanatory chapters are excellent examples of condensed biography; and he obviously enters his task with humour and enjoyment. '*Bless you!*' the Admiral would no doubt say to the Professor. 'You are the Bovril of Letters! (Copyright in the United States of America!).'[39]

This second volume of Fisher papers brought forth a warming connection between Marder and the historian A.J.P. Taylor, author of revisionist works, then reviewing for the *New Statesman*. 'The most controversial, and controverted, of all our historians' in the estimation of A.L. Rowse,[40] Taylor offered his comments on Marder's work in a review entitled 'A Great Man?' There he posed the question as to how Fisher put his ideas over on the politicians and on the ruling circles of the day. Flattery and winning hearts was one way, and press leaks another. Fisher could turn arguments on their head, noted Taylor. He was never troubled with scruples in carrying his convincing views through. Furthermore, Fisher had some truly foolish ideas, like landing an expeditionary force on some sandy beach in north Germany. Yet he also did much that was good, scrapping old ships, doing more for less, and overseeing every invention from wireless telegraphy to oil-fired boilers. He foresaw the submarine. He imagined the German fleet sallying forth to seize the trident of Neptune, and was at a loss when they remained in port. He was far more creative than his Service contemporaries. 'Who can blame him for being wrong now and then, seeing that, like all the other fire-eaters, he had never heard a shot fired in anger?' Taylor, too, thought that Fisher had only the wistful charm of yesterday's music-hall comedian, for his domination of the seas, much shorter than Nelson's century, had lasted only about ten years.

In early 1959 the final instalment of Fisher letters appeared, yet another substantial volume, with editorial explanations, copious and accurate, said Taylor.[41] Bearing the subtitle *Restoration, Abdication, and Last Years, 1914–1920*, it opens with Fisher's return to the Admiralty as first sea lord in 1914, proceeds to the glowing, early days when he worked in harness with the first lord, Churchill, and then traces the mounting conflict between these 'titans at the Admiralty' over the Dardanelles campaign which – exploding in May 1915 – led to Fisher's departure, or abdication, from his post and Churchill's removal from the government. He brought down the last Liberal government, for there was never one truly like it again. Fisher found inadequate work in heading up the Board of Invention of Research, all the while yearning to return to the Admiralty. Many who backed David Lloyd George in December 1916 hoped to restore Fisher to the Admiralty. Fisher claimed to be the only one who knew how to end the war quickly, and some of his contemporaries believed him. There is sadness to this last volume, for Fisher was invariably on the margins, older and weaker now, declining in force and influence though always railing about matters on which he contended he alone was right. From the beginning, he was strong on convictions, always believing in the rightness of his views, though often charitable to his sworn enemies. In the end, it is almost tempting to dismiss the whole as farce. But Marder never allowed Fisher to be dismissed as an object of amusement.

Invariably the third volume remains timeless because of Fisher's connection with Churchill. Sir Martin Gilbert's companion volumes to these years of Churchill's life are worthy accompaniments to Marder's though show no formal interplay. Fisher and Churchill had much in common. They enjoyed power and responsibility. They exhibited restless energy. They had great popular appeal. They showed true vision, even genius. They held each other in deep respect. But they were similarly ruthless and conniving.

Churchill showed surprising forbearance of Fisher, his difficult colleague, over the growing Dardanelles crisis. And yet Churchill was too often preoccupied with other schemes and adventures, political and military, to run the Admiralty without opposition within. When Fisher changed his mind about the plan to send warships to the Dardanelles, he threw Churchill off balance. Churchill was correct when he complained to Fisher of his 'trying to spite this operation by side winds . . . when you have accepted it in principle.' Fisher's role in the affair has been thought dishonourable, and he resigned in a childish huff: 'I am absolutely unable to remain with W.C. (he's a real danger!).' But Marder's selection of letters enlarges our appreciation of the old admiral, allowing us to see his dilemma in fresh light. Fisher's initial distrust of the idea of the Dardanelles expedition, which involved weakening the Home Fleet in the North Sea, was countered by his affection for Churchill: 'Let us hope that the Dardanelles will be passed and over by the desired date to your honour and glory . . . I earnestly hope this may result!' But every rope yarn sent to Admiral de Robeck would be one less for Jellicoe at Scapa Flow; hence, when Churchill insisted on two more submarines for the Sea of Marmara, Fisher walked out of the Admiralty for the last time. His

Baltic project – to 'Copenhagen' the German fleet in its own ports and waters – seems less harebrained than hitherto imagined and, like the Dardanelles, was dedicated to the proposition that war is a matter of movement and surprise. ('Napoleonic in audacity. Nelsonic in execution. Cromwellian in thoroughness.') Fisher built a large fleet for the intended Baltic operation, with Churchill's blessing, and in the end only one such campaign could be undertaken, and the Dardanelles had the backing not only of the government but of the French as well.

But the real tragedy of Fisher, as revealed by Marder, is the gap between the admiral and the workaday sailors left in control of the fleet. Fisher played to his favourites and shunned his opponents. Then there was Sir John Jellicoe, who made petulant complaints about enemy superiority, and Sir David Beatty, who wrote schoolboy letters, and the nameless admirals who passed unnoticed through the halls of the Admiralty. Fisher, like Churchill, envisioned a mobile war. That was the one they would have hoped to have waged. But neither could control the turn of events, for it was on the generals' ghastly alternative of slow slaughter in Flanders that the war turned. If the generals knew no other way than throwing in more battalions, the Navy had its own schemes, but these, too, were dictated by the movement of enemy forces. Fisher knew that, if the Germans waged *guerre de course* with their U-boats, the nature of sea primacy would change. He even wrote to his old adversary, Admiral von Tirpitz, that, yes, in the circumstance, he would have done just the same thing. And so the war dragged on without Churchill and without Fisher, and was decided by altogether different issues than they had faced together in those late months of 1914. When Fisher died in 1920, he left two memorials: a declining if not vanished dreadnought fleet and his unimpeachable collection of his letters. Marder saved Fisher from complete historical eclipse and in fact gave him a new lease of life.

Having resurrected Fisher through his trilogy, Marder now found himself in a new role, on the radio. He was approached by David Woodward, of the Features Department of the BBC, to do an episode for 'In Our Time' on Lord Fisher. Woodward, a keen naval historian himself, wrote and produced the recording. Marder arrived at Bush House on 25 and 26 August 1960 for the rehearsal and recording, and the programme was transmitted on the Home Service on the evening of 7 September. A rich parade of characters filled the hour. Actors dubbed in the voices of Fisher, his biographer Bacon, various old shipmates, and the journalist Stead. Then there were Prime Minister Asquith (who had ordered, unsuccessfully, Fisher to return to his post), the American prophet of sea power Mahan, the maritime strategist and historian Corbett, Fisher's nemesis Beresford, and even a cool, detached

Admiralty Voice.

Marder was front and centre in the whole thing, adding pungent comments about Mrs Fisher, Jacky's character, and the great material changes in the instruments of war at sea. Yet he found himself but an aspect of the larger, ebullient story that Woodward carefully crafted. Fisher would have approved. A voice from *The Times* had the last word, an epilogue describing the funeral service in Westminster Abbey: 'Yesterday morning the British public showed that it loved and mourned on "Jacky Fisher". Till within the last weeks of his long and bellicose life, Lord Fisher was a stormy petrel, bringing the tempests he rejoiced in. Behind him, he had at first, no one; behind him, he had, in these later years, the whole solid affection and admiration of the people. And yesterday morning the people, in its silent, stolid, reverent British way, wrote its affection and admiration for "Jacky Fisher" upon the social history of our time.'[42] For Marder, the broadcast had given him a huge audience, providing an entrance into British sitting rooms great and small, the strange and glowing aura of Fisher seemingly shining on him. Between new quests and challenges, a time for celebration had come, for, apart from Taylor, Geoffrey Elton, A.L. Rowse, and Hugh Trevor-Roper, few historians were talked about among the general public. Marder's book sales increased, to the delight of his publishers.

The adulation Marder received could easily have spun his head and induced him to take up more popular accounts of naval history, such as a one-volume biography of Fisher. He was not to be deflected, rather preferring to advance towards his intended magnum opus, *The Dynamics of British Sea Power*, the code name, as he put it, of *From the Dreadnought to Scapa Flow*. To his credit, he never became a popularizer. He never had to be. For, in the field of naval history, the subjects of his histories and the remarkable, detached coverage that he gave to character, circumstance, and effect had a powerful unity of purpose and attraction, as if the details told their own story. Marder made sense of Fisher's incandescent life, gave a sense and logic to it. In consequence, Marder's bright, radiant star continued to rise towards its zenith.

In closing, we note that Nina, Dowager Duchess of Hamilton had pressed for complete objectivity in the selection and printing of material: 'I do not think you will find any passage which reflects discredit on the Admiral.' To this she added:

> He always had the highest sense of honour. But – and he and I often talked on this point – he would not have liked the lights without the shade. He himself always said that if there is no shade depicted one

cannot see the sunlight. There were occasions when I suggested the toning down of a letter, when one thought that the recipient would not understand. But the bold directness of his speech and letters were of his very self. He was directness itself, and where and when he thought the good of his country was concerned, nothing else counted, including himself. You know, he always wanted his biography to be written by an American, because he thought English writers would want to cut too much. He did not look upon himself as a saint and would abhor being depicted as such![43]

Chapter 4

Marder: The Ali Baba of Historical Studies

BY LATE 1950, Marder had several chapters of his intended big book *The Dynamics of British Sea Power* in draft form. He wrote Geoffrey Cumberlege, the publisher of Oxford University Press (OUP) at Amen House, Warwick Square, London, to this effect, expressing his usual enthusiasm for work in progress. Marder made clear that he feared that several years would pass before he had a finished product. His reason was clear: the Admiralty remained frosty on access to documents under seal. The material would not be thrown open to scholars in the near future, though there was always the chance that he could get an exception made. Besides – and this he did not have to tell Cumberlege, for the latter knew all about it – he still had other fish to fry, notably his Richmond and Fisher books.

From the very outset of their association, the benevolent and guiding Cumberlege was taken with Marder and his attractive subject. Cumberlege, an army captain from the First World War, DSO and MC, and a veteran publisher in India and the United States before returning to OUP and its London office after the Second World War, spotted in Marder a rising star. His associates in London and in the New York office had similarly high opinions of the man in Hawaii. But, until such time as OUP could bring Marder into the stable, the historian was understandably elusive, often embracing more than one eager publisher at a time. That year, Marder had offered his completed Richmond to OUP, which declined it but agreeably referred it to Jonathan Cape, which accepted it. Marder happily signed the Richmond contract for *Portrait of an Admiral*, and with it the binding provision to let Jonathan Cape have first rights of refusal on a subsequent book. Marder was in agreement with such terms, for, as he told Cumberlege, it seemed only fair that Jonathan Cape be permitted to see the Fisher first in view of its willingness to publish the Richmond. Besides, the author had an ace up his sleeve. Back at Harvard, Professor Sidney Fay, who ran the committee putting up the subvention money for the Fisher project, was prepared to do business with Jonathan Cape if that house wanted to do the Fisher in addition to the Richmond; and that meant that Harvard University Press would handle the American run of the book.

Cumberlege took Marder's news with grace but disappointment, replying that it was naturally rather a shock to hear that Marder had been obliged to give the Fisher book to Jonathan Cape. He hoped that Marder would not have to sign another contract that would give Jonathan Cape *The Dynamics of British Sea Power*, as Marder styled his intended big book. He added that he was certain that Jonathan Cape would publish the Fisher whether Marder had the offer of another book or not. That was flattery. He indicated yet again how very happy OUP would be to see the book on sea power when it was ready, and he asked to be kept informed of its progress.

Months passed. Jonathan Cape and Harvard published the Richmond book. Then the Fisher book appeared and grew from one to three volumes. But all the while Marder, a willing suitor, kept up his connections with Oxford University Press. On 21 February 1952 he fired off a letter to Cumberlege: 'This very day I am beginning serious work on my British sea power tome. The interruptions will, I fear, be many, but I mean to persist.' The reasons for delay included heavier than normal teaching loads because of sickness in the History Department and various speaking obligations. But Marder thought that before long he would have something to show OUP. 'I am writing this book for Oxford, not for Cape, Harvard, or any other publisher. I broached the matter to you first, you were interested, I liked you and [John] Brett-Smith [in the New York office] and the way you do business . . . and that's that. I shall attempt a really good book, one that you will be proud to have on your list.' And even at that early stage Marder wanted to have a style sheet from the publisher, also noting that it was his view that footnotes were then being overly done, even comically so, and he was leaning to eliminating the whole footnote apparatus except for quoted and controversial material. Cumberlege agreed with the absurdity of meticulous acknowledgement of every word that has been borrowed and with Marder's alternative plan to use footnotes only for two purposes: to cite the source of a quotation running to more than a sentence or so, and to cite authorities for controversial matter. Marder aimed to be sparing, jesting that he would like possibly to eliminate even those two categories. He promised a thorough bibliography, however.[1]

In the early 1950s Marder's progress showed all the erratic nature of a historian with too many projects on his hands, too many other academic commitments as a senior professor,[2] and too many difficulties in his way to complete his big book. Despite his abundant energy, his driving zeal, and his systematic approach to research and writing, there were limits to what he could accomplish and he prided himself on first-class work. Fortunately, he had a sabbatical leave in late 1951, and this he spent in Los Angeles. From what he told Cumberlege, it seems to have been a busman's holiday: auditing a number of courses outside his professional interests at the University of Southern California, doing some broadcasting at a Los Angeles radio station, and reading proofs of his Richmond. In what little leisure time he had, he caught up on much miscellaneous reading. 'But I am enjoying it all!' He had early plans to start work on *The Dynamics of British Sea Power*. This was encouraging, though the problem of document access persisted.

There was another difficulty. With the Cold War heating up, the Special Committee on Un-American Activities of the House of Representatives in Washington had begun its searching inquiries. FBI agents swept through unsuspecting college campuses and Hollywood film studios, unions were closely watched, and professors, actors, publishers, broadcasters, and others found themselves pitted against Senator Joseph McCarthy. In Honolulu a Japanese male, previously a card-carrying Communist, wrote a pamphlet exposing the movement and thereby set a cat among the pigeons. The battle spread first to a local union of longshoremen and then became part of the national campaign to expose and root out Communists. The debates generated more heat than light but were no sideshow in the run-up to debate on statehood in Hawaii, then a territory of the United States.[3] The Hawaii Department of Public Instruction, with powers throughout the islands, had prevailed on the university administration to put pressure on Marder, a long-time student of Russian history, literature, and film, as well as a lecturer in Russian history and commentator on Russian affairs in the Honolulu press, to offer a radio credit course for schoolteachers on the ABCs of communism. That meant a long summer spent on preparing a book of readings, seeking permissions, and compiling a syllabus of lectures and assignments besides readying the lectures, twenty in all, for delivery on the radio. Marder was no apologist for communism; rather, he was a well-informed commentator on it. Then there had been phone-in programmes, with Marder fielding questions from listeners, including commie-haters, McCarthyites, sympathizers, and others. By New Year's Day, he announced to Oxford University Press, he was a wreck.

'I think Marder is quite unnecessarily gloomy,' wrote Brett-Smith to Cumberlege on receipt of the most recent report from Hawaii. 'He is obviously worn-out, and hasn't done as much as he had hoped, but he has produced a surprising amount, and is clearly a performer. Moreover, the rough work he has submitted reads very well and is of the greatest interest;

Fisher, of course, is a fascinating figure, but Marder makes the most of him.' Brett-Smith did not yet know Marder as well as he might, but he was beginning to appreciate just what volume and quality of work Marder could accomplish, even under the severe pressure of other obligations. He was prepared to wait for the book, knowing that the Fisher would write itself, as he breezily put it, and that 'our book' would naturally come on later at the appropriate time. He did worry that the Fisher might swell up until it swallowed or rendered unnecessary the separate publication of *The Dynamics of British Sea Power*. But the chapters that Marder had sent were a fine example of work, though not up to what Marder said was his pre-announced high standard. He hoped that OUP would be satisfied with the final results.

On a certain night in May 1955, towards midnight, a sleepy Marder answered a phone call from the president of the University of Hawaii, Dr Gregg Sinclair. The president was then attending a large party in honour of 'Admiral So-and-So'. During the evening, he had casually remarked that his faculty included a historian of the Royal Navy and mentioned Marder's name. The admiral knew Marder's work. Could he meet the historian? And so Sinclair had phoned. Marder arranged a meeting with 'Sir Geoffrey' (in fact, Vice Admiral Sir Geoffrey Barnard, the admiral at the British Joint Services Mission, Washington) at his Pearl Harbor cottage, where the latter was guest of the commander-in-chief of the US Navy's Pacific Fleet. The next afternoon, Marder spent a most enjoyable two hours with the admiral and Lady Barnard. As he was leaving and about to step into his car, Barnard called out, 'I return to Washington in two days. Let me know if there is anything I can do for you.' Marder regarded this as the usual sort of polite gesture, nothing more. 'But I had an inspiration,' recounted Marder: 'I wheeled around, "Yes, Admiral, there *is* something you could do for me!" You know, of course, what I had on my diseased mind! The Admiral listened patiently and with interest. "Why", he said, when I had told him of my difficulties with the Whitehall bureaucracy, "you've come to the right man. I know the officer at Whitehall who usually has the last word in such matters. I'll see what I can do."'[4] That officer was undoubtedly the first sea lord, who in turn would have had to consult others.

In Honolulu, Marder waited anxiously for a long twelve months for the admiral to deliver. On a glorious day in June 1956, he received a telegram from Washington saying that all had been arranged, and soon afterwards, an invitation from the Admiralty to come to see them and to resume his work.

Once again Marder had mounted the parapet. To that time, Admiralty papers were under lock and key, though shipped to the Public Record Office (PRO) if not needed for government purposes or otherwise under security wraps. Not until 1958 did Parliament enact the 50-year rule. That meant that the records of 1914 would be unavailable until 1965. And so, at last, Marder got to the innermost papers of the Admiralty – that is, those the Admiralty Record Office was prepared to show him – the El Dorado of documents he had long needed for his sequel to *Anatomy of British Sea Power*. Fifteen years – for Marder assuredly an eternity – had passed since his last access to the same sort of files. Special pleading on his behalf had got results, and gained him special scholar status. An opportunity not to be lost stood before him.

The next month Marder phoned G. Wren Howard at Jonathan Cape. He told him, perhaps sheepishly, that over a considerable period of time he had had correspondence with OUP about the projected *Dynamics*. Now that the Admiralty had granted rights to certain original papers and records, Marder's ten-year delay was at an end, and the book could be written. He wanted to go with OUP. Wren Howard understood Marder's dilemma but was reluctant to release him; he even suggested lunch with Cumberlege at the Garrick Club to sort out the tangle. Cumberlege declined lunch. He played firm and fast: he wrote to Wren Howard that OUP was very unwilling to release Marder from his commitment. It agreeably had passed the Richmond book and the Fisher book to Jonathan Cape, he said. But the book in question was of a different character and OUP had been looking forward to it for a considerable time.[5] Thus did OUP lure Marder from Jonathan Cape, with whom four acclaimed volumes had been published and considerable cordial relations established, something Marder could not ignore. Even so, Marder wanted OUP, for, as the largest publisher of academic standing with worldwide circulation, and undeniably hot for his work, it would promise great things for him. He was not to be disappointed, and subsequently, in one of the great partnerships in English publishing history, nine different volumes were to come forward under the newly forged relationship.[6]

Marder lost no time and by August 1956 had made his first sortie in the precious Admiralty records. His spirits ran high, his dreams fulfilled. Visions of new documentary treasures danced before his eyes. One day that month he took time for a very long session in London with Cumberlege and John Brown, who that year had succeeded Cumberlege as publisher at OUP. They went over the book's details and plans. Marder, they found, was most enthusiastic about the book's projected contents, though it was clear that three or four years would be needed to complete the whole project. Marder, true to expectations, had unearthed masses of documents and letters in the Admiralty records room. Then there had been finds at Windsor Castle and various other places. Not absolutely clear to Cumberlege and Brown was that the book might not find its way into the hands of rival Jonathan Cape, though to that point the London office had done everything possible to keep it in OUP's hands. 'Marder professes his determination to offer it to us first but there seems to be some fairly well concealed tie that pulls him towards Cape.' Then there was a distant connection with Alfred A. Knopf, which had initiated his *Anatomy* project. Knopf wanted the United States rights; OUP wanted to publish the book under the same roof everywhere. 'But all this is a very long way off. I think the book will be exciting for there is no doubt he can write, as you will remember from the specimen chapters that he sent us. He is determined that it shall be one volume.' Soon OUP spoke to Marder of paying him an option, or advance, and wanted to be fed with a duplicate typescript as it came off his typewriter. 'What you sent us a long time ago as a sample has whetted our appetites.' They were now talking of 12½ per cent royalties on up to 3,500 copies and 15 per cent thereafter, with half-royalties on export copies. The parties entered into a contract on these terms; the delivery date of the typescript – now titled *From the Dreadnought to Scapa Flow* – was set at year-end 1960.

With the thoroughbred in the stable, OUP left Marder alone and gave him the time and scope to finish his book. By 30 April 1959 he could write to Brown, who was handling matters, that he was right on schedule, for a change. He had trimmed the material previously sent, had polished it, and had incorporated some important material from the German Ministry of Marine Archives. His secretary was typing final copy in May and into June. All was going well, with top copy of all the 1904–14 material, or 60 per cent of the book, being sent to Brett-Smith on completion. The latter, providentially, put his read text in the safe for safekeeping. Peter Gretton, from his busy post at the Imperial Defence College, was providing comments as the progress continued on the last pre-war chapters, and duplicate copies were being sent to Brown and to Brett-Smith. Marder's goal was a one-thousand-page typescript, or about 250,000 words, as agreed.

Marder was still plagued by the size of the manuscript and had been glibly optimistic in thinking that he could wrestle the whole project to the ground in one volume, especially by including the years 1914–19. He had made many cuts along the lines that Gretton had suggested. Now, he reasoned, a 1904–14 volume might be suitable on its own, even though a little long. He had begun serious work on the last part of the book, though he was setting no goals – 'having finally learned something from experience!' he chirped. When Marder had seen Cumberlege in New York a year previous, the latter had asked, 'Why not two volumes?' Mere mention of this might spoil Brown's day, Marder reported, but he indicated that he was still doing his very best to hold the line at the projected quarter of a million words. He even asked for help in this resolve.

A month passed with no exchange of letters. Marder continued his work, routinely tidying up tail ends of the semester's teaching. He marked his students' examination papers. On about 12 May he gave instructions to the janitor of the University of Hawaii's Crawford Building, where his History office was, to cart away two boxes filled with the term's marked examinations papers. Leaving nothing to chance, or so he thought, he brought him into the office and pointed out the two boxes – just inside the door. The janitor said that he would take care of it when he cleaned the office during the course of the next week. A disaster was in the making, and all of Marder's hurried plans and urgent labours were about to be set back considerably, possibly forever.

During the week in question, the janitor was off sick, and his duties devolved to a janitress, to whom he had given instructions to take away the boxes, and to her assistant. In other words, three janitors were involved in the following scenario. Marder takes up the story, in a letter to his publisher, Brown:

> BUT THE STUPID PERSON PASSED RIGHT BY THE TWO EXAM BOXES, SEARCHED AROUND FOR TWO BOXES, SPOTTED A PAIR (OUT OF SIGHT) & HAULED THEM OFF. I discovered that happened this afternoon . . . too late: it's been all burned up: ALL MY RAW MATERIALS FOR THE June 1915 – June 1919 chapters!!! The work of years. Luckily, the notes for the chapters through Fisher's resignation in May 1915 were elsewhere. I can, of course, and will carry the story that far – to Fisher's resignation. But it must end there, with an explanation in the preface of the tragedy. I could never find the time, patience, and funds to collect this material a second time. PLEASE, PLEASE assure me that you will publish this truncated MS. It's the Fisher Era properly speaking, 1904–1915, though I wanted so badly, as you know, to bring the story past the war. I'm just plain ill . . . A note from you with a bit of cheer is about all that will keep me going – till time has had its chance to set me right.[7]

When Marder had returned to his office on the very afternoon of the tragedy, he had been horrified to find out that the wrong cardboard cartons had been taken. His colleague, John Albert White, who was in an adjacent office at the moment of 'discovery', said that Marder emitted an anguished groan, rushed into the department corridor, and frantically called the city dump from a pay phone (at that time an individual telephone was not a perquisite of every faculty member). He reached a sympathetic operator, but the swift intervention proved unavailing. The precious cargo, he learned, had been consigned earlier that day to the municipal incinerator.[8]

That evening a broken-hearted Marder returned to his typewriter. He rewrote the preface. He altered the table of contents. To his editor by covering letter he explained the change in the conception of the work. He tampered with the title, and even suggested to the publisher that it might be *The Fisher-Churchill Era in the Royal Navy*, thereby working his story more around the strongest first sea lord and first lord, respectively, in the history of the Navy. The book would then end in May-June 1915 and centre on the naval careers of the two titans at the Admiralty. Marder would be teaching that coming summer (and the load would be heavy then and in the subsequent term), but he was hopeful to have the redesigned book completed by the early spring of 1960. In the end, author and publisher decided that the volume would close with an analysis of the British and German fleets in 1914 and the coming of the war. Born out of the catastrophe of a fire was a new logical demarcation. The burning of papers also gave incandescence to the Marder motif, for, phoenix-like, something emerged from the flames of even greater proportions and certainly with better coverage of topics than ever imagined.

The preface of the first volume of *From the Dreadnought to Scapa Flow* bears the date June 1960. Of the tragedy it says this: 'Owing to a dreadful accident reminiscent of what happened to the manuscript of Carlyle's *French Revolution*, most of my material for the 1915–19 years was destroyed in May 1959. I am re-doing the lost work and hope to complete the volume on the naval aspects of the war and its immediate aftermath before too long. Meanwhile, there seems little point in withholding publication of the completed portion of the manuscript.'

Marder knew what had happened to a text of the historian of the French Revolution, Thomas Carlyle. The first volume of that work had been lent to John Stuart Mill for reading but a housecleaner thought it unwanted papers that had been left about the house and so burned it. Marder might also have known of T.E. Lawrence's text about his experiences in Arabia, which had been left for but five minutes in a case on the railway platform at Reading but then vanished. These were devastating losses to their authors, who nonetheless redid their work. Marder's experience was in the same category as Carlyle's and Lawrence's but differs in the remarkable support that came to him so as to reconstitute the lost material. It differs, too, in the resistance put up by his host patron, the University of Hawaii, which sought to limit its liability.

The publisher made the necessary, sympathetic accommodation. The title had been agreed on at the time of contract – *From the Dreadnought to Scapa Flow* – with the subtitle *The Royal Navy in the Fisher Era, 1904–1919*. Now the work was to be divided, with volume 1 to be called *The Road to War*,

1904–1914. The young assistant publisher at OUP, Geoffrey Hunt, nervous about growing length, had all along continued to press for a single volume, but he found that this could not be: now there would be two volumes. Hunt did not want Churchill in any subtitle, thinking it needless to bring in that name. He carried the day on this point. The incineration scenario strangely solved the nagging problem about a lengthy text that had gone beyond reasonable proportions, and now gave Marder a hoped-for chance at a second volume to complete the work.

The Road to War appeared in 1961. When the second volume, *The War Years (To the Eve of Jutland (1914–1916),* appeared, in 1965, and a third was soon promised in what Marder imagined now to be a trilogy, all his hopes (and poor Hunt's, too) for doing the work in a single volume had long since vanished. At the outset of volume 2 he apologized to his readers for his innocent assumption that he could complete the war years in one volume, but doing it all in three volumes now seemed likely. Yet following volume 3, *Jutland and After (May 1916-December 1916),* there came not one more but two: 4: *1917: Year of Crisis,* and 5: *Victory and Aftermath (January 1918-June 1919).* 'Five children born in the same labour' is how he described the quintuplet.

The immense trial of having to redo the initial volume and make it into two (and more) had subsided by Trafalgar Day 1964. On that day he wrote in his preface for the second volume these memorable, gracious lines: 'I must also pay tribute to the three University of Hawaii janitors of imperishable memory for services above and beyond the call of duty which, to their surprise and mine, proved a boon to the project.'

The destruction of historical material had tested Marder's every resolve. The janitors had made an appalling mistake. A week later, the initial shock and numbness caused by that stupid tragedy having nearly passed, he wrote to President Laurence Snyder of the University of Hawaii. He was no longer reading the Book of Job, he said. He had decided that he owed it to himself and to the many kind persons, institutions, and foundations who had supported his research and writing to make a serious effort to redo the destroyed work. 'If three conditions can be met I would be prepared, though without much joy in my heart, to begin re-reading all those books, newspapers, periodicals, and documents! These are: (1) If those who let me see important collections of unpublished papers would extend the courtesy once more; (2) if the University will give me some time off from my teaching chores next year; (3) if I can get the State to award me damages sufficient to make possible a year's study, most of which would have to be spent in England.' Hawaii's government did not reimburse university faculty for non-state travel; that meant that persons such as Marder had to gather funds where they could. Marder's attorney, Axel Ornelles, a former student of Marder's, discussed the matter of damages with the attorney general's office, and Ornelles held the opinion that Marder had a strong legal case for financial compensation. This could lead to support from the university's Board of Regents for time lost. Marder told Snyder that there could be a true mitigation of damages only if a full year's salary plus round-trip travel expenses to England could be paid. And Marder refreshed the president's memory with the following details:

> To make sure there would be no misunderstanding, I brought him [the janitor in Crawford Hall] into my office and pointed out the two boxes in question . . . Whether through poor instructions or through her own gross negligence or abysmal stupidity I don't know, the janitress did not take the two boxes I wanted removed, although they were just inside the door and on the filing cabinet, a position from which she has removed similar exam boxes in the past. Instead she looked around, spotted two likely boxes in my bookcase, and out they went and into the city dump incinerator. The two boxes with my notes were clearly marked 'Personal Papers – Very Important'. Even a second glance into the contents would have convinced the janitress that the materials were not exams.[9]

The University of Hawaii faced a problem unprecedented in the history of academe. Snyder and the Board of Regents were reluctant but in a bind. They could not deny some recompense to their high-profile star, now a senior professor, a rare distinction. Nor could they shirk the obvious fact that some of their employees had damaged the work of another, though they would not take any part of the blame. Marder, under legal advice, sued for damages and was awarded nearly $2,000, perhaps enough to cover out-of-pocket expenses for research over the past many years. Ornelles told the author that the state sought an appeal to have the damages lessened but this was thrown out. As for the university, the Board of Regents did not award the requested full year off, though reasons were not given. Marder had to settle for a semester. The university, within two months of the conflagration, sent this memorandum to Marder, pointing out its own interest in the research to date:

> The Board of Regents of the University of Hawaii, at its last meeting, approved of granting you a leave of absence with pay for the second semester of the academic year 1959–60, in order that you may complete the research of your final volume in the field of British Sea Power. No

administrative official of the University or any other person is authorized to make any commitment or agreement with regard to your leave or the possible extension of the leave in addition to the terms specifically stated in this letter.

As you can appreciate, the reasoning back of this action of the Regents was that in effect the University itself, and hence that Regents as Trustees, had a very real and material interest vested in the research material destroyed in the unfortunate incident last semester. It did not represent an assumption of blame for the inadvertent destruction of your notes. They felt therefore that permission for you to replace the material without seriously damaging the teaching load of the department was a prudent and justifiable action and use of University funds.

The memorandum came from the Office of the President over the signature of Provost Willard Wilson, acting executive officer of the university.[10] It is hard to gauge Marder's response to this feeble gesture. His character, however, suggests that, as with the several rebuffs and setbacks of the past, he would accept the obvious and move on with the next challenge. That is exactly what he did.

Sympathy poured in from various quarters. Rear Admiral Gretton at the Imperial Defence College, by this time historical counsel as well as personal friend, delayed his response to Marder's first letter saying that he was abandoning the project and, instead, awaited a second from Hawaii. Gretton had reckoned, correctly, that if he had written, 'Go on with the book and start afresh on your material', Marder would have had every right to tear up such a letter and possibly their friendship. He had hoped that time would heal, and that when pain and grief wore away Marder would reconsider. Gretton was delighted that Marder had decided to go on. 'You see', he advised, 'the period 1915 and onwards to 1919 is in many ways the most important of the lot. It will include Jutland and the lessons of the battle, and it will also have the great convoy controversy. From these two incidents, I believe we can still learn much – and there is no one in this country who is qualified to do the job of describing them. All our people have axes of some sort to grind. Pro or anti Beatty, pro or anti Lloyd George, or in many cases, just plum dumb ignorant of the truth. You are the only historian who is unhampered by prejudice and who has also taken the trouble to get at the facts, at the raw material and not to copy what a lot of ignorant and very biased biographers have thought up as excuses for their heroes' failings.'[11]

Gretton was sorry to hear news of the disaster. 'It must be almost too much to bear.' But he urged Marder to finish the project, fully aware of the difficulties of doing so and the sadness and trials of having to redo such an immense amount of work. From the British Museum, Department of Manuscripts, came sympathy, encouragement, and promises of nominal support; the librarian at Windsor Castle sent similar greetings, as did the archivist at the National Maritime Museum and various private persons. And perhaps the most helpful letter of all came from the first lord of the Admiralty, the Earl of Selkirk, who said how sorry he was to hear about the destruction of the material. It was a tragedy, a subject of personal loss, 'but it is certainly impossible to think of your abandoning your work after all you have done over the past year'. He also said that, under a recent act of Parliament, certain Admiralty records for 1915–19 were being transferred to the PRO, and access would normally not be allowed there until the papers were fifty years old, that is, 1965 and after. Special authority could be granted by the Admiralty, Selkirk advised, and if Marder were able to visit the Admiralty in the near future he would see that the PRO's keeper of records would be informed so that Marder would be allowed access to the 1915–19 records. Selkirk made clear that Marder would have to consult the Admiralty files in the PRO, then in Chancery Lane, but he said that arrangements about microfilming could be made nearer the time of visit. Marder was now getting the inside track even though the rest of the qualified readers who would have adored seeing these same documents were denied the same.[12]

Marder's supporters ranged far and wide, extending far beyond the immediate circle of staff at OUP. The pursuit of necessary funds to carry on such work from such an improbable distance as Honolulu never ceased. Marder went after Fulbright scholarship money. He came up dry. He had used up his Guggenheim Foundation allocation, his third, in 1958 and could not apply there. He turned to the Social Science Research Council with success. Yet again he approached the American Philosophical Society, in the junior ranks of funding, and it never failed him, even giving him a substitute grant so that he could do research for the materials lost and, later, an unprecedented fourth grant so that he could complete the grand work. The reason for Marder's abundant success is clear: not only did he have good skills in grantsmanship, but he kept a sterling track record inviolate. Backing his applications were superb referees, top American historians. Langer, his mentor, said of Marder that he wrote fine examples of scholarship, enthusiastically reviewed in Britain as in the United States, and that he was recognized as the outstanding authority in this important field. Crane Brinton, Robert Albion, David Owen, and, later, in London, Gerald Graham all came to his support, with glowing letters noting Marder's achievements despite his Honolulu handicap. Owen said that Marder was the most distinguished authority,

British or American, on modern British naval history before 1914. The referees invariably mentioned his use of some collections, including the Admiralty, not always so hospitable to investigators. But the loss of documents to the incinerator plagued Marder for years, and even when he was completing the fourth volume of *From the Dreadnought to Scapa Flow*, nuggets previously gathered could not be found or replaced. Conversely, however, new documentary jewels kept coming to light from private sources, while others were finding their way into libraries, archives, or the National Maritime Museum.[13]

From the Dreadnought to Scapa Flow: Volume I: The Road to War examined the pre-war antagonisms between Britain and Germany, principally the naval rivalry and its dreadnought race. August 1914 formed the end point of the study. Admiral Fisher, single-minded in his service to his one and only love, the Navy, dominates the first half. In Marder's view, 'to him who loves much, much may be forgiven' because, though he was not blind to the admiral's obvious faults, he could condone them in consideration of his achievements. The verdict of history, according to the author, is that in Fisher, who was seventy-three when the war broke out, the Navy and the nation found their man. Winston Churchill, first lord of the Admiralty, dominates the second half of the work, and though a very young politician – in contrast to the ageing sea dog Fisher – he directed the government's naval armament policies and won ministerial and parliamentary approval for them. Marder took pains to describe the revolutions in material: the changes in ships and guns and the coming weapons of under-sea and over-sea warfare. The dreadnought, for all its superiority over its predecessors, virtually eliminated at one blow the whole of Britain's naval lead, enabling Germany to start its arms race at a closer distance behind. The pre-war leaders had conflicting opinions on the effectiveness of the submarine, and they clearly misunderstood the potential it would have in enemy hands. Not even Churchill could conceive the damage these raiders of the deep could do to Allied shipping. The other major conception of the time was that Germany's High Seas Fleet would come out sooner or later, probably sooner, for a head-on collision with Britain's Grand Fleet. There again the British were wrong, for although the German fleet eventually sortied in 1916, at the Battle of Jutland, the dreadnought race had been lost to them by 1914 and they and the kaiser knew it.

Much of the book is devoted to Fisher and his methods within the various contexts in which he had to work, that is, with the sea lords, a succession of first lords of the Admiralty (including Churchill), the Committee of Imperial Defence, and shifting public opinion on naval matters. Marder's tour of the horizon contained examinations of key episodes or issues in naval policy making; the struggle with the insubordinate Admiral Lord Charles Beresford, who in 1907 began the feud with Fisher over the disposition of naval units in the Channel and Home fleets; the weakening of naval strength in Asian waters; the revolution in diplomatic affairs, that is, how previously solitary Britain made alliance with Japan, then France, and then France and Russia in combination; the likelihood of a German invasion of the British Isles by surprise – 'a bolt from the blue'; Fisher's wild concept of 'Copenhagening' the High Seas Fleet in its home ports (a repeat of Britain's punitive destruction of the Danish fleet in 1807); and – perhaps of greatest interest to a reading public long attracted to the subject without having adequate coverage of it – the grave naval crisis of 1909, when Germany's capacity to lay down dreadnoughts threatened British supremacy at sea. Fisher had a violent hostility to Germany, thought war with that power to be inevitable, and came close by months to predicting Armageddon. In Admiral Sir John Jellicoe he thought he had found a new Nelson, and by the close of the book all is seen as in place for the titanic struggle on and over the seas.

'Professor Marder is the Ali Baba of historical studies,' proclaimed A.J.P. Taylor on 8 September 1961 in his *New Statesman* review of Marder's book. 'The Fifty Year Rule operates implacably against all other historians. It has no terrors for him.' He went on to say that the rule laid down that no unpublished official papers were to be used until fifty years had passed, 'even if ministers and service chiefs carried them off improperly and they are now in private collections.' No English historian could dare to violate the rule. But Marder, an American, not only disregarded the rule, 'he is abetted by the Admiralty which has given him the free run of its archives.' Marder could, and did, quote freely from the Admiralty files, also from the secrets of the Committee of Imperial Defence. He had also got into the Royal Archives. Yet neither he nor the publisher would be prosecuted under the Official Secrets Act. What Marder possessed was a passport, one not vouchsafed to others. Taylor wondered if Marder realized the extent of his achievement.

To Taylor's trumpeting of Marder, which led to the curmudgeon of historical studies forging a powerful connection with Marder that would lead to the American being interviewed some years later on the BBC's Radio 3, was added almost unbounded praise for the first volume from influential critics. Professor Michael Lewis in the *Listener* (28 September 1961) noted Marder's impressive use of sources, especially the private ones that allowed the reader almost to eavesdrop on the scene in the prime minister's study when Asquith broke the most unwelcome news to Reginald McKenna, first lord of the Admiralty, that he was to be replaced by Churchill. 'It is seldom indeed that the outsider can listen in to the private talk of such exalted company in such sacrosanct surroundings.' Marder's attention to persons in preference to plans and policies made for great interest and good history. Fisher's faults were soft-pedalled and Churchill's trumpeted – an error of emphasis, not of fact.

In the *Naval Review*, Captain A.B. Sainsbury covered volume 1 extensively, matching in length Admiral Richmond's review of Marder's *Anatomy of British Sea Power* of nearly twenty years previous.[14] Sainsbury, a naval reserve officer, magistrate, and university registrar, who served as trustee of the *Review*, knew the British naval historical scene as well as most naval planners and historians. Reviewing Marder's book was to Sainsbury a privilege, and he noted, correctly, that it was a sad reflection on English scholarship that an American scholar had written it from the unique 'corner' that marked this part of British history. The lucid treatment and the scope of the account of events and policies formed the book's chief merits, and Marder's appreciation of Richmond as possessing all the assets of a great historian – 'a passion for discovery and spread of truth, a succinct and lucid style, the brilliant ability to analyse situations, and to deduce from them fundamental principles, and a keen sense of the great importance of sea power in British history' (these are Richmond's words) – also applied to Marder himself.

This was the highest praise indeed, coming as it did from such a keen appraiser of historical literature. Sainsbury was right on mark here. Marder's book was no drum-and-trumpet history; rather, it was a fine demonstration of the truth of the statement – which Marder quotes in his preface – that 'the art of telling a story is an essential qualification for writing history'. Among the numerous points examined by Sainsbury, the following is particularly apt: Sainsbury said that reading the book made him feel that the recent past was now appearing in a new light. Gone were the self-serving perspectives of memoirs and of official biographies. A new view of the younger Churchill had been presented, alone making the book valuable. Beresford had been given surprising latitude. Fisher came off well. The details of the German naval menace were given as never before. Public opinion was carefully recorded, with ample assessment of it from the zealous, perceptive Marder. Sainsbury concluded with reference to Richmond, entirely appropriate for the *Naval Review* or, in fact, any other publication: Richmond had wondered if Britain would ever see a true history of the war published. Sainsbury proclaimed that the spotting of the Richmond diaries by Marder had brought that claim to light. It now remained to see if a concluding volume of Marder's book would bring the long awaited true history, said Sainsbury. 'The accident which has delayed its publication can only increase our impatience, but it may have the compensation of making more sources available. If it is as good as Volume I our founder would probably have been satisfied.'

The Admiralty had a vested interest in Marder's research and his findings. The board and the secretary – and their staff – worked within government constraints, rules, and regulations. Unpleasant memories of the official naval history of the First World War, by Henry Newbolt and Julian Corbett, lingered still: the Admiralty had differed with Corbett's underlying appreciation of how the Navy had waged war – and said so in an official disclaimer published in the book.[15] Besides, the dispute about the Navy's conduct at Jutland, when it failed to defeat its German rival, had been public, acrimonious, and never-ending. Churchill's role as first lord of the Admiralty during the First World War had been much debated, and Marder's treatment of such episodes as the escape of the German ships *Goeben* and *Breslau* to Constantinople – thus bringing Turkey into the war as an enemy – the humiliating loss of Rear Admiral Sir Christopher Cradock's forces at Coronel to the German East Asiatic Squadron, and the devastating horrors of the ill-conceived Dardanelles campaign ('by ships alone', Churchill imagined) were surely all again to be revived by Marder's work. An undeniably conservative organization with a history to protect – its own and the Navy's – it also was obliged to deal with matters such as legislation and practices on official secrets, Cabinet Office procedures, and ministerial privilege. All such departments of state shared these worries. In 1955 a former intelligence officer had his flat officially raided, even though he had submitted his memoirs to the War Office before publication. Government issued 'D-notices' halting publication; insider Chapman Pincher quarrelled with Harold Wilson over this matter, in 1967. Similarly, a retired army colonel was prosecuted for a copy of a report he wrote on the Nigerian civil war. Authors, like government, were under the gun, so to speak. Newspapers and book publishers were aware of such difficulties. So was Marder, but he did not take the matter on directly, only tangentially.

In his preface Marder kept from public scrutiny his tangles with the Admiralty censors. But in later speeches to naval historians in London and to members of defence institutes, he began to disclose his hand. In 1965 Marder wrote a retrospective piece on his work as a historian, to be used in such venues as a talk. One of the segments was on 'The Censors and I'. In it he refers to the fact that the historian of the present and recent past laboured under many handicaps, not least the danger of running afoul of censorship imposed by authorities. He does not seem to have worried about the Official Secrets Act, though other military historians, writers, and civil servants did.[16] His concern was Admiralty zealousness in protection of its own property. 'I have, luckily, had few such run-ins with authority, but these few have been painful.' He had been under obligation to submit his manuscripts to the Admiralty for clearance prior to publication. The Historical Section of the Admiralty had read the second volume of *From the Dreadnought to Scapa Flow* in typescript in 1963. No alterations had been suggested initially, though one or two factual errors were called to his attention. But some 'higher up' was not satisfied, and when the book was in page proof, in March 1964, the Admiralty asked for a fresh look. As Marder recounted, it found the following objectionable:

(1) A 1916 statement by the C.-in-C., Grand Fleet, Jellicoe, very critical of the Admiralty, was blue-pencilled. He couldn't have meant what he said – not really. Would I reconsider a rephrasing along these lines . . . ? I tried to debate the issue but got nowhere. There were other, vastly more serious, objections.

(2) In a remarkable display of ineptitude at the outbreak of the war, the British Mediterranean Fleet had permitted the powerful German battle cruiser *Goeben* and the light cruiser *Breslau* to escape their clutches and to come to rest at Constantinople – an event that had much to do with precipitating Turkey's entry into the war as Germany's ally. The British Second-in-Command in the Mediterranean, Admiral Troubridge, was tried by court martial for giving up his pursuit of the fleeing enemy ships. My account of the escape of the *Goeben* was based on the *Goeben* Court Martial *Proceedings* of November 1914 – the first time that this material had ever been used in a published work (or even seen by a scholar, to my knowledge). The Admiralty was incensed: the document had never been published in any form, and I should never have seen it, let alone have quoted from it! Wasn't I aware of the 100-year rule on court-martial records? I would be allowed, as a concession, to *paraphrase* the quoted material and *not* to indicate its source in my footnotes. I was *shocked*. I had written the chapter in good faith. The authorities had permitted me to consult the Court Martial *Proceedings* and nothing had been said about any restrictions on its use. To have met the Admiralty's wishes at the delicate stage in which the book was would have meant a costly resetting operation and, more important, would have robbed the chapter of much of its historical value. The debate on this raged on, involving, before it was over, the top officials in the Ministry of Defence (of which the Admiralty became a part in the defence reorganisation of April 1st, 1964). Simultaneously,

(3) The Cabinet Office (not so much the Admiralty) was raising hell over my quoting from, and citing in footnotes, the unpublished *Proceedings* of the Dardanelles Commission of 1916–17. This Commission had tried to get to the bottom of that disaster. (The British and French, you will recall, had failed in a series of attempts during 1915, first naval, then amphibious, to force the Dardanelles and knock Turkey out of the war. This was in large part Churchill's magnificent strategic conception. (The execution was something else again.) The Dardanelles Commission had in 1917 published two reports in which were quoted a few passages from the *Proceedings*. But the document itself, which runs to over a thousand loosely printed pages of testimony, has to this day never been published.[17] Here again, I was told, I should never have seen this material, since it was a *Cabinet* document. From March 1964 to September 1964 there was guerrilla warfare between myself, my publishers, and certain highly placed personages upon whose assistance I had called – between us and the forces of darkness, the bureaucrats of the Admiralty and the Cabinet Office.

The eventual solution to the *Goeben* issue was the result of the intervention of High Authority, which over-ruled the lower-echelon bureaucrats. Since the 100-year rule on courts martial was not promulgated until *after* I had seen the *Goeben Proceedings*, the chapter could be published as was! As for the Dardanelles Commission, I had to be satisfied with a half-victory. Here I was really dealing with very unsympathetic and remote Cabinet Office officials, with the Ministry of Defence (in effect, the Admiralty acting for the Cabinet Office). These chaps are extraordinarily sensitive about scholars seeing and quoting papers in their custody. (The Dardanelles *Proceedings* I had seen was a copy in the Admiralty archives.) The quoted matter could stand, but footnote references to the *Proceedings* of the Commission and to the two published reports would have to be cited as 'Dardanelles Commission' and without page reference. In the words of what amounted to a take-it-or-leave-it proposition, 'There must be no ready means of distinguishing the material drawn from the unpublished *Proceedings* from that drawn from the published *Reports*.' In other words, the reader would not readily know whether I was quoting published or unpublished material, and the more stupid among them might not even realize from the fuzzy substitute footnote I had to use on page 201 that I had seen and made full use of the complete *Proceedings*! My comforting Editor wrote me afterwards: 'The footnotes do look odd in places, but that is due to the Ministry: the discerning reader will surely realize what the situation is, and if the question of a reprint comes up after some years we can approach the Ministry again.'

Tenacious as Marder was he could not win all contests. Yet he won his share and more. In public he would make only two further points about these matters: first, the second volume was delayed for six months, and not published until spring of 1965; second, notwithstanding these unpleasant experiences, he remained grateful to the Admiralty, whose splendid cooperation over the years had made it possible for him to see virtually everything in their records of relevance to his work. It had also assisted his work in all sorts of other ways. 'My 1964 experiences were not typical of my relations with the Admiralty and with the Royal Navy.'[18]

The second volume — the one that had caused Admiralty censors such agony — was published in 1965. Like the first volume, *The War Years: To the Eve of Jutland (1914–1916)* garnered glowing reviews both in the leading British newspapers and in well-informed and influential magazines. It contained all the choice particulars about Turkey's entry into the war, the tragedy of Coronel, and the avenging triumph of the Battle of the Falkland Islands, when von Spee's East Asiatic squadron was destroyed and dispersed. But central to this volume were the unhappy Dardanelles affair, the decision to undertake it, the faltering progress of it and Gallipoli, and the resignation of Fisher and the resulting exit of Churchill from the Admiralty. There was much political history here. Marder termed it 'the war behind the war'. Fisher said, inimitably, that a miasma had descended on the Admiralty. The insistence and persuasion of Churchill led to the decision to begin the Dardanelles campaign. The failure of it was due to faulty planning and preparation, delays in execution, lack of offensive spirit by the commanders, and half-hearted support of Churchill by those concentrating the war effort in home waters and on the Western Front. There was much relief in higher circles when Churchill made his forced exit. Admiral Sir John Jellicoe, commander of the Grand Fleet, placed there by Churchill on the eve of the war, summed up one view when he said that he 'thoroughly distrusted Churchill because he constantly arrogated to himself technical knowledge with all his brilliant qualities I knew he did not possess.' When Churchill exited, in Fisher's wake, the Admiralty was placed in more cautious hands. Balfour replaced Churchill and Admiral Sir Henry Jackson succeeded Fisher. Much drive and energy departed naval affairs with the leaving of the two titans, and for much time after there was chat that Fisher ought to return. There was little talk of Churchill returning to the Admiralty; in fact, the prevailing mood was relief at his departure. As to this dynamic duo, Marder quotes each on the other.

Fisher: 'I backed him up till I resigned. I would do the same again! He had courage and imagination! He was a war man!' Churchill: when Admiral Sir Roger Keyes remarked that Churchill had 'nursed a viper' after recalling the old admiral in 1914, Churchill replied without hesitation, 'And I would do it again; he brought such fire and vigour into the production of ships.'

Volume 3 of the series, *Jutland and After*, appeared, at publisher's request, on the eve of the fiftieth anniversary of the noted battle between the Grand Fleet and the German High Seas Fleet. It was the book of the day. The climacteric event of the dreadnought era, a nexus of Royal Navy history, and the solar plexus besides, Jutland is a beloved topic of aficionados of Britannia's glory, who talk about it much as they do the triumph of Trafalgar or the sad loss of the *Hood* in the Second World War to the guns of *Bismarck* and *Prinz Eugen*. Jutland has special fascination. For it was a defining moment, perhaps the greatest crisis of Britain's sea supremacy, when great battleships and battlecruisers so long moving towards a great encounter met at last, only to be then slowly phased out of the primary role of battle at sea.

The Kaiser's Navy sailed out of Wilhelmshaven into the North Sea on 31 May 1916. The Grand Fleet, commanded by Admiral Sir John Jellicoe, made its own sortie the same day to cruise to the Danish coast of Jutland, with Vice Admiral Sir David Beatty's battlecruiser fleet already out on a coordinated sweep. By accident, British scouting forces encountered German battlecruisers and other units under Admiral Franz von Hipper. Beatty engaged von Hipper's ships, then lured them and the German heavy units following them and led by Admiral Reinhard Scheer towards Jellicoe's heavy units. In these circumstances an annihilation of the Germans might have been expected; this had all the appearances of Jellicoe's day of destiny. But the German commander, Scheer, artfully redeployed his forces after the initial, desultory encounter, then released his destroyers and their torpedoes, which served to ward off Jellicoe. In the mists and decreased visibility of evening, Scheer then made his escape by crossing Jellicoe's line and making a safe, night-time run for home. When darkness fell, Scheer had ordered his ships to harbour; the Admiralty made a mess of transmitting to Jellicoe the German radio messages, which were picked up in London. These indicated the route plotted by Scheer for his escape. It was too late by the time Jellicoe knew the precise details. The Germans were home free.

A battle there had doubtless been, but the losses, in tonnage and men, were greater on the British side than the German. The High Seas Fleet easily had the better of the Grand Fleet, said Marder, who was meticulous in his accounting: 14 British ships of 111,000 tons as against 11 German ships of 62,000 tons. The British lost the battlecruisers *Indefatigable*, *Invincible,* and

Queen Mary, three cruisers, and eight destroyers; the Germans, the old battleship *Pommern*, the battlecruiser *Lützow*, four light cruisers, and five destroyers. Total casualties were similarly proportioned: the Grand Fleet had 6,784, or 8.84 per cent of the total strength of the ships' companies (60,000), the High Seas Fleet 3,058, or 6.79 per cent of the ships' companies (45,000). The day in question was a might-have-been in British naval history, one that could have provided – if things had turned out differently – the ultimate justification for the millions spent on dreadnoughts.

Yet Marder refused to accept Jutland as a defeat, quoting one of his sources, Admiral C.V. Usborne, who reminded him, 'In chess you may lose innumerable pieces, but provided you checkmate the king you are the winner.' Neither fleet was able to inflict a crippling blow on the other, and so, from a tactical point of view, the battle consisted of a series of episodes that are the rule in naval warfare. But, from the point of view of strategy, 'which is what really matters', the Grand Fleet was the winner, beyond a shadow of doubt. '[Admiral] Scheer, who had set out to cut off and overwhelm part of Jellicoe's advanced forces, had been compelled to retreat to his harbours. Albeit a successful retreat, it had not changed the naval position. The British control of the sea communications was unimpaired.' And not only was sea command unimpaired. The results of the battle ensured that it would remain unimpaired. Still, there were severe disadvantages in the British not having won a decisive (and long-predicted) victory: there was no moral victory that would have heartened the nation, the Empire, and the Army in the field; no forces used in defence of the home islands could be released, for the threat of invasion continued; the Baltic as a place of sea operations was still closed, or imagined to be closed; support for U-boats still continued in the form of the High Seas Fleet; and, last, a point Marder gained from Roskill, British light forces could not be deployed for convoy-protection work and the deadlock in France and Flanders persisted, contributing to the carnage of the land battles of 1917.[19]

Marder's book on Jutland tackled the problem of how the Navy's officers dealt with the Grand Fleet's voluminous battle orders (GFBOs). Marder had always been keen to portray officers as uneducated in thinking about principles of war, something endemic to their training. With the GFBOs there was a breakdown on the day of battle: they were explicit in their instructions on the importance of keeping the commander-in-chief informed of all enemy sightings and movements, but on this so-important day they were honoured only in the breach. Jellicoe might have acted more decisively if kept better informed. In the circumstances, Marder concluded that it was difficult to see what more he could have done to force the action to a successful conclusion. Then there was the deplorable failure of the Admiralty. The tragedy of the story was that Room 40 of Naval Intelligence (the Admiralty's secret intelligence department) intercepted and deciphered seven signals, but 'Operations' did not send any of them to Jellicoe. Scheer's signal asking for an early-morning reconnaissance by Zeppelins over Horns Riff had been deciphered. An unmistakable indication of Scheer's route back to his Wilhelmshaven base had been given. There was plenty of time to transmit it to the *Iron Duke* and allow Jellicoe to get to Horns Riff before Scheer. Those indecisive actions of 31 May could then have been supplemented by a full-scale battle in the early morning of 1 June, when conditions of visibility would have been no bar to efficient shooting. Marder put the blame fully on the Operations Division of the Admiralty, and it was a failure that had tragic implications. It denied a naval victory.

Oxford University Press had announced the date of publication of Marder's book to be 26 May 1966, perfect to get media reviews for the eve of the battle on the 31st. The BBC showed interest and the press too. OUP decided to have a high-level book launch at Ely House, Dover Street, its Mayfair, London, address and to invite Marder's friends in the Royal Navy, mainly admirals, and others who had helped him, plus leaders of the publishing world. A gala affair, it brought together the who's who of the British naval world.

On 31 May the *Evening Standard* covered Marder in its long-running feature, 'Londoner's Diary'. Entitled 'America's British Naval Historian', the story seemed to be all about Marder as America's greatest expert on Nelson's lover, Emma, Lady Hamilton – but, in response to the reporter's questions on Jutland, Marder made clear his view that the Battle of Jutland remained a puzzle. 'The great enigma of the battle', he said, 'the answer to which we will almost certainly never know, was that the Admiralty Operations Room never passed on the information which they had about the German movements which would have enabled Jellicoe to prevent them reaching home. The Germans didn't want to fight. They just wanted to get away.' The reporter found Marder an attractive figure, bespectacled, balding, in his mid-fifties, and married with three children. The newspaper photographed him in a canvas chair in sunny Hyde Park, as children and parents strolled by. This was an unlikely pose for Marder – Hyde Park was the last place he would be on a London weekday afternoon – but he looked professorially relaxed. 'I'm a people's historian,' he was quoted as saying, 'I write about human relations. And I'm a romantic in the sense that I'm deeply intrigued by the men who made the Navy of that time what it was. Unlike the officers of the present day – and I've met quite a number of them – they were true individualists.

Those were the days when an Englishman really could afford to walk with his head high, apologizing to no one.' The *Evening Standard* ran a side panel giving the essentials of the battle and ended with a discussion of Admiral Jellicoe, who, it said (quoting Winston Churchill), was the only man on either side who could have won or lost the war in an afternoon.

The Jutland controversy slumbered from the 1930s but never died. Hope existed, Marder recalled, that it had expired on the occasion of the fiftieth anniversary of the battle, but it was not to be. On the evening of the 31st, there was a dinner party at the smart London club Boodle's in honour of the anniversary and Marder's just published Jutland volume. It was, Marder wrote, 'a marvelous party attended by a dozen of the Navy's most distinguished admirals, the civilian head of the Admiralty, and the 2nd Earls Jellicoe and Beatty. Champagne flowed freely. At one point, Lord Jellicoe, with emotion, called for a toast. After paying a handsome compliment to my book, "written without bias", he proposed (seconded by Roskill): "To the end of the controversy!" Glasses were clinked — those of Jellicoe and Beatty most resoundingly — and their contents drained. This euphoric atmosphere lasted 2½ years until December 1968, when the Navy Records Society published a sort of last will and testament of Admiral Harper.'[20] (The story of refighting Jutland is told in chapter 9.)

The same evening of the Jutland anniversary, Marder appeared in a pre-recorded television programme on BBC1's '24 Hours'. The fan mail poured in. Captain Geoffrey Bennett, author of various works on naval history (including 'a damn good one on Jutland', Marder noted privately), wrote to say that he did not see Marder on the BBC, for he was discussing Jutland at precisely the same time on Independent TV. But he noted that, 'having just finished reading your Volume III, I must ask you to accept my unqualified praise and unstinted admiration. No words can adequately express what I think of your achievement. It will assuredly never be bettered.'[21] Bennett sent him some minor comments, and Marder took note of these for a possible second edition, as he did of all useful incoming information.

On 2 June BBC Radio Home Service aired a sixty-minute drama that had been taped on the 31st: 'Jutland Fiftieth Anniversary: Professor Marder's book *Jutland and After*', adapted and produced by David Woodward, naval historian himself. Marder read passages from his book. Ten or eleven professional actors represented the leading participants in the battle — Scheer, the U-boat voice, Jellicoe, Room 40, and so on; the exception was Beatty, who was not named but identified as a 'British Staff Voice'. Marder described the experience as 'delightful, if exhausting'. Two weeks passed. Then Woodward sent Marder a copy of the BBC's confidential audience-research report, which, he said, 'coming from this outstare outfit . . . constitutes a rave notice.'

Indeed it did. Jutland had generated much interest and comment, generally of an appreciative kind but including many sad recollections on the fact that, British victory or not, the battle was a grossly mismanaged affair in which great bravery, dash, and superb seamanship went all for naught as a result of simple stupidity, which could have been catastrophic for the Grand Fleet and for which Britain paid dearly in the loss of life and ships. The foul-up in the use of naval intelligence at the Admiralty, and the failure to get proper intelligence to Jellicoe from London (as told in Marder's account), brought this comment from an engineer and radio officer: 'I think [the programme] gave a very good and clear description of the uncertainty and darkness which seem to have pervaded the whole affair. Those bloody signals . . . ! Nelson on his last stay in Portsmouth was concerned with improved signals.' Other listeners offered praise. One, a retiree, expressed delight at hearing Jellicoe justified by the author; another, an artist, thought the programme balanced and restrained, with good, vivid, but unsensational writing and excellent editing; and a third, a telecommunications expert, commented that, without modern, scientific apparatus to aid them, the British did a wonderful job. All thought that the programme's narrative flow had never faltered and that it had vividly captured some tragic moments, such as the almost instantaneous destruction of the battlecruisers *Queen Mary* and *Indefatigable*.

Admiral J.H. Godfrey, one-time director of naval intelligence, congratulated Marder for having explained some of the British Navy's difficulties to the world: 'I thought your broadcast [BBC1] was admirable – a masterpiece of condensation with all the salient points explained so lucidly to an audience who knew little about the sea and much less about the fog of war, cordite fumes and funnel smoke.'[22] That letter came from deepest Sussex. From other remote locations in the British Isles came similar comments, some written the very night of Marder's Jutland broadcast. Witness this, from Captain Graham Donald, one-time Flight Lieutenant RN, DFC, resident in Isle of Islay, Scotland, to 'Professor Marlowe':

> As one who occupied a well-nigh unique 'front seat view' of the Battle of Jutland, may I give below an extract from my diary of today's date? 3:30 p.m. (B.S.T.) – 50 years ago at 2:30 p.m. (G.M.T.) I was 5½ miles in front of Beatty's Battle-Cruisers – in a very small aircraft-carrier (H.M.S. *Engadine*) when we spotted some funnels (of Hipper's Light Cruisers) on the horizon. As the ground-swell was growing heavier we could only get *one* of our float-seaplanes off. As we were

picking her up about 3.20–3.30 the first dull thumps and the overhead 'whoosh' of the heavy stuff became quite noticeable. As the average age of 20 it seemed – to us – to be a glorious afternoon. Within an hour – by 4.40 p.m. – we had seen 3 of our grand Battle Cruisers blown to glory – and with them 3500 of our own great lads. But it was still a grand afternoon. Why? Because the German Fleet was *already* trying to make a getaway – and the German gunners were getting '*rattled*'. [He describes the erratic German shooting, then:] For most of the action we were able to keep 'close station' with the grand old *Lion* – only 400 or 500 yards off – and could watch David Beatty (the grandest wee fighting Admiral since Nelson) hopping back and forth on his open bridge like a cat on hot bricks. When a German shell peeled the 3½ inch mild steel lid off the *Lion*'s 'Q' turret (the Marine turret) like the top off a bloody sardine tin, we covered our eyes and said 'Oh Christ – the *Lion*'s GONE!' But she wasn't gone. We could see the column of yellow cordite smoke belch up out of the open turret – while that useless 'tin lid' lay on the deck – but the very gallant Marine Major ([F.J.W. Harvey] posthumous V.C.) had enough life left in him to telephone down to the Chief Gunner (our very good old friend Mr. Grant) to 'Flood Magazine'. This he immediately did – so that when another shell landed into that gaping open turret the magazine did not explode – and the *Lion* did not blow up.

Captain Donald thought Jellicoe late in arriving, certainly 'too damn late to be of much real use'. 'There was some Grand Fleet slackness somewhere,' and he pointed out that even the seaplane carrier *Campania* was left behind, forgotten at the Scapa Flow naval base. 'Her small deck-launching facilities would have been an absolute god-send to us', for the sea had become too rough by 3:30 or so to launch water-launched seaplanes. By then the Germans had lost all cohesion, were hell-bent on escape. By nightfall, the British fleet were sole occupiers of the North Sea. 'David Beatty (OUR David) made utterly damn sure that never again would the North Sea be the "German Ocean".' And then: 'Ah well – as I am 70 – with two Wars behind me – I trust you will pardon the ramblings of an ancient "has-been". I must buy your book on Jutland. I wish it luck.'[23] Marder used some of these details in the second edition and systematically set aside Captain Donald's letter and many others for this purpose. They survive, in toto, in his archives collection in California.

A further expression of admiration came from Harvard, and bore the signature of Marder's mentor, William Langer: 'You are the most incredible person: how can you turn out volume after volume of this quality and still live here among the mortals? It beats me, but I am very proud myself of your achievement and certainly want you to know that my warm congratulations go with this.'[24] The newspapers, too, were effusive in their praise of Marder's work. The hugely influential if irksome Taylor said that Marder's volume 3 maintained the high standards of its predecessors. Marder had stated modestly that he had not written the definitive account of the battle. Taylor responded by saying that Marder's account was likely to be as final as any account could be. The narrative was cool and oftimes technical, but the wonderful level of accuracy, clarity, and scholarship were Marder's trademarks, amply demonstrated. Taylor, like other reviewers, awarded top marks to Marder for using almost every source, official and private. 'He is master of every aspect from materiel to personalities. Above all, he has perspective . . . He can place Jutland in the long record of naval development.'[25]

Marder had taken away the old lines of battle – for or against Jellicoe – and, though he could not be said to have ended the debate, which still rages, he had diffused it. His unremitting search for sources was triumphant. He had left few stones unturned. The liveliness of his style showed no trace of combat fatigue. 'With unusual success', Rear Admiral P.W. Brock noted in the *Mariner's Mirror*, 'he has striven to avoid the wisdom of hindsight, and in criticizing he seems to have taken note of [Admiral] Scheer's caution against being too positive that different decisions would necessarily have given better results.'[26]

Roskill proclaimed Marder as 'the greatest living authority on the British Navy in the late 19th and early 20th centuries.' What researchers since Sir Julian Corbett and Sir Henry Newbolt in the early 1920s had been unable to do – get access to Admiralty documents – Marder had been able to accomplish. The only limitation of his account, said Roskill (and perhaps others thought similarly), was that he handled Jellicoe and Beatty too tenderly. 'Nonetheless, this is history on the grand scale, and it has been a stroke of great good fortune for the Royal Navy that the exposition and explanation of its triumphs and tribulations, its frustrations and its failures, has fallen to a writer of such skill and understanding.'[27] This was fine praise, coming as it did from the leading British historian of the Royal Navy.

But Marder's trenchant attempt to clear the names of both Jellicoe and Beatty was not, and could not, be successful in all quarters. Try as he might to calm the waters, the legacies of Jutland remained. There were reputations to protect still, and it was not until 1967 that Admiral of the Fleet Lord Chatfield, the last great British sailor at Jutland – he was the finest of the admirals of the interwar period, Marder said – died, thus opening the floodgates of history. As we will see in chapter 9, this led to the publication of what are known as the Harper documents; that account and its ramifications need not concern us here: they belong best in the story of Roskill and his biography of David Beatty. But, at the time that *Jutland and After* was published, Marder obtained a particularly amusing bit of information. In March 1936 Chatfield, then first sea lord, had received a sharp letter from the dowager Countess Jellicoe imploring him to prevent Beatty being buried next to her husband in St Paul's. She did not get her way. Chatfield explained: 'I have been . . . in communication with the Cathedral authorities as you wished me to. They say it is most undesirable from the point of view of the Chapter to inter Lord Beatty in a corner other than the Naval one. It was for this reason *alone* that the decision was made to bury him next to your husband . . . The question of consulting you arose, but the Cathedral authorities said it was a 'national question' and they had to decide the matter on Cathedral policy. Under these circumstances Lord Borodale [the 2nd Earl Beatty, the admiral's son] also consented . . . The Admiralty was not either the advising nor the deciding voice in the Cathedral decision.' Lady Jellicoe's reply read: 'I do appreciate the fact you and the Admiralty are not to blame about St. Paul's. Strange that the Church instead of giving you Peace of Mind should destroy it.' Chatfield's son Ernle, the 2nd Baron, told Marder that his father had always thought it was the wives who had exacerbated the Jellicoe-Beatty dispute.[28]

May 1968 found Marder at the US Air Force Academy in Colorado at a high-ranking conference on military history, 'Command and Commanders in Military History'. Marder was in good company, for Admiral E.B. Potter, the American naval historian, was there to talk about the command personalities of various US naval officers of the Second World War, and Noble Frankland, director of the Imperial War Museum and co-author (with Sir Charles Webster) of the official UK history of Bomber Command, was present to talk on the combined bomber offensive in Europe during the Second World War, all about Arthur ('Bomber') Harris's Bomber Command and the US Eighth Army Air Force under General Ira Eaker and General Carl Spaatz. The fireworks were reserved for Frankland's appearance because an American professor, Robin Higham, emphasized the criticisms of British and American bomber commands. Then it was Frankland's turn to speak. 'Before I could rise [Frankland wrote in his memoir *History at War*], General Eaker stood up and declared that he had had enough of college boys and would have preferred to hear about the bomber offensive from someone who had been there.' Eaker turned on his heel and strode out of the vast concourse of military historians and service people, followed by Spaatz. 'As they passed the rostrum Eaker looked daggers but Spaatz winked,' recalled Frankland, who added: 'As they disappeared, I took the stand and declared "I was there." A resounding yell of maybe 800 voices rose to the roof . . . it was the only truly dramatic success I have ever had on stage, and off it I fear that General Eaker must have heard the tumult.'[29]

Marder's address on Jellicoe and Beatty as commanders-in-chief of the Grand Fleet was much less controversial. Though he acknowledged the differences between Jellicoe and Beatty, he softened them, emphasizing what the two admirals had in common. Jellicoe made a great fleet out of a heterogeneous collection of ships and squadrons. He met the supreme test of a commander at Jutland and afterwards capitalized on the material, tactical, and other lessons of that battle. As for Beatty, for two years to the end of the war, he kept the morale and efficiency of the Grand Fleet in high order. Marder's conclusion was, 'The Grand Fleet went through the war without fighting a decisive battle, and yet it was the dominating factor all the time. For this achievement Jellicoe and Beatty were equally responsible.'[30]

It fell to Donald Schurman of Queen's University, Kingston, Ontario, to comment on Marder's address. Schurman, a student of the history of British maritime strategic thought, remarked that Marder's paper was like an iceberg, with only the tip of erudition and judgement presented. 'Enthusiasm has inspired him, diligence has marked him, judgement has grown upon him, and magnanimity has rustled the banners of his accomplishments.' This was the first time that Marder's greatness had been proclaimed in his native United States. Schurman continued: 'Although assurance has marked Arthur Marder's publications, I do not think he suffers from undue vanity. He is enough like the subjects of his Nordic sagas that he will be suspicious of too much flattery, and he is enough of the general historian to beware of Greeks "bearing gifts". So much for praise, but it is, as everybody here knows, merely his due.' Marder had come perilously close to qualifying for the title of second 'Official Historian of World War I at Sea' as practised by the Royal Navy, said Schurman. Marder had shown Jellicoe and Beatty not as 'men for all seasons' but eminently, as Correlli Barnett (in *The Swordbearers*) had pointed out in Jellicoe's case, solid men of their time. Marder's address had taken students of naval history away from the old Jellicoe-Beatty 'paper war'. It had obliged historians to mount the ladder in Whitehall 'when they are dishing out responsibilities for things that went wrong' and not to blame commanders on the spot unnecessarily.[31]

Additional comments, by admirals Sir William James, C.M. Blackman, and Sir Angus Cunninghame-Graham — all in the Navy in 1916 and some at Jutland — added piquancy to the discussion but took no issue with Marder.

All steered away from the old stormy waters that imagined that Beatty, with all his zest and charisma – he was a foxhunting man, so they invariably say – would have steered a better course than the cautious Jellicoe on that remarkable day unlike any other in history of British sea power, when Britain came perilously close to losing the trident of Neptune.

With the account of Jutland behind him, Marder dated the preface for the next volume Trafalgar Day 1968. He dedicated the work to his young and growing family – Toni, Tod, and Kevin – 'who suffered through it all with patience and understanding'. Volume 4, *1917: Year of Crisis*, related the story of the Navy from Jellicoe's arrival at the Admiralty to cope with the U-boat menace until his dismissal a year later. If Jutland was the expected battle, the struggle for the sea lanes – the war against the U-boats – was the unexpected one. The war at sea took on a new and critical character, in which the very survival of the home islands was at stake. The convoy system was instituted, after much opposition, and then came a turn of the tide in hunting enemy submarines. Marder's narrative moved freely among the personalities in Whitehall and then shifted easily to the war at sea. Prime Minister David Lloyd George pressed for introducing the convoy system, pushed on by Colonel Maurice Hankey, the secretary of the War Cabinet, with the great anglophile Captain (later Admiral) William Sims, USN, assigned by Washington to consult and advise, giving distinguished advice in the corridors of power. However, as Marder showed, the Admiralty, following Jellicoe's laconic minute of 27 April ('Approve'), had already ordered the instituting of convoys as a trial measure before Lloyd George descended on the Admiralty on 30 April to tell the board to 'act or go'. Marder makes clear that the prime minister later claimed credit for instituting the convoy system, whereas in fact the Admiralty had already put it in place, if on a trial basis. As Edward Carson, the first lord at the time later revealed, the claims of the 'little popinjay' regarding convoys were 'the biggest lie ever was told'. Marder navigated his way successfully through these shoals, letting the details speak for themselves. He noted that the guerrilla warfare continued between the admirals and the politicians, for Lloyd George 'was not at all convinced that the Admiralty's death-bed repentance was sincere.' Hardly noticed by reviewers, his sharp analysis was probing and exact.[32] It remains convincing, though the ghost of Lloyd George making his solemn descent on the Board of Admiralty that unusual afternoon still haunts the corridors of the Old Building in Whitehall.

In September 1969 Marder penned the preface to the last volume of his quintuplet, *Victory and Aftermath (January 1918-June 1919)*. He dedicated the work to his parents, who had given him all that mattered, and he quoted

Archibald Hurd, the venerated historian, who had written that he would have given a king's ransom to be the historian who, once all the secrets became known and public, wrote the history of naval war free of political strife and Service in-fighting. Marder had fulfilled Hurd's dream. But the conclusion of all the great labour brought on a feeling of undeniable sadness. Marder quoted Gibbon, who, in his autobiography, described his feelings after completing the last volume of his *Decline and Fall:* 'I will not dissemble the first emotions of joy on the recovery of freedom . . . But my pride was soon humbled, and a sober melancholy was spread over my mind by the idea that I had taken an everlasting leave of an old and agreeable companion.' 'I am no Gibbon', concluded Marder; 'but for this remark I confess a fellow feeling.'

Marder's last volume showed the Navy triumphant, if not wholly jubilant. The convoy system had brought its rewards. The US Navy had arrived in European waters, serving with the Grand Fleet and elsewhere. The Royal Navy raids on Zeebrugge and Ostend in April 1918 were striking exploits that raised morale but at horrid cost. Marder's last volume was inevitably anti-climactic in the story it told, for Jutland had been fought, or rather not fought. Beatty and the Grand Fleet reconciled themselves to the sad fact that the decisive battle would never take place. They had been trained to expect a day to annihilate the enemy at sea. In November, Beatty received the surrender of the German High Seas Fleet – such bitter sweetness – and there was interminable talk at Paris ('the sea battle of Paris', as Marder dubbed it) about the disposition of the fallen kaiser's naval assets. Then came Germany's scuttling of its ships at Scapa Flow, the British naval base in the Orkneys where the High Seas Fleet had been interned, an event that provoked a flurry of recriminations; naval affairs through and after the Armistice; the naval terms of the Treaty of Versailles and the peace treaties more generally; and the dawn of post-war problems. Now the British had to face a new rival at sea, the United States Navy. Marder's era had ended, and Roskill's begun.

Marder's verdict on the Royal Navy was that it was unfailingly conservative in strategy and tactics, but that this was remarkably but not unreasonably so. The Navy's material was not up to that of Germany. The Navy was dominated by an overly centralized administration, abysmal staff work, under-educated naval officers, and leaders with little ability for creative thinking. There were many lessons to be learned, but they were taken aboard slowly. Of all of them, it was the business of convoys that the Admiralty learned reluctantly and, perhaps, incompletely, for, as Marder argued, you did not actually have to sink U-boats in order to have a safe and timely arrival of clustered and guarded merchantmen: it was the protection of shipping that mattered. Merchant seamen were keen to applaud his perspective.

Marder's summary had a retrospective air to it, and, true to form, he reverted to Jacky Fisher. 'I have said it before and I now repeat: the name of "Fisher" will forever be connected with the Royal Navy at the apex of its power.' He quoted the eloquent tribute of *The Times* (14 July 1920) after the admiral's death: 'Let the schoolmen say what they will . . . this man's fame is safe with history. The people knew him and loved him. His body is buried in peace, but his name liveth for evermore.'

Marder had brought his ship into port, finally, as F.H. Hinsley noted, and against expectations it had ended up as a five-decker. The most recent addition, and its predecessor, had preserved the fine lines that were built into it from the beginning. The paint work might be a little less than perfect, said Hinsley, for such terms as 'a smashing success' and 'through for the war' were unworthy of such a gifted writer as Marder. That aside, the prominence of Marder's flair for taking previously distorted issues and re-examining them had shown through. Historical perspective had been supplied on previous misrepresentation by Service and press over fifty years. The splendid bibliography, with its comprehensive list of manuscript collections, demonstrated Marder's immense care in the making of his own history. It became a guide to all who had business, naval or otherwise, in the years 1904 to 1919; it also lit the path for future researchers, even giving new status to naval history. In other words, Marder's work transcended the usual bounds of naval history, bringing it into the larger world of historical scholarship, no easy feat.[33] Reviews and tributes were unceasing in their praise.

Oxford University Press had reason to be very pleased. Sales figures matched the reviews and were unheard of for serious, definitive naval history. Marder had been right to choose OUP, though that house had no clear track record in the field of naval history and was attracted to it because of its star historian. Its academic record was first-rate, however, and Marder's distinguished books had added to its laurels. The press worked diligently to meet deadlines, make corrections for new printings, send errata slips when required, and issue press releases. It also eased Marder's burdens by cooperating in the sending out of book copies, funded, naturally, at the author's expense. OUP may have grumbled but it did not resist or falter. The publisher's files make for compelling reading: these show the enlargement of the project, with its increasing number of volumes – one becoming in the end five! – and an appreciation exhibited by editor Geoffrey Hunt that this historical enterprise was one for all time and would not likely be replicated. The attention to photographs, permissions (arranged by the author, to add to his other burdens), numerous maps, and indexes was all exemplary. One wonders why the volumes were never reprinted, though admittedly volume

3, *Jutland and After*, the most popular, did go to a greatly expanded second edition (1978).

Although the publisher was keen to do a one-volume abridgement, suggesting it in 1972 as a paperback, Marder wanted no part of it. He had other fish to fry and, besides, it would have been uncharacteristic of him as the sort of scholar he was, right from the outset: he never wrote survey texts or textbooks, and he never wrote for popular magazines. There was talk, too, of a German edition though the five volumes seemed prohibitive as a translation project. An abridged English version was a different matter and kept popping up: OUP wanted it badly. Accordingly, even before volume 5 was out, a unique partnership was forged with the competent and popular naval writer Richard Hough, through the latter's literary agent. Marder disliked the 'messy details' of the pending financial arrangements. He held his ground, gaining 3½ per cent royalties on all copies sold, based on net receipts. Hough's proceeds are not known. Marder was also concerned about what sort of acknowledgement Hough would give to him in the preface of the book: Richard Brain, a senior editor at OUP handling the matter, said that he was sure such a notice would be 'a full and generous one, and justly so'.[34] Hough used Marder's documents and notes, including some for intended revisions of the book – this was part of the agreement – and then wrote up a summary under the title *The Great War at Sea, 1914–1918*, published by Oxford in 1983. By this time, Marder had died. Hough dedicated *The Great War at Sea* to Marder's memory, and he wrote a generous tribute to his late associate. He was obviously beholden to Marder for previous work, but later he would assume a different perspective, giving an off-colour review of volume 2 of the posthumously published *Old Friends, New Enemies*, of which more later. For the moment, however, Marder and Hough forged a useful and amiable partnership.

The five-volume work – 'a monument of scholarship worthy of its subject', said Michael Howard[35] – brought Marder many subsequent honours. Among the first to pay respects was the Admiralty Board, that ancient and venerable institution which in late years had been reconstituted into what amounted to the old Navy Board of an earlier era.[36] It still retained its much vaunted autonomy but was now restrained within the inter-services environment of the Ministry of Defence. Its successive secretaries, librarians, and archivists all knew Marder personally: they had responded to his persistent badgering and incessant inquiries. Their superiors, the old lords of the Admiralty or their successors, knew Marder either personally or by reputation, and on 1 July 1970 they decided to bestow a special accolade on him.[37] Only a few weeks before, in May, Marder had been in London signing copies of volume 5. Senior officers and many others readily snapped these up. Now it was time for the Admiralty Board to express its admiration of Marder's accomplishment, though it was quite uncustomary for it to issue a notice of appreciation to any civilian, let alone an historian. Thus this letter, from the secretary of the board:

Ministry of Defence
Main Building Whitehall, London, S.W.1

1st July 1970

Sir,

I am commanded by the Admiralty Board to say that they have noted with pleasure the recent publication of the fifth and final volume of your history of the Royal Navy 'From the Dreadnought to Scapa Flow'. You have thus brought to a successful conclusion a work of outstanding scholarship, illuminated by both judgement and humanity and a deep understanding of this important period of the Navy's history; and the Board wish to take this opportunity both of offering you their congratulations on the completion of your task and also of expressing their warm appreciation of the service which in their view you have thereby rendered to the Royal Navy.

I am, Sir,
    Your obedient Servant,
    S[idney] Redman

Probably by way of *The Times* naval correspondent, a copy of this minute came into the hands of the writer of the 'Times Diary', who seized on it and suitably headed up his entry 'Ah, Marder!' He noted that the Admiralty Board had sent an unusual letter of glowing praise. From Roskill, he solicited the view that the letter was 'exceptional and possibly unique'. When asked his opinion about Marder's achievement, Roskill said, 'I agree with the congratulations. When I reviewed the book, I called it [a] masterly accomplishment. Marder is a remarkably energetic, thorough and persistent researcher, and writes in a fluent, easy style which makes him a pleasure to read. I gave him the whole of my World War I material, including unique material on the Battle of Jutland.'[38] Yes, indeed, Roskill had a claim to share in Marder's glory. Even so, and for the moment, Roskill fought back the tendency to tell all.

Chapter 5

Roskill and the Politics of Official History

Nowadays it is customary to assume that Roskill was the first and most logical candidate to write the volumes on the maritime war for the Military Series of the *United Kingdom Histories of the Second World War*, generally known as the Official War Histories. He was neither the first nor the most logical. His appointment resulted from the timely coincidence of his being available at the right moment and the Admiralty's pressing need to recommend a candidate to the board, or panel, supervising the official Military Histories. As with Marder, chance dictated his future prospects. That Roskill filled the bill more than adequately, even brilliantly, is now generally recognized. Yet, in his work as so-called official historian, he was certainly not official and had no such standing in law or practice. In fact, in this post he was buffeted by the winds of fate.

Roskill listed himself as 'official naval historian' in his *Who's Who* entry. The title was self-ascribed. He was never the official naval historian and certainly never the official historian of the Royal Navy in the Second World War. He was merely on salary with the Cabinet Office. Further, in British circles a considerable battle then raged about what was 'official history' and also what an 'official historian' might be. Roskill himself was aware that the Military History Series was often referred to colloquially as the 'Official Histories', although that description was in fact incorrect.[1] Professor Sir Michael Howard had initiated a discussion on this point in a *Times Literary Supplement* review of Noble Frankland and Sir Charles Webster's *The Strategic Air Offensive against Germany 1939–1945*,[2] when he said that 'official history' contained a self-contradiction: no government wished to admit the failures of how the war was conducted and therefore would shy away from admitting to muddle, inefficiency, and waste. The editor of the Military History Series, Sir James Butler, made clear that 'official history' was work commissioned by government which then opened records for the purpose and took responsibility for the competence of the author and the editor.[3] Roskill himself was aware of the ambiguities of 'the public's adoptive description of our work'.[4] The government might authorize the work in question but it would never say the work was authorized. The individual author was left hanging out to dry, so to speak. This was the case with Roskill. His appointment and career as 'official historian' shows all the perils imaginable, including considerable interference from Sir Winston Churchill, then in his second premiership, and a quarrel with Lord Mountbatten regarding his powers as supreme commander, South East Asia. This inside story of the politics of official naval and maritime history redounds to the credit of Roskill, and it demonstrates his persistence and courage in the face of onslaught from powerful forces.

Roskill's *War at Sea* was published by Her Majesty's Stationery Office (HMSO) in three volumes, the third in two parts. Volume 1, *The Defensive*, appeared in 1954; volume 2, *The Period of Balance*, in 1956; volume 3, part 1, *The Offensive, 1st June 1943 – 31st May 1944*, in 1960; and volume 3, part 2, *The Offensive, 1st June 1944 – 14th August 1945*, in 1961. The whole, including indexes, ran 2,013 pages in print, and Roskill estimated the total work at three-quarters of a million words. Its size alone commands attention; the contents, undeniable admiration. From the points of deepest despair and difficulty through the period of equipoise and then to the final stages that led to defeat of the enemies, first Italy, then Germany, and finally Japan, the narrative flows in a logical pattern. Throughout the conflict, and almost to the final days in the maritime war, the Navy faced formidable opposition and often defeat. This was no victory parade, as Roskill saw it, the facts and materials presented making it clear that the outcome was achieved at considerable cost, the age-old price of Admiralty. The respective volumes form more of a seamless whole than separate accounts revealing distinct stages in the struggle. Although stressing that the British often worked with Allies, Roskill made certain that he would tell the British story. He also made it an undeclared statement of faith that he would not give excessive attention to the role of the Royal Air Force's Coastal Command in maritime operations, notably in the war against the U-boats. Nor would amphibious operations involving the the placing of soldiers ashore, or the retrieving of them, provide the focus. He wanted – against the odds – to tell the Navy's side of the story. In a way, the final result was a rescue operation for naval history, deliberately manipulated by Roskill with effect.

The uniformly fine reviews enjoyed by the volumes[5] mask the many difficulties Roskill faced in the research, writing, and acceptance of the work. In later years he became rather cavalier in dismissing these problems. This cannot be sustained by a close reading of certain surviving cabinet and

Admiralty papers and other sources. These files reveal the politics of official history and show Roskill under attack from various quarters. He defended himself stoutly and with the crisp precision that was his hallmark. On more than one occasion, he got riled, mainly by injustices thrown his way, and in such circumstances had to be restrained by avuncular associates and superiors. In one instance, as will be seen, he even talked of going public on the matter in dispute. His battles as official historian brought him in touch with many of the political leaders, private secretaries, armed Service brass, and military and naval historians of the day. The story of his *War at Sea* stands as a chapter in how the state tries to own its history and yet how a individual historian, such as Roskill, can shape that history.

This story began in the closing years of the Second World War, when literary and historical minds turned to the question of who would write the official history of the maritime war. Already the government had decided that the History of the Second World War as an official project would come under the direction of the Cabinet Office. There would be a Civil Series and a Military Series. Irrespective of this decision, the Admiralty, proud of its own achievements and wary of mischief that might befall the story if under exclusive inter-Service control, intended to have its own project, as was its right. C. Northcote Parkinson, the historian, had an interest in it, and Arthur Bryant, doyen of popular history, was thought by a flattering Parkinson to be the obvious choice. 'I don't feel I'm at all the person to do a tactical and technical volume on this naval history of the war,' replied Bryant to an inquiring Parkinson. He hoped Parkinson or Captain John Owen, RN, an expert on Queen Anne's naval war, would undertake it. Bryant had made known his views to the Board of Admiralty and there his advice lay.[6] Possibly the Admiralty had asked Bryant to let his name stand and, had the book been completed, their lordships would have been the laughing-stock of future generations, for the pro-fascist turned boot-licking defender of government – the switch occurred in 1942 but was not then disclosed – became discredited in professional historical circles. The Bryant project was set aside but only after £50,000 had been spent. Questions were raised in Parliament, for public expenditures were involved.

Lieutenant Commander Peter Kemp, of the Admiralty's Historical Branch, came forward to produce in record time *Victory at Sea, 1939–1945* (1948). A fine survey in its own right, which forthrightly cast doubt on the Board of Admiralty's actions in the fiasco of the scattering of the convoy to north Russia, named PQ.17 (of which more presently), Kemp's study was a naval book for a naval audience. In his hands, the Admiralty's positions and policies were safe. The work, however, was only a precis of the naval war. It did not rival the work then being developed for the Cabinet Office.

In assuming responsibility for the Official Histories, the Cabinet Office supplanted the Committee of Imperial Defence, which had been authorized to produce the various service histories of the First World War. The grand enterprise was to be under ministerial control, though the Cabinet Office would have to liaise with various historical branches and secretariats. Joint operations now ruled and so, too, inter-Service cooperation, real or imagined. The administration of the Official Histories was kept out of the hands of individual armed services and raised to another level. It was hoped that incomplete volumes would be a thing of the past, while overly extended treatments would be curtailed, departmental interventions and disclaimers avoided, and internecine feuding circumvented. A central command would ease the passage of work and acceptance. The project, except for its secretariat, was to be run by committee, a circumstance made palatable only because of the editorship and chairmanship of Butler, who in November 1946 had been brought from Trinity College, Cambridge, to head up the Military Histories Series. Butler, emeritus professor of modern history at Cambridge, was given the title chief historian of the United Kingdom Official Military Histories. He and his committee, and key civil servants of the Cabinet Office where the operation was overseen, housed, and funded, decided on a number of volumes on Grand Strategy, including one on the approach to war and others on several campaigns such as Norway, the Mediterranean, and the Far East. Before long, a team was assembled consisting, on the one hand, of academic historians, most of whom had some Service experience, and, on the other, of retired officers in the regular forces.

For a time, the search for a suitable candidate for a historical work on the maritime war from the British point of view languished. Urgency soon stalked the halls. In the Naval Historical Branch, staff were preoccupied with questions raised by the official historian of the United States Navy for the Second World War, Rear Admiral Samuel Eliot Morison. The draft of his first volume of *History of the United States Naval Operations in World War II* was approaching readiness, and the whole project was far in advance of anything the Cabinet Office or, for that matter, the Admiralty had in mind. The hot issue in Morison's text was the disaster that befell the PQ.17 convoy in July 1942. The Admiralty's role and particularly that of the first sea lord, Admiral Sir Dudley Pound, in the 'convoy is to scatter' order made for a major headache for the chief of the Naval Historian and Information Branch of the Admiralty.

Morison, Trumbull professor of history at Harvard, had been at work on his mammoth project since 1942, when President Franklin Delano Roosevelt appointed him official historian of the US Navy. In fact, he had been there at the creation, as it were: convinced that too many naval histories were written long after the events, when the sailors had been discharged and the ships broken up, he had gone to see Roosevelt just after the attack on Pearl Harbor. The president was enthusiastic, and Morison was commissioned lieutenant-commander of the US Naval Reserve (USNR) and given the mission to write the naval history. 'Morison's history' was born. For more than half of the remainder of the war, Morison was at sea. He witnessed the North African invasion, sailed in Atlantic convoys, and saw combat in the South Pacific. At war's end, he emerged as captain with seven battle stars on his service ribbons and later retired as rear admiral, USNR. His histories were not, he reminded readers, official histories. 'The Navy has given me every facility, but has not attempted to prejudice my conclusions or set the pattern of my writing.' 'Nobody in the Navy has ever suggested that I cover up blunders or play down errors.' He knew that luck plays a great part in naval warfare, and that under enemy fire even gifted officers can make mistakes. Thus, he was more charitable than armchair authors 'who never get their feet wet'.[7] Morison had as his directors of naval history two naval officers who were scholars themselves and with whom he had served as shipmates during hostilities – Rear Admirals John B. Heffernan and Ernest M. Eller. Working quickly and with the assistance of many fine, well-educated sailor historians, Morison managed a highly successful collaborative enterprise and is not always given the high marks that he deserves on this score. He had been writing about British naval responsibilities in the worst convoy disaster of the war, that of PQ.17, and in the less troubling Operation Torch, the invasion of North Africa, before a suitable British historian was even found and appointed. Morison, in his draft, had stated that the Admiralty mismanaged the convoy in question, and this was bound to spell trouble in Britain if published.

PQ.17, a convoy bound for Russia, destination Archangel, sailed from Iceland on 27 June 1942 despite profound misgivings in the Royal Navy about the continuation of the Russian convoys in the long hours of summer daylight in high latitudes. But a growing backlog of ships carrying Lend Lease cargoes waited in Iceland and Britain. The Allied leaders, particularly President Roosevelt, desired the continuation of the convoys, and the hard-pressed Russians, then facing the German summer offensive, demanded it. PQ.17 consisted of thirty-six merchant ships and an Anglo-American cruiser-destroyer force made up of four heavy cruisers under Rear Admiral L.H.K. ('Turtle') Hamilton, flying his flag in HMS *London*, and the USN's *Tuscaloosa* and *Wichita* plus three destroyers; this was to provide cover as far as Bear

Island. From then on, the commander-in-chief, Home Fleet, Admiral Sir John Tovey, in the *Duke of York*, with the American battleship *Washington* and various other cruisers and destroyers, would provide a distant covering force in the waters northeast of Jan Mayen Island. This was the first time US naval forces were placed under British orders for an operation of this nature, and, though Roskill could never find any confirming evidence, Churchill possibly surmised that the American participation in the event may have been a new factor that influenced Admiral Pound's subsequent actions.

German air and naval forces had been strongly reinforced. Land-based Luftwaffe bombers could be expected when the convoy came near the occupied coast of Norway and U-boats would be lurking along the way. These and the threat posed by U-boats based in Norway were givens. The known presence in north Norwegian waters of four German heavy surface units, including the powerful new battleship *Tirpitz*, were an additional risk since they might move even father north to strike at the Allied convoy as it moved through the dangerous area between Norway and Spitzbergen. A close escort under Commander John E. Broome in HMS *Keppel*, including an American destroyer, fought off air and U-boat attacks until the convoy passed north of Bear Island. Now came the decision that led eventually to the destruction of the convoy. Acting on incomplete signal intelligence, which convinced him that the German heavy units were at sea, Admiral Pound, the first sea lord, ordered the cruiser force to withdraw westward at high speed. Subsequently, he issued a rare 'convoy is to scatter' order. The vessels of the convoy were to proceed independently to Russian ports if they could make it. Commander Broome had the unpleasant duty of bidding farewell to the convoy, leaving it to its fate. When the battle was over on 15 July, PQ.17 had lost twenty-four merchant ships and 65 per cent of its cargoes. Pound, burdened by many responsibilities, had not acted hastily but rather deliberately. Still, he had to shoulder the blame for the consequences of his fateful and controversial decision.

When Morison's draft of his first volume arrived at the Admiralty for the requested speedy review, delivered by a US Navy courier direct from Washington, the Admiralty found itself in the uncomfortable position of having to censor an Allied historian without doing so blatantly. There were other considerations. One fellow working in the Admiralty's intelligence department complained about the work: 'It is considered', he moaned, 'that the eye-strain involved in studying this document is an outrageous imposition and that in any case a fortnight is far too short a time to give the Admiralty a considered opinion in the matter.' More serious was Morison's indirect accusation that the escort commander, Admiral Hamilton, exhibited cowardice. Morison's text never obtained Admiralty approval, nor did it get the immediate benefit of an ally's historical naval department's knowledge or advice. The special courier returned to Washington empty-handed.

The Admiralty needed to keep face so it now effected damage control in these matters. A promise for quick review was given the Americans and the Naval Historical Branch soon dispatched a list of corrections and suggestions to Heffernan, the director of naval history. As an added bonus, and likely as a sign of good faith, the Admiralty sent copies of captured German documents related to PQ.17. These Washington would have had already, as part of the microfilming project of the papers captured in Tambach Castle in 1945. Many of the suggestions were designed to protect the Admiralty from having to address thorny questions concerning the actions of key figures. For example, the Admiralty requested that Morison change his description of the abandonment of the convoy by the escort from 'he [the escort commander] elected to retire' to 'he elected to detach his destroyers to support the cruisers in the expectation that action with the superior enemy forces was imminent, leaving the submarines and the thirteen smaller escorts to provide what support they could to the scattered enemy. In the event, since no surface action materialized, his decision may be open to question.' In the end, Morison held his course but avoided shoals and sandbars, and his subsequent and final wording reads, 'He decided to pull his destroyers out to support the cruisers; this created a near panic among the armed trawlers and other weak escorts and they too scattered.' He said, in reference to German surface units, that the Admiralty overestimated the enemy's aggressive intentions. Morison also, in a footnote, included this historical nugget, Hamilton's message as recorded in *Tuscaloosa*'s war diary: 'I know you will all be as distressed as I am at having to leave that fine collection of ships to find their own way to harbour.'[8]

Morison duly made accommodations but only to satisfy the British suggestions. Requirements of Anglo-American accord counted mightily in the Cold War era. More important, the two naval historical branches maintained high professional standards and were sticklers for accuracy but they still had reputations to protect. The ordeal of PQ.17 would never go away as far as Naval Historical Branch was concerned, and Roskill found himself drawn into it several times. All these are discussed below. The Morison history, proceeding at full speed, revealed the Admiralty's problems.[9]

In the meantime, the Admiralty asked Captain R.K. Dickson, former chief of naval intelligence, to let his name stand as a possible author of the history of the maritime war. Dickson had a reputation as a talented writer. Rear Admiral Royer Dick, director of the Tactical and Staff Duties Division, had suggested him for he selfishly, as he admitted, wanted to ensure that the *naval* view would be put forward to the public. It would be safe in Dickson's hands.[10] Vice Admiral Sir Maurice Mansergh, naval secretary to the first lord of the Admiralty, raised the matter with Dickson but found him strongly opposed to the proposal. The appointment would take him away from a sea command (and future promotion prospects), and besides, he said, he was not the right person. The explanation given Butler was that Dickson could not be released from other duties.

The Admiralty's gaze went elsewhere. In view were two retired officers, Rear Admiral A.J.L. Phillips and Captain F.J. Wylie, recently of HM ships *Norfolk* and *Mauritius* respectively. Perhaps either of these experienced officers would suit? They were of reasonable age – in their fifties – and in good health. Mansergh forwarded the nominations to the Cabinet Office.

Butler, now at last in possession of names to consider, consulted Admiral Sir Geoffrey Blake, who might be called an old beagle of the Navy, a gunnery specialist who had served under Jellicoe and Beatty. Wise, energetic, and always on the scent (he was father-in-law to another official historian, John Ehrman), Blake sat on the Advisory Board of the Official Military Histories but was clearly no toady of the Admiralty. Phillips would not do, said Blake, though he gave no recorded reason, and Wylie was being considered for appointment to the Joint Intelligence Board. Blake consulted with Mansergh, who offered to suggest some other well-qualified, competent naval officer. The tough-minded permanent secretary of the Admiralty, Sir John Lang, tried to advance the process. Nothing would gel.

Even as the search for an author proceeded, without results, the Cabinet Office, not the Admiralty, made plans for an official history of the maritime war. In May 1948 the Cabinet Office circulated to Service departments a prospectus 'Control of Sea Communications'. This was written by Captain John Creswell, RN, a noted historian, an expert in naval tactics, and afterwards a confidant of Marder's. Creswell's scheme, which was adopted, adhered to cabinet guidelines for the Official War Histories, namely, examination of sea-control efforts in all theatres, with primary attention to the coasts of France, the Mediterranean, the Indian Ocean, and the British Isles. Creswell thought the seas historically divisible (his reasons were literary) and that one volume ought to tackle the seas of northern Europe; another, the rest of the world. This oddity probably reflects departmental advice and Creswell's own wide-ranging interest, for he was shortly to publish the first global history of sea warfare in the Second World War.

The Advisory Board reviewed this portfolio at its meeting of 1 June 1948. By this time, Creswell had given notice that, owing to ill health, he would accept the position of author only if he could work at home, in Cattistock, near Dorchester, travelling to London as required. Blake and Rear Admiral R.M. Bellairs, who headed the Naval Historical Branch, baulked at Creswell's working-from-the-country alternative. The required research papers in the Admiralty Record Office could not be allowed to leave London. Questions might be asked in Parliament, and answers rapidly given. Staff naval histories had to be written. Government departments might need to consult the files. Creswell's offer was declined with regret. As to Creswell's proposal about the two theatres and two volumes, the board recognized that spillages would occur and that a work on sea communications would likely involve a measure of overlap with the theatre-focused volumes. The board added that it wanted more emphasis on the Norway campaign and on the US entry into the war. Thus the project had the green light; its dimensions and themes had been adopted. As of that date, Roskill was nowhere in the picture.

But changes were in the wind. On 17 February 1949 Roskill's name came forward to the Advisory Board for consideration. The nomination was championed by Commander Robert Aubrey, who thought Roskill was not only drawn to the project but was superior to any in the running. Although Roskill had written no naval history, said Aubrey, the latter had seen a number of his articles in the *Naval Review*, and these showed him as an attractive writer. Roskill, for his part, had made clear to Aubrey that he was not prepared to move from Blounce to London or to commute to London on a daily basis. The board accepted this: Roskill lived within easy reach by train, and he could come to town as required. Butler met with Roskill, who showed him some of his articles; Butler was pleased. At the board, no objections were raised; perhaps there was just relief. Roskill was appointed there and then.[11] But it was made clear that no documents were to be taken away.

Roskill was told later by Admiral Sir Geoffrey Oliver, a member of the Board of Admiralty at the time, that Roskill's Bikini report had caused the board to nominate him. Roskill believed this to be true, though on this point the paper trail runs dry. He always claimed the Bikini report to be something of a best-seller in the United States, an exaggeration. Roskill believed that it was Captain (later Admiral Sir) Richard Onslow who put his name forward in 1948, and Aubrey may have been the nominator. Whatever the case, Roskill was available; a suitable historian had been found. Alan Pearsall, archivist at the National Maritime Museum at this time, told me that it was his impression that Roskill was 'pretty well wracked up' owing to his war injuries.[12] Still, he must have been sufficiently healthy to be selected, and, in any event, there was urgency to the appointment: Morison was pressing ahead while the

Admiralty had not got off the starting blocks. The Cabinet Office needed to move on these fronts. What the other United Kingdom Service departments thought about these delays can only be imagined. In any event, Roskill was not the Admiralty's man, though his nomination came via that department of government. His every sentence and every historical judgement would be evaluated and questioned. In fact, all Service historical branches, the Cabinet Office secretariat, the Advisory Board, and Butler would scrutinize his work before publication.

Roskill, age forty-five, had landed on his feet. From no prospects he had been given an immense opportunity for a new career or at least a job for five years at £1,200 per annum. Fortune brought the appointment: he was just the right person at the right time. He felt largely inadequate when he assumed his task, he later told an audience at the Canadian Command and Staff College, Toronto. His literary attainments at the date of appointment were few, mainly in the line of reviews and comments in the *Naval Review*. In the early 1920s he had written an essay on Jutland for the Admiralty's annual prize competition. This had shown sufficient promise that Richmond, the principal judge, had asked to see him. Still, he was largely untested in the historical line or on current naval questions, and he was inexperienced in researching and writing anything of the magnitude envisaged. He had read Mahan, Corbett, Richmond, and other naval historians, and, from his own time in the Service, he knew the history of various battles and campaigns.[13] Nonetheless, the prospect of a multi-volume work for the Cabinet Office was daunting, to say the least. A person of lesser abilities and courage would easily have shied away from this immense challenge. Roskill was determined to do justice to what he knew from first-hand experience to be a story immensely worth the telling.

Within days of his appointment, Roskill took up a ground-floor office, Room 54, in the Cabinet Office in Great George Street, adjacent to Parliament Square. He spent his preliminary week reading Mahan, Richmond, and other naval historians. The reconnaissance yielded results, including an appreciation of the historian's problem of framing large works. He surveyed the Naval Staff histories and summaries. Then he began searching out archival materials in the Admiralty and the Cabinet Office. Who helped him, or how he was treated, is not known. But he assumed an official position with as much weight to his office as he could muster, and commenced his duties aggressively and with deliberation.

Roskill knew that he could expect to face bureaucratic indifference and procedural problems. Above all, he was alert to possible political interference. He expected trouble from the Admiralty, he told his Canadian audience. He knew a lot about the difficulties encountered by Sir Julian Corbett with the Admiralty over the Official History of the First World War, and so considered himself forearmed against the difficulties he felt sure he would encounter with the Admiralty. 'Luckily . . . I learnt something of Corbett's difficulties from his great friend Sir Herbert Richmond – perhaps the profoundest thinker and writer on maritime affairs of this century.'

All arrangements of a financial and material nature were administered by A.B. Acheson, head of the Historical Section of the Cabinet Office. A brilliant and supportive civil servant, Acheson was a hands-on administrator, keen to assist and give advice when asked. Butler, who worked only half time as general editor of the Official War Histories, could hardly have performed his tasks without the relief provided by the indomitable Acheson. Roskill was a further step removed from Acheson but the relationship with Butler was similarly smooth. Roskill's links to Butler were distant at first, but they soon became close partners in the process of getting the Advisory Board's approval for volume 1. They were drawn together by unforeseen circumstances and difficulties.

Roskill spent a miserable Christmas 1949 in hospital, nursing war wounds and pondering the enormous task ahead. He could not, for the life of him, see his way to covering so vast a subject in the allotted two volumes. As he explained to Acheson, the naval side of the war could not possibly receive its due under this arrangement. Already a number of volumes had been allotted to theatres where soldiers had been in charge. Butler, considering this, told Roskill he would back a redesign at the board but that Roskill would have to make a case before it. Admiral Blake advised against enlargement on the grounds that the work should, in his view, be tightly controlled around the central theme of sea communications – essentially the Creswell design. He wanted no unnecessarily long campaign accounts, no battle description, and no analysis – just a spare, straightforward narrative. In any event, at its meeting of 18 May 1950, the board agreed to Roskill adding a third volume and Blake backed down. He warmed to the idea that detail could now be given so as to illustrate the thematic points he so desperately wanted covered.

Everything Roskill wrote had to be read and approved by the Advisory Board. At the outset, discussion focused on the title of the work. Roskill suggested these: Maritime Warfare, The Struggle at Sea, Maritime Control, The War at Sea, and Control of the Seas. The last was his preference. The board decided on The War at Sea, with dates 1939–1945, and so the title was determined. In obvious hurry, the board also called for the draft of Roskill's first chapter to be submitted by 22 March 1951. Then it would be circulated, as were all texts for all the series, for review, discussion, and defence, followed by modification and final approval.

Roskill did not, contrary to the editor's statement in the book as eventually published, have a free run of the various surviving historical documents needed for his research. He faced many of the same constraints as Marder but would have had greater access given his Cabinet Office status as temporary employee. Even so, from Admiralty files he could draw only three files at a time. All copies had to be made in the Admiralty Record Office. Many of the expected documents had been removed or 'weeded', he later claimed. He found that the daily War Diary of the Operational Intelligence Centre of the Admiralty had been destroyed after the war. It was an archival holocaust, he later stated. The only surviving documents of use on the intelligence side in regard to naval operations were the 'dockets' of in and out signals arranged chronologically by date. Even these were hard to locate if they still survived. He had no access to ULTRA documents, that is, the British and Allied intelligence of decrypted German Enigma ciphers; neither could he get at the personal and private correspondence of the first lord or the first sea lord, all kept under close wraps in the Admiralty Record Office's special vault, 'the Cage'. Roskill, to widen his sources and get independent advice or opinion, wrote to admirals and other officers concerning their activities. But this avenue of research was limited, for he depended on the services of a ministerial secretarial pool. He had to fight for typing services. He wrote his letters and text in longhand, then realized, as many have, that it would be best to hire his own personal secretary even at personal expense. Mrs Edith Eales – he called her, affectionately, 'Ealey' – became his devoted servant, even moving to Blounce to be with Stephen and the family. He built up his own library of reference and documentary files and, in developing his own filing system, displayed keen archival instincts.

Roskill's work was solitary, always against the clock. He drove himself hard. He travelled from Blounce to London early on Mondays, stayed overnight at his club, the Travellers, worked in his office Tuesdays, and returned home that same evening. Wednesdays would find him in the country. Then on Thursdays he would repeat the itinerary and schedule of early in the week, and was back home on Fridays. By this regime he could get in four days of work in London in a week.

When in London he worked long days and often ended his writing in the club library in the small hours of the night. He took typescripts to the country for weekend review, or he would begin or complete sections of the book there. His health suffered, leading him to abandon evening work. Then he developed an ulcer and late one afternoon collapsed in his office. Commander Geoffrey Hare, appointed his assistant to ease the burden, chanced upon Roskill lying unconscious on the floor. Roskill was rushed to Westminster Hospital and shortly afterwards was ordered to take a holiday. 'A paid holiday?' asked Roskill, the answer to which came happily in the affirmative. Stephen and Elizabeth toured southern Europe, while Roskill nervously worried about the progress of his history.

Roskill's preliminary chapter came to the Advisory Board for discussion on 20 April 1951, with Roskill present by request. The chapter was 'Maritime War and Maritime Strategy'. Butler, in the chair, reminded the board that the purpose of such discussions was to enable members to make points they thought might assist the historian. He went further: it rested with the historian as to how such suggestions would be reflected in the work under review. Butler himself was writing a volume in the series, and he had prepared written guidelines for all official historians in the Military Series. He skilfully guided the process.

Hardly a theme or concept in Roskill's chapter escaped the attention of the board members. With thoroughness matched with good intentions, each managed some sort of evaluation. First off the mark was Air Chief Marshal Sir Guy Garrod, who proudly talked about air power reducing U-boat numbers and effectiveness. Then it was the turn of General Sir Ian Jacob, a pit-bull in these matters of the official line (and a trusted insider of Winston Churchill). Jacob, giving fair warning, reminded Roskill of the pressure under which those responsible for conducting the war lived, and he even quoted Churchill to that effect. Others, in succession, wanted Roskill to explain naval and maritime matters to the general reader. Queries were raised about the author's terminology, including 'strategic defensive' and 'strategic offensive'. What were these? Another, 'limited war' (coined by Corbett), caused anxiety. So did 'concentration of force'. Were other service members trying to give the Navy lessons in strategic terminology, one wonders? Members of the board quarrelled about who should be thanked in the preface and acknowledgements.

Roskill must have felt as if in the dock under cross-examination during that first meeting. He took it in his stride. With tact and care, he eliminated doctrinal terms of the Service and simplified his draft, making the chapter leaner, more direct. In the end, this opening chapter constituted an epitome of the theory and practice of the British Empire, the United States, and their allies in waging a maritime war against a continental power. Corbett's *Some Principles of Maritime Strategy* (1911) shines through here. No less important was Roskill's use of history to explain principles in operation. In its time, the opening chapter was a brilliant exposition, and it still is worth close study. It explains the three phases of the maritime war that Roskill developed for his work – Defensive, September 1939 to December 1941; the Period of Balance,

January 1942 to mid-1943; and the Offensive, mid-1943 to the end. After the introductory material came discussion of British organization for conduct of the maritime war, the development of sea-air cooperation, and British and enemy plans and preparations. These were all preliminary to how to deal with sea warfare as such, where Roskill had to take into account chronological dimensions with area concerns. Usually he moved from home waters, to broad oceans, narrow seas, then the Mediterranean, and later the Far East, all the while taking note of how to deal with specific events such as Dunkirk and the *Bismarck* episode.

Two years passed from Roskill's first chapter being accepted to the hoped-for approval of the complete volume 1. The delays were not of Roskill's choosing. In one case, the Admiralty intervened and strenuously objected to Roskill's account of events leading to the dismissal of Admiral Sir Dudley North from the Gibraltar command in September 1940. The issue, which is treated in more detail below in chapter 8, was whether or not North, who allowed a French squadron to pass unmolested from Toulon to Dakar at the time of the Free French-British expedition to get General Charles de Gaulle a foothold on recaptured French soil, was the scapegoat for the British mishandling of the expedition. Churchill, then prime minister and minister of defence, had had a hand in the firing. Butler accompanied Roskill to the Admiralty to see Sir John Lang, the permanent secretary, who opened the discussion with 'we don't like this', 'we won't have that', and so on. Roskill takes up the story of how he defended himself:

> I gently asked whether he was speaking for the Board of Admiralty, and if so did he not realize that I was a servant of the Cabinet Office, not of his department. I then asked what he would do if I declined to accept his views, and he thumped the table and said 'We would put in a strengthened disclaimer.' I turned to Butler and said 'I don't know if you are aware of it but that is exactly what the Admiralty did to Corbett's Vol. III on Jutland, and it discredited the book forever.' Lang realized that he was beaten, walked over to his safe and produced Churchill's letter to the First Lord demanding Admiral North's dismissal – which I had always believed to exist but had failed to locate. So the meeting ended amicably with an agreement that if the Admiralty would send me a list of any points they wished me to reconsider I would do my best to meet their views. Actually I altered very little.[14]

Another issue arose, during the summer of 1953, when the Advisory Board began closely examining Roskill's text and, in the process, became embroiled in highly politicized discussions. At the core of this stood Churchill, now once more prime minister and author of the best-selling *The Second World War*. Churchill's goal was to dilute any of Roskill's statements critical of his book or of his actions during the war. He sought zealously to guard his reputation, and he had people to do his bidding on this score. Two such persons, sometimes mistakenly called toadies, feature prominently in the inner war over *The War at Sea*, volume 1. The first is Sir Norman Brook, the powerful secretary of the cabinet. He served an odd double-role in the issue at hand: as adviser to Roskill and as censor of the book. A graduate of Wadham College, Oxford, Brook was a capable civil servant and gifted administrator. Despite other toils, he took keen interest in the Official War Histories. As noted by his associate, Sir Burke (later Lord) Trend, 'authors and editors alike paid tribute to the generous spirit in which he made time, among many weightier preoccupations, to deal with their problems, to help them with their researches, and to ensure, so far as he could, that their work measured up to his own high standards of historical accuracy.' Brook, admired by Churchill, had learned from experience that once Churchill had made up his mind no one could make him change it. The second key person in the struggle was the man in the shadows, Sir Eric Seal, deputy secretary in the Ministry of Works and Churchill's trusted private secretary. Seal, like Brook, was a veteran public servant though of a slightly older, stiffer breed, having begun in 1921, after time in the Royal Flying Corps, in the Patent Office. Seal knew all about the politics of the Navy, for he had been tied up with its administration since 1925, especially when Churchill returned to the Admiralty in 1939, and had headed the Admiralty delegation to Washington during the Second World War. In the careful crafting of history of which Churchill was master, Seal, who doubled as civil servant and Churchill's close adviser on public affairs, was brought in to unearth the facts. If Brook was guard dog, Seal was ferret.[15]

In May 1953 Roskill delivered his final text typescript to Butler, who first passed on it, then sent it to Acheson for circulation to the board. Copies went to Brook and Seal, both of whom spotted contentious matters requiring clearance and modification. Brook asked to see Roskill in the Cabinet Office, a serious matter to be discussed, as Roskill suspected. Roskill's galleys lay on his desk. Roskill takes up the story. '"Look here old boy," said Brook, who always addressed me in that manner, "I must show these passages to the Prime Minister (Churchill)." "Very well," replied Roskill.' If the prime minister showed errors of fact or identified passages that were unbalanced, then he would alter the text; but if disagreement between the prime minister and himself was of a subjective nature, then he would have no reason to change his wording. How to get these difficult passages past Churchill was the issue. Most serious were the hard-fought but unsuccessful Norwegian campaign, the loss of the battleship *Prince of Wales* and battle cruiser *Repulse* off the Malayan coast in December 1941, and the dismissal of Admiral North already alluded to. Roskill had asserted that political meddling contributed to these disasters. The discussion of them was of high sensitivity, for coming next for review in the succeeding volume would be Roskill's treatment of the scattering of PQ.17, wherein the first sea lord, Admiral Sir Dudley Pound, would be up for close examination. The Dieppe raid would also be in volume 2, another possible headache for the prime minister and the government.

These subjects – that is, those in volume 1 – needed resolution so as to avoid public controversy and protect Churchill. Roskill threatened to go public with a letter to *The Times*.[16] If the volume were published with Roskill's allegations of political interference, Parliament and press would be in an uproar. As a result, on 10 August 1953, Acheson requested Brook to raise the matter with Churchill at Chequers. They were due to meet the next day.

Brook brought the issues up with Churchill, and the matter was referred to Captain Gordon Allen, Churchill's naval assistant in drafting segments of *The Second World War*. Allen had sure knowledge of the episodes and issues under review, and he had a clear, generous appreciation concerning the individual historian's role in writing 'official history', for he himself was one such, working on *Victory in the West*, all about the European campaign. He did not share Churchill's restricted view of official history.

Churchill grudgingly recognized that the increasingly technical conditions of naval warfare had changed the nature of communications between the Admiralty and naval commanders, and that meant, therefore, that the assent of the commander-in-chief – the senior operational commander – must be assumed when orders bypassed him and were sent direct. Clearly, this was Churchill's way of attempting to dismiss Roskill's accusation regarding his subversion of the normal chain of command; it was also an explanation of how Churchill might dominate Pound. Churchill added, in scoffing tones: 'The object of the writer [Roskill] is evidently to show that everything that went wrong was due to civilian interference. I am not aware, however, of any instances during my tenure at the Admiralty in either war of any orders being sent out without the approval or against the advice of the First Sea Lord or the Vice Chief of the Naval Staff. If there are cases I should be glad to be reminded of them.'

Churchill also had objections to Roskill's account of the sending of the battleship *Prince of Wales* and the battle cruiser *Repulse* to the Far East. These ships, which formed Force Z, were sent to Singapore in October 1941, to be what Churchill later called 'a vague threat' to Japanese military aspirations. The reason they were sent was entirely political, and Churchill had overridden the Admiralty and Admiral Pound, the first sea lord. Regarding the *Prince of Wales* and *Repulse*, Churchill commented that Roskill's text

> . . . is very misleading and is again devised with the intention or at least with the effect of throwing the blame upon civilian interference with the Naval Staff's wisdom for political or diplomatic reasons. When one has lived through the anxieties of which a couple of first class ships can produce as long as their whereabouts at the moment are not known, one does not underrate the fact that similar reactions can be excited from the enemy. I should like to know if there's any evidence that I at any moment departed from the idea that the PRINCE OF WALES and the REPULSE, if possible with the [aircraft carrier] INDOMITABLE, should go to Singapore, [that they] should be known to [have] arrived at Singapore, and should then disappear in the immense archipelago which lies within a thousand miles of it. Thus they would have exerted all the deterrent effect upon the Japanese in any movement to attack which TIRPITZ and at other times other vessels have brought to bear on us. The last thing that the Defence Committee wished was that anything like the movement which [the commander-in-chief of Force Z] Admiral [Tom] Phillips thought it right to make to intercept a Japanese invasion force should have been by his two vessels without even air cover. My view was always, in the words attributed to General [Jan] Smuts, 'as long as the two ships were unlocated they would exert a profound influence.' I may well have explained this to him. I certainly contemplated the furnishing of remote and secret anchorages. The statement that the policy of 'London' was almost the opposite to this is, I am sure, capable of disproof. I am however obliged to the author for inserting that 'the Prime Minister remarked that ships' whereabouts should become unknown as soon as possible.' This was the only intention which animated the Defence Committee.[17]

Meanwhile, Allen, on Churchill's bidding, had investigated the matter. He read Roskill's text, and then met with him. Roskill, who rather disliked and mistrusted Allen, said that he wanted to see a copy of what Allen intended to give to the prime minister. In fact, Allen's views did not contradict those of Roskill, but Roskill was on the verge of a physical breakdown and under a great deal of emotional strain.

Before long, Roskill was in receipt of Churchill's own written appraisal (independent of Allen's investigation). He took issue with Churchill's views, and in a meeting of 20 August Roskill told Butler, his editor, that no Defence Committee orders existed for the *Prince of Wales* 'losing herself' somewhere in the archipelago. Ever the naval officer with an eye to detail, Roskill noted that, had this been the case, refuelling arrangements would have to have been made. Yet no such references existed in Churchill's published account, an omission that confirmed Roskill's suspicions.

Now, therefore, Allen also had to deal with Roskill's response. He was sympathetic to Roskill and well aware of his fellow officer's difficulties in the historical line. On 24 August, Allen submitted his observations to Churchill. He chose his words carefully. He began with assurance that Roskill surely never intended to attribute all that went wrong to civilian interference overriding the considered views of the Board of Admiralty. He had discussed these matters with Roskill privately. 'Naturally, there were occasions when in the course of debate you [Churchill] persuaded the Chiefs of Staff and others to agree to a line of action contrary to their own first declared views.' He added, 'It would be surprising if this were not the case'. Allen warned Churchill that, as prime minister, he and his ministers possessed the ultimate responsibility for any decisions although these decisions also carried with them the implied approval of the Service chiefs. In discussions with Roskill, Allen had taken the position that the dispatch of Force Z was a deterrent, a political act. This meant 'if in the view of the author, a view which he stresses in the text, the decision taken constituted a departure from sound principles of maritime strategy, he may be entitled to make the point, but then it would seem equally advisable for him to refer to the wider responsibilities of Ministers, who may decide to accept the strategical risks involved. The reader could then draw his own conclusions.' This need for balance, Allen reminded Churchill, lay at the core of the prime minister's view that an official historian should state both sides of the case but not judge the issue. In other words, Churchill would have to allow Roskill certain latitude. This was the position that Brook and Butler were to take, too.

Allen had gone searching for documents but could find nothing about the two capital ships 'disappearing into the archipelago'. He therefore found Roskill wrong or misleading on this score. No reference to such a disappearing act appeared until 1 December, by which time the ships were at Singapore. Allen's problem was how to placate Churchill on the business of undue political interference. He told Churchill that Roskill had agreed to changes, especially to remove the offending statement that London's policy was the opposite of furnishing remote anchorages.

Allen now shifted to an equally sensitive topic, the conduct of the Norwegian campaign. Here, Roskill attacked Churchill over alleged interference with naval commanders afloat. As the situation in Norway worsened, Churchill, as first lord of the Admiralty, had inserted Admiral of the Fleet the Earl of Cork and Orrery into the command structure. This officer was to conduct operations in the Narvik area, which was already under the designated naval commander-in-chief, a more junior flag officer. Moreover, this admiral of the fleet was several ranks senior to the designated military commander, a major-general. These unusual arrangements reflected Churchill's own involvement in the disastrous Norwegian campaign. Allen again chose his words carefully, for he knew that Churchill was on record as believing that the Admiralty interfered unduly with the commanders afloat on this occasion. Roskill had commented on Churchill's constant interest in the direction of this campaign, but, said Allen, this did not imply criticism.[18]

Churchill rejected Allen's arguments out of hand. The matter went back to the Cabinet Office secretariat, to Brook and Butler, who were working hard to get revisions made and the book into print. Already production was lagging. Printers and binders were awaiting final text. But Churchill still had the final word. Brook told Butler that he could not promise that Churchill would release the volume without Roskill redoing the Norway account. By now, the Roskill text had become a subject of intense backroom manoeuvring. Butler, fearing intervention from high places, insisted that all printing authorization go through him, as series editor, instead of via the Prime Minister's Office, as Churchill preferred. Acheson, meanwhile, kept Roskill unaware of this, so as to ensure that he would complete any demanded revisions when the time came and, above all, not blow his top if he knew political interference was in the offing. He sensed Roskill's nervous and tired disposition.

Now it was Brook's turn to play his hand. Brook suggested that there should be no problem in allowing Roskill to quote Churchill directly. As to the Norway segment, Roskill had not distinguished between civilians and sailors, nor had he suggested that, as first lord of the Admiralty, Churchill had sent orders without the approval or against the advice of the naval staff. Roskill had merely stated that the force of Churchill's personality had made an impact on the naval staff. This could not be denied. Brook offered this vintage advice to Churchill: 'While you may not agree with this summing up there is nothing in it to which you could properly take exception.' Churchill, placed in a corner, acceded. Brook took the same line with how the public would view the loss of the two capital ships. Arguments about the sending of the ships would continue irrespective of what the official historians say about it. 'He has now considered your comments and after discussion with the editor has made some adjustments . . . The responsibility for presentation and for judgements rests with the author: I understand that you should leave it to him to carry it out.'

Brook, who knew how to finesse these sorts of issues, took nothing for granted. 'My position in this matter is not easy,' he confided to Churchill. 'I am, as I know you will understand, most anxious to safeguard your personal interests. On the other hand, as an official, I have some responsibility for the Official Histories; and I cannot go beyond a certain point in pressing the Editor or Author to alter what they believe to be a fair representation of history.' He knew that Churchill would have to accept Roskill's views, as much as he might object to his interpretations. Churchill had always wanted documents to speak for themselves and disliked editorial comment and historical analysis by official historians.

But further delays ensued because of Churchill's health. In June 1953 Churchill suffered a stroke and those closest to him kept it secret. Not knowing of the prime minister's illness, Roskill became increasingly restless and interpreted Churchill's silence as ominous. And he worried that others, too, would demand new wording, under the heading of 'suggestions'. Working on Brook's side as well was Seal. As Churchill's private secretary at the time of the Norwegian campaign, he knew of Churchill's every movement, every decision, and every influence. He summed up the matter to Churchill:

> It is abundantly clear both from the documents and in the recollection of both Admiral [Sir Ralph] Edwards [at the time Captain Edwards, deputy director of naval operations (home)] and myself that the dynamic force behind the Norwegian campaign was yours, but there is not one single jot or tittle of evidence or of recollection to suggest that your interference was improperly used. I would have said that you were always anxious to stimulate the offensive fighting spirit of the fleet, and to leave it to fight untrammelled by detailed orders. There is perhaps grounds for the accusation that the Admiralty at that time had a tendency to interfere somewhat too freely with the authorities afloat, but there is no evidence for saying that your influence was exercised in that direction.[19]

That Churchill held up the book from May 1953 to the end of that year is certain. He was said to feel very emotional about the matter of Roskill's treatment, which confirmed his suspicious of retired officers who had become historians of the Military History Series: in Churchill's view, they bore grievances and prejudices that coloured their work.[20] But, in the end, Butler and Brooks carried the day, aided by similar assurances from Seal and Allen. Advised that the pressures against him were formidable, Churchill agreed to let Roskill's account of the loss of the *Prince of Wales* and *Repulse* stand. He did so reluctantly, however, and not until he had downed two or three double brandies.

Roskill, for his part, continued in poor health. His enforced furlough was insufficient. John Ehrman, whom I quizzed on this matter, told me that Roskill was very ill from the ordeal, and he became inflamed and irrational when the subject of the book's progress came up for discussion.[21] Ehrman's evidence is insightful, for he had faced similar problems as a official historian, author of one of the Grand Strategy volumes. Ehrman told me that Roskill was very close to Blake, Ehrman's father-in-law, who sat on the Advisory Board. But this counted for nothing in dealing with Churchill. It was Norman Brook, 'a smoothie', who knew how to handle Churchill, and this is confirmed by the literary trail. Brook, like Blake, was sympathetic to Roskill, as he was to all historians in Cabinet Office employ. As for Churchiill, he wanted no more to do with historians after this, and William Deakin, a historian working for Churchill, and later head of St Antony's College, Oxford, said that historians' correspondence was always put at the bottom of Churchill's pile – the lowest priority and the most disagreeable. Ehrman reports that, though Brook stood up for him, Roskill was so distraught as to be past caring: he was beyond reason at this point. However, we do know that he corrected proofs in early 1954 and then went to Nuffield Hospital to get treatment for his war injuries and also relief from the strain and anxiety over his history.[22] He was still recuperating when the volume was released in May. Later that month, Churchill wrote to his wife about Roskill: 'Talking of War historians, I have an overwhelming case against the Admiralty historian. He belongs to the type of retired Naval Officers who think that politicians should only be in the Admiralty in time of War to take the blame for naval failures and provide the Naval Officers with rewards in the cases of their successes, if any.'[23]

The first volume of *War at Sea* was a triumph, securing Roskill a place as a widely accepted and acclaimed historian. As he himself realized, he was now a national figure. The book became one of the best-sellers of the Military History Series and was reprinted after five months, with strong sales continuing for many years. Ehrman says that, without Roskill's firm and fierce response to demands for changes to the text, the final result might have been different: 'The example was not lost on those concerned, within the war histories or among those affected by them.' Ehrman also says that the quality of the book gave a huge boost to the rest of the Military History Series. Sir Basil Liddell Hart, the famed historian and strategist, wrote to Roskill in 1957 praising him for having seemingly negotiated his way through censorship, 'the heaviest handicap on official history'. How Roskill had kept free of inhibiting factors was a matter for congratulation, Liddell Hart said. 'I am sure I am far better placed than Corbett was,' Roskill replied. 'For one thing I have Butler behind me, and for another Sir Norman Brook (Secretary to the Cabinet) has always been most helpful and understanding. Furthermore I am sure that naval senior officers of recent times are more open-minded and less prone to claim infallibility than those of the previous generation. None the less at the beginning I had to fight very hard to establish the principle of independence, the Admiralty made several unsuccessful attempts to treat me in exactly the same manner as they treated Corbett! I expect you know that Richmond and others held that the Admiralty killed Corbett.' The trouble was not with the sea lords but with the secretary of the Admiralty and his department who constitutionally controlled all the Admiralty records and strongly disliked an outsider extracting what he wanted out of them. 'I fear they will never forgive my success in defeating their purpose of suppressing whatever they didn't like.' Roskill prided himself as having established an important principle.[24]

Reviews drew notice to the contentious points that had previously attracted Churchill's attention and had often been explained away by him. Uniformly good reviews noted how Roskill had pointed fingers at Churchill, and in the *Naval Review* Admiral G.C. Dickens provided this well-informed commentary:

> Captain Roskill places on Sir Winston's broad shoulders a share of the responsibility for the confusion caused by the numerous operational messages sent by the Admiralty to the Fleet, over the heads of the Commanders-in-Chief, particularly during the unhappy Norwegian campaign. It is perhaps unfortunate, and unfair to Captain Roskill, that the sensational organs of the press have chosen to seize on the paragraph in which he makes that criticism, and have totally ignored the instances he quotes in which Mr. Churchill's overruling of service opinion (for example over the 'Tiger' convoy to Egypt) are [sic] shown to have proved splendidly correct. The reason is, presumably, that any historical criticism of the great Prime Minister's actions is 'News', whereas mere agreement with the version published in his own memoirs does not carry any such journalistic commendation. None the less it is a fact that certain

'popular' organs have given a very distorted impression of what Captain Roskill has to say on such matters while it has been noteworthy that the more thoughtful reviewers have appreciated and accepted the balance which the author has obviously tried to maintain without concealing what he believes to be the truth.[25]

Roskill's remaining work on *War at Sea* continued despite ill health and Churchill's holding up publication of the first volume. He needed to go to Washington to see documents unavailable in London and to consult with Morison and his team working on the US naval history. Wanting to avoid difficulties with the United States and possibly with Morison, he wrote to Acheson seeking approval for intended expenses, giving this explanation: 'Many of the disagreements between the Admiralty and the Navy Department can only be dealt with fairly if one has seen both sides of the case.' Roskill knew that he was writing a form of alliance history, and he wanted to solve problems before they arose. There were five major issues: 1) delays in getting escort carriers into service, a subject of dispute between the two naval administrations: what experience did the USN have with these ships?; 2) the Moroccan sea frontier in 1943–45, a separate US sea command and 'a thorn in our flesh'; 3) Anglo-American differences over the Sicily, Salerno, and Anzio landings (the RN and British command had been attacked in the United States for allowing the Axis armies to escape from Sicily, a matter with little foundation, Roskill contended, but he needed to check with informants in the United States); and 4) the British Pacific Fleet under the command of Admiral Chester Nimitz: how did the US Navy Department react to its dispatch and arrival in its strategic theatre?

Roskill's 1955 visit to the United States was authorized by Brook, Butler having supported Acheson's original approval. He flew on a US Navy transport aircraft via the Azores (getting a glimpse of Trafalgar Bay from on high) and reached Washington after a long flight of many legs. Elizabeth was at the Metropolitan Club to greet him.

Roskill began his inquiry by a round of calls, to Admiral Sir Geoffrey Barnard of the Joint Services Mission; Commodore Peter Gretton, the British naval attaché; Sir Roger Malkins, the British ambassador; and Admiral John Heffernan of the Navy Department's Office of Naval History. Morison was then in Maine at his summer retreat, so Heffernan gave Roskill the run of his American opposite's office, a palatial affair by Great George Street standards. Friends put an automobile at his disposal.

Roskill worked daily in the Navy Department, got his questions asked, and even helped with proofs of Morison's tenth volume (*The Battle of the*

Atlantic Won, May 1943–May 1945). Roger Pineau, Morison's assistant, took Stephen and Elizabeth to Annapolis, where he was introduced to 'the class' of 3,600 midshipmen of the Academy. Roskill found his first volume much in demand, though with a sizeable mark-up in price, something he saw as HMSO profiteering. Then he was off to Jefferson's Monticello before returning to Washington for a few more days' research, as well as a visit to the White House to meet Commander Ned Beach, the submariner and author, then serving as President Dwight D. Eisenhower's naval aide-de-camp. He eventually caught up with Morison in Harvard's Widener Library (Marder's famous haunt), but by then most of his questions had been answered by Heffernan and the Navy Department. Returning to Washington, he met the chief of naval operations and the powerful people of the Naval Historical Foundation ('consumption of alcohol was up to best Washington standards'). During his last days in the city, Roskill also met with Vice Admiral Harry DeWolf of the Canadian naval legation, who told Roskill that he hoped he would come to Ottawa next, his way of saying, noted Roskill, 'Please don't ignore us next time.' Roskill and his wife departed New York in the *Queen Elizabeth*, happily raised to first class. The voyage home was tonic to a hard-pressed but endlessly profitable tour of historical duty. Roskill had met those who counted in his line of work. 'Americans do of course indulge in outrageous flattery,' he commented. 'They love nothing more than a "lion", and even if the lion is only a diminutive cub they try and pretend he is a full grown specimen. Yet, after making an allowance for this failing, I admit I was touched by the interest shown in the work I am trying to do. I was also pleased to feel that the British Mission was very glad that I had come over.'[26]

On the passage to Southampton and home to Blounce, Roskill must have wondered about the status of his own texts and drafts. In due course, he received comments from US and Dutch historians about the draft of his second volume, and he considered them. But, as he put it, 'as this was a British history he would not be able always to reconcile his views and conclusions with those of foreign historians; and that to go too far in the attempt to do so might be dangerous.' He explained this to the Advisory Board, and received its support. Telling the story from the British viewpoint was correct, though the board cautioned that if a conflict existed he ought to mention the alternative view. Then there was the RAF, which would have preferred to see more details about air operations as part of the maritime war. Roskill would have been happy to comply were it not for space limitations. Finally, Roskill was still awaiting comments from Mountbatten on his final account of the Dieppe raid.

Roskill attended to some minor, mandated revisions as suggested by the board for volume 2. By August 1956, he had signed the preface. The text had gone through the customary review, and during the course of it two matters drew the most attention, again because they were potential dynamite in the political arena and in the press: PQ.17 and Dieppe. The first involved the Americans; the second, the Canadians.

The completed text had been passed to the Admiralty for clearance. Intervention by the Admiralty was always Roskill's principal worry. Now he had confirmation of his fears. 'Our main objection is to the account of convoy PQ.17,' wrote Lang from the Admiralty. It will be recalled that the first sea lord, Pound, had sent a message to Admiral Hamilton, in charge of the covering cruiser force, to clear away westward and had also ordered the convoy to scatter, leaving the merchant ships to disperse to their fate. 'It is our considered view that the story [Roskill's], while still reaching the conclusion that the Admiralty decision to order the convoy to scatter was the main factor leading to calamitous losses, could be told just as effectively with less emphasis on the personalities taking place. The construction of the narrative as it stands seems deliberately to emphasise personal blame attaching to Admiral Pound and, to a lesser extent, to Admiral Hamilton.' The Admiralty did not try to shrink from blame, but it did not know at the time what would happen: the evidence spoke for itself. What the Admiralty objected to was the introduction of new, after-the-event documentation that gave a different appreciation from what the commanders involved had under consideration. (At least one other 'official history', it may be noted in passing, refused to admit any post-facto documentation.[27]) In particular, their lordships objected to the introduction of Admiral Sir John Tovey's recollection about what had occurred. Tovey had concluded that the convoy would be destroyed if scattered. The Admiralty maintained, however, that Tovey could not have known in advance of the order what would happen. How could Tovey be so sure, it wondered? Surely the Admiralty did not regard this as a true state of affairs, for if they did such an order would not have been given. Thus they tweaked Roskill's words: instead of 'It is of course plain . . .', it suggested 'those looking back on the unhappy event will realize that . . .'

Roskill could agree to minor editorial changes but major, substantive material was not up for consideration. Finding himself in the middle of another literary firestorm, he would not agree to lessen his emphasis on the blame due to Pound. He put it this way:

> Rather the reverse is the case; for I have been at some pains to explain that the decision to scatter the convoy, though an inescapable

responsibility of the First Sea Lord, was not taken as a 'snap' decision as has been implied . . . but was considered action taken after a naval staff meeting . . . I have emphatically relieved Admiral Pound of the untrue suggestion contained in Volume IV, p.236, of Mr. Churchill's memoirs. It would seem fairer therefore to say that my account relieved Admiral Pound of such portion of the incubus of blame as can be taken off his shoulders. [As for Hamilton] It is . . . hard to see how a historian of integrity can do more than include in his account Hamilton's reasons for his actions, and that I do, after discussing it with him.

As to Tovey, Roskill had met with him and taken his views into consideration. In fairness to 'that distinguished commander', his views needed to be mentioned. In fact, Tovey's recollections could hardly be called into question, Roskill replied.

Roskill knew that Lang and the Admiralty worried about counterattacks from the press, in Parliament, and elsewhere. He had thought through his answer in advance: 'If a counter-attack of the nature such as Lang fears were to take place the Admiralty can, as has happened before, very reasonably deny responsibility for this history. I realize of course, that it is almost inevitable that the official histories should sometimes cause embarrassments to departments. But I'm not sure that in the long run this embarrassment may not prove more acute if facts already known to some people are suppressed. The omission of the notorious Jutland deciphers from the 1st edition of Corbett's *Naval Operations*, volume III, seems to me a case in point.' Roskill stated that he had made those corrections that he could, and he told Butler that it was time to proceed to print. 'As I have met all the points now raised by the Admiralty, so far as I feel compatible with an historian's integrity and independence, I hope you will agree that we can go ahead with printing as fast as possible.'

Butler came to Roskill's aid. To Lang he replied that Roskill did not seem to have stressed the personal element unduly. 'There is no imputation on the personal honour of either Admiral, but where technical errors of judgement leading to serious consequences have been made by officers in high command I think that to suppress or minimize their personal share in the decisions taken would be wrong from the point of view alike of the student of military history and of the other actors concerned.' As to Tovey, his testimony was material to the story, and if that testimony should induce others to present contrary evidence, from the historian's point of view, so much the better. Roskill could not have wished for a more supportive editor. Bulter urged that the Admiralty not press its remaining points. The Admiralty relented, but it expressed satisfaction that a particular conversation that Tovey had with Pound had been dropped from Roskill's account as requested.

Now Brook, the Cabinet Office, and Churchill had to be brought onside. Butler chose his words carefully in warning Brook what to expect:

> A Convoy to Russia – PQ.17. This is the stuff of which headlines are made. The passage deals at some length with a convoy sent to Russia in July 1942. While it was on its way its commander received orders from the Admiralty to scatter. The result was disastrous, many of the ships being sunk and many lives lost. The responsibility is attributed in the main to an error of judgement on the part of the First Sea Lord, Admiral Pound.
>
> The Admiralty did not like some things which were included in the first draft, and Roskill in revision has gone far to meet their wishes. They have now written . . . to say that 'Although we would not want to go on record as accepting the points which you and he make in your letters, we have no further comments to make.' In other words, they do not wish to press for any further modification.
>
> . . . Roskill quotes a statement in Sir Winston Churchill's volume IV, p. 236, where he says that he never discussed the circumstances in which the order to scatter was given with Admiral Pound, and that it was not until after the war that he learned the facts. This, Roskill says, is a lapse of memory, because on the 1st August 1942 events occurred which led to the despatch of the order. I attach a copy of the record of his statement. It was at a meeting of the War Cabinet at which Sir Winston Churchill was present.[28]
>
> This reference to Sir Winston Churchill's book seems to me to be rather dragged in. But Roskill is anxious to retain it. Some people might read into the passage in Sir Winston Churchill's book an implication that Admiral Pound, having realized that his judgement had been at fault, deliberately concealed the facts from the Prime Minister; and Roskill says that that conclusion was actually indicated in an article published some time ago in the *Daily Telegraph*. The Admiralty were so incensed at that article that they considered the question of issuing a public statement. However, on learning from Roskill that he was proposing to state the facts in his volume, they decided to say nothing. Roskill therefore feels that he must include this paragraph in justice to Admiral Pound and in fulfilment of his obligations to the Admiralty.
>
> Since the facts seem to be clear, I do not think that objection can be raised to Roskill's account. But I thought you ought to be aware of the

matter in case you might wish either now, or shortly before the book is published (which will not be for about 8–10 months) to inform Sir Winston Churchill about it, so that the headlines which will almost certainly appear in the press about his lapse of memory will not take him by surprise.[29]

The term 'lapse of memory' was a gentleman's appreciation of something overlooked. Brook closed the file with this note of approval: 'I don't think I can raise objection in this. But I should wish to warn Sir Winston as soon as the book is published.'

Fully a year later, Brook gave Anthony Montague Browne, Churchill's secretary, the promised 'heads-up': volume 2 was about to be published with its account of PQ.17 and the disastrous result. Brook explained why Roskill had written his account and why the prime minister shared more of the responsibility for the disaster than previously known:

> Sir Winston has told his story in the fourth volume of his book (chapter XV) where, in explaining that the main responsibilities for the decision to disperse convoy must rest with the First Sea Lord, he said that the First Sea Lord had never discussed the matter with him, and added – 'Indeed, so strictly was the secret of these orders being sent on the First Sea Lord's authority guarded by the Admiralty that it was not until after the war that I learnt the facts.' This observation has been interpreted in some quarters as implying that Admiral Pound, having realized that his judgement had been at fault, deliberately concealed the facts from the Prime Minister.
>
> The official historian (Captain Roskill) in the course of his research, found a War Cabinet minute recording that at a meeting on 1 August 1942, over which Sir Winston presided, the first Sea Lord gave the War Cabinet an account of the circumstances in which the order to scatter was issued. He has thought it right, in justice to Admiral Pound, to include in his history a reference to this official record, and has said that the statement in Sir Winston's book must presumably be attributed to a lapse of memory.
>
> I enclose a copy of the record of the War Cabinet discussion. You will understand that there is no ground on which official objection could be taken to Captain Roskill's account. But as the personal reference to Sir Winston may be noted in some of the newspapers when the book is published, I thought you should know the precise facts.[30]

Dieppe, the first major European amphibious landing of the war, on 19 August 1942, was the next burning issue. Lord Louis Mountbatten, as director of combined operations, was responsible for planning the Dieppe raid, otherwise known as Operation Jubilee. The episode was a disaster: of 4,963 men of the Canadian Second Division, which bore the brunt of the fighting, 3,369 were killed, wounded, or made prisoner. Roskill took the view, one held generally, that although the price of the raid had been high, the recommendations made in the after-action report were all put into effect by the time the landings of D-Day took place. A landing could always be achieved regardless of cost but it was the second phase – exploitation – that invariably proved more difficult. Roskill stated that, but for sacrifices made in this operation, other landings, including Husky (Sicily), might have ended in failure.

The 'watery maze' of amphibious operations lay largely outside Roskill's knowledge but on closer study he acquired a modicum of the details. As to the ability of a maritime power such as Britain to put small numbers of well-trained men on an enemy's shore and take them off again, he appreciated that this was a time-honoured business. He quoted Nelson's journal entry (25 July 1797) regarding the unsuccessful attack on Tenerife: 'We got within half gunshot of the Mole head without being discovered, when the alarm bells rang and 30 or 40 pieces of cannon, with musketry from one end of the town to the other, opened upon us.' Threat of a raid forced the enemy to commit sizeable garrisons to guard various places of possible attack.

But Dieppe, more than a military event, had political overtones related to Allied strategy. The Germans were pushing even deeper into Russia, which urgently demanded an invasion in the west by the Allies. Roskill discounted contemporary support in Britain for a Second Front. He bluntly described it as a 'widespread, if ill-informed, agitation, fostered by persons whose political positions lay far to the left'. And he held firm to his views. When Brigadier-General Harry Latham, then working in the Cabinet Office on official histories, noted that Roskill's account of Dieppe had included an 'undignified attack on many who not only conscientiously felt that a second front was then possible, but who were prepared to take a leading part', Roskill did not modify his text. But he did take into account Latham's view that those controlling the war effort knew the consequences of their actions and because of this a 'second front now' option – Sledgehammer – was set aside as militarily impractical in 1942. Roskill touched on the political problems of the government: 'The Cabinet and Chiefs of Staff were, of course, fully aware of these perils; and, although the agitations of the left had no influence upon their deliberations, there remained in their minds a desire to do all they could to discourage the Germans from reducing their garrisons in the west to reinforce their armies in the east.' What Roskill did not state was that the Canadian-born Lord Beaverbrook, publisher of the *Daily Express*, though hardly Communist-inspired, was a tireless agitator for a Second Front. In due course this matter became one for serious jousting – Beaverbrook versus Mountbatten – but Roskill was not drawn into that controversy.

Later, when David Irving entered the fray, claiming that German intelligence knew that the Dieppe raid was going to occur, Roskill did battle with him in the *Daily Telegraph* and the *Evening Standard*. This, notably, was Roskill's first public spat with Irving and began a long, disputatious relationship. The Canadian Broadcasting Corporation (CBC) was similarly interested in the Dieppe controversy, particularly about the matter of German foreknowledge; Roskill became an authority for the CBC to consult. The Canadian official historian, Colonel Charles Stacey, found no evidence to support any claim of German foreknowledge.[31] Roskill made public his special report on this matter, countering Irving and placating the CBC. Yet Beaverbrook would not stand aside, and he came to regard the British policy as deliberate, for which Canadians paid a heavy price. Mountbatten fared poorly under the assault, but Roskill kept clear of this. He preferred to go after Irving. The influential *Der Spiegel* raised the matter as one that Beaverbrook had promoted, finding in Irving an ideal ally against Mountbatten. And so Roskill avoided attack from the CBC and from Mountbatten, but at the same time refrained from levelling blame. Churchill, incidentally and surprisingly, did not know of the raid in advance; in fact, he posed many sharp questions as to why he was not so informed. He had no objection to Roskill's appraisal of Jubilee, only to his treatment of the PQ.17 'convoy is to scatter' order.[32]

Despite mollification by Brook, backed by Butler and others, Churchill took exception to the Roskill account, and at one meeting with Brook made known his views. John Ehrman told the author that Brook had to get Churchill's permission to have the work released. Already printed and bound, it still needed clearance from Churchill, no easy matter. Brook chose his time perfectly. Just at the time Churchill played his victory stroke in a game of croquet – a game that he let the prime minister win – Brook told him that no further obstruction could surely occur. He took Churchill's grunt as assent and the book was published.[33]

A rare, behind-the-scenes view of Roskill and his uneasy relationship with the Naval Historical Branch is displayed in the papers of Commander L.J. Pitcairn-Jones, the man assigned to help Roskill with his work – and to keep eyes on him. At a party hosted by Butler in 1957 to celebrate the publication of volume 2, Roskill and Pitcairn-Jones talked about points of difference in Roskill's recent volume. Naval Historical Branch had sent a long list of corrections and clarifications regarding Roskill's draft. Roskill valued Pitcairn-Jones's advice and help on the *Bismarck* chapter and others. But somehow Pitcairn-Jones had upset Roskill, which brought forth this to Pitcairn-Jones: 'I wonder, after Butler's party[,] whether you had been serious or were teasing me on the matter of accuracy or lack of it in my work. Maybe you were joking – in any way partly . . . I know I have made some mistakes, and I do acknowledge with heartfelt gratitude what you and all in H.[istorical]S.[ection] do to save me from blunders . . . I really go to enormous trouble to avoid blunders . . . I feel very humble about my capacity for the job.'[34] Roskill always expressed thanks to the Naval Historical Branch for its help, especially in answering his many questions, but that same branch sent lists of contentious matters directly to the Cabinet Office, which was part of the process. Roskill's response to Pitcairn-Jones was not over-reaction but rather a legitimate attempt to secure his own autonomy against attempted interference.

In his work on volume 3, Roskill encountered opposition to two separate chapters. The first, which needs only brief mention, dealt with Operation Avalanche, the Allied landings at Salerno on 9 September 1943. The Allied force was on a shallow beachhead under heavy enemy fire. Five days later, the supreme commander, General Mark Clark, US Fifth Army, ordered his naval staff to prepare plans to withdraw either the American or the British assault force and land it again in another sector. This could be a recipe for complete disaster, since re-embarking heavily engaged troops was certainly impractical and probably suicidal. The British senior naval officer, Commodore George Oliver, was alarmed by Clark's order and made clear his views to Admiral H. Kent Hewitt, USN, the overall naval commander. Clark's plan died there and then. In writing the history of this event, Roskill was again on touchy ground, for Clark could be shown to be incompetent. Roskill, however, stated that the matter might be blamed on Clark's staff, who were working under terrible pressure; further, such problems were also owing to lack of experience. At the same time, he sent Oliver's after-action report, the main document for the British appraisal of this crisis, to Hewitt, who supported it as completely correct. Hewitt had been involved in the discussion; in fact, he had arranged the meeting with Clark and Oliver. The War Office objected to Roskill's account, but, backed by Butler, who reviewed the evidence, Roskill stuck to his guns, as he put it. This potentially touchy treatment of Anglo-American combined operations was not flattering to Clark, and it came at a time when the commands of the North Atlantic Treaty Organization (NATO) in the

European and Mediterranean theatres were being strengthened in the face of an increase in preparation and readiness of Warsaw Pact forces. There was a lesson learned from all of this, and Roskill took the opportunity to lay it forth: 'The greatest danger to a combined operation will always arise when a strong counter-attack is launched before the build-up of troops is complete. But once troops have been committed to a landing on a big scale, the issue must be fought out where they stand. Withdrawal in the face of heavy pressure could only result in utter disaster.'[35]

Next came a quarrel with Mountbatten, who was now first sea lord. He took serious exception to Roskill's account of the trouble that had arisen between Admiral Sir James Somerville, the commander-in-chief, Eastern Fleet, and himself as supreme commander, South East Asia, and asked Roskill to call on him. This Roskill did. The interview was not very satisfactory, Roskill recalled: it consisted almost entirely of Mountbatten giving a self-justificatory monologue. When he declared that, at the Second Quebec Conference (September 1944), the chiefs of staff approved a request by him that he should have authority to dismiss any commander-in-chief of the three services whom he found unsatisfactory, 'I must have shown surprise, if not disbelief.' Mountbatten shot back, 'If you don't believe me you can ask the three Chiefs of Staff.' Roskill decided to do so. That day, Roskill chanced upon Lord Portal, the former chief of air staff, at Roskill's club. Roskill took him aside. He repeated Mountbatten's story to him. Portal firmly said that it had no foundation in fact, and Roskill got from him a promise of a written statement to that effect. Then Roskill wrote to lords Cunningham and Alanbrooke, the respective heads of the Admiralty and the Imperial General Staff at the time, and received equally emphatic contradictions of Mountbatten's story. Roskill now sent copies of all three chiefs of staff letters to Mountbatten but received only a grudging and partial withdrawal from him. On the basis of this garnered evidence, he let his version of the high-level squabble stand. Roskill placed copies with Sir John Wheeler-Bennett, adviser to the Royal Archives, Windsor, to be filed with Mountbatten's report on his service as supreme commander.[36]

One final brush with the Cabinet Office occurred in the review of the draft text of his concluding volume. The defeat of the U-boat arm of the Kriegsmarine was never as absolute as generally assumed. On 5 May, as Roskill knew, twenty-five U-boats were in inshore UK waters or in passage to them, tying down 400 anti-submarine vessels and 800 aircraft. 'We never gained a firm and final mastery over the U-boats,' wrote Roskill – a frank assessment, surely, but one that was politically explosive. Germany was now rearmed and a NATO partner. Senior British officials, says Marc Milner, Canadian expert on the war against the U-boats, 'wanted to ensure that there were no illusions about its [the German Navy's] defeat in 1945'. The Cabinet Office forced Roskill to change his wording to the following: 'We did not gain so high a degree of mastery as would have forced them to withdraw from our coastal waters – as the heavy losses inflicted in the Atlantic in May 1943 forced them to withdraw from that ocean.' This was equally correct but at the expense of the Roskill edge. Some critics, Admiral B.B. Schofield being one, would quarrel with Roskill's account of the Battle of Atlantic and say that the work would have to be redone. Others would complain that, as a gunnery man, Roskill knew little about anti-submarine warfare and learned everything he knew about it from the Admiralty's and Naval Historical Branch's experts, Commander Fred Barley and Lieutenant Commander D.W. Waters (known in the inner circle as 'Barley Waters'; Marder dubbed them 'soft drinks').

In defence of Roskill, the sort of the history he was writing, with its broad coverage, dictated the piecemeal treatment he gave to the story. That story was essentially the British contribution and it did not go out of its way to showcase the Canadian contribution. But it did, oddly, give more attention to the American contribution than may be warranted. Canadian and other historians, recognizing this deficit, have since written the history of the Royal Canadian Navy's decisive role in the outcome of the Battle of the Atlantic.[37] Another issue on which Roskill was challenged was his criticism of the American chief of naval operations, Admiral Ernest King, for his alleged recalcitrance about introducing convoys along the American seaboard. In 1958 Morison corrected his British historian counterpart by saying that King was slow to organize convoys because he had not the means: the US Navy had not anticipated the need for corvettes and other small, fast escort vessels. Convoys, King told General George Marshall in 1942, were not only a way to protect shipping but the only way. Roskill later took care to stress that Anglo-American cooperation in the war at sea was far more significant than many historians and commentators, mainly American, were prepared to concede.[38]

By 1961, Roskill's career as 'official historian' was drawing quickly to a close, for in a sense he had worked himself out of a job. He had done so in fine fashion, and the reviews and appraisals were of the highest and most satisfactory order. His third volume, especially its second part and its conclusion, showed the Royal Navy triumphant on all seas, though heavily mauled in the Indian Ocean and in the Pacific. But there was more to this book than campaign history, and in it Roskill expressed pride in the officers and men of the Royal Navy and the Royal Marines. This generation of officers had put an end to the quarrelsome tendency that had so marked the

Fisher era and after, when devotees of Jellicoe had quarrelled with those of Beatty. The admirals of the Second World War were as combative in nature as before, and Roskill thought Marder's parody of Virgil's *Tantaene animis caelestibus irae* (Can such anger dwell among heavenly minds?) justified. In addition, some admirals were pompous and exhibited a high degree of self-importance, said Roskill. But junior officers who served at sea under David Beatty, Reginald Tyrwhitt, Ernle Chatfield, William Fisher, Andrew Cunningham, James Somerville, and Bruce Fraser 'could not but feel that they were commanded by great leaders who well deserved the confidence they felt in them.' Roskill singled out Philip Vian, William Agnew, Tom Troubridge, and Geoffrey Oliver. Similarly, destroyer flotilla commanders or escort group leaders such as Richard Onslow, Robert Sherbrook, Peter Gretton, and Donald Macintyre all exhibited qualities that stood comparison to Nelson's 'Band of Brothers'. They showed integrity and modesty – two qualities that, along with professionalism, were paramount. 'I shall always feel grateful for having known them', Roskill said, 'and I have served with or under some of them.'

The Navy of Roskill's time tolerated intellectual gifts, often with a touch of cynical amusement; it did not appreciate that such could contribute to the Service's health and efficiency. What was lauded and encouraged was character and this at the expense of intellectual achievement. Since the Second World War, however, Roskill noted that intellectual gifts had come to be more highly valued, probably as a result of the enormous increase in higher education in the United Kingdom, and indeed by 1981, when he last mentions this in his writing, the possession of a university degree was regarded as an enviable and advantageous qualification. A champion of intellectual attainments in the Royal Navy, and a frequent commentator and writer on education as opposed to mere training in the Service, Roskill was not alone in his views but he was a clear leader. The battles he fought on this score are still being waged in armed services in the United Kingdom and beyond.

Roskill had immense pride in the success of the Royal Navy and his role in telling its story. In late years the spit and polish had disappeared and some of the style and panache too, but he recalled with delight the sight of the 1st Battle Squadron in Malta's Grand Harbour or of destroyers, stern first, entering the same island's port of Marsamuscetto. 'Thus in my generation nearly all of us felt pride in the community to which we all belonged, and in the cause for which we stood – namely the British Empire.' In Roskill's life, as has been said before, there was something of eternal England, and in his goodbye to the Second World War's sea warfare the two are beautifully melded. This is not the place to discuss Roskill's careful sheltering of the details of ULTRA, if indeed he knew its secrets – he was bound by the Official Secrets Act. But his history does not suffer from lack of disclosure of specific details; rather, we take it for what it was at the time – a superb review of a great and perilous achievement brought to successful conclusion against skilled and dogged enemies.

Roskill's knowledge of the documents of British naval history for the Second World War was unrivalled, for, out of necessity as well as interest and experience, he had amassed a vast personal archive. This, when matched with his formidable memory, made him not only the ranking authority but a fount of knowledge. Among the most engaging documents he had worked through were signals, both German and British. The German documents he found predictably cool and turgid; moreover, he expressed no desire to interview German naval survivors of the war.[39] The British documents, often echoing eternal England as well as Nelson and his 'Band of Brothers', sometimes expressed arid mirth and not infrequently magisterial understatement. Roskill found these a joy. In the former category was Admiral Cunningham's dry report to the Admiralty after the victorious night action against the Italian Navy in the Battle of Cape Matapan, one with phraseology right out of the eighteenth century: 'the enemy sunk as per [list in] margin.' In the latter category was the wry statement, also by Cunningham: 'Be pleased to inform Their Lordships that the Italian battle fleet now lies at anchor under the guns of the fortress of Malta.'

At age sixty, Roskill closed another chapter of his life. His second career had come to an end. But already a new opportunity had come his way when William Collins, the publisher, offered to publish any books he should care to write on the subject of naval history. His history of the battleship *Warspite* is only one of several books he wrote or began to write at this time. With his own documentary collection and rich resources at his disposal as a Cabinet Office historian, he was uniquely placed to explore various historical episodes, among them (in *The Secret Capture*) the story of how HMS *Bulldog* seized a U-110 and carried away to safety an Enigma machine and German codes.

By now, Roskill was becoming increasingly keen to write the naval story of the period after 1918 and leading up to the outbreak of war in 1939. This was a black hole of British naval history wherein some light might be shone. The work would be a prelude to his *War at Sea*. He sought to distance himself from Marder, with whom he had, so he claims, a verbal agreement that the American scholar would not encroach on the post-1918 period. But Roskill did not seek to launch out fully as a private researcher: for all the problems he had had with officialdom, he was still keen to have some sort of official imprimatur on his intended book. There were so many potential files to exploit; he was sitting on a literary gold mine. In 1961 he sought and got permission to use certain Admiralty, Air Ministry, and cabinet papers so as to make the book, eventually published as *Naval Policy between the Wars* (two volumes), an authorized one. That was his intent. He reasoned that it seemed odd that official military histories appeared to deal only with periods of war and neglected those of peace. But the Cabinet Office, now headed by Sir Burke Trend, who had succeeded Norman Brook, when considering Roskill's request to make his book 'official', expressed wariness of any arrangement that would involve a partnership with a commercial publisher, especially one that had contracted with Roskill for a book at 17½ per cent royalties. A book published solely by HMSO, such as *The War at Sea*, might be another matter. At one time, Trend offered Roskill 'official historian' status, in effect making his position retroactive. But Roskill would not cut his ties with Collins, and the reason seems to have been the bountiful royalties.

Of greater complication, and here the Cabinet Office was in an embarrassing position, one more so if the matter became public, was Roskill's access to documents denied others under existing rights of access rules and legislation.[40] An employee in the Historical Section of the Ministry of Defence, whose opinion was asked, made clear that no favouritism ought to be shown Roskill – he was worried about charges of unfair discrimination; as he put it, 'we don't want another Marder case on our hands'.[41] The worry in the Cabinet Office about Roskill was that this historian had been given access to the documentation when in its employ, and now that he was out on his own, so to speak, he would be seen to have been given special consideration. To add to Roskill's woes, the Cabinet Office now talked of claiming a share of royalties for the crown copyright on documents used by Roskill. The files show that Roskill had paid a lump sum of £100 to satisfy copyright claims with HMSO in lieu of a share of royalties for *The Navy at War*, the summary or epitome of *The War at Sea*. These dark files also show that HMSO claimed one-third of royalties from Kemp for *Victory at Sea* and other amounts from other historians.[42] What they might claim for *Naval Policy between the Wars*, with its heavy use of Cabinet Office and Admiralty papers, could only be imagined. The security mandarins grew nervous, and there was talk of expunging direct quotations from the first volume and otherwise eradicating source references – in other words, sanitizing the text. Government clearance would be required.

The Roskill problem (as seen from viewpoints of the Cabinet Office, the Ministry of Defence, and HMSO) was circulated through cabinet and sent up to the prime minister, Harold Wilson. Although there were sympathetic murmurings, especially from Trend, nothing could be done. At that moment, historians D.C. Watt and Herbert Butterfield were chastising the government for keeping to the 50-year rule, which seemed to serve the interests only of the state. American files were open when British ones were not. But still ministerial privilege had to be maintained, and it was not until the 30-year rule was brought in, in 1967, that amelioration occurred. For the interim, therefore, the Cabinet Office would not sanction the Roskill project as one of its own, though the correspondence on this dragged on for some time. At one point, Trend told Roskill that no sanction could be given to his project, a position Roskill accepted most reluctantly. Trend and the Cabinet Office, armed with supporting documentation from HMSO and the Ministry of Defence, had thus put Roskill out into the street as a historian without special status or privileges, and Roskill had gone grudgingly into the night. When it came to clearance of the final text of the first volume of *Naval Policy between the Wars*, he was not required to delete or amend a single word; knowing the rules of the game, he had already cut out the attributions and potentially embarrassing items that Trend and others had worried about in the first instance. That first volume differed greatly from *The War at Sea* in character and scope. It probed all sorts of difficulties: treaty arrangements, enforcement and compliance, fights with the Treasury, interservice rivalries, Singapore and the Dominions, Anglo-American problems and rivalry, and so on. In all it was a tortuous story: Britannia's trident was being turned into a toasting fork, as one reviewer put it.

Roskill bore grudges on account of the fact that he had got no royalties from *The War at Sea*. He estimated that sales and official issues of the four volumes had reached nearly 30,000 copies and grossed over £70,000.[43] He was also missing out on a civil-service pension, another source of complaint. He felt used. As for those on the receiving end of his complaints in correspondence and interviews, including in one instance Roskill's claim that he could almost write *Naval Policy between the Wars* from the American documentation he had seen, D. Woods at the Ministry of Defence said that this was 'just a Roskillian argumentative extravagance'.[44]

What percentage of royalties or what lump sum he eventually paid for use of crown copyright documents is not known. As soon as he left Cabinet Office employ, he had become, on invitation, a feature writer for the *Sunday Times* and later the *Sunday Telegraph*. He was well launched on a career as a private historian. But writing as a commercial venture could not pay the bills – he was still keeping up his country property at Blounce – and Roskill began to fret about his lack of prospects. Just then, however, history repeated itself in the form of an offer from Cambridge.

It was at this point that the paths of our two protagonists, Roskill and Marder, began to cross. In the late 1960s and at mid-passage in their careers – and the mid-point of this book – Marder and Roskill had names that were on the lips of all serious students of British naval history and affairs. Giants in their respective fields, essentially pre-1919 and post-1939 respectively, they were shortly to eye each other as wary boxers. Hardened to the task of getting approval to use documents and to fending off censors and meddlesome civil servants – in the case of Roskill, the prime minister, Winston Churchill – they were not easily to be deflected by rival positions. Marder, in particular, had fought his campaigns in print or in correspondence that did not see publication. Roskill was much the same, as his files on the 'official history' attest. They were well trained for the bouts that lay ahead. Before long, they turned on each other.

Chapter 6

Marder Ascendant: Swaying Palms, Instant University, and Dreaming Spires

IN 1964, at age fifty-four, Marder stood in his prime as publishing scholar and dynamic teacher. His high reputation, won twenty years before when his first book appeared in 1940 to flattering reviews and his first book prize awarded by distinguished peers, had only grown with the Richmond and Fisher portraits and even more so with the lead volume on the Fisher era of the Royal Navy. By 1960, among historians, especially naval and British historians, his reputation was already golden. Reviewers, especially those in Britain, continued to marvel how a scholar from Hawaii, of all places, could use Admiralty documents closed to others and similarly delve into private collections in the safekeeping of admirals' widows. This was Marder's alluring mystery: it added fascination to the wonder of his sterling books. Not much was known in Britain about Marder's academic life, and few bothered to inquire. They would hardly have known that he had a firm base at the University of Hawaii – where he was a star and only one of six senior professors (made such in 1958) out of a faculty of four hundred – and was well known in Honolulu; that he had set down roots there, more deeply nourished than since Boston days; and that twenty years had passed since his arrival from Hamilton College in upstate New York.

Even so, he was unsettled and away from centres of American historical affairs. How much the inadvertent burning of his research notes and his narrow treatment by the University of Hawaii (which, as we have seen, forced him to take the state to court for damages) had to do with his plans to leave the islands is not known. But, knowing Marder, these likely counted for nothing: from misfortune and disadvantage he moved on to the next challenge, as was his pattern.

Early in 1960 Marder began raising the possibility of a move to 'the mainland'. One of the people to whom he spoke about this was John Semple

Galbraith, internationally known historian of the British Empire, then a prominent professor at University of California, Los Angeles, or UCLA, who, in addition to his recent chairmanship of the History Department, was a key player in the expansion plans for the University of California system of multiple, semi-autonomous campuses. Galbraith and Marder had exchanged summer teaching assignments, and on one occasion Galbraith chatted about Marder taking up an appointment in the University of California. Galbraith could not yet open doors for Marder, however, for two assistant professors could be hired for the price of Marder's salary. Accordingly, Marder coyly hedged his bets by saying that, whereas a decade previous he would have jumped at a chance to shift to another institution, for the present he was content with life in the islands; besides, there was a new East-West study institute in the making, a most promising development.[1] Not least, Honolulu was the family home.

Galbraith kept all these things in mind as he went about his work at the University of California. That university, with its first campus at Berkeley, had expanded first to Los Angeles and then, with the rapid growth of the state's population in the mid-twentieth century, the need for further campuses became manifest. A model size of 27,500 students as placed on all campuses mandated new locations where population growth necessitated. Thus, the University of California, Santa Barbara, and others at Riverside and Davis were all brought into existence, always with the most careful planning. Yet these could not meet the rising demand.

The University of California system was headed by Clark Kerr, articulate spokesman for higher education and a great leader in the advancement of the university (Marder thought him among the most intelligent persons he had ever met). Kerr turned Galbraith to working on plans for a new campus south of Los Angeles, in Orange County; this became UC Irvine (or UCI). At the same time, Galbraith planned for a campus at San Diego. Indeed, Galbraith himself might have gone to Irvine but circumstances made him vice chancellor – later chancellor – of UC San Diego.[2]

Meanwhile, Marder had received approaches from Yale and especially from Duke, while Harvard, too, was making attractive but unconfirmed noises.[3] In each case, these universities wanted the world-class scholar but their needs had to fit with Marder's interests, and it was not always easy to find departmental consent. Naval and military history was not a high-demand subject in university recruiting, but rather the reverse: social history and quantitative history were in the ascendant. Civil rights and ethnic demands were also driving curriculum needs and hiring priorities. Marder never taught naval history; in fact, he shied away from this speciality as a teaching subject, only later offering a senior course on the British military tradition. His bread and butter were made on the basis of courses given since his teaching career began: in Russian, French, modern British, and world history. More particularly, he had twice given courses on Russian history through film at Harvard as a summer course; he had offered French and modern European courses from his Harvard teaching days (he specialized in international relations and British foreign policy within the framework of nineteenth-century Europe); and he had mounted a 'British Traditions' course as his stock-in-trade for two decades. His senior undergraduate offerings invariably included a tough course on historians and historical method. Only serious undergraduates studying history were willing to confront him several times a week, we are told.

But these courses were not Marder's full slate of offerings.[4] Surprisingly, and contrary to what might be expected, Marder's greatest teaching contribution was at the preliminary university level, where he offered an introductory course on world history that he regarded as crucial for historical understanding (and central to university undergraduate experience). Integrating European and Asian history, this was the first world-history course anywhere, presaging wholesale developments much later, in the 1990s. His knowledge of the Japanese language and Japanese history, in addition to all his other fields of knowledge, made him a unique instructor. At Hawaii he created the curriculum for world history with an immense syllabus (he referred to it as 'the bible'), which sadly has not survived, and his colleagues, who had to listen to the Marder boast that he had conquered the course, attest to the fact that he was the pioneer in the field. This is a telling point considering that today the University of Hawaii ranks as leader in world history; it has top historians in the field, operates the East-West Center (established in Marder's time) and the World History Institute, and publishes a world-history journal.

At the University of Hawaii, Marder had the uncanny ability to make relevant the local to the global. A brilliant lecturer, he had a wide following in Honolulu and the islands, one of his colleagues calling him 'Mr History'.[5] His regular 'Professor's Notebook' in the Honolulu *Sunday Star-Bulletin*, his leadership on campus amply displayed, his friendships with the great and the good in the islands, and his reputation as a Chinese cook and a dedicated gardener (he said it freed him up from dishes detail) made him a luminary in the eyes of the administrators, faculty colleagues, staff, and students of the University of Hawaii. He had but two framed certificates on his office wall: one, that of the Chinese cooking school; the other, a graduating notice from a Hawaiian hula institute. Star British naval historian he might have been, but in Hawaii he was Mr History.

Nonetheless, events were to overtake him. The story again shifts to Galbraith, a curriculum innovator himself. Marder's scholarly reputation made him an attractive catch but so too did his dedication to foundations of historical study. Galbraith, who had taught a summer session's work in Hawaii, knew of Marder's many professional strengths first hand, including his work on world history. What better person to start a new history programme than Marder? Getting wind of Duke's rival bid for the great talent, he phoned Samuel Clyde McCulloch, himself a British Empire historian of note and newly appointed dean of humanities at UCI, to tip him off and urge him to act. In late October 1963, on Galbraith's recommendation, the vice chancellor of the new Irvine campus, Ivan Hinderaker, urgently sought the opinions of others, Roskill included, regarding Marder's qualifications as a teacher and scholar, and as a person. Professor Gerald Graham, Rhodes professor of imperial history at King's College, London University, replied that Marder was a scholar of international reputation, possibly better known in Britain than in the United States through his books on British naval policy. He thought that Marder had dynamic elements which might well set fire to his words on any platform. His generosity and warmth compelled friendship. 'Every university, in my opinion, should be able to afford one or two eccentric stars; Marder is a real star without being noticeably eccentric.'[6]

On this and other warm recommendations, with keen support given by Dean McCulloch, Marder was offered the post at Irvine. In fact, he became the first faculty member (non-administration) appointed to the new institution. Although in the run-up to this appointment Marder and his wife Jan agonized over whether or not to make the move from Hawaii, in the end the decision in favour of the new venture was made. Years later, with typical jocularity, Marder joked to Graham that the latter's letter had rescued him from paradise![7]

When news broke in late May 1964 that their star was soon to decamp, colleagues at Hawaii were crestfallen. Charles Moore, for instance, expressed sorrow about the serious loss that would accompany Marder's departure. Moore styled Marder an excellent teacher and a superb scholar with a complete dedication to every aspect of his profession – a rarity. Moore was not alone. A farewell party was given to Marder and Jan on 2 June 1964 and many fond goodbyes were said. Cedric Cowing sent his aloha from Europe: 'The department is losing its best teacher of World History and half its bibliography! You will be a hard man to replace!' The university's president, Thomas Hamilton, wrote that all in the university were most unhappy that

Marder had decided to accept the very tempting offer from California after many years devoted to the University of Hawaii. 'You have contributed a lot to this University not only by your writing and brilliant teaching, but also through the suggestions and constant winnowing of ideas with regard to the total life of a university and ways in which it can best develop in this mid-Pacific setting.'[8]

Marder and his family arrived in southern California in the hot summer of 1964. They took up residence in a three-bedroom ranch-style house with a U-shaped driveway at 1726 Skylark Lane in the Westcliff area of Newport Beach, a quiet, modest location. Home contrasted sharply with workplace, then a great construction site — parched, dusty, and noisy. A short commute in his Volkswagen Beetle brought Marder to the burgeoning university campus, a 1,000-acre former cattle ranch of the Irvine Company. The campus itself was designed by the noted architect William Pereira in strong southern California Brutalist style (to reflect permanence) and featured the positioning of buildings around a vast, sloping central open space of Mediterranean-like grass and parkland. Views to the distant hills were enchanting. The newly appointed chancellor, Daniel G. Aldrich, Jr, embraced Galbraith's idea of a fresh start for all undergraduate curricula with a view to developing breadth of study. Marder, given the chance, fought hard to have Asian history included in his core world-history foundation course but did not carry the day among the administrators and academics who met that August to define the requirements for undergraduate degrees. He stood ahead of his time, and the later Asian majority of students at UCI would see the rationale of his thinking about global history. Truly world history, with Asia included, would arrive there only in the 1990s.

Aldrich also took up a second idea shrewdly advanced by Galbraith. This was to showcase an academic talent to the community at large. Orange County, an ultra-conservative jurisdiction, had reluctantly rallied behind the idea of having its own home university (with an odd-ball, even radical, faculty) and embraced the idea only after some urging from the twenty-five-year old Joan Irvine Smith, a director of the Irvine Company, and boosters in the local newspaper. Aldrich needed a luminary academic to sow further seeds of acceptance. He turned to Marder, appealing for a series of six public lectures. Galbraith's spirit was in the background, for Galbraith had told Aldrich of Marder's unique abilities as a compelling lecturer and a fine brain. Marder consented, choosing for his subject the Western tradition, opening with the Tudors and proceeding through the ages. The lectures were a triumphant success, and what made them novel was that on each of the six occasions a separate dean drew the assignment to introduce Marder. That meant that Marder became known far beyond the History Department and Humanities Faculty, a UCI star right from the start. Many deans became converts to history. With considerable flair backed by facts and interpretations, Marder wove his spellbinding tale to an ever-growing audience. For him, talking history was shoptalk, as Noble Frankland recounted to the author; here in front of hundreds of awed listeners, some never before exposed to the mind of a PhD, he laid bare his ideas of history. Of the opening night, Aldrich wrote to Marder: 'The whole event went according to my fondest expectations and I know you have contributed greatly to the idea that the University is really a wonderful thing and how proud the people are that it is located in Orange County.' Of the series, the dean of biological sciences, Edward Steinhaus, sang Marder's praises: 'Any series we initiate must not be compared to the Marder lectures if we are not to fall into an irreversible inferiority complex.' From the public came laurels: a citizenry largely aloof from, even indifferent to, the university now shared the excitement which the faculty seemed to radiate at the idea of being present at the beginnings of a great institution. Marder helped 'the Instant University' into prominence, first in the community and then in the research ratings.[9] Within a decade, UCI had become rated an I-1, in the top seventy American universities.

At the time of his arrival at UCI, a battle ranged about breadth and depth requirements for projected undergraduate degrees. Such discussions were going on at every American college campus, led by Harvard, which was then advancing 'general education' requirements that were to be completed in the first two of a four-year degree programme. At Irvine the academic Senate had the chance to start afresh. 'I am amused when you tell me that you are suffering from battle fatigue, caused by the business of putting out a better mousetrap,' a far-off associate replied to Marder in soothing tones, reminding the man in Irvine of how fatiguing mending an old mousetrap could be. The vice chancellor at UCI, Jack Peltason, was chairing the committee on undergraduate curriculum requirements. To him and the committee Marder put in a plea for the student to be given more autonomy in choice of courses for a liberal education, although the student should be made aware of the expected goals. From his memo we learn that he was keen not only that a student should know about Western civilization but also that he or she should show an appreciation of a non-Western culture. 'We have a mandate to experiment, to try the uncommon and the extraordinary. Let us, then, not be afraid to be venturesome. We can always rescind any policies that don't work. But once in the well-trodden academic groove of rut, it is much more difficult to initiate anything that is "difference". Now is the time. Down with restrictive rules! Up with more student responsibility! Workers in the academic vineyard, unite! We have only our chains to lose!'[10] On this point, as on inclusion of a non-Western ingredient in his world-history course, Marder failed to carry the day. Without remorse or regret he turned to the next challenge.

All the while, the new history department was taking shape. McCulloch was in the department nominally but preoccupied with administration. His first task after hiring Marder was to lure Henry Cord Meyer, originally from Colorado but a German and American historian of note, away from Pomona College in Claremont, California, to be chair. We have met him before. Meyer, it will be recalled, had been with Marder as a research analyst in the Coordinator of Information Office, working with Sherman Kent; and it was Meyer who had crafted that prescient review of Marder's yet to be written book on the Imperial Japanese Navy. Other new hirings in History in these early years included Keith Nelson, Alan Lawson, Gerald T. White, Arthur Joe Slavin, Spencer C. Olin, Jr, and Lewis Hanke – all of them stars, large or small, in a department in which Marder was prima donna. Many were freshly minted PhDs with a perspective on undergraduate education different from that of Marder. Here in this new, instant university the combatants fought on a level playing field where there were no old boys, so to speak, with preferential positions.

Meyer had an ambivalent view of Marder: he recognized Marder's scholarly qualities but was annoyed by his personal attitudes. Marder always jockeyed from one square to another. '[My relations with] Arthur was like Bradley dealing with Patton,' Meyer said, he was 'a hell of a guy to live with'. When Marder, angry over losing his plum corner office to the incoming chair of philosophy, threatened to leave Irvine for UC San Diego, Meyer told Marder: 'No one admires your work more than I do. We've got work to do. Give us four weeks notice.'[11] Marder got on the phone to a sympathetic Galbraith, then made a fast visit to San Diego. Geoffrey Barraclough, a quick-witted, highly intelligent Englishman who had left the Royal Institute of International Affairs, Chatham House, London, to take up a professorship at San Diego, shunned Marder by failing to appear at a formal luncheon of introduction. Barraclough was restless, suspicious, and querulous.[12] He sensed that Marder was about to be foisted on his department and become a brilliant and distracting rival. His 'no-show' had the desired result: Marder returned empty-handed to Irvine, his hopes dashed. He shifted to temporary office quarters, a balcony room in one of the new dormitories. For some time afterwards, he considered removing to yet another of the University of California campuses, Riverside. Nothing ever came of it.

MARDER ASCENDANT: SWAYING PALMS, INSTANT UNIVERSITY, ETC

That first year at UC Irvine was the year of planning and preparation, and in September 1965 the first class of undergraduates, 1,589 in all, arrived. Only a month earlier, the faculty had moved from temporary quarters to six sparkling new buildings. Marder's key course on Western civilization was the core of the general curriculum, and he and his colleagues ran the usual array of offerings at the lower-division level. This academic year, 1965–66, was a year of unique demands on campus, with deans and faculty fully attendant to their start-up duties. Marder was hugely influential with that first class; indeed, the head of student affairs, Donald Walker, soothed Marder (who could not attend a certain meeting) by writing: 'You communicate with splendid influence on students in a thousand ways. We view you as a "Jewel in the Crown."'[13]

All this term, amid the incessant roar of bulldozers and the dust of afternoon winds, Marder put finishing touches to the third volume, *Jutland and After*, for *From the Dreadnought to Scapa Flow*. He worked to deadlines: checking final details, supervising the drawing of maps, proofreading copy, and reviewing publisher's promotional material. So that there could be no calamity, Peter Gretton kept a second, complete, and up-to-date copy of Marder's typescript. Then *Jutland and After* was put to bed.

Marder could not easily dispense with obligations at his university in California so as to hasten to London for the book launch and Jutland anniversary; it took some considerable wiggling to get release from his teaching duties. He had to give assurances that his students would not be short-changed. Meyer as chair and McCulloch as dean backed his case, confident that his teaching obligations would be looked after in advance. Meyer wrote of Marder: 'Marder's work is some of the best modern history that is being written. The fact that his publishers wish to confer an honor upon him, the fact that he has been asked to participate in a national commemorative television program in an area where he ranks as one of the very few authorities in the field: these are events in which I would like to see him participate; they also bring distinction upon our University.' McCulloch reinforced Meyer's recommendation, and on the strength of this the vice-chancellor, Peltason, granted the request, adding that Irvine picked up reflected glory through Marder's accomplishments. Marder thus was able to leave campus early that spring of 1966 and to begin his research time in Britain in advance of expectations.[14]

He arrived in London by air on Sunday, 29 May, just in time to get ready for the demands of the week. He fetched up at the Penn Club, Bedford Place, convenient to all his history business haunts. There followed a day of phone calls and consultations. Then came the anniversary of Jutland, the launch of his book, and the attendant appearances on BBC radio and television.

Marder remained in London for seven and a half weeks, combing various collections for his book, also gathering volumes and manuscripts for the UC Irvine Library. He attended the sixtieth anniversary photographic exhibit at the Imperial War Museum, making the acquaintance of the director, Noble Frankland, the air historian. He gave advice to Professor Michael (later Sir Michael) Howard's graduate students in military and naval history at London University. He attended the annual Anglo-American Historians' Conference, at Senate House, and participated in the stimulating discussion about Admiral Jellicoe. He advanced his knowledge about Study Abroad programmes for American university students. He went to Oxford, and while there made it his business to inquire about the teaching facets of Oxford life — the pro-and-con specifics. He told Clark Kerr: 'Since I was thrown into the company of a couple of dozen tutors, fellows, masters, and one domestic bursar — historians mostly, but not entirely — I was able to acquire a number of insights and some food for thought. We could profit from some of their methods and outlook — as indeed they could from ours.'[15] What Marder did not say, for modesty forbade it, was that he had been honoured by a reception at Oxford University at which every distinguished historian in the university was present to congratulate him.[16] It could have been later on this same day, or perhaps on some similar occasion when in Oxford, that Frankland had Marder as his invited guest at his nearby Thames House in Eynsham: 'I well remember him sitting on a low stool in the centre (of course!) of my drawing room here after dinner vigorously arguing points of naval history with me and my other guests until 2 o'clock in the morning. Everyone enjoyed it and no one got tired.'[17]

Colleagues and administrators at Irvine took due observance of Marder's breathless rise, noting that his eighth book had appeared to rave reviews and that his scholarly production was unparalleled in the university, or elsewhere. His dean, McCulloch, proclaimed that the Jutland book established Marder as the greatest of English naval historians. Step by step, Marder advanced in the internal levels of full-professor status, and on one such occasion he wrote to his supporter Galbraith that his 'elevation to Olympus was approved without fuss or feathers'.[18]

At this point, I made my own Hitchcock-like appearance in the Marder story. In late August of the same year, 1966, just before departing to study under the naval and imperial historian Gerald Graham in London, I travelled to hear Marder at the Pacific Coast Branch of the American Historical Association meeting in Portland at Reed College. In the history business

Marder had assumed star status, and not just as a naval writer: he was one of the greats of the profession. Oddly, or more likely whimsically (for that May he had told the *Evening Standard* that he was the world's greatest expert on Emma), he had chosen Nelson's lover, the infamous Lady Hamilton, as the subject of his lecture. Many have wondered whether, if there had been more Emmas, there would have been more Nelsons. What was her power and influence, and how was she seen in biographies of the greatest naval commander? Marder, who had not long previously penned a study of Nelson as leader, published in the *Naval Review*,[19] chose Emma as a problem of history under the title 'That Hamilton Woman: Clio and Emma Reconciled'. Emma, said Marder, was far from the social distraction often portrayed in the life of Nelson. She was devoted to the naval service and to Nelson, the embodiment of British naval mastery. Naval wives and concubines, Marder liked to say, were 'a special breed of cat' – loyal and devoted to the Service: they often wore more gold braid than their men.

His appearance at Portland was by invitation, giving credence to the observation that, in contrast to parvenus who study how to show themselves off so as to get a place in the limelight, Marder seemed to study how to avoid it. 'He was a man of truly impeccable taste, a perfect gentleman both in his outward appearance and even more in his inward disposition. Yet his reticence and modesty made both his clothes and his attitudes so inconspicuous that one hardly noticed them at the time but thought about them only in retrospect.'[20] On the day of his address, he arrived punctually, and, because dilatoriness was anathema to him, he started on the dot and proceeded in low-keyed fashion with the assurance of the true professional. As on other such occasions, he was well prepared, took nothing for granted, and was methodical. Clearly, he had examined every scrap of evidence and knew the literature on the subject. He was dressed impeccably: Marder loved sartorial elegance, but nothing fancy, preferring the simplest and the best possible quality. He stood at the lectern, master of all he surveyed. The crowd was spellbound, and I experienced how history can be communicated compellingly.

Even before the event, publishers had sought a book from him on Emma or other women associated with noted sea commanders. Marder did not take up their offers, but invitations from publishers, universities, and learned societies continued to arrive on his desk thick and fast. On Stephen Ambrose's recommendation, Marder was asked to take up the Ernest J. King chair of maritime history at the Naval War College in Newport, Rhode Island. Marder declined. Naval Institute Press asked for a one-hundred-year history of the Imperial Japanese Navy ending with the launching of the attack on Pearl Harbor. Marder declined. Sir James Butler, Roskill's old supervisor in the Official War Histories, asked Marder to give the Lees Knowles Lectures on a subject of military history at Trinity College, Cambridge. Marder declined. Methuen sought a work on sea power in the twentieth century. Marder declined. Kenneth Macksey, editor of *Purnell's History of the First World War*, wanted a summary article on Jutland. Marder declined. Hutchinson Publishing asked for an authorized biography of Mountbatten. Marder declined. He declined reviewing books, owing to the press of business. He was too busy working on the next volumes of *From Dreadnought to Scapa Flow* to be sidetracked by any of these allurements. He would read a friend's draft manuscript and help many a fellow scholar and young researcher, and he did accept Peter Kemp's invitation to do the Jacky Fisher entry in the *Oxford Companion to Ships and the Sea*.[21] Otherwise he stuck to his task.

When, however, he received word from Brigadier John Stephenson of the Royal United Services Institute (RUSI) that he was to be awarded the cherished Chesney Memorial Gold Medal, he accepted, provided (so as to avoid distractions) that there be no publicity before he arrived in England that July 1968. But the *Daily Telegraph* leaked the story, and before long the *Daily Pilot* of Newport Beach, California, ran it, thus blowing Marder's cover. At Irvine the tributes were glowing. The award for 'very outstanding services to military literature' had been awarded only fifteen times since the first, in 1900, and only once to a foreigner. That was to Mahan, who completed his studies on the historical significance of control of the sea with *The Life of Nelson* (1897). Churchill had been a recipient and Corbett, Richmond, and Liddell Hart, too. Marder stood in exalted company. His Jutland book was a new dawn in British naval history. At the prize giving, Peter Gretton, now Vice Admiral Sir Peter Gretton, referred to Marder's 'superb sense of balance in his writing, his complete objectivity, fairness, and justice in all he wrote, and the trust with which owners of private papers allowed him access in the knowledge that he would never take an unfair advantage or present an unbalanced picture.' Turning to his many works of history, Gretton held them up as models of lucidity, accuracy, and scholarship, confident that in their field they would remain the ultimate authority. He praised, too, Marder's dedication to his self-appointed task and the industry with which he performed it. Marder replied with graceful tribute to the many who had helped him, particularly widows and relatives of the men of whom he wrote, whose generosity and memories had been placed so unreservedly in his hands. He pointed out that history, and particularly Service history, was more than an account of battles and campaigns or the great events that stir a nation; true history was as concerned with times of peace as it was with times of war.[22]

Meanwhile, an honour of another sort was slowly passing its way through Byzantine corridors. Henry Allen Moe was the godfather of American scholarly genius. A Minnesotan, he was a naval veteran of the First World War, having commanded a US destroyer. He had been wounded in action. Later a bright university undergraduate, he was talent-spotted by the New York bibliographer Carroll Wilson, a Rhodes scholar, who arranged for Moe to go to Oxford on a similar scholarship. Returning to the United States, where he was called to the bar, he nurtured his Oxford connection and for years served on the Rhodes Scholarship Trust, whose American secretary was Courtney Smith, the president of Swarthmore College in Pennsylvania. Moe operated from 551 Fifth Avenue, New York, headquarters of the munificent John Simon Guggenheim Memorial Foundation, where, as administrator, humanist, and later president from 1925 to 1963, he disposed of funds to the cream of applicants for scholarly research. He later headed up the American Philosophical Society in Philadelphia. In early 1940 young Marder paid Moe a visit to report on scholarly progress and prospects. They had naval history in common, admittedly, but Moe saw something else in Marder: a prodigious talent. Marder's applications for Guggenheim funding to complete his *Anatomy of British Sea Power*, to do his Richmond and Fisher books, and to begin *From the Dreadnought to Scapa Flow* all met with success against tough competition for the most prestigious of research awards.[23] British naval history à la Marder floated on American philanthropy. Moe watched Marder's rise with avuncular pride, though without favouritism, for what he did for Marder he did for many another writer and scholar, including at the time the playwright Arthur Miller.[24] Marder was unusually young at the time he won his first Guggenheim, and he called on Moe to show his appreciation. Subsequently, Moe was on Marder's list of persons to receive his naval histories upon publication, without expectation of reward: they were sent as thanks. Moe not only read them, he studied these works as they came from the publisher in steady succession.

Late 1966 found Moe at Rhodes House, Oxford, and talking business with Brigadier E.T. Williams, head of the Rhodes Trust and Courtney Smith's opposite in Britain. The specific matter of discussion was a possible candidate to be appointed to the George Eastman visiting professorship. The chair had been endowed by the Kodak king, Eastman, who, on the recommendation of others, decided that a distinguished American scholar be appointed each year to the University of Oxford and to Balliol College, the holder to come from some different location in the United States and to be in a different field than the previous holder. Other than being able to meet Home Office security requirements, no other qualification existed. The selection was by a committee of five, representing the university, Balliol, and the American Rhodes group. The first holder had taken up residence in Oxford in 1930, followed thereafter by a steady stream of top mathematicians, physicists, and chemists, many Nobel Prize winners; historians selected to date included Wallace Notestein and Garrett Mattingly. Moe pressed for Marder, and, so as to get Oxford academics on side, he discussed Marder's prospects with the historian Sir Isaiah Berlin. To the university registrar, Berlin wrote that 'a wise old bird, Henry Allen Moe', had suggested Marder, whom A.J.P. Taylor had been praising so passionately in the newspapers, including the *New Statesman*, and he thought it a good idea worthy of circulation to the committee. The Chichele professor of war, Norman Gibbs, ought to be consulted. Another candidate, Robert Lopez of Yale, noted scholar of the Italian Renaissance, Berlin did not think would meet with demands for racial purity, 'as I fear he may be Italian by origin'. As odd as this may seem — Berlin himself was a Jew — the Rhodes Trust seems to have favoured Anglo-Saxon and Germanic candidates, though this is now no longer so.

In the meantime, Moe was working his own magic. He sent greetings to Marder at Christmastime, inquiring as to health and progress, nothing more, and received a full report from Marder, saying that the fourth volume was dragging its feet. Marder explained: 'Being a founding father of a new university (and one dedicated to doing things differently and, hopefully, better) is a time-consuming and energy-draining affair.' But blue skies beckoned, Marder told Moe, for ahead lay a full term's sabbatical in England the following autumn. He intended to get the next volume finished by June 1968, so that publication could coincide with the fiftieth anniversary of the scuttling of the German warships in Scapa Flow, though he exhibited customary caution about meeting that target date. Marder told Moe that A.J.P. Taylor had named the most recent volume, *Jutland and After*, in *The Observer's* Books of the Year as 'the best work of history published in 1966 ("straight history", as he puts it, to distinguish it from biography). This may only prove that old Taylor is getting soft in the head.'[25]

Months passed and by May 1967 Marder had received the invitation to go to Balliol for the academic year 1969—70. The invitation, most kind and flattering, he called it, came as a total surprise, and was too interesting to turn down. Now plans had to be recast for the intervening summer and subsequent academic terms. After a whirlwind holiday in France and Spain, mainly retracing his 1938 steps to Mont St Michel and then to Brittany exploring medieval sites, he, Jan, and their son Kevin planned to arrive in

Oxford in good time for the beginning of term in October. The others, Todd and Toni, did not join them; they were at university in the United States. To his friend John Creswell, naval historian and a retired captain in the Royal Navy, he wrote: 'The appt. is a most prestigious one and I am deeply flattered. At the same time I don't know what I'm doing in the company of the Nobel Laureates and other greats who have held the position (all Americans: one a year since 1930)! But we live in a mad, mad world, and long ago I stopped trying to find explanations for the inane things that happen almost daily!'[26]

Eastman, who believed that the progress of the world depended on education, had scattered the wealth of his photographic enterprises to good effect. He had designated an adequate endowment for the Eastman chair. The holder, he specified, was to receive a salary equivalent to an Oxford professor's, plus supplements to raise it to the prevailing American standard, and a free residence. Eastman took a specific interest in Eastman House, insisting that the heating and bathroom facilities be of best quality. He remembered his own travelling days in England: 'I want to make sure that the American professor has a place to live in where he will not have to wear a shawl over his back while he is eating his breakfast, or wait ten or fifteen minutes to get some hot water from the tap.'[27]

Arthur, Jan, and Kevin arrived in Oxford in mid-June, registered Kevin in Magdalen College School, and then headed for the continent. They were back among the dreaming spires by 10 September. Eastman House, Jowett Walk, was nothing short of heavenly, unlike many another don's residence. There were extra bedrooms, abundant heat and running hot water, a Balliol green field behind, and a college housekeeper and college gardener to look after the establishment. Jan seemed in seventh heaven, Marder wrote to friends at home; as for Kevin, unused to English school ways and uniforms, he recalled it as the worst year of his life. Arthur and Jan looked forward to welcoming many guests from far and near. By this time, Marder had determined that he would run a full slate of offerings: an undergraduate seminar in the first term on British foreign policy, 1898–1907; a course in the second term on British and foreign defence policy, 1898–1914, consisting of one lecture a week for eight weeks; and, in the spring, a graduate seminar on historiography and British history in the nineteenth and twentieth centuries. He took on more in the line of teaching than Oxford ever expected of him.

Marder's appointment was announced in *The Times* on 20 October 1969 (delayed at his request). Also joining Oxford was another historian of world repute, Hamburg's Fritz Fischer, Volkswagen professor at St Antony's, best known for his reassessment of German war aims in the First World War. 'It is strange that an American historian who spent 20 years as a professor at the

University of Hawaii should have made almost a corner of this period of British naval history,' wrote the author (Kenneth Rose) of *The Times Diary*. The article went on to say that Marder had just finished an article on the Royal Navy and the Abyssinian crisis of 1935–36 and planned, when the documents became available, the 'fun project' of a book on Churchill and the war at sea in 1939–45.[28]

This is the first public inkling that Marder was going beyond 1939, on which more later, and it spelled trouble with Roskill. Even so, he had no plans for anything more than an article or two, he told A.B. Sainsbury privately in February 1970, also indicating that his Abyssinian article, the subject of which had first engaged him when he was first researching in London at the very time of the events studied, would soon appear. Sainsbury urged him not to give up his unique interest 'in our naval history'. For the moment, Marder could do nothing about any further research, since he was fully preoccupied with finishing his magnum opus. In addition, the editors of the *English Historical Review* were pressing him for a piece, and this – on Winston Churchill's return to the Admiralty in 1939 – he had promised.[29] These commitments aside, however, on at least one occasion Marder told a friend that, for a variety of reasons, personal and professional, the concluding volume of *From the Dreadnought to Scapa Flow* would be his last book. He intended only to do shorter pieces: in fact, that is what he did until he got on to *Operation Menace* a few years later and even more especially *Old Friends New Enemies*.

Marder found Balliol perfectly to his liking, and the dons rallied to his friendship and openness. At the official reception for the Eastman professor, the master, the historian Christopher Hill, recounted how a recent *Times Literary Supplement* noted that the three great American naval historians all had surnames beginning with M: Mahan, Morison, and now Marder. What set Marder apart was that he was an American historian of the British Navy. The Jutland book was 'an enthralling detective story with that apt compound of analysis and narrative which marks historical mastery.' During the Oxford year, Marder's fourth volume would appear and then a fifth: 'We hope that he will find Balliol an agreeable fuelling station meanwhile.'[30]

One reason why Marder requested delayed announcement of his presence in Oxford was to steer clear of distant invitations. His policy was to accept invitations from Oxford colleges (twenty-two acceptances in all, runs the tally) and to decline any that would keep him away – London, Manchester, and Cambridge, for example. This was sound, though it did not preclude visits elsewhere for research or recreation. The same policy held true for other invitations, such as one from Richard Hough for the launch of his Fisher biography in Fisher's old office in the Admiralty. Once made, his plans left little room for manoeuvre (the naval historians' dinner at the Garrick Club was an exception). The Oxford year – 'I have been lunched and dined to death,' he told a friend – left Marder with much less time to visit his faithful friends such as Hough, Kemp, Sainsbury, and others as he would have liked.

Taylor, then in London, was dying to chat with Marder, and suggested, through Hough, a lunch in town. In the end, that had to be squelched, and instead Taylor came to Marder on 5 December. 'A funny thing happened to me last night at Magdalen, where I was A.J.P. Taylor's dinner guest,' he reported to Robert Webb, editor of the *American Historical Review* and then publishing his Abyssinian piece. 'We were discussing the Middlemas/Barnes *Baldwin* and its treatment of the Ethiopian business. "Why doesn't somebody do a study of the Navy in the Crisis?"' Marder had the pleasure of telling Taylor that he already had done so, soon to be published. Of the encounter with Taylor, Marder wrote a file memo for himself: 'A.J.P. Taylor to me – after dinner at Magdalen (he was my host) & a 3-hour chat: "It isn't often I meet an equal!" and repeated it, the nicest thing anybody has said to me in ages!' To this Marder added: 'I guess what he meant was that he wasn't able to talk me down!'[31]

Taylor's version of the meeting was somewhat different. He had admired Marder's work for a very long time, he told a friend, later his wife, Eva, shortly after the Magdalen dinner, 'and was even more impressed when I met him recently.' 'I said to him: "It is good to meet an equal." He said: "It does not happen enough and I feel the same."' Taylor told Eva that Marder had 'the quiet confidence of a great scholar without being in the slightest degree arrogant.' Taylor and Marder enjoyed each other's company, and they were later to meet on occasion. Taylor was a believer in the accidental in history, and it was perhaps the role of the random principle that sparked Marder to point out the part that fate had played in his own life. Be that as it may, the two shared the contention that, as historians, they must be accurate chroniclers of the evidence and come to that evidence cleansed of likes and dislikes, with accuracy the greatest virtue. Taylor, with his left-Liberal and Labour views, and his anti-establishment, incisive critiques, was distrusted by the historical establishment, such as it was; and it is natural that he found in Marder a progressive force for the writing of British naval history. However, he did think that Marder was a bit soft on the admirals: 'Marder is right at the top of historians . . . Though he is an American, for some reason he is in love with the British Navy, and our admirals are lucky to have him as their historian.'[32] Taylor was correct: Marder was enraptured by British admirals and made no attempt to deny it; they were, he thought, a much nicer breed than the German generals of the same era. As for Taylor, he could often be seen in Charing Cross bookstores selling his copies of books he had reviewed. But he kept all of Marder's, a rare tribute.[33]

'Have just been reading A.J.P. Taylor's review [of *From Dreadnought to Scapa Flow*, volume 4]. As regards your accomplishments it couldn't have been better or more truthfully worded.' So wrote the faithful Creswell, who continued, in reference to Taylor:

> When it comes to dealing with events he is not so good, as seems so often to happen when writers who have not specialised in naval affairs air their views on them. To say of the two (which he calls three) Norwegian convoy disasters that 'the lessons of Jutland had still not been learnt' is just silly. As regards the L[loyd] G[eorge] v. Jellicoe on Convoy, I reckon that what you have written puts the matter very fairly. As you say in your last letter, nobody can know for certain. It might have come anyway, but probably L.G.'s influence did something to hasten things. His story certainly had a good start and I am fairly sure that round about 1930 we all thought that it was he who had done the trick. But at that time no one had gone into the matter as fully as you have.
>
> Taylor must have been interesting to have a real heart to heart talk with. With such a flow of popular history maybe you found it difficult to pin him down on details, but he is evidently very readable so perhaps as a conversationalist too.[34]

Marder's college rounds brought him into contact with many historians. Of young Paul Kennedy, he had the highest opinion, and, in correspondence and discussion, Kennedy shared with Marder many references on German naval history of the period. Much mutual profit resulted. The same was true with Martin (now Sir Martin) Gilbert, recently appointed, in succession to Randolph Churchill, official biographer of Sir Winston Churchill. Marder and Gilbert met at Merton, the latter's college. At All Souls, Max Beloff, historian and specialist in government, sought Marder's commiseration about some heavy-handed review he had received. Michael Howard, the military historian reviewing Marder's books, was a fellow there, too. Gretton was now at University College as bursar.

And so went this Oxford year of delight and discussion. It was all potentially very heady. There was the Rhodes Trust Dinner with the Eastman professor in his rightful chair, New Year's Day dinner at Balliol, then the Royal Navy Club of 1765 and 1785 banquet in the Connaught Rooms, Kingsway, London, on 5 February 1970, with Captain Andrew Yates presiding, and other events, including the annual Balliol 'gaudy', or year's end festivities, for members of the college. But too soon the academic year concluded, with Marder making his quiet exit from Eastman House in July, destined for Irvine and its mounting problems, notice of which he received from Sam McCulloch and others. Campus problems in the United States were rampant as Marder headed home; they would only get worse.

Of Marder's time in Balliol, one of its fellows, the historian Richard Cobb, wrote with deep affection:

> The Arthur that we came to know in Balliol seemed far removed from the exalted personage of immense public reputation that had preceded him like a light cruiser scouting squadron. He was quiet, gentle, and rather stately. In any room, he was a presence, even before he opened his mouth. He loved Oxford and loved Balliol. What he most enjoyed were public occasions, the more elaborate the better. He seldom missed Thursday guest nights, which he invariably enriched by his urbanity and by his eagerness to communicate; and he was deeply shocked, even outraged, when the College, in one of its intermittent bouts of self-punishment and pleasure-hating, decided to suppress free wine at the Consilium Dinner. He did not protest publicly about this act of uncouth Puritanism; he was far too conscious of his status as a visitor to the College ever to make such a public stand. But, in private, he did not hide his feelings of outrage. It was not what he would have expected of Balliol, or of Oxford, nor would it have happened in the wardroom of a battleship. He complained quietly, but in measured and stately tones. His own enjoyment in College life was matched by the enjoyment that Jan and he had in entertaining Fellows and their wives and University colleagues at Eastman House. Lunch or dinner there was an elaborate exercise in courtesy and sheer enjoyment. Arthur's gravity would combine quite admirably with Jan's warmth and easy friendliness. In this, as in all their life together, they were ideally suited, complementing each other in a way that made their company delightful, rewarding, and memorable.[35]

Cobb recorded how, on Wednesdays and Fridays during term, an unusually large crowd of historians could be seen emerging from the lecture room beneath the Senior Common Room of the college. Marder, gowned and senatorial, would be among them, carrying a pointer in one hand, a roll of maps in the other, rather as if Europe and the world, oceans and continents had recently been disposed of in his lecture. His fame spread throughout the university, so that, in direct opposite to the usual pattern, an increasing number of students, three times more than he had started with, jammed the room.

Marder's renown and his friendships multiplied in consequence of *Jutland and After*. His friend Jack Gallagher, the Empire historian and a fellow at Balliol, loved the excitement that Marder's book, like Mattingly's on the fate of the Spanish Armada, generated. Marder's telling had set the complexities of naval history aside. And, although Marder had told a riveting tale, Gallagher delighted in saying that Marder's volume on Jutland was best savoured when one was tucked up cosily in bed, as the east winds howled round his bedroom in the tower of the Balliol library staircase.[36]

The Oxford year brought unintended dividends. When OUP published volume 5 of *From Dreadnought to Scapa Flow* in 1970, Taylor put it atop that Christmas *Observer*'s Best Books of the Year. The publisher was ecstatic. Then the BBC invited Marder to record a conversation with another historian about the five-volume work, how it started, its conception, its execution, and its achievement. The producer, John Fox, thought that the partner in the discussion might be Taylor, and if Marder agreed then Taylor would be asked. Marder agreed, and in due course that production was aired on Trafalgar Day 1971. The account included the basics of Marder running down the steps of Harvard's Widener Library and knocking down and 'almost maiming' Langer, dean of modern European diplomatic historians. The editor of the *Listener* could not resist getting in a dig at Taylor, who had in a notorious book portrayed the coming of the Second World War as a great accident. 'For Taylor', the editor said, 'the [Marder] story confirmed his view that 'most of history is shaped by accident'.'[37]

Marder was back in California when the 1971 New Year's Honours List was published, with himself as the recipient of a CBE (Honorary Commander of the Most Excellent Order of the British Empire), rarely given to Americans and still more so to historians.[38] Marder received early notice of it through the British Embassy, Washington, and replied with words of profound gratitude to the queen. Notice of the award brought a flurry of fan mail, and many were the jokes in Irvine about 'Sir Arthur', a prospective elevation to the House of Lords, and so on.

Marder was speechless by the announcement of the CBE. Even so, the awards and notices were rolling in steadily. The Royal Historical Society elected him a fellow. The Royal United Services Institution named him an honorary life member. The prestigious British Academy, highest level of literary attainment, elected him a corresponding fellow. The first sea lord and the lords of the Admiralty, subsequent to their minute of acclaim of 1 July

1970,[39] entertained him to an official banquet held in his honour in the hall of the Royal Naval College at Greenwich, beneath the portrait of Nelson. In the United States, where his meteoric rise did not go unnoticed, the American Philosophical Society elected him a fellow on William Langer's esteemed nomination. The American Academy of Arts and Sciences followed suit. He was nominated for the presidency of the American Historical Association Pacific Coast Branch, and this he accepted. He was chosen, too, for the council of the parent American Historical Association, a distinction reserved for first-class historians. In Hawaii his friend Gregg Sinclair, past president of the university, nominated him for an honorary doctorate: without success, as it turned out, but no disrespect to Marder, for the university was awarding none such in those days.

Then in late January of the same year, 1971, came news that Oxford University Convocation was to confer honorary degrees on such notables as Mrs Indira Ghandi, Edward Heath, Lars Onsager (a Yale scientist), W.H. Auden, Sir Anthony Blunt, Sir Steven Runciman, and – to give him his nominal Oxford designation – 'Professor Arthur Jacob Marder, MA, Balliol College.' (Marder's MA had been granted without fee upon taking up the Eastman professorship and becoming a member of the university.) He was in fine company. Tributes flowed from both sides of the Atlantic. One of his new Oxford friends reminded Marder that the degree was a mark not only of his distinction as a historian but also of the esteem and admiration which his year as Eastman professor had left behind. Now Marder was 'of Oxford'. There were strange costs to this distinction, as a friend mused: 'But you do realize that you will not now be able to write your projected book about Oxford?'[40]

June 23rd found Marder at the Encaenia – the pageant of learning, C.S. Lewis called it – with Auden, Blunt, and Runciman, all finely regaled, all in receipt of the degree of doctor of letters, *honoris causa*, and all standing in the highest favour: Auden, the noted poet of his age; Blunt, the professor of art history in London and surveyor of the queen's pictures – and soon to be exposed as a traitor to the state; and Runciman, the noted historian of the crusades. In this exalted company, Marder was not out of place. The oration in his honour spoke of the accident on the Widener Library steps and how his professor got him to set German generals aside for Haldane's mission to Germany: 'This proved to be the thread of Ariadne that led into the labyrinth', an adoption of Marder's own metaphor. Much else followed, including notice of the five-volume masterpiece, a quinquereme, so to speak, with its enormous personnel, painted in bold and clear colours. 'The waves which Britain once had seemed to rule throughout the world (Charles II's adaptation of Virgil, *Ecl.* I, 66), now seemed to be ruled by an American in a chair at Honolulu. So far had sunk the splendid isolation of the sceptred Island of the Blest to become the pabulum of research. But we are still blessed in that in the centre of his great canvas he has put the Battle of Jutland, which he examines acutely and fairly, apportioning blame and praise, and from it some glory to shed upon us. But narrative is his prime interest, not so much of materials and shipbuilding as of men as their various characters and abilities led them to act.'[41]

The great book on Jutland had given Marder star status in Britain, of that there could be no doubt. Marder entered history with it. Taylor's trumpeting did no harm, for the great popularizer, who claimed that he had been slighted in his own profession, now turned to be kingmaker for the American successor to Mahan. The British press and the BBC added to the chorus. But this was all on the best of authority, mind you, for the reviewers proclaimed Marder's histories as not only the latest word but likely the definitive one. Britain placed the mantle of historical authority on Marder's shoulders as no other nation could do for its own naval past, especially the faltering years of Fisher and Churchill and of the Dardanelles, Jutland, and convoys. This was Marder's achievement.

Part Two

Collision Courses

Chapter 7

The Fight for Hankey's Secrets

NOTHING can be as important to a working historian as sources – and being first to get to them and above all to use them. Attesting to this is the queue of impatient seekers waiting to read soon-to-be-released documents that can still be seen at the National Archives, the old Public Record Office, Kew, on the appointed day. Hired agents and eager researchers are on the hunt for such documents as are about to appear, for a fresh story is what a reading public demands and expects. Nowadays an annual prize cluster of documents on, say, the Profumo affair may be released by the National Archives on the day in question. Details of many such similar secrets remain under lock and key until the release date. In other cases, documents remain sealed forever, the national interest requiring it, or so it is said. Private researchers, in these circumstances, have been driven farther afield, to family papers, there to uncover literary nuggets, and lucky is the historian or biographer called upon to do an authorized work, for he or she has first and perhaps complete access to the trunks and files of a dear one recently departed. Often under such circumstances a sanitized version of a work appears, and something that could have been warts and all now looks more cleaned up, more saintly, more noble.

Marder and Roskill shared the quest of all good historians: they were on the hunt for new material hitherto unused. In their day, concepts of 'the end of history', 'post-colonialism', and 'deconstructionist theory', the last essentially the rethinking and repostulating of known material rather than the taxing quest for new, were only faint rays of new suns rising. The reading publics of the United Kingdom, the British Empire and Commonwealth, and the United States were served by a transatlantic publishing industry that wanted to know all about the First and Second World Wars and about political leadership. The phenomenal publishing sales of Churchill's *Second World War* reflected this and so, too, Roskill's *War at Sea*. Roskill noted privately that HMSO made a fortune out of his book, and this explains why he was able to demand unimaginably high royalty rates for the books subsequently published by Collins – 17½ per cent. Marder's publishers,

Jonathan Cape and Oxford University Press, likewise gained mightily from the books on Fisher and the Royal Navy in the First World War, though Marder's royalty rate, at 12 per cent, was nowhere as high as Roskill's. The point is that there was an eager reading public awaiting the newest approach to the past, and in the years Roskill and Marder were writing for this market, the publishing pastures were green even if inflation was driving up the costs of books. Each knew the merit of new material hitherto unused: such material gave freshness and vitality, insights never before imagined, good lines to quote or summarize, and, above all, authenticity – the hallmark of the historian.

Clouding the horizons for Marder and Roskill were the restrictions of successive Public Records acts, the Defence of the Realm Act, 'D-notices' and regulations concerning what the press could or could not print, and ministerial and cabinet regulations and controls. The Official Secrets Act hung over their heads and over those in government who otherwise would have gladly helped them and others. A private individual had no right of access to British official archives, though officers in certain ministries had power to grant access to certain individuals. The chilly effects of the Cold War were felt by Marder and Roskill in small, incalculable ways. Neither would – or could – reveal anything that might expose the government or its allies. Each of them knew the protocol of abiding by the rules of the game on the use of secret materials, and it must be remembered that Marder had worked in the OSS, the precursor of the CIA, and that Roskill was not only formerly a deputy director of naval intelligence but later in the employment of the Cabinet Office.

Marder and Roskill shared a zealous desire to get at unused sources, and it is that which resulted in the gathering storm and sparring match that constitutes the second part of the book. They came from different schools or training grounds of history and historical study, and this, too, bears on their gradual separation. Marder was all Harvard and all American university scholarly training. Most prominent in the influences of his training as a historian was the school of Leopold von Ranke, the German historian of the mid- and late nineteenth century who had insisted that all sources be examined and that the historical argument be derived from them. Here was a school of history desiring no great thematic whirl, no counterfactual treatment, and hardly any 'what might have been if?' This was straight-ahead history written in the best of narrative style and arranged systematically in a form of undeniable order and clarity. Marder prided himself in gathering together Ariadne's thread – the linking of it all – and he also prided himself as a teller of story, often quoting his favourites Sir Charles Firth and Sir Lewis

Namier on the merit of the narrative. With no moral axe to grind, no clarion call to trumpet, and no other historians to tangle with (his school of history had been trained to fight battles not in the text but in footnotes), he proceeded rather merrily on with his method before such time as Roskill made his challenge.

Marder's technique, essential to our understanding of the gathering storm, was based on two kinds of research, one public and the other private: the first involved visiting owners of records to see what documents they had, exploiting the Admiralty Records Office by special permit when the Public Record Office was unavailable, and examining every scrap of printed evidence; and the second consisted of corresponding with persons who had been participants in events, afloat or ashore, following up letters from persons who had read his books, heard him on BBC radio, or seen him on BBC TV, and, above all, exchanging rapid correspondence with a tight cluster of historians, all of whom became friends and some very close ones, on the evolving chapters and sections of Marder's books in the making. Among the latter – for they had ringside seats – were Peter Kemp, Peter Gretton, and John Creswell. Kemp had an entrée to other naval historians, to serving or retired members of the armed services, and to others of use in the line of history.

Because Kemp and Gretton were close associates, especially at the Royal United Services Institution, and reading the same script as Marder was feeding them, they often compared notes: on one occasion it seemed that Marder was treating Jellicoe too harshly, and the combination had to set him straight. Brought into the golden circle later – in fact, he volunteered – was Captain John Creswell, expert on naval tactics and a good hand at drawing plans and maps. Creswell had been touted to be Cabinet Office historian for the *War at Sea*; in fact, he had written the first prospectus for the book. Illness had kept him from being 'official historian' but it did not stop his historical endeavours, including the publication of *Sea Warfare 1939–1945: A Short History* (1950), which Marder critiqued in draft at Creswell's request. Among members of this well-developed committee of quality control and historical industry, the Royal Mail speeded circulation of Marder's chapters. Winter storms, railway stoppages, postal strikes and other inconveniences threatened progress but Marder and his guides pressed on. Beyond this inner ring there reached wider circles. Customarily, Marder would send segments of a chapter – maybe even a paragraph or two – to one of his informants. His object was to make sure that he had the details correct and also the right slant on or appreciation of the matter under consideration. Another exchange would follow the revision, and sometimes a third. Marder left nothing to chance in his quest for authenticity. His devoted minders insisted on nothing less.

In 1960, in the run-up to the publication of the first volume of *From the Dreadnought to Scapa Flow*, Marder requested that Roskill read its last three chapters. He consented. Marder was immensely grateful, as he was to all who critiqued his work. With customary pains, Roskill made various comments of use to Marder. By this time, Roskill was just launching his lucrative career as a reviewer for the *Sunday Telegraph* and was already reviewing for the *Economist* and the *US Naval Institute Proceedings* besides various non-paying journals. This meant that he had various perches from which to observe Marder's progress. Even so, he was compromised as reviewer for having already read Marder's work in draft form. This explains Roskill's ready acceptance of Marder's books once in print.

Roskill's reviews of Marder do not stand in stark contrast to those by other reviewers. But, as an author, Roskill distanced himself from Marder, citing him only when absolutely necessary and keeping him at arm's length when giving thanks to American foundations or grants agencies – Rockefeller and the American Philosophical Society – which, on the basis of letters from Marder, had opened their coffers and allowed visits to Washington. The distancing began in 1966, for Marder had stolen the show with his *Jutland and After*. He had snatched the crown jewels of modern British naval history, no small achievement for an American, and he still had two more volumes to write in the same great series. But Marder was not blameless in the developing rift: his pressing demands for comments on his work were beginning to grate on the otherwise receptive Roskill.

Roskill's background in historical method was based on his preparatory schooling and days at Osborne and Dartmouth, his independent investigatory pursuits dating from the interwar period, and his own self-development alongside certain naval officers, principally Stephen King-Hall, who were mentors or models. His viewpoints probably owed much to the legal world in which he was born and also to his mother's strong sense of liberal progress and enlightenment. Roskill had no academic training in history, historical method, or historiography, a disadvantage. Probably less well served in public education than Marder, Roskill learned from masters of the authorized curriculum at Osborne and Dartmouth. His history masters were particularly fine, but surely no better than Marder's either at Boston English High School or in Harvard College. On the other hand, his Service time gave him a familiarity with government ways of communication in print media. As we have seen, by the time he was chosen as a Cabinet Office historian to undertake the *War at Sea*, he was a known writer in select naval circles but had no wider constituency and had published nothing of a commercial nature. In the Cabinet Office he had the advantage of access (on application) to the Admiralty Historical Branch's case files, histories, and weekly and monthly summaries of the naval war. He also had access to those who were writing these summaries and historical appreciations. He had to jockey for secretarial help but, while in Cabinet Office employ, had a full-time assistant, Commander Geoffrey Hare, who drafted and assembled material for his consideration, checked quotations and details, and helped with indexing. Hare would stay on, in a private capacity, long after *War at Sea* was completed, a heroic twenty years in all. Indeed, prefaces of Roskill's several books published in this period – HMS *Warspite* (1957), *The Secret Capture* (1959), and *The Strategy of Sea Power: Its Development and Application* (1962) – show Hare as Roskill's right-hand man. Edith Eales, his devoted secretary for seventeen years, handled correspondence and text with ease and flexibility.

Roskill's output was prodigious at the time he commenced reading Marder's drafts. He was then completing *War at Sea*. Even before the second part of the third volume was published, in 1961, the books mentioned plus another, *White Ensign: The British Navy at War, 1939–1945*, had appeared. Roskill already had *The Art of Leadership* on the stocks and was drawing up plans for the first volume of *Naval Policy between the Wars*. He may well have written more than Marder did in the same time but the work was discursive and the themes and subjects necessarily various. Roskill had no inside track with the governmental records still under close guard, and he had to write under the rules incorporated in the 1958 Public Record Act (6 and 7 Eliz. II, c. 51), whereby 'authorized officers' of government departments were allowed to open official records before the expiration of the fifty-year 'closed period' then in force. In Roskill's case, the 'authorized officers' were Sir John Lang, permanent secretary of the Admiralty, Sir Maurice Dean, permanent secretary of the Air Ministry, and Sir Burke Trend, secretary of the cabinet. While writing *Naval Policy between the Wars, Volume I*, Roskill received that privilege on condition that he submit his typescript for scrutiny.[1]

Correspondence for September 1961, just as the first volume of *From the Dreadnought to Scapa Flow* started to receive its fabulous reviews in British papers, shows Roskill showering praise on Marder. At the same time, however, Roskill issued two words of caution to the professor: the first, about Admiral Sir David Beatty, and, more forcibly, the second, about a line being drawn in the sand where Marder must stop and Roskill begin (note: this was Roskill's idea and not shared by Marder).

Dear Marder:

It was most kind of you to have told the publisher to send me a copy of your new book, and I shall hope to get the author to inscribe it the next time he is in this country. I had actually read it, with great interest and admiration, and I really do congratulate you on a first-class piece of writing. I have reviewed it for the *Sunday Telegraph* in which I understand it will be given some prominence tomorrow, and I feel sure that it will be equally well received in all the other papers.[2]

That letter bore the date 9 September and the review appeared the next day. The *Sunday Telegraph* had just made its debut, and Roskill, a *Sunday Times* contributor for the past decade, was announced to be regular naval writer for the new paper. He had been lured there, into phase two of what he called 'high-class journalism', by a lucrative retainer.[3] The review itself was full of praise and contained no substantive criticism. It made a couple of points about Fisher and Churchill and of Marder's brilliant treatment of the strategy under which the British fought the First World War at sea, and commented on Mahan, on trade defence, and on the strength and weaknesses of the Royal Navy on the eve of Armageddon.

Marder wrote to Roskill expressing his renewed thanks and gratefulness for the complimentary review. He thereby elicited this long, engaging reply, dated the 29 September, from the Cabinet Office:

Dear Marder:

Many thanks for your letter of the 25th. I did not exaggerate at all my admiration for your book. Indeed if anything the reverse was true. I have a feeling that one or two of, what I might call, the Beatty gang got to you between typescript and publication, as I noticed you had amended your remarks about his part in strategy and tactics. That is a very complicated issue, which still arouses passions over here. Though on the whole I think you have been fair, I hope you will not mind my giving you a word of warning for your next volume. Beatty was a fine leader of men and a romantic character; but his morality was certainly not of the highest, and it is very unwise for the historian to accept the view of people who fell under his spell.

I am horribly busy, as I have begun research on the records of 1918–39. This is to be my main work in connection with the Fellowship to which I have been elected at Cambridge, and my intention is to try to fill the gap between the Official Histories of the First and Second Wars. *That fits very well with your project, as it will mean that is where Marder stops Roskill begins* [emphasis added].

My Cambridge lectures of last June have been expanded into a short book called 'The Strategy of Sea Power' which Collins are publishing next February; and I have a good many other projects in hand. However I cannot return a dusty answer to your request to read your new typescript, so send it along when it is available; but please do not harass me to do it quickly. I marvel at the speed with which you have been able to recover from the loss of your notes. Such a disaster would have set me back for good.

Roskill closed his cheery letter with a postscript that Marder's book awaited inscription from the author, and he thanked him again for the copy sent as a gift.[5] It will be noted that Roskill did not tie the line of demarcation, the beginning of the interwar years, to the lending to Marder of his papers on Jutland, as he later claimed.[6]

To this point in time, cordiality and generosity marked relations between them. Marder, having no early warning signs, continued at customary high speed, and naturally kept asking Roskill to review his texts – and the latter always agreed. The reviews, all of them glowing, especially of *Jutland and After*, appeared in steady succession. Mutual appreciation and admiration covered their relations. Roskill was wearying under the work of reviewing Marder's texts, but, still, he carried on.

Meanwhile, Marder wanted to know from his inner circle what sort of fellow Roskill was, for the comments Roskill sent him were often critical, opinionated, and even censorious. Creswell, in response, gave Marder this assessment, dated 1 March 1963:

Yes, I should say Roskill is an independent. He certainly tends to be hyper-critical, though in all sincerity and without any hard feelings, and he seems to find it difficult to clear his mind of hindsight. He writes a very good narrative but to my mind his judgements smack too much of the staff officer analysing a fleet exercise and making points for his C in C to drive home when summing up at the post-exercise conference. Just the thing for those occasions when everyone expects mistakes to be pointed out and no one expects to be patted on the back, but perhaps less suitable when writing a history of war operations with their dangers, complexities and strains. Yes, I'm an independent, in that I admire Jellicoe and Beatty about equally.

Shortly after *Jutland and After* appeared, John Ehrman, naval historian and former Cabinet Office historian, close associate of Roskill, and Admiral Sir Geoffrey Blake's son-in-law, hosted lunch at his London residence. Blake, who had been powerfully influential in the help that Marder received, and who also had been the naval representative on the Cabinet Office subcommittee overseeing the Official War Histories including the *War at Sea*, was there. So were Marder and Roskill. In other words, the two historical giants of modern British naval history were at a social event together for the first time. David Erskine, secretary of the Navy Records Society, was there, too, and Roskill's wife, Elizabeth. 'Had a pleasant quarrel with S.R. on Beatty', Marder confided to Creswell in a letter later that day.

> He said I missed an important facet of D[avid] B[eatty]'s character in [volume] III – that he was 'arrogant'. This I wouldn't accept. No arrogant Commanding Officer could win the devotion & affection of officers & men as Beatty did. Neither of us convinced the other! On D.B.'s refusal to sack [Captain Sir Ralph] Seymour [who Beatty claimed had cost him three victories], I said it was because *au fond*, D.B. had a soft streak in him. No, said S.R., he wouldn't sack him because of the 'class loyalty' factor (or some such words) – that Seymour was an aristocrat, which appealed mightily to D.B. Rubbish, said I. And so it went. An interesting lunch![6]

Early next year, Marder revealed even more to Creswell about Roskill, for the first volume of Roskill's *Naval Policy between the Wars* was now complete and due at press.

> His 1st chapter & my last (or penultimate) one, post-Armistice, overlap; he tried to persuade me to stop . . . at the Armistice. I said I couldn't & wouldn't: the logical conclusion is the Scapa business in June 1919. And besides, I told him, the sub-title of the work gives 1919 as the terminal date. I gather that his treatment of Nov. 1918-June 1919 is much sketchier than mine will be. The Jutland controversy, post-war, was supposed to have been a chapter in R[oskill]'s 1st vol. But he had a second thought & decided against it. There may be some mention of it, but not the full treatment he had originally planned.[7]

Traces about Marder now began to appear in Roskill's correspondence. Roskill disclosed a growing grudge against the American – as in this letter to Captain A.B. Sainsbury of the *Naval Review*:

As to Marder's request, between ourselves he is rather a nuisance to busy working historians like myself. Though he is a nice man his knowledge of British naval history is not sound enough to enable him to write with confidence and accuracy. He always asks me and various other people to read and check his typescripts. He has done this with every book he has published, and at the present time some 1,500 pages of typescript of his new book is coming to me in serial form. My difficulty in dealing with it really arises from the fact that I see on nearly every page how incomplete Marder's knowledge is, and I really have not the time to give his drafts the careful reading that they need.[8]

Nonetheless, Roskill needed Marder's patronage and help, since he was then seeking American Philosophical Society money to fund his next visit to the United States, this one for research on his second volume of *Naval Policy between the Wars*. He had Admiral Morison, Sir James Butler, and Marder as his referees. The grant was awarded, though Marder thought the figure requested immodest. In any event, Roskill completed the book and sent Marder a copy. Marder acknowledged receipt, with thanks. He also sent Roskill references to an important collection of papers of Edward Carson, sometime first lord of the Admiralty. 'If successful, this will save me a great deal of trouble,' wrote Roskill to Marder in thanks. Then, he turned to Marder's next visit to the United Kingdom, one that included Cambridge on a tight itinerary: 'You will of course realize that I have been keeping in touch with the Librarian here [Churchill Archives Centre] about your forthcoming visit, but I must admit that I think you are trying to do far too much in too short a time, when you say you will only be coming on a Saturday afternoon. However, that is your affair, and I know that you are accustomed to moving at the speed of an inter-continental missile.'[9]

Thus did the exchange of letters continue, with Roskill thanking Marder for photocopies of more documents, specifically the Committee of Imperial Defence subcommittee's juicy report on the vulnerability of capital ships. 'I knew, of course, of that committee', Roskill wrote once again to Marder, in thanks, 'but had not had the documents actually copied. I am afraid it is one of the problems that besets us poor Englishmen at the moment – that ever-rising costs prevent us making the fullest possible use of such facilities. You Americans are lucky in that respect, so if you have any more documents of the 1930s you do not want, I would be delighted to have them.' Roskill's pay-off was a flow of documents from Marder.

This was the last letter before the blow-up, and is dated 2 January 1969. Roskill was then critiquing the draft of Marder's last volume of *From the*

Dreadnought to Scapa Flow. As if that were not enough to preoccupy him, besides getting ready for his next research trip to Washington, the awkward, difficult business of publishing – through the Navy Records Society – sections of the papers of Captain John Harper relating to the tortuous Jutland controversy (see chapter 9) had blown up in his face. Roskill was working under tremendous strain, with too many irons in the fire. Still, he kept on with new projects, with others in view. He completed *Naval Policy between the Wars, Volume I*, and now found himself stymied by inability to get access to departmental records after about 1934; they had not yet reached the Public Record Office. The second volume he had to put on hold.

At this very moment, the grandest of opportunities was offered – a welcome invitation from Robert (Robin) Hankey, 2nd Baron Hankey, and a senior British diplomat, to write the life of his father, the famed Maurice Hankey, colonel in the Royal Marines and secretary of the Committee of Imperial Defence – the man who knew more secrets about the conduct of what he had called 'the Supreme Command' than any other person in the war ministry of the First World War and throughout the interwar period and well into the Second World War. This was an opportunity Roskill could not refuse. 'After visiting his home and finding that his papers were quite untouched I accepted the job on two conditions,' Roskill recollected in 1975 as part of his record of his blow-up with Marder. 'The first was that the family should accept that there would be no censorship on what I wrote, though I would show them the typescript and consider any criticisms or suggestions they had to offer. The second condition was that the Hankey copyright should in effect be leased to me for a peppercorn while I was working on the biography. These conditions were accepted by Lord Hankey's family and I went ahead.'[10]

Marder, however, had preceded Roskill in the use of the 1st Lord Hankey's diary, drawing on it for *From the Dreadnought to Scapa Flow*. As we have seen, in Marder's volume 4 of that work, page 164, he mentioned Lloyd George's famous visit to the Admiralty on 30 April 1917 on the subject of the adoption of convoys as a means of protecting shipping from the depredations of U-boats. Lloyd George, as Marder pointed out, later misrepresented his role in the change of policy. 'Hankey's testimony is unimpeachable,' proclaimed Marder in defence against the claim of Lloyd George's biographer as to how the prime minister had 'invaded' the Admiralty and 'dragged forth the truth' about the necessity to impose convoys. In the same volume (page 334), Marder also made direct quotation from a diary entry for 26 October 1917, in which Hankey, a significant figure in the movement towards adopting convoy as policy, was harshly critical of the Admiralty's slothfulness. Describing one devastating attack on merchant shipping that was inadequately protected by warships, Hankey wrote sardonically: '[The Admiralty] . . . had been fully warned by highly secret, but absolutely reliable information [from Room 40, the intelligence gathering centre], of the probability of an attack on the Norwegian convoy, and had neglected to act. [Sir Eric] Geddes [first lord of the Admiralty] regards this as an example of [the First Sea Lord] Jellicoe's lack of energy, if not timidity, and wants to replace him by Admiral Wemyss.' Hankey's testimony was indeed irrefutable and vital to Marder's line of inquiry. However, Marder also provided — on the basis of more solid evidence of those in the Admiralty at the time (his key witness, so to speak, was Admiral Sir Alexander Duff, director of the Anti-Submarine Division) — a stout defence of Jellicoe and those of the naval staff. In this he had been helped by Lady Duff, another spirited naval widow.

In the warmth of the southern California sunshine in January 1969, Marder was dealing with various points and corrections sent from Roskill, as from others, about volume 5. Along with Roskill's comments on specific matters were such gratuitous points as telling Marder that he was rushing into the post-First World War period in which his information was slim or misguided; Roskill recommended, once again, that Marder stop volume 5 at June 1919. 'In general I have nothing but admiration for this concluding part. I think you have somewhat altered your scale, giving more greater space to comparatively small events, compared with earlier volumes, but that is your affair.'

Then rang the opening bell:

I have one important point about Sources . . . you refer to 'Hankey MSS'. Now these are closed by decision of the present Lord Hankey, whose copyright of course they are, & dozens of request for access have recently been refused. How you got at unpublished parts of his diary I don't know, & I think it better not to ask; but I could not recommend to Lord Hankey to give permission to print them. What he printed in *The Supreme Command* is of course open — but the other stuff definitely is not available to scholars, & I can't agree to exceptions.[11]

Here was Roskill in a new role, as custodian and gatekeeper. And again, on 18 January 1969: 'About the quotations from Hankey's diary, you are in trouble. When I undertook the biography it was definitely understood between me and the present Lord Hankey that his father's papers remain closed until I had finished the job. In consequence we have refused literally dozens of requests for access and quotations, and I really cannot recommend Robin Hankey making an exception in our case, and it would obviously lead to complaints from other writers.' The solution, said Roskill, was for Marder to take out the offending paragraphs from his text. 'I am sorry to be difficult about this, but shall stick to my guns. Nor do I think it will in any way vitiate your story to take out the few unpublished extracts. I myself have had some copyright refusals, and I always acquiesce without complaint when that occurs, annoying though it is.'[12]

Marder's professional career as an historian, and his secret as the Ali Baba of historical studies, as A.J.P. Taylor called him, was getting access to new, unused sources. He knew well these sorts of scenarios, having fought three decades of battles with gatekeepers and censors. But dealing with Roskill had a new edge to it, a rivalry between heretofore close associates. Now it was Roskill who barred the door and wanted to claw back on earlier material.

'Yours 19th January, with its unfair, illogical, and ungenerous position *re* my use of the few Hankey diary extracts, surprises, distresses, and above all saddens me,' he opened his letter of 23 January to Roskill. Then he got to the main points:

> I am sending a copy of your letter, together with a copy of this reply, to Lord Hankey, and herewith is a copy of my letter to him. I do not want to keep anything from either of you: I have nothing to hide, having acted in good faith in the whole matter. You are *unfair* because you are insisting that an agreement reached between you and Lord Hankey be applied retroactively to embrace the earlier understanding between Lord Hankey and myself. You are *illogical*, if that's the word I want, in insisting on something now that you should have raised a whole year ago: I refer to the 'Hankey MSS' entry in Volume IV, the MS of which you read, with doubtless your usual care, at that time. You are *ungenerous* in wishing to deprive me of the use of material that I consider important for my purposes, even if its removal in the case of Vol. V would not 'vitiate my story'. This I find most uncharacteristic of you. Indeed your letter gives me the impression that it was written by an impostor, not by the Stephen Roskill I thought I knew! The occasional exception made for a deserving scholar is, then[,] anything but unusual. As for the 'complaints' to which you refer, I don't see that they affect the issue. He [Lord Hankey] permitted one small exception in 1966 to a scholar whose work he wished to encourage – and before the New Policy went into effect. This hardly qualifies as a legitimate ground of complaint from anybody. And what if there were complaints?! But why go on. I'm sick about it all.[13]

William L. Langer, Harvard historian (top left); Admiral Sir Herbert Richmond (top right); Peter Gretton (bottom left); Peter Kemp (bottom right).

Discussing Admiralty documents access: Vice Admiral Sir Geoffrey Barnard, Vice Admiral Sir Peter Gretton, and Marder, 1960. *By courtesy of the Marder family*

Marder beneath the great guns of Admiral Tōgō's *Mikasa*, triumphant at Tsushima. *By courtesy of the Marder family*

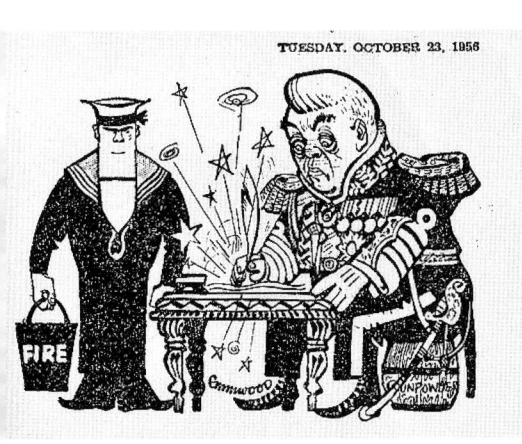

Admiral Lord Fisher writing a fiery letter while a naval rating on fire rescue detail stands by; a cartoon accompanying a review of *From Dreadnought to Scapa Flow* in the *Evening Standard*.

Marder on the eve of the Jutland 50th anniversary heads the *Evening Standard*'s Diary page.

Marder en route to the BBC Studios reads reviews of his *Jutland and After*, 31 May 1966. *By courtesy of the Marder family*

At the Admiralty 1979: First Sea Lord Admiral Sir Terence Lewin (later Baron Lewin of Greenwich) with, left, Lady Lewin and, right, Jan and Arthur Marder. *By courtesy of the Marder family*

Marder at his desk at the University of California, Irvine, 1975. *By courtesy of the Marder family*

Admiral of the Fleet the Earl Mountbatten of Burma with Marder, at Broadlands, 1979. *By courtesy of the Marder family*

Stephen Roskill, about 1920, in naval uniform. *By courtesy of Nicholas Roskill*

Elizabeth and Stephen Roskill on the occasion of their wedding, 12 August 1930. The dalmatian was Elizabeth's, the spaniel Stephen's. *By courtesy of Nicholas Roskill*

A pre-war view of the cruiser HMS *Leander*, without camouflage and carrying a seaplane. She was loaned to the Royal New Zealand Navy in 1941.
By courtesy of Nicholas Roskill

Captain Stephen Roskill, RN, when in command HMNZS *Leander*.
By courtesy of Nicholas Roskill

Admiral of the Fleet Sir Dudley Pound. Portrait by Captain D. Wales-Smith. *National Maritime Museum BHC2960*

Admiral Sir David Beatty, when Commander in Chief, Grand Fleet, 1916-19. Portrait by Sir Arthur Cope. *National Maritime Museum BHC2537*

Dustjacket of Roskill's *Churchill and the Admirals*.

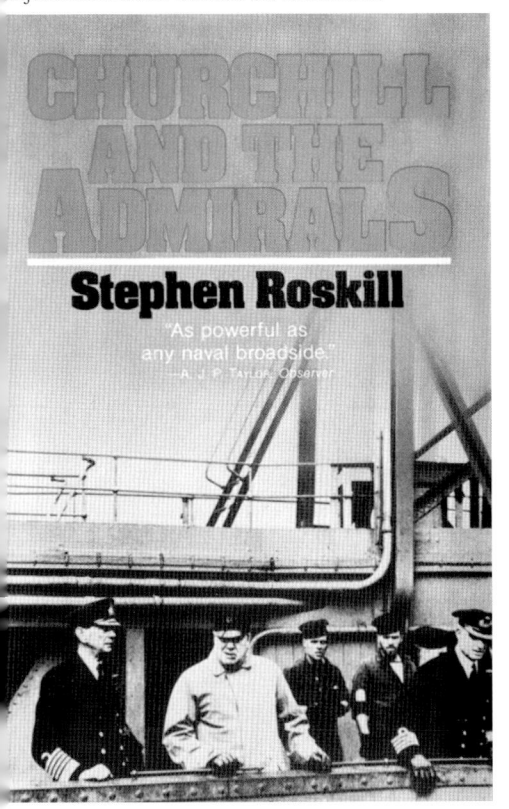

Dustjacket of Marder's *From the Dreadnought to Scapa Flow, Volume III: Jutland and After*.

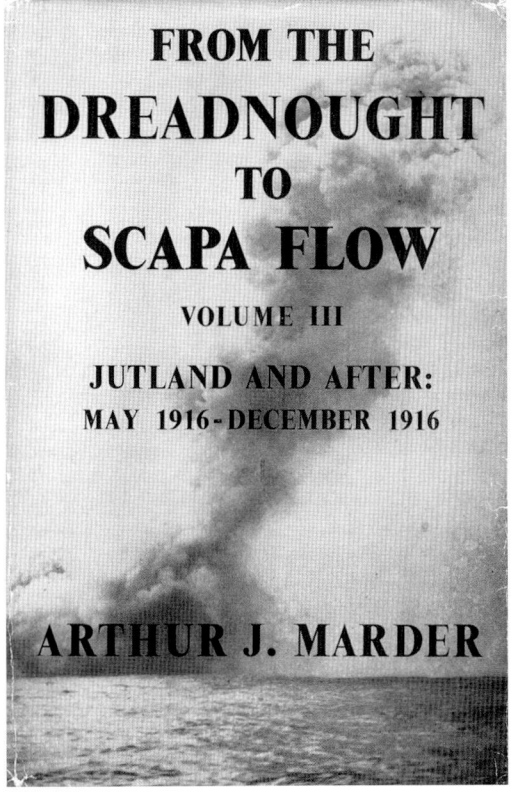

The Roskill brothers on the occasion of th[e] Encaenia, and the awarding of an honorary doctorate to Stephen, 25 June 1980. Left to right: Ashton, Stephen, Oliver and Eustace. *By courtesy of Nicholas Roskill*

Captain Stephen Roskill, RN, Life Fellow [of] Churchill College, Cambridge. By Michael Noakes. Portrait from the Roskill Library. *[By] courtesy of the artist and the Master, Fellows an[d] Scholars of Churchill College*

So ended the first round of this sparring match. The second deepened the crisis, and showed in Roskill a nasty streak about doing work for Marder without recompense. He defended his right as 'authorized' biographer to have full control of the documents, just as Martin Gilbert had for Churchill or Sir Philip Magnus for Lord Esher. As to Marder's charge of ungenerosity, Roskill stated this to be the most extraordinary of all, noting that he had spent weeks going through three bulky volumes of typescript at Marder's request and without payment. 'To put the matter on a purely commercial basis my fee to read a typescript for a publisher (which I am often asked to do) is 25 guineas; and my fee for a consultation (which I am often asked to give) is the same. You have had all these services from me for years for absolutely nothing. I cannot even recall being offered a drink, let alone a meal by way of acknowledgement, though you have enjoyed our hospitality. Again where does the ungenerosity lie?' Roskill acknowledged that Marder had helped him get grants from US foundations, for which, he hoped, he had accorded adequate acknowledgement. (In fact, he did so personally but not in print.) Roskill came to the next point. Recently, the chair of Marder's department had written Roskill as to whether Marder should be awarded senior professorial status. 'Ungenerous of me to respond – again on my own time?' Then he got to an old wound still bothering him:

> Since you raise these absurd charges against me I will mention one, possibly relevant, against you that I have long had in mind. I have sometimes wondered whether Marder, in his avidity to tap unpublished sources, does not show a lack of scruple in his methods. For example after you came here in my absence last summer I learnt to my concern and dismay that you had asked for copies of Keyes papers *which you knew to be closed*, and that the copying of them had rightly been stopped by the Librarian. Are you really so innocent as not to know that the mere copying of those letters without Lord Keyes's permission placed us in breach of copyright with him? I was very angry when I heard about this, and only forbore to tell you so because I heard the story at second hand and, as the copying was stopped, no damage was done. But it left a very nasty taste in my mouth.
>
> If you had asked me, as an old friend, to do you a favour of exempting you from an agreement with Lord Hankey I would probably found it hard to refuse. But not now.[14]

This last remark was disingenuous for Roskill had already stated that he had no intention of letting Marder see these papers.

In the face of this barrage of criticism and abuse, Marder could not stand idly by. He took umbrage at Roskill's intemperate reply, but, truth to tell, temperatures were rising in California as well as in Cambridge. Marder reasserted his points about access and use, but the matter now, sadly, boiled down to generosity and ungenerosity:

> Yes, you ARE ungenerous – in the sense, as I intended to get across to you but failed dismally – in that you have a richly deserved reputation (stated by me publicly) for generosity. You have given freely of your time and your materials. This is precisely why I have not been able to fathom your position in this affair. In short, you have in a sense spoiled those whom you have helped! And in the case we are discussing, I was not asking for anything extraordinary. It is churlish of you to mention what you have done for me. I have repeatedly expressed my gratitude to you and tried to be of such assistance as I could to you and your projects. In any case, I have never believed in keeping a ledger in these matters, since scholars are expected to help each other whenever and however they can – within reason, of course.

Then came Marder's counter to Roskill's stinging blow that he had tried to cheat on access:

> As for your absurd KEYES MSS charge, I had corresponded with the Librarian for months on them. When he referred me to Lord Keyes for the OK, this I did, and RECEIVED WRITTEN PERMISSION FROM LORD K. TO EXAMINE THE PAPERS. This I did at Churchill. When I was subsequently informed by the Archivist that the WWII papers were, under the 30-year rule, out of bounds, I said Fine: please send me the Xerox (I hadn't copied any of that material) when it can be done. This was agreed to, and to use up some surplus funds, I got Dr. [Edwin] Welch [archivist at Churchill Archives Centre] to accept payment in advance. So much for your ridiculous charge about lack of scruple. Really, Stephen . . . An historian should get his facts straight – *always*.

Marder also stated that the chairman of his department, in seeking names of persons with whom to consult as to his suitability for professorial high elevation, had trawled through Marder's various book prefaces. Marder was not aware of the promotion until after the process was done. He could not resist adding, sourly, 'Now that I think of it, the Chairman not too long ago popped in for a chat and, among other things, wanted to know who were the outstanding men in the broad field of military studies. My innocent reply has, I now see, got me into some difficulty. I shall, I promise, be more careful in the future.' Marder was prepared to end it there, burn his correspondence on this heated matter, and leave the decision to Lord Hankey, if Roskill was prepared 'to forget this nasty exchange of letters'.[15]

The story now shifts to Hethe House, near Edenbridge, rural Kent, where Robin, the 2nd Lord Hankey, had returned from winter travels in Sweden only to be greeted to a pile of letters and enclosures from the naval pugilists. Hankey read the boiling correspondence and then spoke to Roskill by phone. To Marder he wrote on 9 February: 'I am horrified to have been connected with such a sharp controversy between two such eminent historians. *Please* both bury the hatchet forthwith!' To Marder he also wrote that he had, in fact, granted permission to use extracts for the diaries, though now wished he had got the matter of permission down in writing. And he said he should have explained the arrangement to Roskill. Hankey's embarrassment is best revealed in his closing remark:

> I must clearly stand by the agreement I then gave that you can publish the extracts you have sent to Roskill and me. But if I stand by also in a white sheet, I must ask you to handle the matter in such as way as to cause the minimum of trouble between Roskill and the publisher of my father's biography. This is fortunately a quite remarkable work, and I find it hard to believe that a book of such breadth and scope will suffer too much from your few quotations. But please play them down and not up, so as to embarrass us as little as possible! I am sorry about all this! I enjoyed meeting you immensely, & you helped us a lot. I hope your book is going well.

Thus closed Hankey's reply to Marder, a copy of which went to Roskill.

Robin Hankey found himself caught between old promises to Marder and new ones to Roskill. But it is clear that Hankey had now given Marder a green light to proceed, though to do so with caution. Marder replied to Hankey in softening tones, suggesting various ways of quieting the overt references to the Hankey diaries, and noting that the editor at OUP might have other suggestions. Marder knew all these tricks, having been raised on them as a publishing historian. Then he turned to the dispute: 'I am sure that Stephen is as prepared as I am to bury the hatchet – not in the other party's head, of course! Despite all the thunder and lightning, I think we share a great respect for each other's work and for each other as persons.'

But Roskill would not play by this rule. He refused to allow the Hankey copyright to be exploited by Marder. 'I told Lord Hankey that I would rather abandon the biography than have our agreement breached in such a matter.'[16] Thus this 14 February telegram, Hankey to Marder: 'Please suspend my letter 9th Feb. Deeply regret that owing further developments I must withhold copyright permissions quotations volume five. Letter follows. Hankey.' That letter was dated the next day. Evidently the publisher, Collins, had waded in, doubtless at Roskill's urging. Now newspaper serial rights were also imperilled, a matter of vital concern as to material untouched since the death of Hankey's father. Even publishing extracts would endanger the book and the serial rights themselves, stated Hankey. 'I really have to choose between your great work on the British Navy and Roskill's life of my father, which is equally a history of an era. I had hoped to avoid this dilemma, but our publicists make it impossible. What else can I do?' 'I intensely dislike "tooing and froing" but I am afraid this has to be my last "fro". I have spent a bad night on it. I am going to have a bad conscience either way.'

'There really isn't much than I can say, is there?' Marder replied to the telegram and letter from Hankey, to which he added, 'I can appreciate the impossible position into which you have been placed by certain parties, and I guess that is that.' He explained how in the interim he already severely cut out Hankey diary entries from volume 5 and eliminated telltale source references or footnotes. Marder closed it all in generous fashion: 'I harbour no grudges or any sort of ill feeling, certainly not against yourself. Indeed, you have behaved like a gentleman throughout, not that I would have expected anything else. For my share of the anguish that you have suffered – I mean my share of the responsibility, excellent though my motives have been – I can only offer my profound regrets.'

Robin Hankey, terribly embarrassed, was full of regrets of his own. But he could do nothing. He was sorry 'things have worked out this way'. All direct quotations from his father's diaries would have to be eliminated from Marder's text. 'Please excuse me for having put my foot in it – but if I *have* even so been able to help a historian, I am very happy to have done so!'[17]

News of the fight reached Gretton, who wrote Marder to the effect that he was not surprised to hear that he was having trouble with Roskill. Gretton was certain of Roskill's key role in the mess surrounding the Navy Records Society's publication of the 'Harper Narrative'. Against this background, the difficulty with the Hankey diaries was true to form. 'The trouble with him [Roskill] is that he now knows that he is the only chap fit to entrust any naval history to, and he obstructs everybody else like mad. I have a tremendous regard for his works and always praise them enthusiastically both in reviews and in conversations, but his self role as doyen and controller of all naval historians is irritating to put it mildly. I too find him most helpful sometimes but impossible at others. I suspect that if he fails to stop one doing a job and one shows determination to plug on, then he gives in and becomes his natural helpful self.'[18]

Many months passed, communications between Marder and Roskill frozen. Marder's volume 4 came into print, and he had his publisher send Roskill – and anyone else who had helped with the book – a presentation copy. Roskill's first volume of *Hankey* was now at press, and Roskill was pleased to tell Marder of progress.

Roskill should have stopped there. He should not have hinted that Marder could now use material as pre-digested by Roskill:

> As I now know where I stand with regard to my Hankey biography I can make you a suggestion to enable you to use in your final volume the quotations you wanted to use from the first Lord Hankey's diary without infringing the agreement I made with the present Lord Hankey. My Hankey biography will definitely be published in two volumes, the first of which is now in page proof. It will be published next spring, and *The Times* has bought the serial rights to it. If you like I will send you an uncorrected page proof, and you can then extract what you want from it if, as I assume to be the case, your final volume will not come out till later in the year. The references should, of course, be to my biography, which will be called *Hankey, Man of Secrets*, not *Man of a Million Secrets*, as in the page proof (Collins, 1970). Perhaps you will let me know if you would like to do this.

Marder, then in Oxford, received this letter in a state of complete amazement. Was it an olive branch strangely offered? He could not believe his eyes. He scratched a large exclamation mark and double vertical lines adjacent to Roskill's handwritten closure 'Yours sincerely' and then wrote this telling comment on the bottom of the letter:

> The bloody bahstud offers me as a great favour what I always claimed as a right!!!
> *Note* that I gave him every assurance that Vol. V would be published after his Hankey, I . . . Obviously, he suffers (and rightly) from a bad conscience![19]

Roskill had the Hankey Papers locked away at Churchill College after he was finished with them. The single volume on Hankey became two, then three, the last published in 1974. Young researchers such as Nicholas d'Ombrain, then completing a DPhil thesis for Oxford, were refused access to the Hankey papers at Churchill. Thus, when d'Ombrain came to finish his work, he had to rely, strangely, on Marder's guidance with respect to what Hankey had been engaged in. The diaries were out of bounds. His *War Machinery and High Policy: Defence Administration in Peacetime Britain 1902–1914* (Oxford, 1973) was a fine book which would have been much better with the insider, Hankey's, revelations. Hankey was, after all, 'the man of secrets'.

Marder dropped all direct references to Hankey diaries in volume 5 of *From the Dreadnought to Scapa Flow*. However, in the bibliography contained in that same volume, he included an entry on the Hankey MSS. With an asterisk he noted, as he did with other similar collections, that these manuscripts were among the documents not available in time to be of use to him or were still restricted. ('I include these references for completeness sake.') He stated that the Hankey Papers might be made available in Churchill College when the authorized biographer, Roskill, was finished with them. 'I was privileged to examine only the diaries of 1917–18.' Marder's same bibliography showed the Keyes Papers, also at Churchill College, to be open, which they were. As to Roskill's papers about Jutland – that is, those lent to Marder and returned – they were listed as 'important unpublished papers and correspondence on Jutland and miscellaneous correspondence and papers on the war'.

Marder's trail of documents leaves no doubt but that Roskill deflected his intention. Roskill's pressure on Robin Hankey, even to the point of refusing to continue with the biography if Marder used previously approved long extracts from the Hankey diaries, determined the nature of the final text of the fourth and fifth volumes of *From Dreadnought to Scapa Flow*. 'Even when I reduced the quoted matter to 25 words, Roskill was adamant, and poor Hankey, terribly embarrassed, cd. do nothing . . . I suppose the uproar may be helping us to sell a few books, but I'm not too happy with the whole business & only wish Roskill wd. go away and bother somebody else!'[20]

By the time Marder's volume 5 appeared, in late 1970, Roskill's *Naval Policy between the Wars, Volume I* had been in print for two years. Marder had consulted it from time to time and found it quixotic yet invaluable; thus this bibliographical annotation (vol. 5, page 393): 'Badly organized and something of a jungle of facts in places, yet an indispensable work for its extensive use of British and American source material and its shrewd judgements. The Armistice period is dealt with in the first seven chapters, *passim*.' Marder meant nothing malicious but with brutal frankness he had made his assessment.

Roskill, unable to leave this alone, took offence. A third party (likely Sir Basil Liddell Hart, who was helping Roskill with his Hankey book at that time) let slip the details of Roskill's displeasure to a columnist at *The Times*. The whole – this 'national chatter' – was covered in *The Times* Diary for 23 June 1971. It makes engaging reading. It is the first public disclosure about the rivalry between the two naval historians – though it did not reveal that the cause of the unpleasantness was the matter of rights to Hankey's famous diary:

'Salty Plows': It seems our ancient universities are indulging in a little gamesmanship in honouring the practitioners in the field of British naval history whom each of them have patronized. Today Oxford confers the honorary degree of Doctor of Letters on Professor Arthur Marder of California University. The same degree (though in his case not an honorary one) was conferred on Captain Stephen Roskill, a fellow of Churchill College, by Cambridge some six months ago.

Roskill was made a C.B.E. in the last New Year Honours List, and the award of an honorary C.B.E. to Marder was recently announced. Last year, when Marder was Eastman Professor at Oxford, the British Academy elected him a fellow. I understand that Roskill's name will now go before the Academy's Council at its next meeting. That will bring the score back to deuce.

Roskill has published many warm tributes to Marder's work, notably in this column last August. It does not appear that Marder reciprocates, however. The only reference which Roskill knows Marder has made to any of his books is the description of his *Naval Policy between the Wars* as 'badly organized' which appears in the bibliography of the final volume of Marder's *From the Dreadnought to Scapa Flow*. 'Perhaps,' says Roskill, 'I could have got it better organized had I spent less time reading, checking and criticising all Marder's typescripts and corresponding with him.' Vantage Roskill.

In the immediate aftermath of the flare-up, correspondence between the two men was always civil if cool. Marder continued to send Roskill documents at the latter's request, but he no longer pestered Roskill to review his texts. This had a twofold benefit for Roskill: it relieved him of an obligation that he had grown tired of, and it eliminated the possibility that his reviews of Marder's future works would be compromised by his comments on the same works in manuscript form. As for Marder, he told Peter Gretton that he and Roskill had suffered a permanent split – 'on his initiative'. 'My conscience is clear. It is, I confess, a relief to know that I'll not be lectured to by him, school-boy style, in future. But this is *entre nous*.'

Roskill makes hardly a mention of Marder's books in his *Naval Policy between the Wars* and in the three volumes of *Hankey*. He meant to distance himself from Marder. Each continued to cite and footnote the other's published work, but no longer would the fisticuffs show up in footnotes or bibliographical annotations. The battle would now be joined in the *Times Literary Supplement* and, even more significantly, in the main bodies of Roskill's and Marder's books. The lightning rods were Winston Churchill's role in the naval war of 1939–45, Admiral Sir Dudley Pound's role in relation to Churchill, and collateral material used by Marder in his study of the Royal Navy's attack on the French Navy in the unhappy affair at Oran. These books became the parade ground for the next phase of the battle: Marder's *From the Dardanelles to Oran* (1974), Roskill's *Churchill and the Admirals* (1977), and Marder's *Old Friends, New Enemies* (1980), where he had the last word about Churchill, Pound, and the Far East tragedy of the *Prince of Wales* and *Repulse*.

The naval world took notice of these bouts, and in certain circles mirth and smiles were evident. Connoisseurs of scholarly disputation looked forward to new developments. Peacemakers made futile attempts. Newspapers followed the growing division, checking their authorities against lines they would print. Hyperbole was not part of the equation to these third parties. Historical controversy was strangely welcome, and there were other combatants besides Marder and Roskill. Two historians of the Tudor era, Jack Hexter and Geoffrey Elton, entered the lists of a protracted quarrel. Hugh Trevor-Roper (later Lord Dacre) found himself in trouble with Africanists when he pronounced that, before European colonization, Africa had no history. A.J.P. Taylor was steadily in the news, especially when he pronounced that the outbreak of the Second World War was if by accident, and he and Trevor-Roper did battle about that.

As for Marder and Roskill, the cause of the bother – the fight for a few though precious excerpts of the Hankey diaries – resulted in what Marder called 'a first class row with Roskill.' It was all in the correspondence, safe from wider viewing at the time. Marder kept it secret, away from the public eye. 'Someday I want to show you some correspondence that you simply won't believe,' Marder confided to Gretton. That correspondence, now disclosed, does seem hard to believe. But it puts paid to the argument made by some that this was a petty spat, not worthy of attention in the historical literature – much spilt ink. It tells not only of the rivalry but of Marder's views of Roskill, and Roskill's of Marder. Deep down it was an unpleasant picture. Roskill had been brutal in his assault on Marder, impugning his motives and his honesty. Marder challenged his rival's charges and would not stand down from a fight. He had had his share of battles with censors, as had Roskill. He could never understand if Roskill's comments on his Jutland manuscript were intended to be helpful or merely a means of slowing him down. Privately, to Gretton, he reserved his sharpest words about Roskill: 'He is one of the most helpful people I know & at the same time one of the most, no, THE MOST, trying person I've ever known.' That was on 3 February 1969, at the height of the crisis. Another letter to Gretton of 11 February bared all: 'He [Roskill] has been abusive & irrational, to put it *mildly*: *hubris* personified.'[21]

Chapter 8

Historians at War: Quarrels over Churchill and Admirals

A SHADOW had been cast on the future when, in 1969, Roskill blocked Marder's use of a snippet of Lord Hankey's diary for the concluding volume of *From the Dreadnought to Scapa Flow*. Marder felt the consequent hurt deeply. Yet it is worth remembering that this, though the primary issue, was not the only cause of the dispute and discord between the two men. The Hankey matter would have been sufficient in itself to cause the deep divide. But added to it was Roskill's simultaneous and unwelcome call that Marder halt his *From the Dreadnought to Scapa Flow* at 1918 rather than 1919 (a design to keep Marder out of the interwar period).

What gave the contest notoriety in the first instance had been Roskill's statement, as quoted in *The Times* on the eve of Marder's being honoured with a DLitt by Oxford University, wherein he complained of labours expended on Marder's behalf at the expense of his own progress.[1] Literary sleuths took note. Roskill's extraordinary remarks surprised many; that Roskill was less than enamoured with Marder's achievement now received additional notice in the *Times Higher Educational Supplement*.[2]

Marder kept silent for the moment. In fact, he told a correspondent, A.B. Sainsbury, a trustee of the *Naval Review*, that it was 'very stupid of the *Times Higher Educational Supplement* . . . to try to build up a professional vendetta.' Connoisseurs of scholarly disputation began to sit up and pay attention: they did not have to wait long for the next instalment. Roskill got the first, unwelcome, indication of Marder's advance into the interwar period when, to his surprise, the *American Historical Review* published, in June 1970, Marder's study of the Royal Navy and the Ethiopian or Abyssinian crisis. For his account of this episode – in which the Navy had counselled no action on grounds of imperial overstretch and growing demands east of Suez – Marder had used many sources for the first time, including recollections of admirals.

But Roskill was unimpressed. The article was an intrusion, Roskill wrote in 1975 in his 2,500 word synopsis 'Marder v Roskill', for Marder must have known that Roskill would cover the same subject in his history of *Naval Policy between the Wars*. 'However I made no protest about that as many years had elapsed and it could well be that he had genuinely forgotten the agreement made between us.' Further: 'I did not put anything in writing about this as it was a "gentlemen's agreement" such as with normal people it is quite unnecessary to put in writing.'[3]

In fact, Marder had begun his foray into what Roskill had regarded as his turf in the 1960s, when he began considering Winston Churchill's tenure as first lord, from 1939 to 1940, and Pound's as first sea lord, from 1940 to 1943. This move, strangely enough, brought Roskill back to the fight with Churchill over various contentious episodes in the maritime war. Here was ample space for opposing sides to be drawn by the duelling historians, with a goodly amount of documentation, some of it new and revelatory, to be examined in order to frame respective historical arguments. What was new to say? Nearly three decades after the events, some of the counsellors of Churchill and those who were at the Admiralty with Pound were still alive; their views could be solicited. Not least in importance, public demand remained hot for new appreciations of how the war at sea had been conducted. It had been a time of setbacks for the Royal Navy – the U-boat sinking of the battleship *Royal Oak* in Scapa Flow, the faltering and eventually failed campaign in Norwegian waters, and continuing successful U-boat attacks on merchant shipping. There were many other events and many other catastrophes. Readers yearned to know how Marder, the supreme historian of the Royal Navy of the First World War, differed from Roskill, the 'official historian' of the same navy during the Second World War.

We can date Marder's return to Churchill as a historical subject to early 1965, in the aftermath of Churchill's funeral. More than twelve years before, Marder's initial publication on Churchill as first lord of the Admiralty from 1911 to 1915, a 1953 article,[4] had given a praiseworthy view of the young, innovative, energetic, and reforming statesman with an old-styled cavalryman's zest for offensive action. Author and subject had much in common. Marder's stunningly sensational initial volume of *From the Dreadnought to Scapa Flow* had placed Churchill alongside Jacky Fisher as a saving guardian of Britannia's power in critical years. Now, with Fisher's legacy having been enshrined in the fifth and final volume, Marder was understandably curious about what Churchill did upon his return to the Admiralty in 1939. He was keen to know, as he told Basil Liddell Hart in 1968, about Churchill's 'naval strategic ideas, relations with the Navy, and, above all, his *influence* on specific events and operations and strategy.'[5]

Any study of Churchill as first lord of the Admiralty in 1939–40 necessarily had to include discussion of his professional naval counterpart, Pound. A torpedo and electrical specialist who had commanded a dreadnought at Jutland, Pound was one of the progressive forces that energized staff and planning development at the Admiralty between the wars, the sort of thing Herbert Richmond had thought so lacking in the First World War. He had gone on to be commander-in-chief, Mediterranean, before being called home to be first sea lord in June 1939. The deaths of many suitable candidates for that post left Pound as the only obvious choice, states one historian of the Admiralty, Nicholas Rodger. That same authority wryly observes, however, that 'Pound was the embodiment of exactly those faults which had been so disastrous in the earlier war.'[6] Besides lacking a sense of humour, Pound – so goes the conventional view (and one shared by Roskill) – was narrow in outlook and an obsessive centralizer. He liked to drive rather than lead. During his tenure, the Admiralty staff, seeming on the defensive, was exposed to Churchill's onslaughts. Certainly, Pound bore a double burden, being not only first sea lord but also chief of the naval staff. In addition, he was chairman of the chiefs of staff committee until Churchill eased him out of this position, bringing in General Sir Alan Brooke (later Field Marshal Lord Alanbrooke) to succeed him in March 1942. By 1943, it is said, Pound was overstretched and ill – hobbled by osteoarthritis and deafness – but he bore his difficulties and his duties with courage, forbearance, and silence.

Marder's perspective was different. He took the view that Pound showed no sign of physical deterioration before his fatal brain tumour was diagnosed in 1943 – a position sustained by Robin Brodhurst in his biography of Pound, *Churchill's Anchor*. Marder's research – and deriving theme – produced adequate documentation to show that the first sea lord won many contests against Churchill's overbearing and nudging propensities, except in the *Prince of Wales* and *Repulse* and PQ.17 disasters, where political requirements superseded strategic realities. To be sure, Marder's evidence did not include that which Roskill unearthed. Before Pound's fatal brain tumour was diagnosed in 1943, a Royal Navy officer noticed with horror that Pound had become a worn-out old man. At a naval staff meeting, another officer observed Pound drooling down the stem of his pipe, and 'out for the count'. Then there was evidence from a naval surgeon to the effect that there were early signs, even before he became first sea lord, that Pound was unsuitable for the post. But Marder learned from Admiral Sir Bruce Fraser, Vice Admiral Sir Ronald Brockman, and Lieutenant General Sir Ian Jacob, military assistant secretary to the War Cabinet, who attended the meetings of the chiefs of staff and of the Combined Chiefs of Staff Committee, and many others that somnolence, real or apparent, did not affect Pound's effectiveness. It is beyond dispute that, in addition to his many troubles, Pound had to contend with Winston's habits. As Robin Brodhurst has written: 'Dudley Pound had to fight Hitler by day and Churchill by night.' The point at issue was whether or not he fought that fight well or, overwhelmed by infirmity, simply succumbed.

In the course of his research, Marder's admiration for the admiral grew; and in the back of his mind was the concept that here was a way of showing that Churchill was not solely at fault for the Navy's misfortunes, and that the Admiralty, and Pound, must bear their share of responsibility. His friend Kemp, then Admiralty archivist and head of the Naval Historical Branch, was already on to this theme, and, as previously noted, in his *Victory at Sea*, published with the knowledge and acceptance of the Admiralty, he had gone so far as to say as much in regards to PQ.17 – a rare public admission of responsibility by an Admiralty officer.[7]

For Roskill, by contrast, the subject of Winston Churchill at the Admiralty was always a source of *admiration* (in small portion) mixed with *irritation* (in large measure): *admiration* at the immense and beneficial influence that Churchill had played in the Second World War effort, and *irritation* at Churchill's several attempts against him to keep inviolate his own history of the war. As we have seen, the Cabinet Office papers on *The War at Sea* show Churchill repeatedly quarrelling with Roskill's historical judgements. Roskill's recollection of his fight with Churchill and his minders (two historians, Alex Danchev and Daniel Todman, call these aides 'the velvet throttle') continued to rankle.[8] Hard-fought battles over the first and second volumes of *The War at Sea*, especially over the Norwegian campaign and the disastrously managed PQ.17, had spread later into a dispute with Mountbatten, Churchill's specially nominated supreme commander for South East Asia, about the extent of Mountbatten's powers to sack British service heads under his command. Roskill had scores to settle. Time and circumstance favoured him, and an opportunity now strangely offered itself to set the record straight about Churchill.

Roskill, like Marder, was on the trail of Churchill. When Roskill became naval writer of the *Sunday Telegraph* in 1961, the editor, Donald McLachlan, was keen to see the 'official historian' turned journalist-historian tackle any subject suitable for a feature article on the naval history of the Second World War. But here we take a useful diversion. McLachlan, historian himself, was one of the brilliant band of outsiders brought into the Naval Intelligence Division at the Admiralty by Rear Admiral John H. Godfrey in 1939. When

Roskill joined the *Sunday Telegraph* team, McLachlan was researching that hitherto closed historical subject — closed in the sense not only of legal constraints but also of honour in not revealing the secret — the use of Ultra in the Battle of the Atlantic. Although McLachlan's *Room 39: Naval Intelligence in Action, 1939–1945* did not appear until 1968 and did not infringe the Official Secrets Act, it is clear that he was keen on, as W.J.R. Gardner puts it, 'driving a substantial dog-cart if not a coach and horses through the wall of silence.'[9] (Even so, not until 1974 did historians refer overtly to the Ultra factor; in that year F.W. Winterbotham's *The Ultra Secret*, though based on slim research, opened the gates to the historical study of Ultra.) McLachlan's career as historian, so promisingly opened with his book on naval intelligence — a subject that he knew first hand — was cut short when, in Scotland, the automobile he was driving smashed into a tree. At the time, he was working on a biography of Pound. His widow, Kitty, advised by a friend in Oxford of Marder's growing interest in Churchill and Pound, subsequently lent Marder his research notes and papers.

Let us now return to Roskill's side of the story. As editor of the *Sunday Telegraph*, McLachlan was an appreciative accomplice for Roskill. Given such freedom and with such an accommodating editor, we might imagine that Roskill would be free of the Cabinet Office's shackles and legal constraints. But this was far from the case, for the intervening power of the state did not confine itself to 'official history' — all of British publishing was subject to the Official Secrets Act. As to subjects, Churchill was a natural first choice: Roskill turned to it with alacrity.

In late 1961, when the last volume of *The War at Sea* was at press, Roskill sent Sir Norman Brook, the cabinet secretary, a request that nowadays seems to indicate that the politics of official history had reached merely another stage, though one less urgently controlled than Butler's Official War Histories as managed by the Cabinet Office. Roskill, now on his own as a private researcher, and without Butler's shock-absorber role, had to deal directly with Brook. We are reminded of Brook's all-seeing and all-knowing manner and his smooth handling of historians in the face of Churchill's attempted meddling in how they saw and wrote history. Roskill knew all about this from the outset of his work on *The War at Sea*. Accordingly, he approached this new round of arrangements with Brook and the Cabinet Office with justifiable caution. The Official Secrets Act had to be observed. He dare not rush into print with a story for the *Sunday Telegraph* without the necessary clearance, mindful as he was that not only was he in the public eye as an 'official historian' but his own credibility as a historian would be up for examination. Now that he was poaching on his own game as 'official historian', he would have to tread carefully.

On 12 December, Roskill sent Brook typescripts of two intended articles for the *Sunday Telegraph*. These, he wrote by way of introduction, were 'designed to amplify matters' discussed in *The War at Sea* but not given full space there. One bore the title 'Churchill and the Admirals', the other 'Sir Dudley Pound, a Balanced View'. Roskill explained to Brook that he did not think either intended article infringed the form he had signed in connection with the Official Secrets Act, but he added: 'It is obviously true that I could not have written them had I not been an official historian.' He thought the Admiralty might also need to see them. 'I hope there will be no objection to publication as they are, I think, historically speaking, quite important.' He asked that the copies be returned in due course.

Brook took Roskill's texts to the country for reading over Christmas. He knew of the battle waged eight years previous between Churchill and Roskill. He must also have thought back to the recent furore over Lord Alanbrooke's frank, even shocking, war diaries, with all their revealing comments on Churchill as published in Arthur Bryant's *The Turn of the Tide* (1957) and *Triumph in the West* (1959). Defenders of the prime minister were resolute in defence of their chief, unforgiving in their attack on Bryant and Alanbrooke. With all this no doubt in mind, Brook studied Roskill's texts carefully.

On New Year's Day, back in the Cabinet Office, Brook had copies made of Roskill's texts and sent these to Sir Clifford Jarrett, secretary of the Admiralty. He pointed out in a covering letter that he, Brook, could have no objection though he wished the articles would not be published while Churchill remained alive. Further, and this was a novel consideration on Brook's part, he wondered about the propriety of Roskill drawing for his own purposes on knowledge gained while working as a historian of one of the Official War Histories under the auspices of the Cabinet Office. This was so close to home as to be discomfiting if not alarming. Jarrett had similar thoughts. That same day, Brook composed a file memo, 'Note for Record', one he shared with Jarrett. It is an epitome of Brook's views on the subject, and tells us a good deal about the 'velvet throttle'. There could be no objection to publication of Roskill's 'Churchill and the Admirals' articles. The first was a little biased against Churchill, especially regarding the 'prodding' communications that Churchill sent to admirals at sea, but Brook was prepared to set that aside:

> As I have said elsewhere, this was an essential aspect of Churchill's personal control of the Government machine: it was not, as some of the

war historians have seemed to suggest, directed particularly at the Service Commanders: it was applied throughout the whole field of wartime Administration and was exercised just as much against Ministers and civilians as it was against the Services. It was natural that Churchill should have felt that it was necessary for him, when he succeeded Chamberlain, to show that there was a firm hand on the wheel; and if the country at large responded to it so well, it seems unreasonable that the Admirals (and the Generals) should have resented this personal *leadership* so much. If I were Roskill, I would not publish this article while Churchill is still living.

Brook took issue with minor matters addressed by Roskill. He thought discussion of 'the Prof', Frederick Lindemann (Lord Cherwell), and his new, sometimes ill-conceived instruments of war ought to be treated over the period of the whole war.[10] As to Roskill's main arguments, Brook believed that discussion of Admiral Pound and the PQ.17 'convoy is to scatter' mess and also the loss of the *Prince of Wales* and *Repulse* offered nothing new beyond what Roskill had written in *The War at Sea* – another way of saying that no official secrets had been breached. The text on Admiral Pound similarly received the green light. Jarrett had raised no objection, and Roskill's articles were cleared for publication.

Not long after Brook eased the passage of Roskill's texts, the articles appeared in the *Sunday Telegraph*: 'Churchill and His Admirals' on 11 February and that on Pound on 18 February 1962. Such hard-hitting pieces, relatively untouched by editorial control, were bound to draw fire. Take this opening salvo from a distressed reader with a filial connection to a distinguished and much lamented admiral: 'I cannot let your article . . . go by without severely criticising your comments. I have always had the greatest respect for your Naval Histories and, since your accounts will go down to posterity, it grieves me considerably to read your views you have expressed on my Father, [Admiral Sir] Tom Phillips [commander-in-chief, Force Z, who died when his flagship, the *Prince of Wales*, out of reach of air cover, was sunk by Japanese Navy land-based bombers and torpedo aircraft off the coast of Malaya].' So wrote Commander T.V.C. Phillips, RN, serving at Supreme Headquarters Allied Powers in Europe (SHAPE), Paris.

'It is all too easy', the son continued, 'to twist opinions to fit in with events, or to be wise after the events, or to judge matters with the knowledge and views of a decade later. I have never before had to defend my Father as his contemporaries have done that with greater ability than mine, but, as time goes on, fewer are left to keep events in this true perspective. History is so often misjudged by those that follow writing erroneous accounts.' Commander Phillips particularly condemned Roskill's paragraph on his father 'erring in his judgement' as to warships working in waters where the enemy held undisputed command of the air. This implied that the father did not hold this view but felt that 'given sufficient resolution on the part of sea officers the air threat could be overcome.' This was not a true statement of the father's position, said the son. He cited two earlier cases – the bombing of the *Empress of Britain* (later sunk by a U-boat when being towed) and the loss of the *Southampton* to air attack – and these were evidence enough to the father that ships could no longer go about their business in that area with the impunity of the opening phases of the war.

Commander Phillips made reasoned points:

> Any officer holding the position of my Father during the first two years of the war, and being involved in the conduct of operations during the Norwegian campaign, could not but be made fully aware of the air threat. That the sequence of naval events at Singapore went the way it did, was not through the lack of appreciation by the Admiral afloat of the effect of air attack but through our forces being extended to the full, so leaving the air defences in the Singapore area lamentably weak with little or no air cover available to carry out innumerable tasks. The events that stopped an aircraft carrier accompanying the capital ships made the movement of these two ships to the Far East an even greater game of bluff.

He closed his letter to Roskill: 'I do not know how your series in the *Sunday Telegraph* will continue or whether you will refer again to my Father, but I hope that, should you do so, your remarks will be more just and more in keeping with your previous books which have given you international fame as a historian.'

With characteristic directness bordering on the abrasive, Roskill replied. It was common for sons and relatives of distinguished officers, he said, 'to rush to the defence of their forebears if any criticism is made of them,' something perfectly understandable so long as they were well informed. Roskill had defended Admiral Phillips on several issues over which contemporaries were severely critical – but that was another matter, he explained. As regards the father's attitude to defence of ships against air attacks, Roskill pointed out that, from personal experience, he was well placed to comment, for he was in A-A gunnery and radar in the Gunnery Division of the Naval Staff from May 1939 until September 1941. Admiral Sir Charles Forbes, commander-in-chief,

Home Fleet, had difficulty with Phillips in the inshore Norwegian campaign. Admirals Sir William Davis and Sir Ralph Edwards, who had read the draft of the article in question, agreed that it was fair. The 'new era of naval warfare' that the son had mentioned had begun in home waters in April 1940, when Admiral Forbes represented that operations such as the bombardment of Stavanger by the *Suffolk* were bound to end disastrously. Yet he was ordered to carry it out.

Roskill stood his ground:

> By the time your Father got to Singapore I am sure he was fully alive to the realities of the air threat – as I made clear in my history. But there are none the less in the 1st Sea Lord's papers some letters from Flag Officers representing that a command such as he was given should have gone to someone who had obtained first-hand experience of conditions at sea during the war. I discounted such opinions, largely because there may have been ulterior motives behind them. What I cannot ignore is that in 1940 he did undoubtedly underestimate the air threat, and overestimate the ability of ships to defend themselves – and Churchill attached great weight to his views, even when they were unsupported by the Naval Staff. Therein may lie the origin of such signals as that telling [Andrew] Cunningham at the time of the battle of Crete that 'risks must be accepted'.

Roskill had defended his turf. He closed his letter with regret that he had wounded the son's susceptibilities, adding, 'I can cite well-considered opinion, as well as my own experience, in support of what I wrote.'

Commander Phillips ended the correspondence in diplomatic fashion, stating that he had underestimated Roskill's attempts at unbiased effort. He also replied to Roskill's request for any evidence of a rift existing between Churchill and his father. 'On the contrary, to my knowledge, the close bond formed by my Father serving Churchill, which developed into a friendship, remained until the end . . . I assume that this idea of a rift was also conjured up for ulterior motives, in order to belittle my Father and to explain how he was given the Far East Command.'[11]

From his 'Churchill and the Admirals' series Roskill moved to other naval topics, some of which were simmering powder kegs and potentially explosive. One of these, of persistent interest, was the loss of the carrier *Glorious* and two escorting destroyers, *Ardent* and *Acasta*, to the *Scharnhorst* and *Gneisenau*. The details may be briefly stated.

On 6 June 1940 Allied governments, realizing the impossibility of continuing the campaign in Norway without adequate air cover against the audacity and speed of the Wehrmacht, backed by the Luftwaffe, determined on withdrawal from Narvik. The Norwegian king, Haakon VII, and his ministers, going into exile, were given passage from Tromso in the cruiser *Devonshire*, destination British soil. British naval units were then strangely scattered in disposition, with the carriers *Glorious* and *Ark Royal* supplying sea-based cover for withdrawal. RAF fighters that had been operating in northern Norway needed to be transported home. The *Glorious*, jammed with evacuated RAF Gladiators and Hurricanes, was fatefully detached with two destroyers as escorts to proceed independently to Scapa Flow. The official line was that she sailed early on grounds of having low fuel levels. (Churchill, acting on the advice of Captain Gordon Allen, his naval adviser for his *Second World War*, would not swallow this line of reasoning: 'This explanation is not convincing,' wrote Churchill in *The Gathering Storm*. 'The *Glorious* had enough fuel to steam at the speed of the convoy. All should have kept together.') Her captain, Guy D'Oyly-Hughes, a submarine specialist, at odds with the officer responsible for air operations, Commander J.B. Heath, had previously landed him at Scapa Flow under a dark cloud to await an official inquiry. D'Oyly-Hughes may have been in a hurry to return to Scapa to settle the matter. In any event, he had no reconnaissance aircraft up; Gladiators were available at ten minutes' notice. Visibility was extreme that day, 8 June, when the *Glorious* was taken by surprise by the *Scharnhorst* and *Gneisenau* then working their way north to attack shipping and bases near Narvik. *Scharnhorst* opened fire at 27,800 yards. All three British warships were sunk, with the loss of 1,474 officers and men, plus 41 airmen, including all but two of the RAF fighter pilots — a calamitous end to an ill-conceived campaign that lacked adequate air protection for the fleet and the expeditionary forces.

In *The War at Sea*, Roskill had expressed his astonishment that the *Glorious*, with sufficient Swordfish aircraft to maintain reconnaissance flights and to form a small striking force should the need arise, had no air cover on the fateful day. 'What is certain is that she was caught not only unawares but virtually defenceless when, at 4 pm, the German battle-cruisers sighted her smoke.' Heath, retired in Somerset, made no response to the official history; he was to play a later role. But Roskill received a resentful letter from the widow, Mrs D'Oyly-Hughes, and later a 'savagely angry' letter from Guy D'Oyly-Hughes's brother. Historian John Winton, a former naval officer, has explained how Roskill met the brother's criticism through a third party (Roskill could not reply himself since doing so would have breached the Official Secrets Act, involving as it did the evidence in the Board of Inquiry's findings, jealously guarded by the Admiralty).

In London in 1963 Roskill chanced upon Mrs Hope Slessor, whose late husband, lost in the *Glorious*, had served with him in the carrier *Eagle* on the China station. She told Roskill that his *War at Sea* was wrong as to the *Glorious*, and through her a communication was opened with Heath, who had kept his own documentary evidence. Roskill, digging further, concluded on the basis of various new papers and interviews that his previous treatment of Captain Guy D'Oyly-Hughes had been far too generous.

Roskill's indictment, necessarily delayed, appearing first in *Churchill and the Admirals* (1977). There he wrote: 'The story of fuel shortage is false. Not only had she replenished at Scapa before sailing for the last time, but the Captain of the destroyer *Diana* took in a long visual signal made by the *Glorious* to the *Ark Royal* asking permission to proceed to Scapa "in order to expedite Courts-Martial".' Roskill gave early warning that he intended a fuller account (but that would have to wait until the widow had died). Roskill's first salvo came in the *Sunday Times* on 15 June 1980, under the heading 'The Cantankerous Captain of HMS *Glorious*'. Roskill appeared in the guise of prosecuting attorney against the naval commanders and those at the Admiralty who had directed the war at sea. 'The Admiralty has tried to suppress the truth for years,' charged Roskill. He thereby opened a subject that would eventually place the Naval Historical Branch, and its historian David Brown, in the hot seat as they stoutly defended the official position that the *Glorious* was returning home because of low fuel reserves. Now it was time for the next generation to defend Captain D'Oyly-Hughes, and his elder daughter, Bridget, Mrs Michael Riviere, replied with a letter to the editor of the *Sunday Times* in which she described Roskill's article as 'an unpleasant personal attack in the guise of naval history.' This brave defence enraged Roskill and he framed a stoutly worded letter that the editor chose not to print (it survives in Roskill's files). So influential on historical grounds was Roskill's case – now made, it will be observed, when he was free of 'official history' duties and had much more documentary evidence at his disposal – that it was taken up first by John Winton and then by Tim Slessor, whose father, as mentioned, had been lost in that incident. Slessor produced a video production on this tragedy and an article that became central to his book *Ministries of Deception*, about cover-ups in Whitehall of certain ill-starred military episodes of the war. The scent on the trail had been laid by Roskill, Slessor states clearly, and Correlli Barnett would mine the Roskill treasures to good effect in *Engage the Enemy More Closely*, pointing the way for future research.[12]

At the same time that Roskill launched his career as a newspaper features writer, Marder was only just completing his second volume of *From the*

HISTORIANS AT WAR: QUARRELS OVER CHURCHILL AND ADMIRALS

Dreadnought to Scapa Flow, from 1914 to the eve of Jutland. But in 1965 he was already turning to some sort of a study about Churchill – the 'W.C. Project' he liked to call it. His correspondence with various admirals and retired civil servants makes clear that he was groping for a book on the theme. His discussions with historians, notably Taylor, Basil Liddell Hart, and Martin Gilbert (all were then working on Churchill books, chapters, or articles), further fuelled his interest and confirmed his predisposition to do a work on Churchill. The fruits of his correspondence gave added certainty as well as uniqueness to the project. There are hints of the work being a naval biography, a study of Churchill as first sea lord or even a work entitled 'Churchill as Naval Lord in 1939–45'. Marder kept the theme close to his chest: he gave nothing away in his correspondence or discussions until he was sure of his ground and direction.

Already the Churchillian field seemed crowded, for not only was Roskill writing his newspaper accounts but Marder's friend Peter Gretton had just issued *Former Naval Person: Winston Churchill and the Royal Navy* (1959). Noted American writer Trumbull Higgins produced an incisive *Winston Churchill and the Dardanelles: A Dialogue in Ends and Means* (1963) and other works that were not carping or hostile to Churchill but showed him as chief architect of mistaken strategies or ill-advised campaigns.[13] Then in his last years, Churchill had clearly become a fruitful subject for historical inquiry, and his death (on 24 January 1965) signalled that it was now time for post-mortems. Churchill's physician, Lord Moran, produced a disparaging account in 1966. This brought a sharp response from 'The Secret Circle'. Brook, Sir Ian Jacob, Jock Colville, and Sir Leslie Rowan (all then in correspondence with Marder about how Winston waged war) gave appreciations in Sir John Wheeler-Bennett's *Action This Day: Working with Churchill* (1969). Such guarded accounts by private secretaries, military secretaries, and prime ministerial aides about their days working with Churchill likewise had become part of the wider account of how the war was waged and won. Taylor was already writing book reviews about Churchill as 'Former Great Person' and was embarking on books about war lords with retrospective glances at Churchill. What was there left to say on the naval side?

Against such a crowded field Marder had to focus on what he knew best – and that was the dynamics of British sea power – that is, who directed the use of naval power and how was it employed (and with what results). Marder drew up two lists of questions for correspondents. The first of these was designed to get surviving admirals' views on other commanders who held prominent positions during the Second World War. The second was of more elastic character and related to decision making and operational effectiveness in campaigns, Norway at the top of the list and of persistent public interest. Over many months and under cover of carefully constructed letters of introduction and inquiry, he sent questionnaires to about two dozen former senior officers or widows or other family members of the same. The various replies not only became the historical essence of Marder's 1972 article 'Winston Is Back' but also had extended value for his subsequent monographic studies and led naturally, in later years, to his study of the tragedy of the *Prince of Wales* and *Repulse* as told in *Old Friends, New Enemies*. Because he had worked so assiduously over the tempestuous relationship of those two titans at the Admiralty, Churchill and Fisher, and the resulting Dardanelles campaign, which led to Fisher's resignation and Churchill's forced exit as first lord, he wanted to explore the possibilities of the relationship of Churchill and Pound. This seemed as natural as it was inviting, for the first phase of the war at sea – Roskill called it the defensive phase – was marked by various tragedies, misadventures, and mistakes. Who was responsible, Marder wanted to know? And who should shoulder the main blame – Churchill or Pound, or both? Scapegoats abounded. But could the truth be unravelled?

Marder was in the minority in believing that Churchill imposed his will on generals and chiefs of staff only rarely. Taylor held a similar view, which further alienated him from those who wanted to see in Churchill the cause of military misfortunes. In their eyes, Churchill directed the course of the war, and did much of the directing. Churchill once said – and Taylor found this a most delightful and characteristic remark – 'All I asked was compliance with my wishes after reasonable discussion.'[14] Churchill was inexhaustible: he wore people down, and, as old Jacky Fisher had complained, he could not out-argue Churchill. Pound had to contend with the same, only this time Churchill was more careful and on surer ground. Dreading prevarication in both military and political spheres, he regarded offensive operations as central to the waging of war. As he told Pound in December 1939: 'An absolute defensive is for weaker forces . . . I could never be responsible for a naval strategy which excluded the offensive principle.' He hated paralysis; accordingly, Alan Brooke had much reason to complain in September 1942: 'It is a regular disease that he suffers from, this frightful impatience to get an attack [in this case, North Africa] launched.' As Martin Gilbert puts it, Churchill wanted to 'drive forward the whole machinery of war-making.'[15]

Still alive to help Marder were retired senior naval officers ('the "semi-extinct volcanoes" . . . the senior officers RN of a bygone era', he fondly called them).[16] He needed to see them in person, and, from an initial encounter, letters and documents would flow his way. Like an anthropologist among survivors of the recent naval past, Marder set to work with zeal though still uncertain of the final result. His immense reputation within the higher echelon of retired naval officers facilitating his passage and inquiries, he extended his search to present and past members of the civil service, principally in the Ministry of Defence (Navy) and the Cabinet Office. Only on rare occasion, for reasons of not wanting to 'go public', would Marder receive a letter of regret. In certain cases, a respondent might report being bound by the Official Secrets Act. Some who declined the opportunity stated that they had thought about writing such a book themselves, but, with so much already published on Churchill, they had stood down. But these persons were few in number. The openness with which recipients replied is testament to Marder's reputation, admittedly, but expresses much more: many wanted their accounts included in the historical record, others the record to be corrected, and still others, in the naval instance, to show a bravado that a retired admiral might well display in a ward room at a reunion. Naval officers had stories to tell; Marder liked to listen but preferred by far the written word, new evidence upon which to frame his historical argument.

Marder first explored possibilities with Creswell, his devoted research associate who had toiled unreservedly and with no thought of recompense on *From the Dreadnought to Scapa Flow*. Creswell offered Marder a pair of stories about his time serving at the Admiralty early in the war, both under the heading 'Master of Negation':

> Act I. In 1940–41 when Winston got bored with the obstructions of those old fogies the Chiefs of Staff (in his view) he used to ask the Directors of Plans – Charles Daniel, [Ian] Playfair (I think) and Jack Slessor – to stay a night at Chequers, hoping to suborn them from their true allegiance. After the third glass of vintage port he would say: 'Good port this. We'll make a first-rate plan on this.' Charles was a connoisseur of port and thoroughly enjoyed the entertainment; but he always kept his head.

> Act II. Dickie Mountbatten had been installed as Chief of Combined Operations and Charles Daniel was his chief naval assistant. Again the same scene is Chequers, where Dickie had been dining. After dinner Winston was looking through an evening paper in which there was a photograph of Dickie and some of his staff attending the first night of a film. Winston looked at this and, pointing, said: 'Who's that? That's so & so, he's my top airman.' And then, pointing to a man almost with his back to the camera,

Winston: Who's that? That's Daniel.
Dickie: Yes, he's my top sailor.
Winston: Why in the world have you taken him on? A master of negation. He would never let me do what I wanted.[17]

Marder's files are thick with this sort of anecdotal evidence, which was tempting for a historian to use to effect but which he largely declined. Other chief correspondents had more weighty evidence for him. In response to a steady flow of urgent queries, Admiral Sir William James, age eighty-four, living in distant Fife, pecked out replies to Marder on a ramshackle typewriter. James, commander-in-chief at Portsmouth in 1939–44 and chief of naval information, never failed Marder as a correspondent and was himself a prominent biographer and historian.[18]

James's letter is a precis of Churchill's actions and innovations on the naval front. These include: 1) a project not in the war plan of gaining mastery of the Baltic so as to free Scandinavia from the menace of invasion and to influence Russian policy and strategy; 2) a proposal to convert older battleships for service in narrow waters by giving them large anti-torpedo bulges, stronger armour decks, and many anti-aircraft guns; 3) a scheme to lay minefields in Norwegian waters in order to compel German ships to leave territorial waters and lay themselves open to attack; 4) a plan for mining the Rhine with fluvial mines; 5) a project for a mine barrage in waters of the North Sea; 6) an inquiry into the welfare of personnel and, as 'an important adjunct of naval life at Scapa', the fitting out of a theatre and cinema on ships; and 7), a scheme to board the *Altmark* and release British prisoners. (Of the above, 1 through 3 were set aside, 4 and 5 were partially implemented, and 6 and 7 were implemented.)

'It was the same Churchill who had been 1st Lord in the 1914–1918 war,' James informed Marder. 'He had a remarkable grasp of sea warfare and always seemed to see a little farther ahead than his professional advisors.' James noted Andrew Cunningham's assessment that Churchill had a striking flair for grand strategy, that he could see the shape of things to come, but that he became restless during the long periods of preparation for the major operations and gave a willing ear to projects which on close examination would be wasteful of men and materiel and not advance chances of winning the war. It was in character, said James, for Churchill to listen to Admiral of the Fleet Sir Roger Keyes, a man after his heart, a man who always wanted to be doing something somewhere. Strangely, however, Churchill did not realize, as the Navy did, that Keyes's obsession was 'seeking reputation in the cannon's mouth', that throughout his career he had been frustrated of winning fame, that he had never been in command of a fleet in combat, and that this was now his last chance.

Keyes stayed at Portsmouth with James early in the war, when the Germans invaded Norway. At that point, Keyes took an early train to London to ask Churchill to give him command of some ships to attack Trondheim. 'It was a mad-cap idea,' James told Marder: 'Churchill had already put an Admiral of the Fleet in command of the Narvik operations [Earl of Cork and Orrery] and if Keyes had got his way there would have been two Admirals of the Fleet commanding small squadrons in the Commander in Chief Home Fleet's command. A truly Gilbertian situation!!' Fortunately, the Naval Staff dissuaded Churchill from giving Keyes this command, said James. He also thought that Churchill made a terrible mistake in placing Keyes in charge of Combined Operations. A commanding officer of one of the commando establishments once told James that it was no use old Keyes coming to inspect them and talking about the Zeebrugge raid of 1918, which they all knew had been a failure: what they wanted was to hear the experiences of an officer who had up-to-date knowledge of amphibious operations. Keyes even got up schemes such as a landing on the Brest peninsula, another hare-brained project, said James, calculated 'to blood the commandos'. Then there was the wildcat scheme (said Andrew Cunningham), Pantellaria, which had forces landing on an island in the Mediterranean extremely close to Italy; the location lacked its own water supply. Churchill fought hard for the operation, but it was squelched.[19] In James's view, it was Churchill's great loyalty to old friends and his eager desire to do something somewhere that led him to listen to Keyes and these impetuous schemes. (Marder, not to be misled by James, demonstrated how little Churchill responded to urgings from the gallant Keyes, who lacked any sense of modesty; in fact, Churchill squashed outright the admiral's proposal for a Norwegian attack.)

James described how Churchill had to be pressed to give support to motor torpedo boats (MTBs), their building, manning, and basing. Churchill had not thought much about their need. James informed him that maritime war always ended in narrow waters – this would be the time when MTBs would seal the victory. Churchill then quickly warmed to the idea, and before long funding was given to a new base, HMS *Hornet*, at Gosport, where officers and ratings trained for the armada of coastal craft required before the war was over.[20]

Marder had asked for Churchill anecdotes. James supplied two. Churchill visited Portsmouth on various occasions, always leaving the naval officers and men all the better for his visits. His vigour was remarkable. On one occasion, he went round the bombed areas in Southampton, then moved on to

Portsmouth, where he wore out his hosts stumping round the dockyard, and ended up at the civic centre to give everyone a talk. 'He got back to Admiralty House at about 4 o'clock and when my wife asked him if he would like a cup of tea he replied after a moment's thought "No, not tea. My doctor has ordered me to have nothing non-alcoholic between breakfast and dinner."' On another occasion, Churchill retired for a spell after lunch and lay down in bed; 'it was this that enabled him to keep such long hours of intense work.' James continued: 'He always had his cigar and rather typically gave one to a dockyard employee who accosted him when we were walking round. But, as I said earlier, my main recollection of his visits is that he left us all feeling a little braver and a little more sure of final victory.'

Other informants told Marder the same: in Britain's darkest hour the light of Churchill shone forth; his urgings were necessary and beneficial. But, as to the naval and military issues of 1939 and 1940, many tales of muddling through came to Marder. Captain John Litchfield, MP, RN (retired), at that time writing his own naval history, advised:

> I hope you will let me see your paper on Winston & Norway when it is finished, as this was one of the most curious & controversial episodes of the war. I still believe that although the COS [chiefs of staff] made a fearful mess of it, they were pushed & prodded into unsound decisions by Churchill: I myself joined the Joint Planning Staff just as it was beginning, & believe me, it was like entering Bedlam: nobody seemed to know who was running the show or what was going to happen next as orders, counter-orders & counter-counter-orders chased each other at high level, & Roger Keyes & Co whispered ideas in Winston's ear! It really was an example of how NOT to run a shop.[21]

Marder toiled away at finishing *From the Dreadnought to Scapa Flow*. Meanwhile, his 'W.C. Project' files bulged with new evidence gathered from admirals who had fought the Second World War ashore and afloat. Correspondence with naval widows – Marder's 'special breed of cat', who tirelessly networked the immediate naval past of their own lives – unearthed many nuggets. Six years of accumulating evidence about Churchill at the Admiralty in the Second World War began paying historical dividends. But the project suffered growing pains. Marder's self-inflicted problem was what to do with the tottering piles of evidence. A timely invitation from the editors of the *English Historical Review* (*EHR*), Professors J. Michael Wallace-Hadrill and J.M. Roberts, solved the problem. Would he write an article on the subject or an aspect of it? Not setting aside a larger project, and once free of *From the Dreadnought to Scapa Flow*, Marder joyfully set about the more confined task. Divide and rule was a good maxim to follow, he knew, and he was mindful of what Professor Langer had told him ever so long ago, his terrible tendency to be prolix.

News of Marder's research on Churchill at the Admiralty in 1939-40 reached Sir Eric Seal via his brother-in-law, Noel Atherton, who had prepared Marder's charts and maps for the quintuplet. Although the importunate Marder had solicited abundant, substantial responses from various admirals and Admiralty secretaries, something quite out of the blue arrived, dated 29 July 1971, when Seal's first letter was delivered to Marder. Seal had served in the Admiralty before the war and was principal private secretary to the first lord of the Admiralty from late 1939 until 1941.[22] 'As such, I was of course in his [Churchill's] complete confidence, until in May 1941 I left for America as Deputy Secretary [of the Admiralty] (North America) in the Admiralty Delegation.' Seal was then writing an account of his own experiences with Churchill which he wanted to see in print; in fact, he offered to send Marder a copy if the latter were interested. Then Seal got to his second point, for he, like Brook, knew of the inside politics of Roskill's *The War at Sea*, having read and commented on it for Churchill before it was released, reluctantly, for publication. He let Marder in on the secret: 'I think I should warn you that Roskill in his "official history" was badly wrong in some of the statements he made about Churchill's interventions in naval affairs in the Norway campaign. The last thing I did for Churchill, when he was Prime Minister for the second time, was to analyse all this. (I was then of course no longer his Private Secretary, but the Deputy Secretary of the Ministry of Works.) Winston was most careful in the second war to leave professional matters to the sailors.'

Marder, sensing a bonanza, shot off a reply by return post to Seal. Could he have more details about Roskill's history? Meantime, as one writer to another, Marder would gladly look at Seal's memoir and would give what comments he could. Thus, Seal's text arrived in California where it was read over the Labour Day weekend. Marder gave its author extensive comments, especially about its publication prospects, which, being more of a personal memoir, he thought slim. He suggested it might be divided, one part being the Churchill story, the other, the career in military and government service. Marder warned that publishers had become particularly hard-headed about autobiographical material. Seal, disregarding Marder's advice, sent his text to Oxford University Press, which declined it. An introduction from Marder did not guarantee any sort of success with OUP, as two other writers, John Litchfield and Donald Schurman, would also learn.

Marder also told Seal of his faltering progress on his study of Churchill. He explained that he was at his wit's end, as he put it, trying to scale his 'WC' piece down to a typescript of acceptable length for the *English Historical Review*. He was struggling with two alternatives, neither pleasing, he said: treating the whole story of Churchill at the Admiralty by thinning the various segments, or singling out for adequate treatment what he considered to be the most important facet of Winston's tenure – his strategic ideas and influence on naval operations – with Norway as the centrepiece. He was hoping that a letter from the editor at the *English Historical Review* would bring helpful advice as to length. Meantime, would Seal give him his comments? Seal replied agreeably (24 August 1971) and offered as much help as he could: 'May I say that I think that I am almost the sole survivor of those who were close to Winston as First Lord senior enough to know what it was all about, and I feel a corresponding responsibility.'

Seal recounted how Churchill had become disturbed by Roskill's *The War at Sea*, 'which enlarged upon the undoubted fact that the Admiralty had intervened seriously in naval operations in the early days and suggested, quite falsely, that the prime factor in this was Churchill's influence as First Lord.' According to Seal, acts of interference from Whitehall were not Churchill's work but the spontaneous action of the naval staff and in particular Dudley Pound and the then vice chief of naval staff, Tom Phillips, 'who certainly had good justification'. Captain (later Admiral Sir) Ralph Edwards, who had been the deputy in the Operations Division in 1940, had confirmed Seal's view on this; thus, Edwards's diary became especially significant evidence to Marder (and to Roskill). 'The plain fact of the matter', reported Seal to Marder, 'was that Dudley Pound, who had recently been C in C Med found it very difficult to keep his hands off the control of the fleet, and he certainly had more and better information. But much suspicion attached to Winston, partly as an echo of the Dardanelles, and partly because it was generally known that he was always in the War Room, to which he was irresistibly attracted. Being aware of the Dardanelles legend, I was very alert to the problem. I am quite satisfied that Winston took scrupulous care not to transgress the proper limits of Naval and Political responsibility, and not to force his view on any professional decision.'

Marder's subsequent text shows Seal's influence on nearly every page, and the essential argument became the leitmotif of the work. Perhaps Marder had developed this already, for Seal's letters, coming late in the game as it were, are more like icing on the cake. (This icing, we note below, was poisonous to Roskill.) Seal had a good sense of history and had recently been reading about Churchill and Fisher at the Admiralty in the events leading to the Dardanelles disaster. He held the opinion that Fisher showed an old man's tendency to change his mind and to concentrate on the facet of the problem uppermost in his imagination. Churchill did not necessarily mislead Fisher, Seal contended, but his relations with the service chiefs were very unusual – 'He was a War man,' Fisher was wont to say. Added to this, Seal reminded Marder, was the fact that Churchill was a most unusual character, and certainly no conventional politician.

Seal had no intention of shaping Marder's research and said so; he knew that Marder had made a thorough study of the matter. But he was keen to make one point clear:

> Forgive me if I say that for me the main interest of the Norwegian period is that it covers an important phase of Winston's development and emergence. There were in fact practically no naval events of consequence. The simple fact is that the enemy by a superior lack of scruple got over their handicap of naval weakness by surprise and initiative; and got there first. The subsequent efforts to dislodge them reflect credit on no one, and the really fascinating fact is that Winston, despite the handicap of his prominent part in this sorry story, was recognized by his Parliamentary colleagues as the man [to lead the government], and rose almost despite himself to power as P.M. There are of course interesting naval sidelines, but they are sidelines, and there is no Jutland story lurking beneath the surface . . . I quite agree with your view that after Winston became P.M. the complexities are immense, and the naval story cannot really be divorced from Dudley Pound, Andrew Cunningham, and I must add [US Admiral] Ernie King!

Seal's correspondence with Marder also opened doors of memory. Seal scurried back to his own files. First he re-read Roskill's account of the Norwegian campaign as found in *The War at Sea*, with particular notice of the proposed attack on Trondheim, Operation Hammer. Then he examined his own papers to find if there was any variance of facts with Roskill: none could be found. What Seal objected to (letter of 8 September 1971) were Roskill's judgements: 'His comments are . . . wide of the mark, and create an unfavourable impression on my mind when it comes to an assessment of Churchill's part . . . It is perfectly true that he spent a good deal of time in the War Room, which had a tremendous fascination for him. To infer from this that he assumed control is, in the circumstances, almost malicious. It is certainly utterly unwarranted, and false.'

Seal warmed to his task. For Marder he recalled Churchill's instructions to go to the Historical Section of the Admiralty and track down any incriminating messages from him if indeed they were to be found:

> I made a careful search of all the signals sent by the Admiralty between the 7th and 19th April [1940], and there were only two with characteristic marks of Churchill's phraseology, which I may say I am pretty competent to detect! One is an appeal for fuller current information, which was I think dictated in the First Sea Lord's presence, but which was sent off from my office as a personal message, and the other is referred to by Roskill on page 186, who clearly did not recognise the First Lord's hand. It is an appeal to the C.-in-C. to reconsider [his strong objections to] the proposed attack on Trondheim, which contains the characteristic Churchillism 'Pray therefore consider this important project further.' Roskill omits the underlined words, without realizing that Pound would never have used this phrase, although his Secretary actually sent the message off.

In the event, Seal had reported to Churchill in carefully chosen, soothing words: 'It might be thought that Captain Roskill himself fails to produce evidence adequate to support the conclusion at which he rather more than hints, namely that the First Sea Lord intended throughout to avoid any interference with Commanders afloat and that you overbore him. I am sure that no one serving in the Admiralty would have supposed that was the relationship between you. There is not the slightest evidence that any operational message issued by the Admiralty did not have the full concurrence of the responsible chiefs of the Naval Staff.'

To Marder, Seal's letters were manna from heaven. Not that he wanted to spike Roskill, for malicious intent was quite beyond him: he wanted to set the record straight, even if it meant correcting *The War at Sea*. Marder now had all he needed.[23]

Meanwhile, the editors of the *English Historical Review*, sensing that Marder's words were golden treasures from the attics of history, and realizing that he was uncomfortable with an article of the customary length, offered to accept the piece as a supplement to the *EHR* of nearly four times the customary length, at, say 20,000 or 30,000 words. Marder, unshackled, took up the offer.[24]

In June 1972 the fruits of Marder's labour, based on such fresh evidence, appeared as a sixty-page supplement, number 5, of the *English Historical Review*. Marder chose for his title '"Winston Is Back": Churchill at the

HISTORIANS AT WAR: QUARRELS OVER CHURCHILL AND ADMIRALS

Admiralty, 1939–40', the first three words being the signal from the Admiralty to the fleet on the evening of 3 September 1939, when Churchill, having accepted the prime minister's invitation to become First Lord of the Admiralty, sat once more in the room in which he had set in motion, a quarter of a century earlier, the first naval stages of the previous war with Germany. (The signal was flashed to the fleet but the hard copy has never been found, much to the annoyance of some historians.) 'Winston Is Back' was subsequently published separately by Longman at what some considered the outrageous price of £1.25. 'When the author is that illuminating American Professor Arthur Marder and his subject is Churchill's return to the Admiralty in 1939, tuppence a page is not excessive.' So wrote Kenneth Rose in his 'Albany at Large' column in the *Sunday Telegraph*, 21 May 1972. Soon thereafter *Navy News* (July 1972) trumpeted: 'Read this account and shudder. The factual account of Churchill's forays into professional realms, and the general muddle of the early war months, requires the reader to remind himself constantly of Winston's morale-building influence, lest the conclusions become distorted.'

Of the many historical jewels Marder brought forward – and we trace the main points below in contrast to Roskill's contrary positions – one of the most illuminating is the following snippet. Marder had dispelled the myth that Churchill overruled his professional advisers as first lord, yet, paradoxically, he also brought up contradictory evidence: for instance, how unfairly he treated Captain A.G. Talbot, the director of anti-submarine warfare. Churchill kept claiming that the Navy had sunk large numbers of U-boats. Talbot, however, in keeping with his department's practice that U-boat 'kills' must be demonstrably proved, insisted on a more modest estimate – and one confirmed by post-war research. On 25 April, Churchill ended a brisk minute on the subject: 'The conclusion to which this officer comes is that all the attacks, except the actual 15 of which we have remnants, have failed. This conclusion leads me to think that it might be a good thing if Captain Talbot went to sea as soon as possible.' It was not in fact until they had another blazing row in September that Churchill, by then prime minister and minister of defence, had Talbot removed at ten minutes' notice. Talbot's successor, Captain (later Admiral of the Fleet Sir) George Creasy, felt that Talbot had been badly treated: 'It was Winston in one of his naughtiest moods.' In late years, Creasy had described the atmosphere in the Admiralty at that time as 'a sea of flame'. His memory might have failed him, and that Marder knew; and, as for Talbot, his sudden sacking did not, happily, affect his career and he ended the war as a much decorated vice admiral. But the event shows the sharp instincts of Churchill that sometimes bordered on the cruel.

'War was his element and Power his objective,' wrote his parliamentary associate Robert Boothby, who had his own axe to grind (for Churchill had not given him preferment in his administration even though he'd been a strong supporter through the 1930s): 'In my heart I hated both. I could never take the streak of cruelty in his nature.'[25] Boothby expressed surprise that Marder, so good on the First World War, had got the Second so wrong. 'He has written that Churchill never interfered with his admirals. The exact opposite is true. He never stopped.'

Those waiting for Marder's reaction to Roskill had no reason for disappointment. His words were oblique but telling. He quoted Roskill's endorsement of the widely held view that Churchill interfered excessively in naval operations in 1939–1940: 'Mr Churchill used, during critical periods of naval operations, to spend long hours in the Admiralty Operational Intelligence Centre and the tendency for him to assume direct control there from is easily to be understood.' Having reviewed the evidence upon which this charge had been based, Marder quoted Seal: 'It is perfectly true that he spent a good deal of time in the War Room . . . to infer from this that he assumed control is, in the circumstances, almost malicious. It is certainly utterly unwarranted, and false.' Seal's refutation of Roskill was given in detail, either in text or notes. Marder concluded: 'Comment would be superfluous.'

'A salty rejoinder is no doubt already being concocted,' said the *Times Higher Educational Supplement* with true foresight. Roskill read Marder's account and became distressed, not least because Seal's investigation in the Admiralty files, at Churchill's request, had exposed a story still kept secret in the Cabinet Papers about the official military histories. This rankled. There were many other historical issues that Roskill needed to address, notably his view of Churchill's overbearing actions and Pound's compliance and weakness, and in his view Marder should not be allowed to go unanswered. But what alarmed Roskill most was Marder's printing of the Seal letter to Marder. This accused Roskill of, among other things, 'near malice' towards Churchill, as Roskill put it. Roskill consulted his solicitor, who remarked that the charge was unquestionably libellous.[26] Roskill had no desire to engage in litigation against Marder. Setting all else aside, he prepared a lengthy and, in his view, reasoned rebuttal to Marder's attack and sent it to the editor of the *English Historical Review*, anticipating the courtesy of acceptance. The decision was not to publish it. Roskill thought this denial of right of reply unique and ethically indefensible. Accordingly, he turned to a friendlier periodical, the *RUSI Journal*. Roskill's reply to Marder appeared in the December 1972 issue as an extended review of 'Winston Is Back', under the heading 'Marder, Churchill and the Admiralty'.[27]

Roskill began his rejoinder with a complaint about how Marder had used his sources. He thought some informants of dubious value, especially those offering evidence dating to years after the event. He then objected to the fact that Marder had not come to him for sources – he thought it discourteous (the public did not know then about the fight over the Hankey diaries, which explains why Marder did not inquire of Roskill this time round). Roskill argued that Churchill meddled in naval matters, that Pound gave way, that Pound interfered unnecessarily with commanders afloat, and, generally, that the Marder view ought to be closely questioned. He closed with the statement that the time had not come for 'reworking' the 'official' naval history of the war. He went further: he implied that what Marder had done was to confirm the view that premature ventures into the subjects covered in his, Roskill's, work ought not to be taken without more thorough research. In fact, Roskill disputed the value of Marder's witnesses, particularly that of Seal. He thought Seal not a reliable source inasmuch as so much had transpired between Seal's investigation on Churchill's behalf into Roskill's account of the Norway campaign and Marder's revisiting of the same topic. Doubtless, Roskill was seeking to protect himself at Marder's expense. Another arrow had been drawn from the quiver.

'I have read Captain Roskill's broadside in your December issue,' Marder wrote to Kemp, who wore another hat as a past editor of the *RUSI Journal*. 'It is about what I expected: interesting, provocative, in places amusing, but telling me more about Roskill than about Winston as First Sea Lord in 1939–40.'[28] To Roskill, Marder wrote on 16 August 1972: 'I did not consult you because it would have involved sending you parts or all of the paper. Given your churlish remarks in June 1971 (as reported in *The Times* of I believe 21st June, or was it the 23rd?), I had no desire to impose on you again, for so you made it seem. It is, I must tell you, the less attractive side of a scholar who, *generally*, is as gracious and helpful as anyone could want.'[29]

In the circumstances, Marder had formed a clear opinion of his opposite. Roskill, he knew, could debate the issues as well as any. He could dig in his heels. What Marder objected to was Roskill's self-styled arrogance. Roskill's attacks in the *RUSI Journal* confirmed this trait, as did subsequent relentless comments by him on seemingly everything Marder wrote about Churchill, Pound, and North. Marder thus had grounds to give Roskill this nickname (as stated privately to Peter Kemp at the time of Roskill's reply to 'Winston Is Back'): Sir Oracle.

Marder's public response came in 1974, when his collation of recent articles and a new piece on Oran appeared in print as *From the Dardanelles to Oran:*

Studies of the Royal Navy in War and Peace, 1915–1940 (Oxford University Press). 'Winston Is Back', now enlarged and partially changed to meet Roskill's criticism, gave no ground when it came to essentials. In fact, Marder found Roskill's fiat that it was too soon to revisit the material covered in *The War at Sea* of provocative, even amusing, value. He drew the reader's attention to it. In a long appendix – 'Musings on a Bolt from Olympus'[30] – to the new 'Winston Is Back', Marder defended Churchill's eight months at the Admiralty as in the main 'extremely beneficial'. He explained further the Churchill-Pound relationship, using evidence gathered from four members of Pound's wartime personal staff still living:

> I would not describe any of these officers as uncritical admirers of Pound. All four categorically deny the truth of Roskill's charge as it applies to their period of service with Pound. The picture that emerges from my correspondence with them is of a very tough officer to whom no one could dictate, least of all, Churchill. He had, as I have pointed out, the common sense to know that a frontal collision would only increase Churchill's obstinacy, so that when one of Churchill's 'prayers' arrived, suggesting some operation, possibly but by no means always tactically advisable, and almost always practically impossible from sheer lack of available means, Pound would have the operation ... 'appreciated', the forces necessary assessed, the scale of expected losses added, and finally showing where the forces would have to come from and what their removal would mean. 'Thus', as Admiral [James Ashley] Waller [naval assistant to Pound in 1941–42] sums up the matter, 'Churchill was brought to a point of saying (nearly), "Who thought up this damn-fool project, anyway?" and it was then dead as a dodo.'

Marder's riposte did not stop with his answers to Roskill, framed as they were on the basis of documentary evidence, some of it new (from Jacob, four admirals, and Kemp). In a grand concluding epilogue, reminiscent of his conclusion to *From the Dreadnought to Scapa Flow*, he made two larger points that he felt had escaped historians of the war. These, he said, put Churchill's role and methods in proper historical perspective.

The first, briefly stated, was that the Navy was not an expensive toy placed at the disposal of admirals in wartime; rather, it was an instrument of national policy. Pound was one of the few senior admirals who realized that the doctrine 'if only the damned politicians would leave us alone to fight our war, we'd be much better off' would not answer. Churchill had a clear idea of what the Navy could do, and his prodding ways, though perhaps overdone, were better than leaving the Navy to do it themselves. ('And I am inclined to think that the Navy needed it.')

The second, arising from the first, was that Churchill, as well as being an astute politician, was a historian of considerable merit. 'It could not have escaped him that throughout English naval history, when the admirals had been left to their own devices, they had made a mess of things, and that it was only when there had been strong political direction at the top, as in the Seven Years War and the Napoleonic War, that the Navy had really achieved the full measure of its capability.' Thus, when Churchill became prime minister, he retained the main direction of war as minister of defence. Marder credited the political control as exercised by Churchill for the fact that the British made fewer blunders during the Second World War than in most wars of the past. He closed his rejoinder to Roskill by quoting Roskill himself: 'Rereading today what I wrote on Churchill, Pound and this matter I see no cause to revise any of it.' Marder was toying with Roskill, taunting him.

Paul Halpern, the naval historian, in a mammoth critique of Marder's book in *Reviews in European History*, September 1976, observed that 'the battle lines are clearly drawn. The final word on the subject has certainly not been said and probably never will.' Halpern was not sure that, given the personality of Churchill, Marder had the advantageous position, 'or that his chapter will stand the test of time as well as the remainder of the book. On the other hand, the debate itself is a fascinating one, and it will be very interesting to see how the subject will be treated in the far distant day when Martin Gilbert's biography of Churchill, with its massive companion volumes, reaches 1940.' In fact, Gilbert's biography took the Marder line; as Gilbert wrote to Marder, his work owed much to the guidance of the American historian.[31] Another historian, Paul Addison, in his review, expressed no quarrel with Marder's surprising conclusion that Churchill did not dominate his professional advisers. 'We are left to think over the conclusion that Churchill's capacity to infuse a new climate of morale into the administration, and inspire others, was his greatest gift . . . Yet Churchill's gift had a dangerous aspect. In a sense Professor Marder's hero in the Admiralty is Pound: that rock of independent judgement, immune to all Churchill's emotional warfare.'[32] Marder had tipped the scale in favour of the professionals. By this time, too, Marder was being read by the professionals: Admiral Sir Terence Lewin, then commander-in-chief, Naval Home Command, cited Marder at length in a lecture at the Royal United Services Institution: 'We must learn the lesson of history lest in our own age we are militarily – and as a consequence politically – powerless to prevent a similar example of aggression or interference backed by the growing Soviet maritime strength.'[33]

Those following the gathering storm since the eve of Marder's Oxford honorary degree, when Roskill made his unappreciative, and some thought unwarranted, comments, waited and watched for the next blast. Meanwhile, Marder had finished yet another book, this one *Operation 'Menace': The Dakar Expedition and the Dudley North Affair* (1976). In theory, the Dakar expedition of 3 July 1940 seemed sound enough. General Charles de Gaulle, newly arrived in London to raise the standard of Free France, could be landed at the Senegal port with a small force. The transporting and covering of the force would be, in the main, a British commitment. Once placed ashore, the force would raise the flag. The locals would rally round the new but relatively unknown leader. A new anchor of a non-Vichy France could be established. Any move by Hitler or Pétain in West Africa would be forestalled. So far so good. The unravelling tragedy had comic beginnings. De Gaulle showed up at Simpson's Piccadilly to be kitted out in tropical dress, explaining in a booming voice that his destination was West Africa. Nearby, in Jermyn Street, Free French officers filled the restaurant Ecu de France with stirring toasts of 'A Dakar!' At Euston Station a case of leaflets addressed 'Aux habitants de Dakar' broke open and scattered in the breeze. Incredibly, neither Vichy nor the enemy got wind of the operation. Independent of these comic turns in Piccadilly and Euston, the Vichy government had decided to send three cruisers and three destroyers from Toulon to Dakar. The British consul in Tangier and the British naval attaché in Madrid learned of the Vichy squadron and independently passed secret messages to London that the French warships would pass through the Gibraltar Straits on 11 September. But the messages sat in an in-tray, and, by the time the Admiralty was alert to proceedings, the French ships were through the straits in broad daylight and facing clear, unobstructed sailing ahead. When the Anglo-Free French force, with de Gaulle, his officers and men aboard, arrived off Dakar, a heavy fog lay off the coast. In a contest with guns ashore, the Royal Navy was on the receiving end of damage. After two days, in a brilliant sunshine, the force made its humiliating withdrawal.

As a military operation, Menace was undertaken at the insistence of Churchill, its enthusiastic chief sponsor, against all professional advice. 'Churchill was eager during July for a military adventure somewhere that might divert the Germans from the British Isles, enhance British prestige and raise morale at home.' It proved a tragic farce. In Marder's words, '"Menace" exemplifies . . . all that can go wrong in warfare: an operation fouled up by unforeseen contingencies, the accidents of war, and human error, and against a background of undue political interference, inadequate planning, and half-baked co-operation between Allies.' Marder's tale was a classic, tragic-comic illustration of the fog of war. On reading Marder, Professor Brian Bond was so struck by the many similarities between Dakar and the Dardanelles that it was tempting to blame the Service advisers of 1940 for neglecting the 'lessons of history'; Churchill had been the prime mover on both occasions, when political considerations overrode professional advice.[34] In fact, the Joint Planning Staff had told Churchill directly that an operation which relied on the cooperation of the enemy (Vichy France) did not provide a sound basis for planning.

Seldom do books of historical scholarship, written by academics, receive exalted acclaim. Yet such was the case with *Operation 'Menace'*. Reviewers such as Litchfield, Sainsbury, Taylor, and Ronald Lewin gave highest praise.[35] They (and others) spoke of the book as being the last word on the subject, the definitive treatment, but they were equally excited about the opening it gave to war, to quote Clausewitz, as the extension of politics by other means. Litchfield wrote, 'Marder, as ever, writes with real understanding of the Royal Navy, of whose ways and leading characters he has, in some miraculous way as an American acquired an extraordinarily accurate perception.' Sainsbury, with a keen eye on the Marder-Roskill dispute, took pains to set Marder's new appraisal against Roskill's 'official history'. Time and new evidence had deepened the story: 'Its construction is a microcosm of Marder's methodology. The diligent use of published sources, the hunting down and use of private papers and of individual recollections; the distillation of all this energetically accumulated evidence into a readable text, spiced with a mixture of some occasionally questionable and other more magisterial *obiter*.' Marder had not told much more than his confrère had done in *The War at Sea*, published in 1954. However, the scope of his treatment offered more promise: 'Hence, we are grateful for his expanded and racier account, with more detail than was available to or could be used by the official historian.' Taylor, comparing Marder's book to *The Guns of Dakar*, written by criminologist and historian John Williams and published concurrently, thought the latter slighter and less austere: 'It also fills Marder's one deficiency: a reluctance to look over "the other side of the hill" to discover what the enemy (in this case the Vichy French) were doing.' Lewin, comparing the same two books, set the tone of his review at the outset:

> Come home, Evelyn Waugh: all is forgiven. How often has it seemed that your brilliantly sardonic and deflationary novels merely present a minor truth about the British at war, whilst ignoring the main point. Your soldiers, hilarious boobies, rarely look like matching up to Alamein or Normandy. But now, on the unimpeachable evidence of these two

books, we discover that your picture in *Men at Arms* of Operation Menace (where you were among those present) is not just one of your idiosyncratic caricatures. As you sit with Voltaire, please accept this signal admitting that you told the truth, nothing but the truth, and a great deal less than the grotesque pathetic reality. After the fiasco, one of *Ark Royal*'s pilots, who had had a rough time, explained: 'Operation Menace' – I call it Operation Muddle!

It is said that at White's, Waugh's club, the story of the fiasco was regular repertoire, and true it is that a script writer had no need to embellish the details. They stood on their own. The particulars and anecdotes were not lost on Marder, who gave them extended life in brilliant description. He had no shortage of eyewitnesses. Though Waugh's *Men at Arms* had enshrined the story, Marder had written the true history.

Marder's book offered a cautionary tale for those tempted to believe that 'war is too serious a business to be left to the generals'. At the same time, the Dakar fiasco showed that war is too professional a business to be left to political strategists. But to this discussion was added a second part, Marder's treatment of the controversial Dudley North affair, which was indirectly connected with the events at Dakar. Marder's book thus offered two tickets of admission for the price of one, as John Terraine noted. Few incidents in the Second World War led to such accusations of injustice, which involved, besides North, Pound and, by implication, Churchill, then prime minister.

After five years in command of the Royal Yacht, North was appointed to Gibraltar as flag officer, North Atlantic. Pound had chosen him for the job, a safe hole and essentially an administrative position. With the fall of France, however, the appointment assumed greater importance. Twelve days before Operation Menace was put in motion, three Vichy French cruisers and three destroyers were allowed to pass through the Gibraltar Straits; North, who had unwisely expressed strong feelings about the Navy's recent attack on the French fleet at Oran, took no steps to intercept them, shadow them, or ascertain their destination. On Pound's advice, their lordships, having lost confidence in North, who failed 'in an emergency to take all prudent precautions without waiting for Admiralty instructions', relieved him of command. But the board went beyond that: it spelled out its reasons in terms that amounted to a charge of negligence. North demanded a court-martial to clear his name. Their lordships declined; North remained alive and proved litigious. Marder followed this saga through its seventeen-year history (eight successive first sea lords were burdened by it), which came to an end only with Prime Minister Harold

Macmillan's decision in 1957 to clear North's name without endorsing his actions. Four years later, North died.

Marder's revisiting of Roskill's treatment of the Dudley North affair enhanced an already public conflict between the two historians. Marder's interpretation – that Pound played the key role in North's downfall – is more convincing, for it rests upon North's limitations as an officer of flag rank and on Pound's own personality traits when confronted by what he viewed as incompetence. Both Marder and Roskill remained conscious that North received punishment far harsher than the rather foggy evidence of his supposed negligence could ever justify. Indeed, all parties involved – North, Admiral Sir James Somerville (commander-in-chief, Mediterranean), the Admiralty, Churchill, Pound, and even the Foreign Office (which neglected to decode promptly the original Tangier message) can all bear some measure of blame in this unfortunate but all too common wartime occurrence when the chains of command and responsibility are not clearly articulated.

Operation 'Menace' received critical acclaim in all prominent papers and journals save the *Sunday Telegraph*. There Roskill gave it only passing marks, finding Marder's detail excessive and his long footnotes – some covering half a page – distracting. Roskill also thought Marder guilty of some highly dubious statements about Sir Desmond Morton (the chief architect of the pre-war Industrial Intelligence Centre) and Admiral Pound. Only when Roskill came to the role of Churchill did he give praise: Marder 'does not pull his punches about Churchill's actions'. He and Marder seemed on common ground at last, with Churchill as the culprit.

But Roskill needed more space to deal with Marder's *Operation 'Menace'* and, for his purposes, he selected a different venue than the Sunday newspaper where he was a features writer. Thus it was that, when Peter Gretton's review appeared in the *Times Literary Supplement* of 20 February 1976, Roskill burst into its pages with his own critique. Gretton's review differed hardly at all from the other glowing appraisals of *Operation 'Menace'*. Accordingly, all we can conclude is that Roskill sensed that here was an opportunity to score points against Marder. With the *TLS* tolerating, even encouraging, disputation and literary rivalry, Roskill's strictures would have been warmly welcomed by the editor.

Roskill objected, in the first place, to Marder's characterization of Pound as furious with North and, secondly, to Marder's suggestion that the passage of the French squadron from Toulon through the Gibraltar Straits provided the needed catalyst for the superseding of North. If Marder had asked to see certain documents that Roskill had in his possession, stated the latter, he would have formed different (and correct) conclusions.

According to Roskill, Marder's verdict that North had failed in his duty was incorrect, for it did not take into account a certain message that North sent to the Admiralty on 11 September. Here was a naval defence of a victimized admiral.

At Oxford University Press, the publicist Elizabeth Knight read the Roskill attack with interest. She sent Marder a copy, adding in reference to Roskill, 'He can't keep out of it!'

Marder's retort now had a note of sarcasm, even cheekiness. He jested that not often was an author honoured by two reviews in the *TLS* – 'the second, in my case, in the form of a long and curious letter from S.W. Roskill (12 March).' He had no reason to change his view on North's being relieved of command: he cited a secretary's vivid recollection of Pound's reaction to North's letter. Pound was indeed 'hopping mad'. Roskill's inability to 'accept as adequate' Marder's statement that the passage of the French vessels was the catalytic agent suggested only that Roskill had not read his tenth chapter 'with care and an open mind. Let him try again.' Further: 'As for Roskill having shown me "[as Roskill said] all I have – as indeed I have done for his earlier works", I am mystified. The only papers he ever showed me were a valuable Jutland set, and that was a dozen years and five books ago. But I must apologize to him for not having made a more regular practice of asking "to see any relevant letters or papers" in his possession. It is very naughty of me. On the other hand, one very disagreeable experience, about which the less said the better, hardly encouraged me to seek material from the Captain for my later books.'

Now it was Roskill's turn. Inasmuch as Marder had made reference to 'the Jutland set' of documents and the disagreeable business of documents shared, it was time for Roskill to lay open the issues:

> When Arthur Marder writes (March 26) that the only papers I ever showed him were 'a valuable Jutland set . . . a dozen years and five books ago' his memory is extraordinarily abbreviated. My copies of Volumes 4 and 5 of his *From the Dreadnought to Scapa Flow* (1969 and 1972) are inscribed in his hand 'with very warm thanks' (adverb double underlined); I have in front of me a receipt signed by him 'with my sincere thanks' for copies of documents sent to him on June 11, 1973; and on his last visit to this college [Churchill] I put out for him the copy of Admiral Sir Ralph Edwards' diary covering the Norwegian campaign of 1940 (without request) in order to show him that the statement that I had quoted from it 'with extreme inaccuracy' (*Dardanelles to Oran*, page 171) was wholly unjustified. I have in fact over

the years put in more work for Professor Marder than for any of the scores of other historians who have come to me for help or advice, and the only thing I have ever refused him is permission to publish long extracts from the diary of the first Lord Hankey which I, who had been appointed his authorized biographer, was about to use in my *Hankey, Man of Secrets*, Volume 1 (1970). Presumably this is the 'very disagreeable experience' to which he refers. His very rude letters to me on that score certainly were disagreeable, and I expect my replies were equally so in his eyes. As I shall be dealing in full with the 'evidence' cited in Marder's last two books in a work called *Churchill and the Admirals* on which I am now engaged[,] I will take up no more of your space on that matter.

'I see that my good friend Stephen Roskill is at it again,' replied Marder in the *TLS* on 30 April. 'I didn't mean to draw blood, being a man of peace. Still, inaccuracies must not be left unanswered, must they?'

Item. The inscriptions in his copies of *Dreadnought to Scapa Flow*, volumes 4 and 5, were for his constructive reading of drafts of these works, and *not* for any materials loaned to me. There were none.

Item. He 'put out' for me a copy of the Edwards diary when I last visited Churchill College. I don't know what he is talking about. The only copy I ever saw and used was the one which is available to every qualified researcher.

Item. The 'long extracts' from the unpublished Hankey diaries which he would not permit me to use turn out to be – I have just checked the point – two quotations totalling *twenty-five words*. Yes, that's what it came down to! And innocuous words at that. The pettiness of the Captain's behaviour on that occasion, so uncharacteristic, was overwhelming.

Item. The intimation that, professionally, our relationship was a one-way street is as untrue as it is contemptible. This is not to deny the considerable help the one-time Official Naval Historian had given me on specific points (and in the case of the Jutland volume the loan of documents) in years gone by. Indeed, I know of no historian, living or dead, who, allowing for an occasional aberration, has been so generous with his time and papers to scholars young and old, British and foreign. If for this reason alone, and despite everything, I wish him well.

Some readers would have thought that the disputation had reached a frightful state of splitting hairs. Others sensed that further unpleasantness lay ahead; and they now knew, for the first time, about the battle that had raged over the use of twenty-five words from Lord Hankey's diary. But, on the broader front of how Churchill waged the war (and interfered, and to what degree) and how Pound had responded to his urgings (some excessive), there existed enough for several disputatious books. With neither contender willing to back down, the quarrel could hardly run to any final disposition. Those who followed the literary tangle knew that another chapter would surely come. They were right.

Some months before Collins published *Churchill and the Admirals*, Roskill wrote to Marder on various naval historical points (Marder had sent him some documents) and told him that he had finished with the book and sent it to his editor. 'As with everything I have ever done', he told the American, 'I dislike it intensely, but I feel that if I go on tinkering with it I shall never get it finished and shall probably deprive it of any merit which it may have.'[36] But at least it was finished; now the critics would decide. Roskill took no steps to tell his opposite that another ticking time bomb awaited him (just as the 'Bolt from Olympus' had startled Roskill). Now it would be tit for tat.

The appendix to *Churchill and the Admirals*, 'A Historical Controversy', in no respects brief at fifteen printed pages, extended and enhanced the Roskill line as first advanced in the *RUSI Journal* in answer to 'Winston Is Back'. It took up various issues in the *TLS* fight and brought in new evidence to counter Marder's positions.

Roskill thought memory a fickle jade. He defended himself as 'official historian' against Seal's visceral intrusions on behalf of Churchill. He did not think that Churchill was much different in the Second World War than in the First. Nor would he alter his opinion of Pound. True, a letter by Roskill to the *Daily Telegraph* about Pound (7 March 1970) had brought much conflicting evidence from officers who had been close to Pound in the Admiralty about his ailing disposition. Even so, wrote Roskill, 'for Marder to write that Pound showed no signs of physical deterioration before 1943 is nonsense.' And again, 'when Professor Marder pronounces on my opportunities for informing myself on the exchanges between Pound and Churchill I can only infer that he is speaking ex cathedra where appeals to reason or to evidence do not lie. But here we are concerned with history.'[37] Alanbrooke's diaries became powerful evidence in Roskill's hands.[38] Roskill laid on the detail about Pound's health and performance at the Admiralty, seeking to disparage Marder's evidence or to set it aside. It is a game that historians play, to their later regret, for one historian's trash may be another's treasure.

To summarize Roskill's assault, the following may be mentioned: 1) Roskill agreed with Marder that Pound was 'the supreme centralizer' ('I recall a late night meeting to which I was summoned to discuss the allocation of Lewis guns to small craft!'); 2) he agreed that Churchill 'never completely grasped the nature of maritime war'; and 3) he thought that Marder exaggerated the degree to which Pound handled Churchill: some naval disasters might have been averted had Pound stood up more resolutely. Doubtless, Churchill was difficult to deal with; at the same time, Pound's loyalty to Churchill was surely to be admired, even though taking upon himself responsibility for loss of the *Prince of Wales* and *Repulse* was overdone. 'But whilst one may respect his humility it is none the less possible to doubt whether he was a big enough man for the job.' Thus closed Roskill's appendix. Readers, though likely weary of the incessant jousting, must have felt a certain appreciation for Roskill's feisty reply. In an age when it was particularly fashionable to doubt the wisdom of superiors, Roskill's views would have had wide acceptance. Nonetheless, his attack on Marder was losing momentum and force.

Gretton, who had reviewed Marder's *Operation 'Menace'* in the *TLS*, now came to assess Roskill's *Churchill and the Admirals* in the same journal. In the issue of 25 November 1977, Gretton wrote that Roskill's evidence showed Churchill's lack of confidence in admirals and generals. 'Taken all in all, Churchill sways somewhat on his pedestal, but the book ends with a most eloquent quotation which leaves him standing firm as a rock.' As to the fracas with Marder, Gretton noted the details of the naval historians' war, above all the supposed new series of signals (unseen by Marder) between the commander of the Norwegian campaign, Cork and Orrery, and Churchill – what Roskill believed was his trump card. 'It would need a braver man than I to adjudicate', concluded Gretton, to which he added, 'But I will allow myself the opinion that it would have been better to reserve the attack on Marder, which is impressive, to some other form than this book. It is sad that our two greatest naval historians should indulge in such quarrels.'[39]

Marder was about to trip himself up. He read Gretton's review and impetuously, not having read *Churchill and the Admirals*, fired off a letter to the *TLS*. 'The good captain has been remiss in his homework. I refer to these signals [a 'Personal and Most Secret' series between the commander of the Norwegian campaign at Narvik, Cork and Orrery, and Churchill], quote from them, comment on their significance, and cite the PRO references to the lot: all on pages 164–5 of my *From the Dardanelles to Oran*.'

Roskill found himself presented with a rare opportunity to correct his opposite in public and the opportunity was not lost on him. He replied that Marder should have read his book before rushing into print with a comment about a 'trump card' having been produced by Roskill in the controversy. The 'trump card' had been produced by the reviewer, Gretton! 'It seems therefore that if there has been a failure to do the "homework" to which Marder refers it was not, at any rate in this case, on this side of the Atlantic.'

Marder knew that his hurriedly crafted letter had backfired, his first misstep. Now it was time to acknowledge his mistake (the only time he ever did so, but to a powerful adversary): 'I have just seen Stephen Roskill's letter (December 9), in which he suggests that I was a bit hasty in commenting as I did on a passage in Admiral Gretton's review of his Churchill book,' he wrote in the *TLS* issue of 27 January 1978. 'I thought I was on firm ground. It may be, judging from Captain Roskill's letter, that I was not, in which case I am indeed sorry. I shall read the entire book, and especially the appendix, which I gather from the Gretton review, is devoted to my sins, with great interest when it finally reaches me. In my next book perhaps the Battle of the Appendices will continue!'

In the circumstances, Sainsbury, Gretton, and others wondered at the time whether this academic fracas was a benefit to historical scholarship. Was it a war without end? It seemed unseemly, a sort on ongoing historical dust-up. Marder had laid out the details almost to excess. Roskill had countered in equal measure. Bryan Ranft, professor of naval history at Greenwich, who also taught in the Department of War Studies at King's College, London, noted of Marder's *From the Dardanelles to Oran* (with no disrespect to the book itself, to which he gave high praise) that it raised significant questions about the value of controversy between scholars and about the problems of historiography confronting writers on recent history. 'Such public controversy can obscure as well as reveal the truth,' he commented, then adding: 'In the heat of argument extreme positions are taken and certainties claimed where the nature of the evidence and the complexity of the situation make it unlikely that either protagonist is completely right.' The relationship between Churchill and Pound may have been more complex, perhaps more symbiotic, than had been allowed – and did not circumstances allow for give and take? Churchill's obsession for offensive action on political grounds might be countered by Pound's professional pragmatism. And, finally, a lesson for all time for any member of a postgraduate seminar or any serious practitioner of the historian's art: 'Disagreement between such eminent scholars raises important questions of historiography. To what extent does the available evidence permit precise answers to the matters in dispute? What different criteria should be applied to the interpretation of official documents and personal papers, and, most important of all, to contemporary historians, what measure of reliability can be applied to the reminiscences of those once employed in great matters?'[40]

In more recent times, the battles continues, not about North (now redeemed) but certainly about Churchill and about Pound. *At the Admiralty*, the documentary record edited by Sir Martin Gilbert, shows no Churchillian heavy-handedness, only gentle nudging of Pound. The *Alanbrooke War Diaries* cast dark shadows across Pound. By contrast, Robin Brodhurst's *Churchill's Anchor*, which appeared in 2000, rehabilitated Pound as a competent administrator but showed him not without fault in the conduct of operations. Vice Admiral Sir Ian McGeoch reviewed it in the *RUSI Journal* and in doing so revived many of the details of the spat between Marder and Roskill. McGeoch held strongly to the view that Pound was medically and professionally unfit to be first sea lord, a position identical to Roskill's. Brodhurst had regretted the fact that the dispute between such eminent historians had reached almost a schoolboy level. This would not do, McGeoch contended, for the credibility of Britain's 'official naval historian' was at stake. Drawing from his own personal experience, he concluded that Pound, as an anchor, failed to check the influences of his political master 'and even with an excessive scope of cable failed to hold him fast.' McGeoch had held up the Roskill line against that of Marder; however, it is clear from Brodhurst's book that Roskill was too preoccupied with Pound's debilities and expressed this in partisan style in subsequent work.[41] As to Marder, Brodhurst, like Roskill, had much evidence to exploit. Thus, Brodhurst and his reviewer revived the Marder-Roskill confrontation, gave it new life, as it were. It was the old battle in new guise.

Doubtless, Marder had inadvertently opened the closed files on 'official history' by bringing to light Sir Eric Seal's telling testimony, which exposed a case of historical misjudgement. This had embarrassed Roskill terribly. Now the hurt, deeply felt, was Roskill's. Marder was the first to dismantle a chapter in the 'official history'. The dispute, entering a new and starker phase, was soon to furnish further historical chapters.

Chapter 9

Roskill: Refighting Jutland

THE struggles between Marder and Roskill over the Hankey diaries and over the interpretations of the roles of Churchill and Pound in the conduct of the Navy in the Second World War would alone suffice to demonstrate Roskill's stubbornness and even, in the eyes of some, mean-spiritedness. His own memoir on the dispute demonstrates that the differences were personal rather than historical, but in fact the one could not be separated from the other. Marder might be accused by Roskill of breaching a gentlemen's agreement and, later, of borrowing but not returning documents, but, truth to tell, Marder turns out to be the aggrieved party – a victim of the more difficult side of Roskill's character. That same side was again demonstrated in the saga of the Harper papers and of the writing of Roskill's biography of Admiral of the Fleet, Earl Beatty.

'Shortly after publication I was informed that the copyright of material, from which I had successfully applied to the third Earl Beatty for permission to quote, was legally invested in the Executors and Trustees of the second Earl, Sir Arthur Collins, KCVO, and Mr David Dixon.' So wrote Roskill in a publisher's sheet tucked into his 1980 book *Admiral of the Fleet Earl Beatty*. 'In these circumstances I would like to acknowledge that the Trustees are the copyright owners of some of the material used in this book and I apologise to them for my mistake.' This, along with a list of errors and misprints, was signed Stephen Roskill. Many students of naval history and biography have wondered about this slip of paper, which was more than an errata sheet.

In 1980 legal action was under way against Roskill and his publisher Collins. The inside story of Roskill's fight with the executors and trustees of the estate of the 2nd Earl Beatty can now be told from the Roskill papers, from Marder's files, and from other personal and private documents. This story, amounting to a secret literary history of the Battle of Jutland, involves the then Royal United Service Institution (now the Royal United Services Institute for Defence Studies), the Navy Records Society, all the leading lights of British naval history of the time, and, not least, the ghost of the admiral who, from his grave, continued to play a remarkably powerful role in shaping the received version of the story of Jutland. Roskill seems to have been caught in the jaws of fate.

Lying at the bottom of all the unhappiness and rancour that involved Roskill and the events of Jutland is the account of J.E.T. Harper and the Official Record of the Battle of Jutland, commonly called the 'Harper Record' – another chapter in the politics of naval history itself but here, also, an essential part of the plot that involved Roskill. Strangely enough, Marder's correspondence provides the hitherto unrevealed inner story.[1]

By 1960, Marder was already in search of everything associated with Jellicoe, Beatty, Jutland, and the rewriting of the history of the battle. His earlier work based on the Jacky Fisher papers had been a timely introduction to many of the surviving naval officers, most of them by this time admirals, who had been at Jutland. Thus, one day in June 1966, he made a country visit to Beatty's biographer, Rear Admiral W.S. Chalmers. Marder's *Jutland and After* had just been released to acclaim. The American had the valued experience of several hours with what might be called a first-class witness and participant in history. 'We enjoyed your visit', confided Chalmers, 'and I am sure you realise that what I told you about Beatty's private life in later years was of course second hand and not for publication.'[2] Chalmers had been with Beatty in the North Sea, on the bridge of the flagship *Lion* – and, loyal to his chief, he had been entrusted with many secrets about the admiral, in and out of the service. Marder did not betray the confidence.

Roskill, by strange reversal of fortune, came to make public the secrets that Marder could not disclose. At this same time, Roskill had to contend with the swift pace set by Marder. Yet Roskill could produce texts for publication equally quickly and obtaining a publisher was not a problem. His publisher had asked for a book about the problematic naval event of the First World War, the Battle of Jutland of 31 May and 1 June 1916, to mark the fiftieth anniversary in 1966. Roskill's first assay into the Jutland story appeared in the *Naval Review* in 1957, 'Truth and Criticism in History – and Jutland'.[3] His work on the capture from a U-boat of an Enigma machine and code books, his further portrait of the battleship *Warspite* (1957), and his projected works on naval policy between the wars were all formulated or launched while he was still nominally toiling in the catacombs of Great George Street doing his Cabinet Office history. But for him the undoubted prize, Jutland, remained elusive, and his profile of the *Warspite* was the closest he could then come to such a study. A biography of Beatty, however, would present a grand opportunity.

In 1963 Marder visited Roskill at Blounce to discuss naval historical matters and told Roskill that his account of Jutland would be very detailed.

Roskill knew that Marder was continuing his volumes of *From the Dreadnought to Scapa Flow* but now he learned that Marder intended a whole volume on Jutland. Roskill takes up the story: 'He told me that his intention was to devote a whole volume to Jutland, and exhibited understandable anxiety about the possibility that I might produce a rival account.' Roskill backed down agreeably and generously, and he even handed his research files over to Marder on loan. These included the only complete copy of the whole list of deciphers which were in the hands of the Admiralty's Room 40 on the night of 31 May–1 June 1916. This unique collection had come to Roskill through his friendship with Edward Clarke, formerly of Room 40, who gave him the whole of his papers (which, of course, he should not have retained). Roskill had also managed to obtain from Jellicoe's former secretary a rare surviving copy of the *Naval Staff Appreciation* of Jutland. As Roskill admits, Marder reciprocated by providing Roskill with certain files, notably microfilms of the Wester Wemyss papers.[4] Roskill, in any case, could not write the sort of book that he intended about Jutland if the Admiralty was frosty on access to its confidential papers, for Marder already had the inside track.[5]

The life of David Beatty is inextricably tied up with Jutland – and its tortuous aftermath that continued long after the war ended and the peace treaties had been signed. Roskill, who finally came to this topic late in life, admits in his biography of Beatty that, at age seventy-seven, his energy and mobility were being curtailed and he was obliged to draw on the help of younger scholars for research and new insights. Roskill's *Admiral of the Fleet Earl Beatty: The Last Naval Hero: An Intimate Biography* lifted the lid of secrecy on the private life of the 'Last Naval Hero', notably his marriage to Edith Tree, née Field, who had divorced her husband to marry Beatty, and his extramarital affair with Eugénie Godfrey-Faussett, wife of a fellow naval officer. Altogether this reflected the direction that biography was then embarked upon as a literary genre, necessarily replete with behind-the-scenes material. Though one could not normally imagine Roskill to be doing studies that not even the society magazines *Tatler* or *Queen* would touch, it is to his credit that he held his course: and naval history is the better for it. Just as Nelson had said that there would have been more Nelsons if there had been more Emmas, so, too, perhaps there would have been more Beattys if there had been more Edith Fields, or more Eugénie Godfrey-Faussetts.

Roskill knew that the history of previous attempts to tell the story of Beatty's life had been incomplete or warped. Geoffrey Rawson had produced an unauthorized biography in 1930, six years before the admiral's death. Then the task of writing an authorized biography had fallen to Chalmers, a friend of the now deceased Earl and a competent writer. The biography, published

1951, with an introduction by C.S. Forester, used letters and memoranda held by Beatty's son David, the 2nd Earl Beatty. But even Chalmers's book differed from that originally intended. Sir Shane Leslie, an Anglo-Irish Roman Catholic and a cousin of Winston Churchill (his mother was Jennie Jerome Churchill's sister), had been asked to do a guarded book on the admiral's social life (which invariably meant private life), and Leslie, a competent writer and biographer, had set to work on it the 1940s. He then gave it up, there being too much pressure from the second Earl to keep secrets away from prying public eyes. Some of the material had then passed to Chalmers for inclusion, with careful, diplomatic touches. A most cautious book had resulted. Leslie's rough text about Beatty devolved to Roskill, who was particularly attracted to its details of the private life of the great sea warrior. Leslie and Roskill discussed these matters. The greatest potential existed, for some 185 letters from Beatty to Eugénie survived, in copies, among the Beatty papers. (Hers do not seem to have survived, sadly.) In any event, Roskill, then gathering as many papers for the Churchill Archives Centre as he could, bundled up the Leslie papers with the Godfrey-Faussett items, and had them catalogued. Leslie's draft biography survives in that collection and after his death became a source to be exploited by Roskill.[6] To be able to write about the Edwardian age of which he was conversant, for it was the epoch of his parents, was an attractive prospect.

Yet another, parallel, prospect was being presented to Roskill on Jutland. This involved analysis of the Admiralty's mismanaged attempt to control naval history. On the eve of the battle, public and press had expected another Trafalgar. They were deceived in their expectations (in fact, even Jellicoe and Beatty were later disconsolate that success had eluded them on that day). Immediately after the battle, the first lord of the Admiralty, Arthur Balfour, hurriedly issued an official Admiralty communiqué. It had been written even before Jellicoe's first report had been telegraphed to London. Balfour's intention was to counter Berlin's claim of victory. He had noted that, among the battlecruisers, the losses had been heavy. He catalogued them. As for German losses, they were serious but he had no specific details available. Press and public sensed that the Grand Fleet under Jellicoe (who had overall command at sea), with its battlecruiser squadron under Beatty, had suffered a serious setback that even amounted to defeat. Once Jellicoe's details came to hand, some amelioration could be undertaken, and Balfour hauled in Churchill, with his golden pen, to write something that would put a more assuring face on the matter. Despite Churchill's incomparable prose, many sensed an Admiralty cover-up. The details of what happened that day off the Danish coast remained shrouded in mystery.

In and out of Parliament, questions continued to be raised. Why had victory been denied? Was British gunnery at fault, or British communications, or ship and fleet handling, or ship design? Was Jellicoe to blame or Beatty? Within the Navy a schism developed. It seemed as if the pre-war rift between admirals Fisher and Beresford that had long divided the Navy had erupted again, in a new form.

The Admiralty assigned the director of navigation, Captain (late Vice Admiral) John E.T. Harper, RN, a New Zealander, a highly regarded officer with command experience, to produce a true record.[7] He received his instructions from the first sea lord, Admiral Sir Rosslyn Wemyss, a few weeks after the close of the war. If Harper could produce a straightforward record, free of judgements, based on ships' logs and track reconstructions (no oral evidence to be accepted), Wemyss hoped that an end would be put to the schism deriving from disputes over the events. Harper had not been at Jutland, an advantage. What was perhaps not known at the time was that Harper was keen to defend himself against any manipulations to the record. He intended to do his job confidentially (as was his remit), completely, and correctly. He started by obtaining the longitude and latitude of where the battlecruiser *Invincible* went down, had divers verify the wreck, and squared all navigational reckonings of Jellicoe's *Iron Duke* and Beatty's *Lion* against the wreck location.

Harper, heading a team of four, completed his assignment on 3 October 1919. This is called *The Official Record of the Battle of Jutland*, or, more generally, the Harper Record. Wemyss intended to release it without its being shown to either Jellicoe or Beatty. Its future date of publication and its authorship were reported in Parliament (thus blowing Harper's cover).

However, on 1 November, when Beatty succeeded Wemyss as first sea lord, the Harper document lay on his desk. He read the proofs, diagrams, and charts. He took exception to certain passages in the narrative. The locations did not fit well with his recollection as to where the battlecruisers had been; certainly, the naval units under his command were shown in a bad light. Various admirals serving at the Admiralty, all of whom had been with Beatty at Jutland, made their observations in writing. Ernle Chatfield and Osmond Brock did not like the tone, critical of their chief. Chatfield held that British battlecruiser gunnery was better than that of the Germans; Brock held that the Harper Record showed that a great battle had taken place in which the British got the worst of it. Harper had pointed out that the Grand Fleet battleship *Hercules* had been straddled at 6.15 p.m. Beatty wanted this deleted. Harper demurred, and Beatty remarked as a softening blow that 'there was no harm in the public knowing that someone in the Battle Fleet got wet, as that is about all they had to do with Jutland.'[8] To some of the demanded changes, Harper could not agree. Beatty intended to write the preface. Then Walter Long, first lord of the Admiralty, intervened and, hearing what an alarmed Harper had to say, sided with him. Meanwhile, Jellicoe, who had heard of Beatty's intention to make changes, issued his own statement of dissent to Long and, upon getting satisfaction, sailed for New Zealand, there to take up the governor generalship. The Harper Record was in limbo.

In Parliament, the controversy persisted, while gossip circulated through the Service and the clubs about the non-appearance of the Harper Record. The press gave the matter full attention. Seeking a way out of the difficulty, Beatty wished the official historian Sir Julian Corbett to write an introduction to the Harper Record in which Corbett would explain the role of British gunnery at Jutland in the light of failure of British shells to penetrate German armour. But Corbett was not to be hoodwinked, for he intended to avoid any obligation to Beatty. Jellicoe advised Corbett to decline. By a phone call to Brock, the deputy chief of the naval staff, Corbett explained that Longmans, his publisher for the official history he was doing for the Committee of Imperial Defence, would object to a rival account – he was already under contract to complete *Naval Operations* with them. In the circumstances, it was agreed that Corbett would get access to all of Harper's documents. The press was sniffing around the fringes of this matter, which was, as Corbett informed his friend Sir Henry Newbolt, a real 'mare's nest'. Harper aided Corbett in the process, and in June 1921 he left in Corbett's hands all his papers relating to Beatty's efforts 'to cook the Jutland plan and the Sea Lords' comments'.[9] The Admiralty seized on this opportunity strangely offered and used it as a pretext to shelve the Harper Record.

At this juncture, a fresh wind blew through Admiralty corridors. In the absence of a proper historical branch, two brothers who regarded themselves as a special gift to the historical profession, captains A.C. and K.G.B. Dewar, set about preparing the *Naval Staff Appreciation* as aforementioned. The resulting work, full of errors, invited Jellicoe's objections and those of Sir Hugh Evan-Thomas, who had been a rear admiral commanding the 5th Battle Squadron at Jutland. The *Naval Staff Appreciation* unjustly blamed him in regard to two occasions when the distance between Beatty's battlecruisers and his battle squadron had opened to such a degree that visual signalling was impossible; Evan-Thomas contended that the fault was Beatty's because of the laxity of his signalling arrangements.[10] Thought to be too controversial to be distributed – it would have huge ramifications in the fleet, to say nothing of Parliament and press – the *Naval Staff Appreciation* was ordered destroyed by Beatty's successor as first sea lord, Admiral Sir Charles Madden, in 1928, though, as we have seen, Roskill obtained a copy. So, too, did Winston

Churchill, who used it profitably in *The World Crisis* (1923) and thereby credited Beatty at the expense of Jellicoe.

Meanwhile, for the Committee of Imperial Defence, in 1922, Corbett brought his Jutland volume, the third volume of his *Naval Operations,* to completion, but he was circumscribed by the Admiralty on the key point involving the interception and deciphering of German signals: he could thus not reveal to the public that the failure to pass the most important of these to Jellicoe was responsible for the escape of the High Seas Fleet during the night after the battle. The 'egregious blunder' by Captain Thomas Jackson, the director of naval operations, resulted in Jellicoe and Beatty not knowing the locations of their enemy opposites, giving the impression that the enemy would not be encountered for some time.[11] Blind to the enemy's movements and position, they encountered the German fleet by chance. Corbett had to remain silent, perhaps to protect Jackson, the naval operations division, and Room 40. Even with adhering to as much as he could of the Admiralty's demands about his text, Corbett did not come off unscathed. A prefatory note by the Admiralty disclaimed responsibility for the accuracy of Corbett's book. It even declared that 'some of the principles advocated, especially the tendency to minimise the importance of seeking battle and endeavouring to force it to a conclusion', were directly in opposition to its views.[12] Jellicoe praised the Corbett interpretation. Other books added to the conflagration, including Admiral Sir Reginald Bacon's polemical *Jutland Scandal* (1925) and Carlyon Bellairs's scurrilous *The Battle of Jutland, the Sowing and Reaping* (1920).

Thus did it come about that in 1924 the Admiralty's sanitized *Narrative of Jutland* appeared, being a reworking of the *Naval Staff Appreciation* (Roskill called it the 'de-venomized' version). This contained an introduction which explained away various issues and minimized the value of ships' logs, captains' observations, and admirals' dispatches. It made dubious the Harper account: there were discrepancies of time and place that cast doubt on its narrative of events. Signals and wireless intelligence, though valuable, was incomplete. Then came the savage blow: 'Captain J.E.T. Harper's record and diagrams of the battle really represent the first stage of this work. But there is no such thing as finality in historical work, so there are certain points where the record is considered open to revision, more particularly in its representation of the movements and courses of the German fleet which differ widely from those of Admiral Scheer.'

By now, Harper was preparing to take retirement. Once returned to civilian life, he added to the controversy with a pro-Jellicoe book, *The Truth about Jutland*, published in 1927. For safekeeping, Harper deposited his typescript of the original Harper Record, printer's proof of the same, and various pieces of Admiralty evidence of tampering, plus other correspondence of relevance including his own hard-hitting indictment of Beatty's 'fudging the record', in the RUSI in Whitehall, safely under lock and key. The only way to get it out of there, Harper said, was by burglary. This collection was not to be opened until his death and the death, in fact, of anyone named in those documents; then and then only would a disposition to be made. There sat these treasures.

Marder had been on the hunt for the Harper documents but could not find them before his *Jutland and After* was published in 1966. There, he stated that he would gladly leave the details of that unsavoury affair to Roskill, who was then investigating the subject. However, while subsequently toiling through Cabinet Office manuscripts in the Admiralty Record Office, he chanced upon a copy of a full Jutland Admiralty file that included the precious document. It was the key, because it told the inside story – though the keeper there did not know anything about its existence or use: 'It's a slow-motion, play-by-play account of poor Harper's tribulations, supported by documentation' was Marder's description of it.[13] Marder knew that the originals of the Harper papers (including the key one) held at the RUSI were bound to come into the public realm soon, for Admiral of the Fleet Lord Chatfield (Beatty's flag captain at Jutland) had died in 1967, thus clearing the way for disclosure of the inside history of the Jutland controversy. Who would be first to make the astonishing story public?

In late 1967 Marder wrote another one of his enthusiastic letters to his associate Vice Admiral Sir Peter Gretton, mentioning that he had found Harper's secret history of the history of Jutland. Gretton, closely connected to the RUSI, had seen the document (that is, Harper's original) in question. 'You certainly are the most competent "ferreter outer" in the world', Gretton replied, 'I am horrified to hear that you came across *a copy* [emphasis added] of that terrible Harper paper – terrible because of the story it tells.' Marder was then playing with the idea of using Harper's story as an appendix in a projected second edition of *Jutland and After*, but he would still have to get a release from the RUSI. Gretton contacted Peter Kemp, the Navy librarian who was also editor of the *RUSI Journal*, who in turn told Gretton that he would be advising Marder to write formally to the RUSI, in whose care the original was, and that the naval members on the RUSI council would decide. Gretton told Marder that he hoped the answer would be 'No', for, inasmuch as the Navy was having a rough time at that moment, he did not want to see this large blot on its escutcheon revealed, as he put it. 'I have not seen the Harper paper for several years and cannot remember much about it, but I think that it showed a disgraceful fiddling of the Jutland record which I still find astonishing. We were brought up in the Navy to consider such behaviour impossible. And I am glad to say that nothing like that happened in WWII. At least, I know of no example.'[14] Marder faced a closed door – some thought it about time.[15]

Eight years before, in 1959, Roskill had attempted to get access to the same Harper trove at the RUSI but was denied.[16] Geoffrey Bennett says that he saw these papers, sometime before 1964, and he wrote in his history of Jutland that he thought they were of little interest except to a biographer of Beatty or to some student of Admiralty administration in the years following the First World War.[17] Even so, Bennett covered his tracks carefully, and there is no evidence that he actually saw the critical papers in question. Who else saw them in addition to Gretton and the director, librarian, and staff of the RUSI is not known. The secrets lay hidden. There were no leaks and no copies made.

How was the RUSI to deal with the most contentious document of modern British naval history? To compound the institute's anxiety, word was out that books and possibly historical manuscripts were going missing from the RUSI library and being sold. Marder's relentless quest for the Harper materials at the RUSI was perhaps a blind for events that were unfolding with speed. It was not Kemp's doing that the Harper documents were kept away from Marder's hands – Kemp was preoccupied with his aged mother's health – but rather the actions of Kemp's assistant editor of the *RUSI Journal* who doubled as the research assistant at the institute, David Erskine. He was aided, even led, by Roskill and the two now formed a powerful combination.

It so happened that the Navy Records Society was about to publish its second of two volumes, edited by A. Temple Patterson, of *The Jellicoe Papers: Selections from the Private and Official Correspondence of Admiral of the Fleet Earl Jellicoe of Scapa*. Erskine and Roskill were able to facilitate the liberation of the Harper documents from the RUSI for printing by the Navy Records Society, despite the added costs a larger book would entail to an already financially strapped organization. To many, especially Roskill, it seemed a golden opportunity to insert a special appendix of Harper documents. Temple Patterson did not resist the pressure, though his section of the book on the Jutland controversy – all about Jellicoe – had already been put to bed. Our story now shifts to the Navy Records Society.

The NRS was established in 1893 for the purpose of printing rare or unpublished works of naval interest. Guiding lights in the early years were Professor Sir John Knox Laughton of King's College, London, Admiral Sir Cyprian Bridge, and Corbett, among others.[18] Over time, the NRS had issued many treasures – volumes on the Spanish Armada, the English Civil War, the Dutch wars, and others. It had printed many works on the sea kings of Britain, notably lords Spencer and Keith, and a volume of Nelson's letters to his wife. By the 1960s, with Pax Britannica a fading memory, the NRS was well into volumes on the modern era, with plans to print some of Jacky Fisher's papers (edited by Kemp) and perhaps a collection of Roger Keyes's papers (by Professor Paul Halpern) and a projected volume or two by Roskill on the Royal Naval Air Service. The NRS worked bit by bit, responding to the needs or more likely the opportunities of the day as they arose. It was Roskill's zeal and wiggling that brought about the Harper opportunity. No publishing programme could avoid the Beatty papers, and, dating from the early 1960s, the NRS had a project in mind for this, with John Barnes, a lecturer at the London School of Economics, as editor. The papers were largely out of bounds for the present, under lock and key in Chicheley Hall, Newport Pagnell, Buckinghamshire, largely unavailable to the public though private researchers such as Barnes obtained limited access to them. In fact, the 2nd Earl Beatty had given permission to borrow a selection for editing and printing under NRS authority. Roskill was active in the cataloguing of these.

In 1968 the NRS was under the presidency of Lord Carrington, first lord of the Admiralty. His role in the unfolding events was far from titular. The secretary was Erskine, already mentioned, a genial man, who, when he took my two-guineas' membership subscription, warned me that meetings were invariably dull and that I need not bother to attend. Safeguarding the purse strings was Bernard Pool, expert on naval contracts. Former secretary of the Admiralty Sir John Lang, who knew all about Admiralty secrets, was a valued councillor. There were at least three admirals: Sir Henry Moore; Sir Arthur Hezlet, the submariner who had been out with Roskill to the Bikini atomic-weapons trials and had since become an expert on nuclear power and naval warfare; and P.W. Brock, whose last command had been in HMS *Kenya* in the Korean War and a trustee of the National Maritime Museum. There were several captains: A.B. Sainsbury of the *Naval Review*; Geoffrey Bennett, historian of the First World War; Taprell Dorling, who wrote books about destroyers in the First World War that he knew first hand; and Roskill. Commander John Owen, historian of Queen Anne's navy, was there. Lieutenant commanders included the submariner Kemp, Naval Librarian in the Ministry of Defence and editor of the *RUSI Journal*, and George Naish of the National Maritime Museum. There were a cluster of professors: Gerald Graham, A. Temple Patterson (the editor of the Jellicoe papers), Christopher Lloyd and Brian Ranft of Royal Naval College Greenwich, John Bromley of Southampton, and Michael Lewis of Britannia Royal Naval College,

Dartmouth. Part of this illustrious group, too, were E.K. Timings of the Public Record Office; the Reverend J.R. Powell, expert on the seventeenth century; Sir Michael Cary, former secretary of the Admiralty; Piers Mackesy of Oxford, expert on the eighteenth century and the Norwegian campaign in the late war; Alan Pearsall, archivist at the National Maritime Museum; and Dudley Pope, the historian and novelist. Academic authorities included Anthony Ryan, Jonathan Steinberg, and Glyndwr Williams. Also on council were John Ehrman, official military historian and biographer; Dame Veronica Wedgwood, historian of the English Civil War; and Oliver Warner, essayist and biographer. Daniel Baugh, Donald Schurman, and James Goldrick provided overseas representation. Council's membership was naturally in flux and changeable from year to year. Most influential on the council were Erskine, for he was also research assistant at the RUSI as well as assistant editor of the *RUSI Journal*, Ehrman, for his opinions counted strongly not only as a naval historian but as one who knew about official historical matters and law, and Roskill. Erskine was the fixer in the unfolding events, led by Roskill.

Roskill became a member of the NRS council in 1956 and was ten years in that role, becoming a vice president in 1967 and an honorary life vice president in 1976. In 1968 he chaired the all-important publication committee. He exerted considerable influence, even domination, in the society's affairs.[19] 'Having been on the Council of the Navy Records Society [twenty] years before he [Roskill] was a member', Rear Admiral P.W. Brock wrote me, when I had wondered why his name had been dropped from the council's list and if he would stand for renomination, 'I have not been childish enough to let that rascal Roskill make me tender my resignation but having been on the Council at a later stage under his overbearing and mannerless dictation, I have no ambition to serve on it again.' To this he added: 'I think that what really gets under my skin about him is the thought of the time and heat I once expended upon people who warned me that he was one of the less carefully Chosen!'[20] But Brock returned to the council at Erskine's request and resumed his helpful position: the *Mariner's Mirror*'s preferred reviewer of Marder's *From the Dreadnought to Scapa Flow*, whose perceptive points always sent Marder back to his notes so as to defend himself or make corrections. He had as thorough a knowledge of the history of the Navy during the twentieth century as that of any who graced the NRS table.

Such was the roster of the NRS when, in 1968, I ventured into the old exhibition room of the Public Record Office, Chancery Lane, for a council meeting. The council had assembled to review the accounts, to discuss the state of pending projects, and to make plans for the future. With little control over recalcitrant volume editors, save for sending warning messages or cancelling contracts, the group turned to more urgent business. Though Roskill represented the publications committee, everyone present knew that he masterminded the committee's business and the publication agenda. He showed every attention to detail that one would expect of him, coupled with exactitude and order. His hearing aid gave him trouble, as such contrivances often do. But his deafness allowed him to fend off approaches and inquiries and so to carry the day unmolested and unmoved. Though in private his elliptical charm and engaging manner won many friends, in a vaulted Gothic council chamber such as this, flanked or faced by councillors who knew the style of the man, there were no takers to pick a quarrel or even to verify a point.

The NRS had decided to publish the key Harper documents, and to do so with the RUSI's approval and blessing. The expression 'rushed into print' is not inappropriate here. The NRS wanted the documents published before some other publication was undertaken beyond their control – and by that was meant Marder's rival project. It would solve a problem for the RUSI, too. The NRS could not publish all of the documents, for there was insufficient room in the already crowded *Jellicoe Papers II*, then at press. Accordingly, an appendix was determined upon, tacked on to Temple Patterson's selection of documents about Jellicoe and the Jutland controversy. An introduction to the Harper material was quickly crafted by Patterson, aided by Erskine, who supplied a footnote or perhaps more, and by Roskill, though we do not know the exact apportionment of responsibility here.

In any event, the selection of Harper documents in question as published by the NRS contains Harper's sworn testimony, dated 13 September 1935, that the statement of facts dealing with the compilation of the Official Record of the Battle of Jutland as prepared by him was true and correct under the terms of statutory declarations legislation. The companion item – that is, 'And the Reason it was not published' – was the troublesome one. Equally hot was HP 4, with all the Admiralty correspondence hitherto under wraps (most damaging to Beatty), and HP 5, Harper's true and sworn statement. These, taken together, the printer and editor decided to call, as a sort of catch-all, 'Harper's Narrative'. The title of the book was changed to reflect the addition: *The Jellicoe Papers: Selections from the Private and Official Correspondence of Admiral of the Fleet Earl Jellicoe Volume II 1916–1935, with an Appendix on the Papers of Vice Admiral J.E.T. Harper.*

The material was kept under close guard while proofs were read and the volume indexed. Printers and binders completed their work. Notice of the NRS's next annual general meeting was given the membership. Early alarm bells sounded. As a form of damage control or so as to answer criticism in advance, Barnes, as closest to the Beatty papers project, was designated to write an article in the upcoming *RUSI Journal* to explain the situation and the process. Much to Roskill's disappointment (and that of many others), that article never appeared. An explanatory note would have been useful to the NRS during the difficult times to come, when it had to contend with the anger of the 2nd Earl Beatty.

It was known in naval historical circles that explosive Harper documents would be included in the volume. Word travelled quickly. The 2nd Earl Beatty, determined and desperate to put a stop to publication, made his appearance at the meeting of 9 December 1968. It was a meeting of fireworks finished only by a vote of those in attendance. He made his objections known. Roskill did not wither and was not moved, and, as the 2nd Earl would have it, actually turned off his hearing aid in the middle of the heated discussion.[21]

The next day, Roskill wrote to Marder: 'At yesterday's AGM of the Navy Records Society the decision to publish the Harper paper was supported by an overwhelming majority. I am afraid David Beatty is annoyed, but I really do not think he has a leg to stand on; and in my view there is a good deal to be said on Harper's side, though he certainly exaggerated some of his criticisms. What a colossal waste of time the whole controversy now seems!'[22] This was probably the first that Marder had heard of the release of the Harper materials from the RUSI. Whether intended or not, Roskill had stolen a march on him.

A review copy of *Jellicoe Papers II* went directly to *The Times*, and on Saturday, 14 December, the storm broke with publication there of a large article (part description and part book review) under the sensational heading 'Beatty Shown as Falsifier of Jutland Record'. The writer was Basil Gringell, who doubled as Admiralty correspondent and Church of England correspondent for *The Times*. (It is said that once, rather confusing his two portfolios, he addressed the first sea lord as 'Your Grace'.) Gringell was no neophyte in naval history, rather a reviewer of naval works in that newspaper, including Marder's books.[23] The article itself was an even-handed exposé but dynamite in and of itself. The truth, or at least Harper's version of it, was now out, the missing piece as it were.

The 2nd Earl Beatty, continuing his objections to the NRS having published the Harper account, replied to the Gringell review with a letter to *The Times*. This attacked the reviewer and said that the Harper Narrative contained accusations not facts. Beatty's worry was that in future historians would quote from Harper out of context. He had already made this point to the NRS, without success. He had fought a losing battle.

Over the next week or so, other letters appeared. Admiral Sir William James, the historian, age eighty-eight, wrote to say that no evidence existed that Beatty had 'fudged' the naval records of Jutland. Young Nicholas Beatty, age seven and a half, wrote from Chicheley Hall defending his grandfather. Barnes wrote to say that the full story about Beatty had yet to be told, and that the intended publication of the Beatty papers by the NRS would make clear the details. It was too late.

Roskill's letter of 10 December was not the only perspective that Marder received about the NRS decision. Kemp wrote on 6 January:

> I am so disgusted with the NRS over the Harper business that I almost wrote cancelling my subscription. We had an up-and-downer at the AGM (Beatty was there) and the objectors were soundly outvoted. I suspect that Erskine considers it a 'scoop' for the NRS, as though we were a daily newspaper. Oddly enough, Roskill was in favour of this method of publication in the Jellicoe volume, which surprised me. Barnes, as you know, was supposed to produce an article for the *RUSI Journal* for last November, but nothing arrived. I only hope he produces something for the next issue, but of course it will be too late to do any good. It is the lack of justice which riles me in this method of publication. As anyone could have seen, to produce Harper in that form was an open invitation to journalists to write the sort of comment they did. 'How Beatty Cooked the Books', and so on.[24]

In the next issue of the *Naval Review*, Captain A.B. Sainsbury, the reviewer of *Jellicoe Papers II*, classified Harper's Narrative as 'a pathetic and disappointing little collection'. What was intriguing, said the same commentator, was the document's inclusion in the Jellicoe volume so as to avoid risk of publication, possibly in extracts, elsewhere in the near future:

> Surely this apprehension seems a thin excuse rather than a convincing explanation. Why, one wonders, did the RUSI not publish the documents, with or without a commentary by a competent historian, either as a supplement to their Journal or as an occasional paper? . . . Can it be that a pirated publication was seriously feared? That someone had found a duplicate which suggested the existence of yet more copies . . . ? But what has anyone gained by this apparently enforced publication? We know nothing more about Jutland . . . It is to be hoped that the matter may now be dropped in all its aspects – Jutland, Beatty, Harper himself and the very publication of his wretched papers: they have caused enough fuss.[25]

Marder followed the eruptions from a distance. Having been out-manoeuvred, he could do nothing more than open a stream of letters complaining of the NRS's actions and the public aftermath. Admiral Sir Angus Cunninghame Graham, one of his correspondents, wrote with news that it seemed a pity that Harper's papers should have been published by the NRS.[26] Richard Hough wrote at the same time: 'We shall be talking (as is the whole country) about Beatty and the Harper Memo. It has had a lot of space and you have been much quoted in *The Times* letters as the final word. Beatty made a very dignified reply to a rather outrageous piece in *The Times*.' A few days later A.J.P. Taylor, answering a query by Marder about American actions in 1917, commented: 'We are in the midst of a scare here over the Harper record. No-one has remarked that the story has been known for twenty years or more, but, no doubt, to those who write articles in newspapers this would be in itself news.'[27] To Marder, Geoffrey Hunt wrote from OUP that there was quite a fuss in the United Kingdom about the publication of the *Jellicoe Papers II*. *The Times*, he said, had a rather silly article on the Saturday, the 14th, written by Basil Gringell, 'who seems to have been put on to the subject with no background and an inclination to sensationalism which *The Times* seems to favour nowadays.' The *Guardian* had a more sensible article, but it, like that in *The Times*, was exclusively concerned with the Harper documents in the appendix and the charge that Beatty and Chatfield falsified the record when Beatty became first sea lord. Lord Beatty had a good letter in *The Times* that morning, Marder was informed, but surely a review copy of *Jellicoe Papers II* should have been in the paper's hands long enough to give it to someone knowledgeable who would have read Marder's *Jutland and After* at least. 'Even if he [Gringell] had merely looked up the references to Harper in your Index, as I have just done, it would have helped. What you say on p. 201 seems to me absolutely valid and, if the controversy does not die away as quickly as it began, I hope there will be a letter from Roskill, or someone of that standing, to put the matter in perspective.'[28]

The 2nd Earl Beatty wrote to Marder just before year end, in response to Marder's sympathetic notice of Beatty's riposte to *The Times*. 'It has come about as we feared', Beatty wrote solemnly, 'and I regret to say that Roskill as Chairman of the Publications Committee of the N.R.S. is at the bottom of the dirty pot. He has been patronizing and pontifical in his reply to a letter from me! He does not like criticism.'[29] Marder was sympathetic to Beatty, and he pointed this out to Roskill, who replied censoriously: 'I really do not see why you should condole with David Beatty, as he has already made an ass of himself over the Harper paper. And, as you know, there is about 80% truth in that paper. He would have been far wiser to keep quiet and to have accepted my view that John Barnes is a bit of a wash-out. He has never done the article promised for the *R.U.S.I. Journal*, and I have no confidence in the N.R.S. getting his volume of Beatty papers anywhere near the agreed date. I warned David of all this years ago, and offered to find a better editor. He first agreed with me, but then, under pressure from Barnes, changed his mind.'[30]

Meanwhile, Roskill had replied to Marder's most recent letter, agreeing to read the final volume of *From the Dreadnought to Scapa Flow* and noting that he was pleased that he could take his time in doing so 'as the pressure on me really is very heavy just now'. He also added his own perspective on the hornet's nest generated by the Harper documents as published in *Jellicoe Papers II* and gave another insight into the recent fireworks, blaming Beatty:

> I share your astonishment over the Harper business coming up again, but (between ourselves) it is actually the fault of David Beatty. He made an awful fuss about the publication of the paper, came to the A.G.M. of the society, and a motion was put that all copies should be withdrawn. Hardly surprisingly the motion was heavily defeated. Only four people voted for it – namely David Beatty and John Barnes, Geoffrey Bennett (I think because it shows his account of the Jutland controversy to be in error) and, rather surprisingly, Piers Mackesy of Oxford. David Beatty is angry with me, but I have tried to explain patiently to him that it really is no use his trying to say what shall or shall not be published by the N.R.S. Your name did not come into the discussion at all, so you have no cause to worry.[31]

Marder took notice of all that came his way from his editor and his correspondents. He was already at work on corrections for a second printing of *Jutland and After*; in fact, a second edition was then under consideration and would appear a decade later, in 1978. It benefited much from the flurry over the Harper documents but did little to change Marder's view that finger pointing ought not to be the name of the game in British naval historical circles. A likeminded view was held by P.W. Brock, who wrote to me: 'I am glad to have been clear of the controversy about the Harper Papers. I can see no excuse whatever for including it in the Jellicoe book without even some indication of its value (or lack of value). It is an unbalanced attack on Beatty without doing Jellicoe any particular service. In common with the great majority of officers on that confused occasion, they did their best but could have done better with the advantage of hindsight, more practice and better visibility. The rivalry stirred up by their supporters was an unhappy sequel: at this time of day there is no excuse for our continuing the discussion in their discordant tone of voice.'[32]

Similarly, Geoffrey Bennett, when reviewing the history of the Jutland controversy, opined that the story had really been concluded in 1940, with the appearance of the second edition of Corbett's *Naval Operations*, volume 3. The new edition not only took into account the German Official History; it disclosed the signals traffic, deciphered by Room 40, and thereby made clear that the signal regarding Scheer's return via Horns Reef had not been passed to Jellicoe. 'The reputations of these two great admirals could not be charred by raking over the dead embers of a once fierce argument that was kept ablaze for too long by a human weakness in one of them. Beatty may have made use of his position as First Sea Lord to distort the truth about Jutland in his own favour, but lesser men have suffered *folie de grandeur* with smaller excuse. There are aspects of Nelson's life that are open to harsher criticism, but no one questions his right to look down on the heart of London from the summit of a column in Trafalgar Square.'[33] Roskill told Marder that Bennett voted against publication of the Harper documents, and we can be assured that Brock would have joined the other four had he not been out of the country.

Controversy over the Harper material in *Jellicoe Papers II* raged for some time, and the December 1968 flurry in *The Times* caught the attention of the public. In the *Naval Review* and the *RUSI Journal*, some considerable issues were raised, and then the matter faded out as a discussion between Temple Patterson and Geoffrey Bennett, with some involvement by Admiral Sir William James.[34] As for the RUSI, an article, or notice, less window dressing than pure information, appeared in an issue of its *Journal*, reporting on the dispersal to other repositories of the institute's assorted naval and other military manuscripts.[35] The naval manuscripts held at the RUSI went to the National Maritime Museum, save for the Harper documents (the full set), which were sent to the British Library. An unsigned review of *Jellicoe Papers II* appeared in the March 1969 issue of the *RUSI Journal* and served as an exculpation of the RUSI and NRS and provided a comprehensive review of Jellicoe, Beatty, and the Harper saga. Less direct than the membership might have hoped, it may possibly have been authored by Barnes or Erskine.[36]

Roskill paid dearly for his role in having the key Harper papers published in *Jellicoe Papers II*. From Charles Beatty's biography of his uncle the admiral, issued shortly before *Last Naval Hero*, and from Roskill's correspondence with Charles Beatty, we have an unusual perspective about the politics of the literary affair. Charles Beatty says that at one time – that is, before 1968 – the 2nd Earl Beatty promised Roskill a free hand in the writing of a definitive life. But the 2nd Earl dropped his support after the Harper papers' inclusion in the NRS publication, seeing Roskill as the devil in the piece. Charles

Beatty says that Roskill was well into the biography when the second Earl heard of the NRS decision to publish the Harper selection. Roskill wrote Charles Beatty on 22 January 1979: 'It was a source of real sorrow to me that the second Earl chose to pick a quarrel with me because the Navy Records Society published the 'Harper Papers' about Jutland. In fact, the decision to do so was taken by the Council as a whole . . . This quarrel of course made the biography hopeless – especially as I knew David the second Earl had suppressed the draft biography by Shane Leslie because it told about his father's disastrous marriage and hinted at his love affairs.'[37]

The second Earl, a former lieutenant commander in the Royal Navy, a personal private secretary to parliamentary and financial secretaries of the Admiralty, and sometime Member of Parliament, died in 1972. His widow, Diana, who married Sir John Grenfell Nutting in 1973, naturally had a vested interest in the Beatty papers and the memory of both the first and the second Earls. The trustees and executors of the estate held firm copyright control of the admiral's papers. Roskill did not know this.

Denied access to the full collection of Beatty papers, Roskill had to consider alternatives. This brought him into closer cooperation with Leslie and, in turn, those having custody of the Godfrey-Faussett papers. Forced to confine himself to the details of battle and naval politics as provided in the papers already made public, Roskill shifted his attention so as to exploit the papers that Leslie had already used but had been obliged not to publish by the second Earl's injunction. Now Roskill could fight back, using papers outside the control of the trustees and executors. His growing files in the Churchill Archives Centre aided his process considerably, and he seems to have had all the support he needed from his editor, Richard Ollard, and his publisher, Collins. The biography, Roskill knew, could hardly be definitive. But he held the view that he would do the best he could with what he had. In the end, Beatty's relationship with Eugénie was perhaps the most unique and original part of the book; even so, it was splendidly balanced with the naval accounts and details of the admiral's life. Roskill made no attempt to be vindictive against the second Earl. What he did not know was that the third Earl, who readily encouraged Roskill in his good work, was being outflanked by the never-sleeping trustees and executors of the second Earl, who held copyright to the Beatty papers.

Charles Beatty, nephew of the second Earl, was undeterred by the legal difficulties that getting access to the Beatty papers afforded. To his way of thinking, the gathering of information from other sources sufficed for the book he was preparing, which would include a spare narrative of the Battle of Jutland but considerable detail about the admiral's social and sporting life. The Eugénie matter was to be left on the sideline. *Our Admiral*, Charles's book, appeared in 1980, in advance of Roskill's *Last Naval Hero*, but offered no rivalry for the sort of market Roskill aimed for. It, nonetheless, showed Admiral Beatty in a poorer light, for it exposed his mean spirit and cheapness when it came to property and inheritance. Charles's father, a major, David's brother, had died of war wounds after his return to England. Charles fared poorly and expected more beneficence from the admiral. This was not to be. Roskill paid no notice of Charles Beatty's book, and it is clear, too, that Charles did not know as of 1979 that Roskill was writing *The Last Naval Hero*. Perhaps Roskill kept the details under wraps, fearing a legal battle.

The Beatty papers remained at Chicheley Hall. Death duties continued to extract a terrible toll on family fortunes. At one time, Barnes had access to them and even had a selection of them away on loan for an intended biography of Beatty. The NRS wanted to publish some Beatty papers also. These projects became stalled, partly because of lengthy ill health suffered by Barnes, and were a matter of concern and embarrassment. Accordingly, Lord Carrington intervened and had the documents recovered and restored to their owners. It was not until Brian Ranft published the two volumes of *Beatty Papers* (1989, 1993) in the NRS series that the matter was eventually brought to a conclusion.

Meanwhile, following leads that the Beatty papers might be coming up for sale, a duo from the National Maritime Museum consisting of the custodian of manuscripts, Roger Knight, and the archivist, Alan Pearsall, ventured into Buckinghamshire, on 18 March 1978, to examine the papers and to discuss the matter of purchase with what Knight says were the formidable couple Sir John and Lady Nutting. They found a well-rounded collection of the greatest importance. The collection, with all its hidden secrets, lay in a clutter of trunks in the attic. It was clear to them that no systematic examination of them had yet been made by any historian. That increased the value, sparking additional interest.

What price could be put on these documents? What, indeed, would the market allow? There was a danger of the collection being sold abroad. The auctioneers Christie's had given the owners the valuation of £50,000. The Estate Duty Office valued the papers at £17,000, which would leave them not a great deal after sale for such treasure. Returning to Greenwich, Knight recommended to his superior, David Proctor, that the National Maritime Museum acquire the collection, consisting as it did of over a thousand letters, including five from Churchill, twenty from Fisher, forty from Jellicoe, twenty-five from Wemyss, and various other gems, including 1,026 letters from the

Beatty to his wife and fifteen in return. This recommendation was taken up, and soon the National Maritime Museum went shopping for funds to effect the purchase.

Still, the price remained up in the air, vendors and purchaser unable to agree. The vendors therefore sought a competent evaluation, and they turned to Anthony R.A. Hobson of Fordingbridge, Hampshire, an expert in these things. In his report, Hobson said of Roskill that he had used the Beatty papers for the first volume of his *Naval Policy between the Wars, 1919–1929*. However, for his *Last Naval Hero*, 'he appears to have relied on Shane Leslie's copies and other material in his possession and made no application to the Trustees for access to the present archive. His knowledge of the Admiral's letters to Lady Beatty after 1914 seems to be very incomplete and some of his quotations from originals in the Beatty Papers are inexact.' Hobson made clear that Chalmers had omitted any controversial material and anything likely to offend or distress. As Chalmers had explained in his preface, 'it is too near his lifetime to reveal all that he wrote, and his letters alone would fill several volumes.'[38] Hobson valued the papers catalogued at £71,275, a considerable advance on Christie's guide price. The National Maritime Museum was in a bind, and the British Library, which now came into the story as temporary custodian of the papers until such time as the disposition of the Beatty materials could be determined, stood down as a rival buyer. This cleared the way for the National Maritime Museum, but only if a figure could be agreed on. Haggling ensued. The matter went to arbitration, with Ehrman, then of the Historical Commission on Historical Monuments, siding completely with the vendors, much to the surprise of the intended purchasers. Thus was Hobson's valuation made the sale price. By a curious twist of tax law, the Beatty papers were ingeniously and surprisingly valued not as one lot but by the piece, thus avoiding Inland Revenue fees. But, ultimately, all ended well: the Nuttings got a good price, the archival assessor's word was upheld, Ehrman's advice was taken as final, enabling funds came from the intrepid National Heritage Memorial Fund and from the Pilgrim Trust, and, best of all for future researchers and writers, the National Maritime Museum, for £73,200 (fees included), got its magnificent new collection.[39] The Beatty archive was secured to the nation.

The purchase of the Beatty papers was announced in a press release from the National Maritime Museum dated August 1981. The acquisition of the great collection, it said, would enable the definitive biography of the admiral to be written at last. In addition, other major research on the First World War and on the controversy of the capital ship versus the submarine, as well as the reduction of the Navy's manpower and plans for Singapore in the early 1920s, could now be undertaken. Knight, in the *Mariner's Mirror*, November 1981, charted the course for the future: 'Is it possible now, sixty-five years after the Battle of Jutland and forty-five years after Beatty's death, for a generation freed from the violent emotion of the times to produce a more detached assessment? Paul Kennedy pointed out in his preface to *The Rise and Fall of British Naval Mastery* that this country's dramatically changed naval circumstances will mean that "the older historiography needs to be reassessed and the older assumptions need to be modified. Perhaps we will now have more insight into Beatty; but he will still be, because of those changed circumstances, the nation's Last Naval Hero."'[40]

Roskill fared curiously under the purchase of the Beatty papers. He could assert no claim to a definitive life and kept free of the matter. As to use of the Beatty papers for the biography, the legal firm Withers, acting for the trustees and executors of the 2nd Earl, were not satisfied with Hobson's statement that Roskill's use of the papers had not devalued the whole collection. They took the opposite view. Noting that Roskill had used some of the documents in *Naval Policy between the Wars*, they contended that the value of the papers had been thereby reduced by £5000 and demanded compensation in the same amount for breach of copyright. This caused Roskill considerable anxiety, and his brother, Sir Ashton Roskill, acted as his unofficial adviser 'throughout the protracted ordeal of this painful experience,' as Stephen put it. 'Many thanks for your good wishes for 1981', Roskill wrote his confidant Sainsbury, on New Year's Eve 1980, 'though it looks like being a difficult year for all of us . . . I trust most earnestly that our solicitors will get the Beatty executors to accept a reasonable settlement; but I've told them I'd rather be sued than pay £5,000. I think that must have been a try on because the book won't bring me anything like that sum. In fact Collins has estimated that I'll do well if I net about half that sum.' He recounted:

> Not until just before publication did the second Earl's solicitors and executors come up and say that the copyright belonged to them. They asked for publication to be deferred until after the sale of the Chicheley collection on the grounds that it would reduce the price obtained. We took legal advice and were assured that no judge would grant an injunction to stop publication on grounds claimed by the executors, so we 'published and be damned' but put in the corregia slip which you will have noted. So far so good, but last week the solicitors came up with a demand . . . a monstrous claim. We are going to refuse to pay any such sum and if they like they can sue me; but of course the very last thing I want at my age is to be involved in litigation.

News of Roskill's war with the solicitors reached the editor of the *Sunday Telegraph*, and Kenneth Rose, in the widely read column 'Albany', raised the matter under the heading 'Admiral Beatty's Crock of Gold' in the issue of 23 August 1981. 'In spite of completing so remunerative a bargain, the trustees apparently believe that there is still more to be made out of the papers,' stated Rose. 'They are continuing to demand compensation for breach of copyright from Captain Stephen Roskill, author of the recent biography of Beatty – even though Roskill was the victim of a misunderstanding.' Coming to Roskill's defence, the same writer noted that the National Maritime Museum had just announced that much of its newly acquired material had never before seen the light of day, and that only now could a definitive biography be written. 'That does not suggest that Roskill exposed many of its secrets. In any case, the limited infringement of copyright made in good faith by our greatest living naval historian can surely now be overlooked.'

A sudden silence descended on Withers as soon as the article was published. In the end, Withers did not pursue the case. Collins paid £500 as a limited share in the defence and would go no further. Roskill had to put in considerably more, £648.75, though not as much as the sum of costs (£2,433.05) billed by his solicitors, Oswald Hickson, Collier, who waived their other fees in sympathy. The cost of the copyright case rivalled the amount at risk and, besides, cut heavily into the author's royalties. Roskill believed that the publicity given the matter in the *Sunday Telegraph*, and echoes elsewhere in the press, had persuaded Withers to drop the matter.

Roskill maintained that he had acted throughout in perfectly good faith with the 3rd Earl Beatty. However, as he knew, the third Earl had badly misled him when he gave copyright clearance which was not in his right. Roskill contended that no charge of any action even approximating to improper conduct rested against him. How could he have guessed that, in the case of the second Earl, the copyright of his father's papers had descended to his executors? Roskill knew that Lady Nutting had given access to her late husband's papers to several historians who had quoted from them freely in their books and published acknowledgements to her. Why should she have treated him differently from other applicants, he wondered? He gave this as a possible answer:

> In retrospect it seems to me that the only possible grounds for the above attitude lies in the fact that, as Mrs Nutting knew, the second Earl picked a very silly quarrel with me over the Navy Records Society publishing as an Appendix to the second volume of *The Jellicoe Papers* some documents which he considered reflected adversely on his father. I was

Vice-President of the Society at the time in the absence on other business of its President Lord Carrington; but of course Earl Beatty had absolutely no claim to demand what the Society could or should not publish – as was made clear when he brought the matter up and attacked me at an AGM and the members of the Society supported me 100 per cent. Beatty neither owned the papers in question nor the copyright in them, and in truth made an ass of himself in bringing up the matter; but his wife understandably took his side in the dispute. Richard Ollard incidentally agrees that the whole trouble dates back to that unfortunate and unnecessary dispute.[41]

One of Roskill's associates at Churchill College says that the matter distressed Roskill considerably in his later years and may have broken his heart. One correspondent, Sainsbury, received from Roskill a letter in which he clearly indicated that his heart, if not broken, had gone out of any further thoughts of a major book. Perhaps a second volume of papers on the Naval Air Service might be done for the NRS, but nothing more.[42] It was Roskill's view that the third Earl had granted him all the permission he needed; the rub was that this had occurred just at the time that the trustees and executors of the second Earl were demanding their pound of flesh. Roskill, indeed, was caught in a bind, and it was a great pity that he did not obtain written permission to proceed with research in papers that were indeed 'a crock of gold'.

The second edition of Marder's *Jutland and After* had appeared in 1978, a considerable extension of the first – 363 as against 307 pages in the original – but did little to change the general perspective on the battle or the aftermath. Still, as Marder said, 'no book is so good that it cannot be made better.' A reviewer, Sainsbury, wondered if the second edition was worth the price. Marder replied that, although a jacket dust cover usually indulges in puffery, in this case the blurb was indicative of the range of new material: 'e.g. the German knowledge of the R.N.'s secret recognition signals and the effect of exhaustion during the battle, an expansion of my "treatment of personalities", a "broadening of the analysis of important facets of the battle", e.g. as regards the initial contact between the battle-cruiser forces, the operations of the destroyers on both sides, British and German gunnery, why the British battlecruisers blew up. Grand Fleet signal arrangements and enemy reporting, and Scheer's strategy and tactics.' Marder had the answers, all the answers.

Sainsbury had been watching the sniping that went on between Marder and Roskill. He noted in his review that Marder had now dropped reference to Roskill. No mention was made of the unsavoury affair of the Harper papers. There was no sinister intent in this, Marder replied to the editor of the *Naval Review*. He added, 'In the interval between the two editions Roskill abandoned his project of doing a study of the controversy.' Roskill, who followed this correspondence, could not leave this alone, and, characteristically, said that Marder was in error: 'The truth is that the second Earl Beatty proved so difficult over the use of his copyright of his father's papers, and so determined that any criticism of his actions should be suppressed, that I postponed publication.'[43]

Roskill's *Last Naval Hero* received fine, even glowing reviews.[44] This work, it is true, did not portray Admiral Beatty in a warm or gracious light. Roskill thought that Beatty was an unsavoury character or words to that effect, Donald Schurman advises, as well as a terrible anti-Semite.[45] Being Beatty's biographer would always be a difficult, even distasteful task in any event, as a future biographer attempting a full and authoritative life may attest. But one thing is sure: Roskill had set down clearly the relationship of Beatty to his two great loves, a lasting achievement.

Beatty, as Roskill portrayed him, was caught between devotion to Ethel, who had given him the financial underpinning that he had so desperately needed, and his private affair with the beautiful and agreeable Eugénie. Such a lovely contrast of women must have been a torment to the old admiral. As to Beatty and Jutland, Roskill went back to the board for all the details, relying heavily on Marder, with additional information provided by John Campbell's detailed work on British battlecruisers. The narrative is shot through with asides, many generous, about 'Professor's Marder's observations'. For example, Roskill writes on page 180 that 'Professor Marder's account of the seven phases into which that hectic night's events can be divided ... cannot be bettered.' James Goldrick, writing his *The King's Ships Were at Sea*, about the North Sea in the first seven months of the war, brought to Roskill's attention vital points at the proofs stage. Nicholas Rodger at the PRO fed him a stream of documents. On the matter of gunnery efficiency, Roskill benefited mightily from the pioneering work done by Jon Sumida, then not published, and fully acknowledged his debt to his source. That the Admiralty had destroyed various boxes of files concerning Arthur Pollen's invention for fire control of ship's gunnery[46] was a stain on the Admiralty, Roskill charged; he said, recklessly, that this sort of 'weeding' of records was nothing sort of scandalous. We now have, through the NRS's book on the Pollen Papers, edited by Sumida, sufficient evidence for what is surely one of the great 'might-have-beens' in the history of naval affairs – one as intriguing as the question of whether or not better signalling would have affected the outcome of the Battle of Jutland.[47] Roskill makes clear that the communications by signalling and radio were dismal, to and from Beatty, rivalling that to and from Jellicoe or the Admiralty for that matter.

The exercising of command at sea rests with communications, which alone determine deployments and tactics, the root of all the problems at Jutland. Corbett had always stressed communications to be vital: no one doubted this, but, as Roskill explains, the mistakes led to disastrous consequences. A major problem during this dawn of the age in which distant operations could be directly influenced from headquarters ashore was the flow of information within the Admiralty and how intelligence was not passed on immediately to the fleet. The trouble was in the Admiralty, and most blameworthy, as Roskill put it, was the 'staggeringly bad co-operation of the Admiralty's War Staff with Room 40'.[48] But it was Roskill's account of Beatty's loves that was the most original feature of his book, shedding a new light on the women behind, or in front of, the admiral. Roskill's book will be read a good deal in the future because of the insights it brings to these matters. In an important way, his biography of Beatty was path-breaking for it treated naval history as social history – not of classes, mind you, or of inter-class rivalry, but of the social relations of a great commander with two remarkable women.

As to the unhappy matter of the Harper documents, Roskill makes clear that Harper became increasingly obsessive, even neurotic, as Beatty's interference and tampering continued. In Roskill's estimation, Beatty's actions were 'highly injudicious, even reprehensible, interference' in the preparation of the various accounts but he should be generously acquitted on Harper's most damaging charges against him.[49] This author cannot accept this view, which seems odd, even contradictory. It flies in the face of evidence and is at variance with the steady, true course that Harper maintained throughout the long contest. But that is Roskill's adjudication on it, and we leave it at that for others to judge.

When Roskill's *Last Naval Hero* appeared in print, the signals between him and Marder had become fainter and less frequent. Charm and geniality had disappeared from their correspondence, with subjects restricted to historical matters, especially the sharing of documents – for they needed each other. In public, however, Roskill still could not leave Marder alone, and the references to Marder in *Last Naval Hero*, Sainsbury noted, were numerous but restrained. In his review of the book, Sainsbury commented that 'an agreeable and welcome tranquillity seems to be descending on their relationship. Marder's third volume, especially in its revised version, is as definite a work on Jutland as we need or are likely to get and Roskill, though never hesitant to comment critically, seems content to accept it as a basic source.' Nonetheless, Roskill took the bulk of one chapter to quarrel and joust with Marder on Jutland.

Part Three

Closings

Chapter 10

Rising Sun and California Sunset: Marder's Farewell to History

FRESH from his year at Oxford in 1969–70, Marder returned to the University of California, Irvine. He had some inkling as to what might face him, for, on the eve of his departure for England, the general discontent sweeping American college campuses had not escaped Irvine. Because that university was a recent creation, though nonetheless a branch of a well-founded state-wide system, much of what transpired there appeared to be revolutionary even if in fact it wasn't. Orange County was a Republican stronghold, and the state governor, Ronald Reagan, was at war with the university chancellor, Clark Kerr. The faculty generally supported Kerr but could not overturn Reagan's firing of him.

Marder never wrote about the ferment, or what some would call the general malaise that infected society and the university, but it is clear that several interlocking causes lay at the bottom of the problems that he and other senior faculty members faced. Because Marder took seriously his role as a 'founding father' of UCI, he felt the distemper of the times keenly. Pervasive student unrest Marder could deal with in a rational way, but in his department dissension existed between what might be called the old guard and the young Turks. Marder played a prominent role in hiring most of the young assistant professors, and so once these junior faculty members became obstreperous, advanced new theories about the nature of history, or sided overtly with certain students pushing revolutionary positions, Marder became marginalized and ostracized. So many causes were being pursued by student groups at that time – opposition to American policy in the Vietnam War, support for civil rights and gender equity, and promotion of the mores of the new drug culture that encompassed both youth and young adults. All of these – and others – came together in the late 1960s. But it was challenges to university governance by students that Marder found the difficult matter. Marder could not escape the vortex into which he and other senior academics were drawn. It was time to take a stand or to walk away, and Marder never walked away from a problem or a fight, rather the reverse.

The leading champion of student causes at UCI was a brilliant, eloquent PhD student assigned to Marder, Rich Robertson. The clarity of the twenty-one-year old's writings in the campus paper show that he had many of the gifts of his supervising professor. Only a lit match was necessary to bring forth flames to any number of smouldering piles. A young member of the History Department, George Kent, Asian specialist, was up for tenure. Marder declined support for him, possibly on grounds that he was a lightweight in research. The department was split on the issue. To broker a deal and prevent further disaffection from the junior faculty, the new dean, Dr Hazard Adams, had Kent assigned to a new department of culture where he could have a permanent home. Marder had been outflanked. This matter had brought forth a challenge from Robertson, who, in support of Kent, had challenged Marder's authority. Robertson abused Marder mightily in the office of the department chairman and virtually spat in his face (as Meyer put it). Marder, while taking it in good stride, concluded that he could not stand impartially by as supervisor to Robertson and must step down. Robertson found himself assigned to another member of department. Not to be denied, Robertson could not accept Marder's position as constitutionally correct: he contended that faculty such as Marder could not pick and choose their battles.[1] There for the moment the matter rested, with the young faculty increasingly supporting student causes and the older ones resisting the same as well as responding to pressures from the young Turks. Robertson was reassigned – to Meyer.

At Balliol, Marder had come to know one of the fellows, Richard Cobb, noted authority on the French revolution. On returning to UCI, he arranged an invitation for Cobb to be a visiting professor the next year. One would have thought that an Englishman's discussion of French revolutionary history would be welcome among the student body, not least among Robertson and his radical associates. Now it was Robertson's turn to play a constitutional card: if the university were to spend money on a guest lectureship, then the students must have a role to play as to who would be invited. Faculty appointments had to have student consent or support, otherwise havoc would ensue. Robertson and company played up the issue, arguing that they did not have a complete dossier on Cobb, and at the end of the day the invitation to Cobb had to be withdrawn. The matter reached the pages of *The Times* by way of a well-concealed Balliol connection. In the end, the students fielded their own candidate, none other than Robertson, whose nomination was unacceptable to the History Department. 'The whole affair is very characteristic of the inefficiency and deviousness of student bureaucracy,' commented Cobb, no stranger to how revolutions were fomented. As for his own fortunes, a rival invitation to visit India had just come his way, and there he hoped that student control had not yet taken root. The Cobb affair proved embarrassing to Marder and a source of further alienation from his own department and its students.[2]

Adding further to Marder's difficulties at UCI was the general position taken by the department that students be allowed representation at the departmental table – in other words, having a voice in affairs, if not a vote in decisions. Marder was not alone in opposing this but one by one his supporters fell by the wayside. In several 'Cassandra Letters' to his closest friends, he explained that he could not accept these changes and that, in protest, he would attend department meetings out of professorial obligation but would not take part in discussion. He took up a certain position at the table, distant from others, and while they carried on in discussion of pressing issues including matters of protocol and order, he remained silent – the first time since his undergraduate years at Harvard that he would have been quiet in a university setting. His position was ridiculed but to have walked away would have been a sign of defeat.

Marder was seen by younger colleagues, and even some veterans, as a prima donna. That was their view of him. English observers saw him differently, regarding him as modest in demeanour and disposition. Certainly, as a teacher, there was not a hint of arrogance in his performance; he took his classroom duties seriously and attended to them with commitment and zeal. One of his standard offerings at the undergraduate level was a course on British history and traditions, standard fare as seen from the outside but compelling to students. Another staple was his course on historiography, once a requirement for all honours students but which died on his departure. A third course, still remembered with admiration, was on the British military tradition, a senior course based on readings of the authorities of the day – Liddell Hart, Michael Howard, Stephen Roskill, and other stalwarts.

Age had not quelled his spirit as a historian but, predictably, had isolated him from the swirl of events of national and California politics. Yet another issue was forcing his alienation. The curriculum put in place at the time of his appointment only half a dozen years earlier was now being reorganized, with many demands about breadth and depth up for consideration; his Western-civilization course was being reorganized by those who favoured theory-based and comparative research and social science. The replacement course was the team-taught 'Making of the Modern World'. This was based, as Marder saw it, on postulates antithetical to everything he believed in as regard to historical research, which to his way of thinking was document-based. The UCI historians were in the vanguard of many other sweeping changes then reordering the 'history profession', and they had many supporters elsewhere off-campus. To his senior colleagues, Marder wrote privately about his own views on this upheaval:

> I see considerable merit in a program which has a theory *component*; I see little in one which is so theory-*focused*. In all the discussions . . . there has been no mention that the study and teaching of history involve a great deal more than knowledge of the concepts and theories of Durkheim, Weber, & Co. To understand and try to apply Weber's writings on the modes of political domination, or Veblen's analysis of class social psychology, or Fogel's 'counter-factional conditional concept', and so forth and so on, is splendid. It is useful for a graduate student to understand some of this stuff and to try his hand at applying them to particular historical events and movements. It might even lead him into fruitful research paths. But there is so much more to the study of history than this sort of approach. History is also, *inter alia, narrative* – in which the political, social, economic, and cultural threads are interwoven. It is the mastery of the whats, whys, and wherefores of man's more significant experiences. It is poetry and imagination. Yes, and it is Ranke's 'wie es eigentlich gewesen ist'. Durkheim, Weber & Co. can't begin by themselves to do the job that is required! I regard them as aids or tools, *no more*.

With the History Department 'hell-bent on a theory emphasis', as he put it, the study of history at the postgraduate level promised to become a narrow affair. At the undergraduate level, he thought it would be a complete disaster. Marder could not resist a further jibe at his younger colleagues, who seemed to have taken up new causes of history with inconsiderate haste. He quoted a recent address by Louis B. Wright, distinguished historian of American colonization: 'It is astonishing how some historians naively hail the latest fashion in research as the only road to truth. A corollary to this is an intolerance of all those who do not embrace the new faith. The path of historians for the past century and a half is littered with abandoned dogmas that ought to provide a warning against certainty that any one method is the only way to truth.' To this, Marder added: 'Hear, hear!' The bleak job market was further cause for worry. It was all very well for graduate students to prate on how much they loved the study of history but the fact remained that one day they must face the problem of 'how to pay for the bacon and eggs that will enable them to pursue their much-loved interest.'[3]

Marder kept his composure and carried out his many other duties. He maintained his research agenda in the face of several challenges. He kept to his priorities. Fending off numerous invitations, he concentrated on matters at home, including presidency of the American Historical Association, Pacific Coast Branch, in 1971–72. Marder, not distanced from graduate supervision, saw through the work of four budding historians who completed PhD theses. One of these historians, Gerald Jordan, was an expert on Nelson, and two others, Mark Jacobsen and John Horsfield, under whom Marder also lit a fire, were to complete the second volume of Marder's book on the Royal Navy and the Imperial Japanese Navy. The fourth, Jack Gusewelle, wrote on an aspect of the history of India.

At this time, Marder seems to have had no capacity or drive to write another big book; ten had been enough – on average, one every three years. Even so, short studies offered tantalizing possibilities: Jutland and the Dardanelles remained preoccupations, and Jacky Fisher, too. Marder was all the while revising and enlarging *Jutland and After*, which, as noted in the previous chapter, appeared in a second edition in 1978. At Oxford University Press, his editor, Geoffrey Hunt, looked for a new book from Marder. He showed patience and hope. On one occasion, he wrote to Marder to say that good books were hard to come by and that he was prepared to wait for Marder's next. Hunt knew how to lure Marder. Marder, in a moment of relief, proposed a collection of printed articles and yet-to-be-completed shorter studies. In the latter category would be 'Oran, 3 July 1940', subtitled 'Mistaken Judgement, Tragic Misunderstanding, or Cruel Necessity?' – a study of the measures taken, when diplomacy failed, to keep French ships at Oran in North Africa out of German hands. The result, when the larger project was brought to more manageable proportions, became *From the Dardanelles to Oran* (1974), described by one reviewer as 'history at its best'. Yet another book came to OUP from Marder – the already discussed *Operation 'Menace'* (1976). For Marder, these were all short pieces.

All during this time Marder wearily told his colleagues and friends that he would write no more. But the reviews were wildly enthusiastic and appeared in the top British dailies, Sunday papers, and weekly journals such as the *New Statesmen*, the *Spectator,* the *Economist*, and the *Times Literary Supplement*. More was eagerly expected from Marder's pen. His colleagues, friends, and publisher reasoned that he would surely return to his life's calling.

From an unexpected source came the idea for a new book. Admiral Lord Mountbatten, the former first lord of the Admiralty and chief of the defence staff, suggested to Marder that he explore the Imperial Japanese Navy in relation to the Royal Navy. Marder had been approached for a biography of Mountbatten's father, Admiral of the Fleet Prince Louis of Battenburg, and had declined the proposal. Something more current along the lines of his recent Second World War inquiries would be more fetching. Marder talked it over with his young friend Alvin Coox, the military historian of Japan and a professor at San Diego State University. Many years before, in 1948, at the suggestion of his Harvard professor Donald Cope McKay, Coox had visited Marder in Hawaii to seek his counsel about writing Japanese military history. Coox regarded Marder as his intellectual 'godfather', much as Marder looked on Langer as his. Marder, at about the time of Coox's visit to Hawaii to see him, had set aside his desires to become a historian of the Japanese Navy in favour of a return to his first love, the British Navy. Thus the new idea – of linking the Imperial Japanese Navy with the Royal Navy – was for Marder a gift from the gods, particularly if Coox could become the chief counsel and guide to the Japanese sources. The idea for the book embraced new and engaging horizons. Of central importance, Coox could assist with translation (his wife, Hisako, was Japanese) and he could open doors to translators in the United States and Japan.

Marder immersed himself into the interactions and relations, in peace and war, of the Royal Navy and the Imperial Japanese Navy in the critical 1936–45 decade. As Marder rightly reasoned, there was no lack of writings in English on facets of the subject, but no scholar had yet attempted to study the whole story from both sides and with extensive use of both Japanese- and English-language documentary sources and printed materials. In addition to war planning in the lead-up to the conflict and wartime strategy and tactics, he intended to become concerned with the 'psychology' of the two navies: among other matters, the stereotypical views that the RN and IJN held of each other and the values, traditions, and general outlook of the two forces, all treated comparatively. This was a tall order. But it was a new task that had happily presented itself. Marder knew that he would get more data from British archives than he could from the relatively thin Japanese naval archives. The RN's records were voluminous; the IJN's destroyed, either by the bombings of Tokyo in 1945 (and resultant fires) or through wilful destruction on orders of the Navy minister as the war was coming to an end. Marder had some knowledge of the Japanese language from earlier days, and in 1961 he had travelled in Japan. These were added benefits to his scholarship.

As before, Marder's research depended on scholarly grants. Just when he thought preliminary funding secured, in May 1975 the door was closed because of an abrupt altering of the requirements for a university summer-research grant. In any case, he and his wife were then embarked on a cruise to the Mediterranean, part of the alluring Campus Afloat Summer Program run by Chapman College. This is how, in typical Marderese, he expressed the sudden change of plans to John Lawson of the Naval Historical Branch in London: 'The Lord has spoken. I'll NOT be doing that large study of the Japanese Connection, or anything large.' Lawson must have mopped his brow in relief when he received Marder's letter, for, as in the past, he would be obliged to answer a never-ending stream of queries from Marder. Alongside these two sentences of Marder's letter he scratched, 'Welcome news!' Lawson's superior added 'very good news'. But Marder seldom wrote a letter that did not contain some sort of request for information. In the event, Lawson dug into the files as asked and obtained for Marder the naval diving teams' damage reports on the wrecks of the *Prince of Wales* and *Repulse*.[4]

Pleasant cruising in the Mediterranean with Jan that summer of 1975 did not result in relief from fatigue, but before he returned to California he nonetheless made a whirlwind visit to London to consult with Lawson at the Naval Historical Branch, there to ferret out some sources, and to talk to his publisher. He was seeking to determine the dimensions of what was opening before him. Once back in California, he completed a confidential report to his university dean, the sort of thing on which most university scholars customarily put the best face with regard to recent performance and future prospects: 'I have no time-table for this project, nor can I be *certain* at this stage that I have a book, as distinct from one or more major articles. Much will depend on my ability to generate support for research assistance and help with translation and interviewing. Something will depend on my health: I am pretty tired – *mentally* – and need a period of relaxation when I am not striving to meet a publisher's deadline. Indeed, it is for this reason that I have refused a contract from my publisher, Sir John Brown, of Oxford University Press (London). This does *not* mean that I have retired as a scholar – far from it.'[5]

In the late spring and early and summer of 1976, Marder travelled to Japan to interview Japanese naval officers and to gather materials. Now another visit was called for. Reading Marder's successful application to the National Endowment for the Humanities (NEH), for intended research in Japan in 1978, we learn of the extent of his research already completed or yet to be done. On the British side, he had interviewed and corresponded with several British participants and read the various printed materials. Loose ends remained. These included answering a plethora of queries that had arisen, and continued to arise, in the course of research. Several dozen Admiralty and Cabinet Office files had escaped his net, either because they were still out of bounds under the 30-year rule or because they were regarded as too sensitive for release. 'I ran out of time in my last visit . . . so could make no effort to spring these materials. Experience shows that, approached tactfully and with cogent arguments, Authority will bend somewhat.' In any event, new materials would be released on 1 January next. Marder's documentary list looks like an urgent shopping list for groceries. At the Churchill Archives Centre, where Roskill was a principal and directing force, papers of Admiral of the Fleet Sir James Somerville (commander-in-chief, Eastern Fleet, 1942–44, head of British Admiralty delegation to Washington, 1944–45) had become available, having been closed until 1977. Roskill had promised to show Marder material from his own papers about important facets of the story of the Eastern Fleet. At the National Maritime Museum, Greenwich, were papers of Admiral of the Fleet Lord Chatfield (first sea lord, 1933–38, minister for coordination of defence, 1939–40). There were other possibilities, including Admiral Lord Louis Mountbatten's papers covering his tenure as supreme allied commander, South East Asia, 1943–45. These last Marder did not get access to, since they were under wraps while awaiting appointment of an official biographer: this was eventually Phillip Ziegler. In Washington, Marder intended to examine Admiral William ('Bull') Halsey's papers in the Library of Congress and those of Admiral Ernest King in the Naval Historical Center, Department of the Navy. His purpose was to determine RN–USN relations vis-à-vis the Pacific war, and also to see what Japanese naval documents were in the Naval Historical Center. All of this viewed the British side of the story, with a glance at the Japanese.

On the IJN side, Marder had read almost everything that had been published in English, including proceedings of the International Military Tribunal for the Far East, the 'Japanese Monographs' series (prepared by Japanese officials for General Douglas MacArthur's post-war headquarters in Tokyo), and the US Strategic Bombing Survey interrogations of Japanese officials. He had already in Japan interviewed thirty-five officers of the old Navy, corresponded with half a dozen others, and collected a miscellany of source materials, especially from the Office of War History of the Defence Agency. One of Marder's enduring techniques was to exploit official military files, but his search always extended far beyond these self-restricting confines. Drawing on the findings of his research assistant, the amiable and devoted Coox, Marder discussed in his NEH application the various Japanese materials that had survived the systematic destruction – by the highest military leaders – at the time of Japan's surrender in August 1945.[6] Coox helped him make intelligent selections for translation by a hired translator in Tokyo (an IJN commander). By 1978, Marder had made a dent in the eighteen or so volumes in the ninety-six-volume (to that date) official Japanese history of the war pertinent to his subject. These, together with the volumes of the Contemporary History Material series, would be the thrust of his research programme. Much lay ahead for another visit to Japan: the diaries of the late Professor Shigetar Shimada, who when at the Navy Ministry had saved a small portion of the naval archives, and the papers of important admirals (Isoroku Yamamoto, Mineichi Koga-Nori). Then there were holdings in the Naval Library at Meguro, the National Diet Library, various private papers and diaries, and the naval periodical *Hata*. He had, besides, to consult Professor Sadao Asada, of Doshisha University, Kyoto, the ablest of younger naval historians. Also to interview was Professor Tsunoda Jun, foremost scholar of twentieth-century Japanese military and diplomatic history, and various naval officers. He and Jan did a lecturing tour to Australian universities, where they were feted, and they took their regularly scheduled holidays.

Marder, age sixty-eight, now revived if ever he had faltered, set a rigorous research agenda. His plan called for uninterrupted writing, with OUP waiting expectantly for the book though with no firm contract signed. Marder knew that he was onto an original study of relationships – of mutual influencing, as it were, or of how the two navies interacted in peace and in war. He thought 'that inevitable tragedy' might well be the subtitle of the completed study. He wanted to get at the Japanese side of the story, a difficult task as it proved, and to use Japanese sources to enrich and broaden the study. Marder was realistic about his own abilities and what might be the outcome:

> I bring no theories of history to my research and writing, nor do I expect to arrive at any startling conclusions. I am essentially a narrative historian, in the tradition of a G.M. Trevelyan, A.J.P. Taylor, and the late Samuel Eliot Morison. I want to tell a story and to tell it well, and with a liberal infusion of the personal – the human – component, for I can never forget that at bottom history is about *people*, individuals as well as groups. The story that I shall tell is, basically, a tragic one, and with man's limitations all too prominently displayed, such as his moral cowardice at times and his shortsighted thinking. Yet it will also show man at his sublime best, for there are many instances of courage, moral as well as physical, of farsightedness, and of an extraordinary spirit of self-sacrifice.

In Japan, Marder faced the problem of the absence of the naval archives.[7] He shared this frustration with Professor Asada and all others engaged in research in Japanese naval history.[8] This forced him to rely on interviews and correspondence with former naval officers. Asada recalled the limits Marder faced: 'Understandably Japanese naval leaders are extremely reluctant to talk about the war they lost, but Arthur managed to have some substantive interviews with a dwindling group of former officers . . . It is to his credit that he got as much information as he did. Sometimes former Japanese officers are more willing to open themselves up to foreigners, especially scholars of Arthur's distinction, than to Japanese researchers. And Arthur took full advantage of this privileged position.' Marder used relevant portions of important diaries, memoirs, biographies, and a wide range of secondary sources – all translated for him. Among English-language works he used Asada's celebrated study of the relationship of the IJN and the USN, a parallel study to Marder's. 'In a way, Arthur turned virtue out of necessity. His comparison of Etajima (Japanese naval academy) with its British counterpart is simply brilliant.'[9] Marder managed a lecture at Professor Asada's university, Doshisha. 'You certainly covered a lot of ground both in your lecture-discussion sessions and in your ambitious sight-seeing schedule!' said Asada. Marder's visit to Kyoto was a triumph: 'We found your intimate and personal account so helpful, interesting, and (if I may say so) inspiring both to specialists and graduate students.' Asada was profoundly grateful to Marder for suggestions and advice about his own work.

At that university, Asada hosted a lecture, delivered under the auspices of the Japan Foundation, in which Marder talked on the subject 'An American Historian's Love Affair with the Royal Navy: Reflections on Forty-Seven Years of Marital Bliss.' Asada gingerly coaxed the text out of Marder and had it published in his university's journal. The result is the only fragment of Marder's reflections on his engagement with history and his lengthy immersion in Royal Navy history. 'That history teaches us only that we learn nothing from history is a dictum whose truth has been sadly confirmed for me time and time again, particularly in my study of the inter-war period.' He was puzzled by why the lessons of 1914–18 were forgotten, neglected, or not thoroughly absorbed. The Navy had forgotten the success brought about by the introduction of convoys in 1917. 'Why do armies and navies rarely learn from success? In chasing this one down, I found myself lost in a maze of varied explanations, no single one of which represented the *key* to the problem, but all of which brought me face to face with what seems to me to be the central problem of all historical study: human motivations, their sources and conditioning.' The answer to so many historical problems, as Langer had stressed, lay in a much better understanding of man. What struck Marder most forcibly was the extent to which personality affects history.[10]

Also in Japan, Marder visited the naval academy Etajima, modelled along the lines of Britannia Naval College, and there was greeted warmly. Then he discovered that his 1972 publication 'The Influence of Sea Power upon History' – about naval lessons the British learned or neglected from the First World War – was required reading among the naval cadets. Here Nelson was held high as the embodiment of British sea power. Admiral Heihachiro Togo, the victor at Tsushima, was equally venerated as the Japanese Nelson. When Marder spoke to the aggregate officers, faculty, staff, and cadets on his favourite topic of Nelson and leadership in the Royal Navy, all eyes were on him, all ears listening to his every word: he seemed to his hosts to be the next Alfred Thayer Mahan.

While Marder pressed on with his new project, he faced the prospect of retirement. He left the university without regret or rancour in 1977. In announcing his retirement, the university press office recounted the story of the young professor, facing his first teaching assignment and weary after late-night lecture preparations, who had delivered what he thought was a competent lecture on the French Revolution of 1789. His students, however, looked puzzled, and not until the end of his lecture did he realize that he was addressing his class in modern Russian history. So had begun Marder's teaching career. There was news, too, of the fact that the second Lord Fisher of Kilverstone, the admiral's son, had given him a silver model of Britain's first submarine, and this was one of Marder's prized possessions. The model was first given by King Edward VII to Jacky Fisher as a Christmas present in 1909. The son had given it to Marder as a memento of his father in appreciation of Marder's *Fear God and Dread Nought*, the edition of Jacky's letters.

Many tributes and gifts were given to Marder upon his retirement, but none so touching as a Festschrift edited by his doctoral student Gerald Jordan, *Naval Warfare in the Twentieth Century, 1900–1954: Essays in Honour of Arthur Marder*.[11] This volume of writings, presented as a tribute to a scholar by his peers, contained contributions from a dozen scholars from Japan, Britain, Canada, and the United States. Admiral of the Fleet the Earl Mountbatten of Burma provided a glowing foreword; as he explained, Mountbatten had been proud to be associated with Marder's outstanding historical work and his international reputation as a modern naval historian of the highest calibre.

Roskill was not among the contributors, his essay having been declined by the editor as unsuitable. Why? In rejecting Roskill's invited contribution, Jordan chose his words carefully. He had found Roskill's 'Essay on the Writings of Arthur Marder' both stimulating and provocative. But he declined it on grounds that, since so much of it concerned disputes of the kind students of naval history were following in the *TLS*, its contents demanded that Marder be given the opportunity to reply. Jordan had been looking for an essay which discussed and evaluated Marder's work in the context of twentieth-century British naval historical writing. Instead, Roskill had sent a review that bordered on the accusatory, stating how Marder had broken — or forgotten after the passage of fifteen years — a gentleman's agreement to stop *From the Dreadnought to Scapa Flow* at war's end, thus leaving Roskill to fill the gap between the Corbett-Newbolt *Naval Operations 1914–1918* and his own *War at Sea 1939–1945*. Roskill complained of Marder's sparse footnoting. He objected to Marder's importunities to critique his manuscripts. He thought Marder had unwisely yielded to might-have-beens when he speculated on possible results of an energized Dardanelles campaign. He complained vehemently of Marder's use of Seal's very nasty attack on him. He deplored Marder's inaccurate statements regarding the Admiral North affair in the *TLS* (30 April 1976). In short, despite praising Marder's work and wishing him a happy, profitable retirement, Roskill had intended to disclose the details of their dispute as he saw them — a selective assault, mind, for it dodged the unsavory Hankey diary fight. Roskill's essay was a reworking of a 2,500-word memoir he had prepared for posterity, 'Marder v Roskill', dated 1 May 1975. That Roskill felt deeply about his anguished relations with Marder is clear in these writings, but they did not belong in print and Jordan knew it. 'No further action' is what Roskill wrote on Jordan's rejection letter.[12]

While the book was at press, Marder had made one last attempt to smooth relations with Roskill, and for that purpose, among others, had visited Churchill College — with some success.[13]

Meanwhile, at the University of California, Irvine, the Senate had selected him as distinguished faculty lecturer for 1977–78. This, coming from peers, he regarded as the highest tribute paid him. He took as his subject the rise and fall of the IJN, with dates 1941–45. The lecture was printed under title of *Bravery Is Not Enough*, in November 1978. Marder told his audience how the British and American navies had failed to grasp the strengths of the IJN, miscasting the Japanese national characteristic of slowness of mind and underestimating Japanese naval air power, with its high degree of training, efficiency, and ability to sink warships. On the British side, the supreme confidence engendered by their glorious naval tradition — the Nelson syndrome, he called it — wedded to a large measure of ignorance stemming from the near impossibility of obtaining reliable intelligence on the Japanese fleet, were sources of trouble. Then came the great shock — Chuichi Nagumo's attack against Pearl Harbor — and on 10 December 1941 the newly arrived battleship *Prince of Wales* and battle cruiser *Repulse* disappeared beneath the waves of the South China Sea; the aircraft carrier that was to have accompanied the two capital ships grounded shortly after Force Z had sailed to Singapore. Marder told how the British ships were attacked by seventy-five twin-engined, land-based bombers and torpedo bombers of the IJN's 22nd Air Flotilla operating from what is now known as Vietnam. It was a terrible tragedy for British forces, a devastating blow to power and prestige, and the blackest day in the history of the British Empire. The fall of Singapore the following February was the largest capitulation in British history, involving the surrender of 130,000 troops and loss of the only base from which Britain could defend Australia and New Zealand. 'These victories', Marder reflected, 'had a tremendous morale effect on the Imperial Navy, which, drunk with success, now envisaged a short victorious war, not the prolonged pre-December calculations with the outcome in doubt.'

From his description of Japanese naval capability Marder proceeded to explain its fall. In 1937 Admiral Soemu Toyoda, the chief of the Navy Ministry's Bureau of Naval Affairs, had made this pithy observation: 'We lag behind the material agencies of war; we therefore try to keep our personnel equal or superior to that of any other navy.' The superiority in efficiency began at Etajima, where physical fitness, endurance, and toughness were stressed and the cadets were bred to a rigid discipline, one that had its origins in the samurai code during centuries of feudalism. Loyalty, courtesy, valour, fidelity, and simplicity were all instilled, and burning devotion to the emperor constituted the spiritual life of the academy. But honour and duty were not enough, Marder explained, and even though the IJN built the largest battleships (70,000 mastodons, he called them) and had the fastest torpedoes and the most advanced fighter aircraft in the world's navies, and even though they constructed the largest guns (18in), greatest armour, and new weapons in the form of the giant 'cherry blossom' gliding, rocket-assisted piloted bomb and the 'human torpedo', *kaiten*, introduced in 1945, this was not enough either. Nor did *kamikaze* attacks counter the overwhelming superiority of the enemy's forces and reverse the dangerous situation into which Japan had been driven by 1944.

Marder wrote that the fall of the Imperial Navy could not be attributed to being overwhelmed by superior technology and a massive superiority in numbers of ships, planes, gun, and men. Japanese tactical considerations had assumed a knock-out blow as at Tsushima against the Russian fleet in 1905 – and a sudden end of war. The IJN was poor at collecting information, and the Army and Navy had an unsatisfactory relationship. But there were deeper roots of difficulty: the absence of independent rational judgement and too confident belief in superior fighting techniques and fighting spirit. As one commander of *kamikaze* operations put it: 'Right up to the end, we believed we could outweigh your material and scientific superiority by the force of our moral and spiritual convictions.' 'The Combined Fleet will never return,' wrote Masanori Ito in his book *The End of the Imperial Japanese Navy*. This was true. Its existence, its achievements were but a page in history and the blame ought not to be placed upon the enemy who destroyed it but on Japan itself. This was Ito's verdict. It was Marder's as well. It covered the sins of omission and commission and, as he put it, also revealed flaws in the national character which he, too, identified – that is, lack of sound judgement and overstress on spiritual qualities.[14]

If Marder was undertaking an anatomical study, as it were, of the IJN, he was similarly examining the Royal Navy. The misadventure of Force Z and the loss of the *Prince of Wales* and *Repulse* were supreme tragedies in the history of the Royal Navy – indeed in all annals of the sea. Not content with official reports of proceedings and battle summaries, Marder went after those who could shed new light on the past. He showed the instincts of Basil Liddell Hart, John Toland, and others in this sort of work. Using his customary technique of soliciting written answers to questions about such events, Marder wrote to Admiral of the Fleet Lord Fraser of North Cape. He enclosed a list of questions and expectantly awaited answers. Months went by and Marder got no response from Fraser, then aged ninety-one and in Royal Naval Hospital Haslar, Portsmouth. Marder pressed Mountbatten to get the needed responses from Fraser. Mountbatten had been charmed by Marder and had encouraged him in his research. He was eager to help him with his new project inasmuch as he would feature mightily in the narrative when Marder got to Churchill's appointment of him to the South East Asia command. Bearing the historian's commission, Mountbatten visited Fraser in hospital. That evening he wrote Fraser: 'May I urge you to deal with them [Marder's queries] very carefully because he is our most important author of the Royal Navy and the book he is going to do about the Japanese War at Sea may well become the standard work. I have given him what help I can but, of course, your help as Commander-in-Chief, first of the Far Eastern Fleet and then of the British Pacific Fleet[,] is vital.'

Marder had prepared his questions for Fraser (then an admiral of the fleet) with care. He knew that the health of Admiral Sir Dudley Pound, first sea lord, was of material importance, and Roskill thought Pound quite unfit for his job medically (and, as we have seen, had written to that effect in his 1977 book *Churchill and the Admirals*, a riposte to Marder's interpretation). Fraser's replies for Marder left nothing to chance. No, there was nothing wrong with Dudley Pound's health when he was first sea lord. He was mentally alert. No,

Pound was not Winston's 'stooge'. Yes, he would fight hard on strategical and operational policy. Pound put up a very tough fight regarding the *Prince of Wales* – he refused to send out the *Prince of Wales* and *Repulse* until Churchill changed the destination to Australia under the cover of the Royal Australian Air Force. 'Winston's words to me were, "I want to keep a thorn in the side of the Japanese."' In answer to Marder's 'How was the sinking received at the Admiralty?' Fraser replied, 'Like every other sinking.' His relations with the Americans, especially Admiral King, were very good. 'Admiral King was obstructive because he didn't want supplies to the American fleet cut short in any way. When I met him after the war he was very nice.'[15] And so on. This shows what Fraser could provide, but, from the point of view of historical inquiry, it also shows the Marder method, and the results – typical of those produced by his wide-ranging correspondence – provided the new materials for his history.

Many shared in Marder's triumphs as a historian but perhaps none so much as his mentor, Langer, whom he had almost maimed (as the legend now stated) when hurtling down the steps of the Widener Library. Langer had kept in close touch with his prodigy. He marvelled at Marder's ability to collect so much data in the course of a trawl through records offices and private papers, on one occasion jesting that he thought his pupil would have to hire a vessel the size of a large Cunard liner to bring home the spoils. He delighted in A.J.P. Taylor's 'rhapsodizing' of Marder, and he continued to watch, with awe and respect, Marder's prodigious output of fine histories. Marder, whose correspondence files bulk large with flattering appreciations from the likes of British admirals, colleagues, staff, and students, never forgot his mentor, and he converted the honorarium given for his *Bravery Is Not Enough* lecture into a UCI scholarship in Langer's name.

When he retired from the university in 1977, Marder had intended to complete his scholarly agenda. Yet no sooner had he relocated to the lovely Oceanside community of Montecito, Santa Barbara, in 1978 than the promise of a new dawn in connection with a new History Department did not appear so bright after all. It is true that he had an office among the historians at the University of California, Santa Barbara, and kept nominal office hours, all the while maintaining a rigorous schedule of research and writing. But he was often absent or away, and, apart from early warm receptions as an additional star on campus, the aura began to fade. Besides Meyer, Coox, and McCulloch and their wives, few came to call and for the first time in their lives Arthur and Jan had free time on their hands. Then came, upon application, a lovely invitation. He was awarded a three-months' residency at the Rockefeller Foundation's Bellagio villa on Lake Como, and it was there that he wrote three long chapters on the tragedy of the *Prince of Wales* and *Repulse*. Jan was his constant companion, as always. Afterwards, they returned to Santa Barbara and the delightful ambience of splendid scholarly isolation, beautiful walks on paths overlooking the Pacific, and occasional company was both therapeutic and productive of good writing.

In January 1980 Marder sent the first volume of his text on the RN and IJN to Oxford University Press. The dedication read: 'To Alvin Coox with profound gratitude for his encouragement and help, *ab ovo*.' The next month he discovered the awful news that he had pancreatic cancer. He now faced a round of medical examinations, major surgery, and various therapies. There were months of agonizing work as the queries and answers flew back and forth between Oxford and Montecito. He went into remission. Throughout this time, he continued to be a disciplined researcher and writer. He finished chapters one through six and the appendix for the second volume of the RN-IJN study. He even crafted the dedication for what he knew would be his last book if published: 'To Peter Kemp, for steadfast support over a generation, my undying gratitude.' It was his last farewell to history. During one period in these last fleeting months, a final trip to Japan had been planned for more research. Instead, he and his beloved wife took a long anticipated trip to Tahiti as tourists. He died in hospital in Santa Barbara on Christmas Day 1980.

Marder never saw his last work in print. The first volume, *Old Friends, New Enemies: The Royal Navy and the Imperial Japanese Navy, Strategic Illusions 1936–1941*, was published in 1981. His supremely devoted friend and aide, Kemp, saw it through the press and indexed the book. Kemp opened his tribute to Marder by quoting his late associate: 'To look at yesterday with the eyes of yesterday, that is the historian's real task.' Kemp thought this was the reason why Marder could be called 'the supreme historian'. Marder also said, 'It's unfair to criticize a man because you know something he didn't know.' This had come out vigorously in the case of Vice Admiral Tom Phillips in the episode of the *Prince of Wales* and *Repulse*. Kemp continued: 'But there is more to the writing of history than that. The basis of all good historical work is knowledge, and in this Arthur towered above so many of his contemporaries. His appetite for research was prodigious by any standards, and it was matched both by his own energy and by his powers of meticulous organization of the material he collected. The volume of his correspondence was immense . . . and if all this letter-writing produced one small nugget of relevant information, he counted it all worth while. His industry, his dedication, his knowledge, his judgement, his integrity, his happy facility with words, made him one of the giants of his profession.'

RISING SUN AND CALIFORNIA SUNSET: MARDER'S FAREWELL

Kemp's lasting impression of Marder was that he was a man of both great happiness and great courage. He recalled the devastating news that much of the remaining research he had done for *From the Dreadnought to Scapa Flow* had gone up in smoke. It seemed like a blow from which he could never recover. Yet within a month Marder had made new plans to start research all over again in England. 'That was his courage, indomitable, undismayed. His love of life, of his children, of his friends, above all, his constant devotion to Jan, his wife, was his happiness, which is reflected in his work.'

Of all the reviews of *Old Friends, New Enemies*, that by former British naval officer and historian of note Ronald Lewin adds the broadest view and appreciations not found elsewhere. Marder's pre-eminence as master-historian of the Navy in the twentieth century, Lewin said, would seem anomalous were it not that he had been preceded by a fellow American, Admiral Mahan. 'Marder, however, sparkled with a constellation of qualities many of which are lacking in Mahan and some, at least, in his British rivals, among whom Captain Stephen Roskill is – in every sense – outstanding.' He continued:

> He shovelled up facts and formed them into intelligible patterns like those engineers of the US Marines who, almost over-night, bulldozed airstrips out of the Pacific coral islands. His relentless intellectual energy was expressed in a buoyant, athletic style. He was a nonpareil in the use of oral history for legitimately academic purposes; and a predisposition to praise never prevented him from identifying the occasions when, in the conduct of war, man *'like an angry ape / Plays such fantastic tricks before high heaven / As make the angels weep.'* . . . To read the last and splendid work of a great historian fills one with sorrow. But the story he has to tell is itself enough to 'make the angels weep.'[16]

At the memorial service held at the University of California, Irvine, many fine tributes were paid to Marder. His scholarly friends John S. Galbraith, Samuel McCulloch, and Henry Cord Meyer prepared the statement of appreciation. The Arthur Jacob Marder Prize, to be awarded annually for the best historical essay by a student, was announced – this, said Kemp, would surely have given Marder the greatest pleasure of all: 'With all his great qualifications, with all his personal distinctions, he was that sort of a man.' Coox was at the memorial service. He appeared embarrassed and distraught when it was asked if he would be finishing the second volume as he had promised Marder.[17] He had other pressing obligations. For a time, the matter rested, then Meyer took up the scheme with Jan Marder. She was reluctant, justifiably anxious that her late husband's high standards in research and writing be maintained; eighteen months later, under assurances from Meyer, a noted military historian himself, she agreed to the project. Meyer gained the support of Oxford University Press and developed a general plan of work. With Kemp's help and above all the historical labours of John Horsfield and Mark Jacobsen, the second volume of Marder's 'unfinished masterpiece'[18] was completed and accepted for publication. Thus, ten years after the first volume, the second appeared. It was entitled *Old Friends, New Enemies: The Royal Navy and the Imperial Japanese Navy, the Pacific War 1942–1945*.

Jan Marder never lived to see the second volume completed; she died in February 1985, also of cancer. But, to the end of her life, she had been, in addition to much else, the true supporter of her husband's literary and historical efforts. Mark Jacobsen made due notice of this in the book: 'Despite her own misfortunes, she cheerfully supported our undertaking to the end, never relinquishing her faith in those she liked to call "the boys", and steadfast in her admiration for the husband whose work she supported in his lifetime and beyond. Every scholar should have such a wife. Everyone in our position should have such unflinching kindness and consideration behind them.'[19] The research notes were gathered together, and, under the care of UCI's Special Collections archivist Roger Berry, were added to the Marder papers, thus completing the large but by no means complete files.

All would have wished Marder to have lived long enough to complete his last book. But the work as finished was as faithful a substitute as could be expected.[20] Marder's notes, his interviews, his exchanges of letters with survivors, and his jottings about what sort of book it should be illuminated the way for Meyer, Horsfield, and Jacobsen. The vitality of the sources was retained.

Marder had an uncanny gift for coaxing confidences out of sailors. He also had a profound knowledge of ships and the sea. He had sound historical judgement, even if he did not always do battle with other historians' interpretations. Seven Japanese admirals figure among his wide-ranging sources. The research had extended to Japanese as well as to British, American, and German archives. Every major naval engagement between forces of the RN and IJN was described. So were the formation of both sides' naval strategies and the complexities of armament, supply, and intelligence. The appendix, compiled by Marder himself, covered the sensitive point about how the Japanese treated prisoners of war. The concluding chapter analysed why the Japanese surrendered when they did, a continuing controversy. The book bore out Kemp's accolade, as given in the previous volume: he called Marder 'the supreme historian.'

Chapter 11

Roskill at Churchill College: The Laurels and the Legacy

IN 1959, to his surprise and delight, Roskill received an invitation from Lord Adrian, the master of Trinity College, Cambridge, to be the Lees Knowles lecturer in the following year. The lectures were to be under the heading of 'military science'. Roskill joked that he knew little about Cambridge, despite the fact that his son Mark had been a scholar at Trinity. All Roskill's kin had been to Oxford. He accepted the offer, and in doing so suggested that he might take as his subject the last year of the Second World War at sea, the account of which he had just finished for the Official War Histories. He also proposed the month of May as a suitable starting time – he later said that the choice was the most idiotic time of the year, for that is the month of play in Cambridge. In the interim, he got to work and, keeping in mind the sort of thing Sir Herbert Richmond had done in *Statesmen and Seapower*, abandoned the intended discussion of 1945 and instead crafted a cluster of lectures that he expanded into a broad historical study, *The Strategy of Sea Power: Its Development and Application*, published by Collins in 1962.[1]

Roskill arrived at Trinity as college guest. With his customary attention to detail and form, he readied himself for the event. He had lectured on numerous occasions and in many other venues, including command and staff colleges, military institutes, and the US Naval Academy. These events were 'all hands on deck affairs', so to speak, with protocol and precision the order of the day. When the time came for his inaugural Lees Knowles lecture, the first of four, he began punctually, as thirty-two years in the Navy had taught him. But for the next five minutes, the door in the lecture room in Mill Lane banged to and fro as stragglers made entrances – creating such a disturbance that he finally gave up. He waited until calm descended, and then began again. This was his first lesson in Cambridge customs.

One day Sir James Butler, editor of the Official War Histories, vice master of Trinity, and professor of modern history, gave a lunch party for Roskill, and among the guests was John Morrison, senior tutor of Trinity and later president of University College, Oxford. Morrison invited Roskill to walk with him in the fellows' garden, and Roskill agreed; the chance to admire the lilacs was irresistible. But Morrison had something up his sleeve. He told him that a new college, out on a western site adjacent to Madingley Road, was to be founded in Cambridge as the United Kingdom and Commonwealth memorial to Sir Winston Churchill, and that he was to be its vice master. Would Roskill be interested in election as a research fellow? The idea had never entered Roskill's head and, besides, he had no knowledge of what such an appointment might involve. But Morrison provided soothing advice, and Roskill responded that the idea had strong appeal, assuming that Morrison was serious about what he said. Meanwhile, Roskill had been attracted to the prospect of an advertised senior research fellowship at another Cambridge college, King's, but Roskill's application there, so he says in his unpublished autobiography, 'A Sailor's Ditty Box', fell on stony ground. 'My desire to get to Cambridge somehow became almost an obsession.'[2] Butler and Samuel Eliot Morison wrote letters of recommendation on his behalf for the Churchill College fellowship.

Then followed a long pause while the Churchill College electors mulled over the proposition, which Roskill says was an extraordinary one, for why would a naval captain turned historian become a fellow of a new college? But then came a letter from Sir John Cockcroft, the master of Churchill and the nuclear-secrets man, inviting him to take up a senior research fellowship for three years commencing in late 1961. Roskill accepted. Meanwhile, Lord Tedder, the chancellor of the university, laid the foundation stone of Churchill College on 14 October, though Churchill himself was too ill to attend. Roskill's admission to the university allowed him to receive in February 1962 the master of arts degree 'by incorporation', his first degree, and one (he mused) taken without matriculation or O-levels.

Stephen and Elizabeth chose a poor November day to survey the prospects. In teeming rain and with an enormous pile of bricks and scaffolding facing them, nothing at all seemed inviting. He told his wife that he wondered what he had let her in for this time. A cluster of Nissen-like huts stood on the rise, the core of the college, as it were; one of them housed the Combination Room near the grandiloquently named Dining Hall. Nearby, Cockcroft, a stolid Yorkshireman of cool and cold disposition, conducted business in challenging circumstances, rain dripping on his head.

Almost two years passed after his election as a research fellow before Roskill made his first appearance at Churchill, in 1963. He did so in a state of extreme nervousness. He sat beside Cockcroft at his first college dinner, and he found it very difficult to make conversation with him, doubtless

Cockroft's identical view because of Roskill's deafness and the din in the hall. Roskill knew little about the university, its statutes, ranks, and distinctions and what an 'advanced' student was (and who were excluded from this designation). Before long, Andrew Sinclair, the college's director of studies in history, had Roskill supervising freshmen seminars, and George Steiner, a fellow, had him running the Socratic Society. The thirteen other fellows were all in science and engineering and seemed rather suspicious of the stranger in their midst. The first academic crisis came over whether or not to have a Christian chapel on the college site. Roskill was keenly in favour (against decided opposition) and on the winning side. One college fellow resigned in protest against such a place of worship.

These early days at Churchill College were uncertain ones for Roskill, who fortunately had many historical projects under way at the time. The college exhibited growing pains and lacked a centre of gravity such as one would find in a naval wardroom. So much did Roskill feel like a fish out of water, he told the vice master, Morrison, that he thought about leaving. 'Well', replied Morrison diffidently, 'if you went we should only get another chemist,' which seemed to indicate that Morrison wanted him to stay. The circumstances were all a bit lonely or solitary for Roskill, as Zara Steiner, the historian, recalled of those days. The History faculty, though some members knew about his Lees Knowles lectures in 1959, otherwise largely neglected him because he did not have a department membership. Then Cockcroft called him into his lair and, in his inimitably direct way, asked as to Roskill's future plans. Roskill had none, and said so, but he indicated that he and his wife were happy in Cambridge. That sufficed, and before long came news, in 1964, of a five-year renewal of his fellowship and, at the end of it, extension to retiring age of sixty-seven.[3]

During much of this time, Roskill visited Cambridge only when circumstances or appointments demanded, driving the hundred miles each way as required. The Cambridge experience for him in these early days was of a speculative nature, Zara Steiner told the author, but there was a chance of a new career in the making – and no other prospects. James Goldrick holds that Roskill needed to make a home there and that the college became very much part of it, especially the Archives Centre of which he was founding father. In these transition years, Stephen and Elizabeth kept up Blounce as best they could, but the farming life became too demanding and none of the family had an interest in its sinking prospects, especially with other possibilities in view. From time to time, they stayed in a flat arranged for by the college. At length, an end came to itinerancy; a house, Frostlake Cottage, Malting Lane, was acquired and modernized, and a lovely study was built to add to its charms and garden. By coincidence, the house had once been the residence of Guy Pocock, Roskill's history master at Osborne. Blounce was sold, to much sadness, with even more to follow when it was learned that its site was to be divided and many houses built. The long association with the country had ended.

In 1958, before Roskill had given the Lees Knowles lectures, he was well advanced on another topic, one that preoccupied him during the early years of his connection with Churchill College. He, like Marder, was fascinated by naval leadership. He had written an essay for the *Naval Review* entitled 'Thoughts on Leadership', and this had attracted attention among the journal's readership. He followed this with an article on the contribution that psychology could make to the section and training of officers. Roskill had hoped that psychologists would join in the debate, but he was mistaken. It was on his first line of reasoning, from the 'humanist' angle, that his arguments would find resonance with the reading public. The theme allowed him to express ideas and concepts that were derived from his rich knowledge of English history, but, more, enabled him to draw on his personal past, one derived from the fundamental liberalism of his family, more particularly his independent-minded and protective mother and his urbane and progressive jurist father.

As was so often the case with Roskill, opportunity came knocking in the literary line. His *Naval Review* articles attracted notice in the Admiralty, and the personnel department's head, a senior officer, inquired of Roskill whether he would consider writing a book for use in the naval service. 'This suggestion set me thinking furiously', Roskill recounts, 'mainly because, as I stated at the beginning of my *Naval Review* article, to write on such a subject might well appear "arrogant and conceited", and imply that the writer had practised the art of leadership with success.' But, thinking of the benefits to the Service, he wrote the book, *The Art of Leadership*, published by Collins in 1964, became a minor classic. It continues to be used not only in command and staff colleges in the United Kingdom but in Commonwealth countries and the United States, too.

Meanwhile, Roskill gathered materials for his several books and for his additional new venture as a features writer for the *Sunday Times* and, later, the *Sunday Telegraph*. He was in periodic contact with former military officers, politicians, and civil servants. Churchill College's connection with Sir Winston Churchill, and the efforts by Cockcroft and others to increase the college's endowment, favoured Roskill's designs. Soon the temporary archives room bulged with documents, since Roskill knew innumerable admirals, generals, air vice marshals, scientists, and politicians and could assure them that their papers would be in safe keeping. Before the college fellows knew it, Roskill had created something quite disproportionate to their expectations. Papers of Admiral Sir John de Robeck, the commander-in-chief in the Dardanelles campaign, arrived, first of the naval treasures. Then came some of Jacky Fisher's. Cockcroft used his influence, and other important collections found their way to Churchill, including that of Baron Vansittart of the Foreign Office, Earl Atlee's correspondence with Sir Winston Churchill, Reginald McKenna's papers as first lord of the Admiralty, and the papers of Esher, Hankey, Keyes, and A.V. Hill — to name but a few.

At a college guest night in 1961, Roskill found himself sitting next to Sir Anthony Montague Browne, who had been private secretary to Churchill as prime minister in his second administration, and who casually remarked, 'I suppose the College does realise that Sir Winston's papers are likely to come to it one day.' Roskill replied that, not being a member of the so-called Building Committee, he could not speak with authority, but he was fairly sure that the college had heard nothing about such an idea. Next day, Roskill got confirmation from Cockcroft and from the bursar. If the Churchill papers were to be accommodated — there was no doubt but that they would be accepted — the best that could be done was to squeeze them into what had been designed as a sound barrier between the Bracken Reading Room and Wolfson Hall, a lecture theatre. Some mobile shelving was fitted to the lower space, and fellows giggled to think that a keeper might, contrary to the claim, be sandwiched in the stacks as the mechanism rolled one great file bank against another. A strongroom door, burglary and fire alarms, and equipment for binding manuscripts were installed. In 1969 Dr Michael Hoskin, a fellow of the college and historian of astronomy, was asked to become librarian, with a view to constructing an Archives Centre. The Leverhulme Foundation made a grant to the archives project, and a conservationist, Victor Brown, was appointed. In 1969, too, Lady Spencer-Churchill donated her husband's post-1945 papers to the college. Cockcroft went after US ambassadors of the Churchill era, many of whom had deep pockets, asking them to contribute a share of the cost of an Archives Centre. Hoskin, meanwhile, persuaded the college fellows that the site of the centre should be not on the margins but at the heart of the college. Then came the memorable day, 26 July 1973, when US Ambassador Walter Annenberg, in the presence of the Duke of Edinburgh and Lady Spencer-Churchill, opened it.

Roskill's role in these developments was largely unofficial, for he was never archivist or librarian. More likely, as Correlli Barnett, the first keeper, said, he was the elder statesman of the archives. In establishing it, however, and securing so many collections, he played a direct part. He pursued distinguished naval and military officers to encourage them to deed or lend their papers to Churchill. To those who laboured at cataloguing and filing, he not only gave good advice but took his turn, with shirtsleeves rolled up, in the hard grind, even drudgery, of cataloguing collections. Marion Stewart, employed in the Churchill Archive Centre, observed him from first hand. She had an office next door but one from Roskill, and the two of them worked in tandem at sorting and listing of the collections. Roskill did all the naval collections and she did all the political, scientific, and other military collections. He would often talk to her about interesting things he was finding as he worked through a collection, and she would mention to him any items she had found that she thought might interest him. 'He was a most stimulating colleague because of the sheer breadth of his knowledge and his shining intelligence. He could be a bit daunting – there was no room for sloppy thinking with him – but he was very open to receive new ideas and impressions.' Brown, Barnett, Stewart, and Alan Kucia formed the working team at the archives and 'all absolutely adored Stephen Roskill. And we were the ones who were with him on a day-by-day basis. It's an old fashioned concept, but I could honestly say that we revered him. Praise from Captain Roskill was hard earned but generous when it came and, oh, how one prized it!'

Marion Stewart gives a snapshot of Roskill at this time: 'In manner and bearing, Captain Roskill was always very dignified and rather reserved. He gave the appearance of being aloof, perhaps a little haughty and autocratic and one was generally quite formal with him though he did tease each of us, gently, from time to time and he would share something that amused him – in a rather donnish way. I think some of this reserve was due to the fact that he was profoundly deaf so one spoke more slowly and clearly when conversing with him and that had a restraining influence on normal social chat. On the other hand, I can't imagine that Captain Roskill would ever have been much enamoured of small talk.'[4] Kucia, who as a young archivist worked with him, lovingly called him 'the old sea dog' and Barnett said that undergraduates had dubbed him 'the Ancient Mariner'. Fellows and other members of the University found his country attire of a Norfolk jacket to cut an unusual figure in Cambridge.

That was the view from the inside. From the outside, news travelled quickly to military writers in particular and to academic scholars that the Churchill Archives Centre had little-used treasures of great and growing value. Naval historians such as Paul Kennedy, Jon Sumida, Donald Schurman, and James Goldrick came calling from overseas, and persons doing biographies or political studies did likewise. Soon the reputation of the place was high, on a par with the Liddell Hart Centre for Military Archives at King's College, London, and not to be ignored by any serious researcher. The parade from near and far continued in growing numbers. In 1978 the Roskill Library was installed in the Archives Search Rooms, where twenty scholars could, it was said, be accommodated in air-conditioned comfort.[5]

By February 1982, stimulated by Zara Steiner's interview with him and particularly with her statement that a man who had led such a fascinating life ought to write his memoirs, Roskill had drafted the last few chapters of his sizeable autobiography. It appears in various forms in his files but is best remembered, as stated, as 'A Sailor's Ditty Box'.[6] His devoted typist Mrs E.V. Eales ('Eealy'), by this time living in Bridgwater, Somerset, laboured over the drafts, putting longhand text into reasonable order. Roskill intended to show the whole to Collins, his publisher, but was uncertain whether it should be published in his lifetime. He hoped the final result would, at least, interest family and friends. Writing it offered a pleasant distraction from the chore of assembling the second volume of *Naval Air Documents*. The work on the latter was slow and tedious: 'My heart really isn't wholly in it.'

Collins received the typescript of Roskill's 'Sailor's Ditty Box' in April 1982. Shortly thereafter, Roskill met with his editor, Richard Ollard, about publishing it. Ollard was lukewarm at the prospect. At the time, he had in mind a TV series to be called 'The Admirals', to accompany 'The Generals'. 'Well, of course, if *that* did come off we would all be rich beyond the dreams of avarice but these things hardly ever do,' Ollard chortled. It was indeed a wild dream. In any case, the only thing Roskill had on his mind was completing his memoir, for steam had run out of any other projects. It was time to close the file, as it were.

The memoir opens with discussion of his life as cadet and midshipman and then proceeds to sub lieutenant and lieutenant, then to fledging gunnery officer, Far East, and Mediterranean. Following this is climbing the gunnery tree, rustication and recovery (1941–44), home and off again, a new career (as Cabinet Office historian), and then the wind-up, 'groves of academe'. The further particulars need not detain us here, and the major details have found themselves into this narrative. But the Marder references are explosive, and did not go unnoticed by his prescient editor.

Roskill began the assault this way:

When I told him [Marder] about my prospective book on Jutland he showed understandable concern about a rival account being published at the same time as his own; so in the end I agreed to withdraw from the fray and handed over to him all the papers I had collected about the battle. Marder made good use of those papers . . . and I also read the whole of that five-volume work in typescript and sent him many pages of criticism and suggestions. When he very much wanted to move from the University of Hawaii to the mainland of the USA I was one of the referees that got him appointed to Irvine campus of the University of California. In view of all the trouble I took on Marder's behalf it is perhaps understandable that I should have been outraged by his publication, without any prior mention or warning to me, of a very nasty attack (see *From the Dardanelles to Oran*, Oxford 1974, pp. 169–70). This led to a historical dispute and breach of our formerly friendly relations which in retrospect I greatly regret.

The issue Roskill was referring to concerned Sir Eric Seal's criticism of his reliability as a historian; as we saw earlier, Seal believed that Roskill had drawn false conclusions about Churchill, as first lord of the Admiralty, running roughshod over his first sea lord in the Norwegian campaign. It was one of several matters, four in fact, that pitted Roskill against Marder. We note it here as the first line of attack the captain used against the professor. In this case, he was terribly embarrassed by Seal's revelation, and he knew that Marder had solicited, though probably quite innocently, Seal's letter on the subject.

Ollard, proceeding delicately, suggested to Roskill that the treatment of 'your relations with Marder' was, 'probably necessarily', 'a somewhat over-simplified account. Wouldn't it be better to cut it right out and leave it to your biographer to judge between you? I can't think you've anything to fear.' These were cautious words from an editor who always pressed his author about authenticity and tone, but Roskill was, as usual, quick to take offence. In the margin he wrote in a huff: 'I think *stet* [leave as is], even if over simplified. Let a biographer decide!'

But there was more to it than that. Roskill held the deepest suspicion, a pathological one, coupled with anguish about receiving the coveted Chesney Medal of the Royal United Services Institute. This is the second issue. He thought, even in advance of the actual notice of award, that maybe Marder had put him up for it. He was right – but he could not prove it.

In fact, Marder started the nomination process in 1971 or 1972, with a letter to the RUSI regarding Roskill having been passed over for the Chesney. Marder got only the barest of responses. From the RUSI he turned to his correspondent A.B. Sainsbury. He began his letter by stating that 'Roskill is, or can easily be, one of the most difficult persons alive. Though I agree with the appraisal as far as it goes – I have suffered my share from his spleen, his vanity, and his omniscience – I must add that nobody in the realm, or elsewhere, has contributed as much to Military Studies, through helping scholars, young and old, and, of course, through his own considerable published work. His *War at Sea* should, I think, have won him the Chesney – those volumes alone. I would like to think that his work as a scholar is what matters, not whether he could win a popularity contest.' Marder, who had heard that Roskill's health was deteriorating further, thought that the time was right to give his work the recognition it deserved 'while he's around to enjoy the honor'. He encouraged Sainsbury, who was well connected at the RUSI and well placed in naval historical circles, to 'propagandise', as he put it, the nomination.[7]

Marder was crystal clear about the need to get Roskill recognized in his own country as a great scholar. Sainsbury took it up; he wrote to Michael Howard, the most recent recipient of the Chesney, to see if he would back the nomination. Howard, then at All Souls, Oxford, unhesitatingly provided enthusiastic support. 'I felt extremely embarrassed to have received it before he [Roskill] did and assumed that the Council was reluctant to make the award to two naval historians in succession [Marder being the other]. His historical work is outstanding: a man who has produced a double like *The War at Sea* and *Hankey: Man of Secrets*, which between them cover forty years of the history of war with both lucidity and scholarship, deserves recognition from the Services at least commensurate with that he has received from the academic world. There are very, *very* few former recipients of the Medal who are in this class.'[8] There were some rumblings at the RUSI, for the secretary told Sainsbury that the cost of the medal alone would be a staggering £300 and the reception another £150. 'So we are overtaken by inflation,' was Sainsbury's caustic reply; but, in the end, the endowment for the Chesney was increased to cover possible costs. Marder had been right in urging Sainsbury forward with the Roskill nomination: 'Remember the slogan when you get flak: "The Chesney is NOT a popularity contest."' 'The Abominable No-Men are always with us,' mused Howard. 'Anyhow, I shall now feel somewhat less of a fraud.' The nomination met with success, the RUSI council voting unanimously in favour of the resolution. Marder said that it had renewed his faith in man and was long overdue. He also noted: 'I would be horrified – and so would he – if it ever got about that I had anything at all to do with the award.'[9]

Roskill was on to it in a flash, and even before he agreed to accept the Chesney Medal he fired off this to Sainsbury: 'I would make it clear that for many years I did a great deal of work for Marder. He came to my home many times, ate of my bread and drank of my wine – and went away with what he wanted. Of course he has considerable charm and a very glib tongue, which take in many people. My wife however never took to him, considering that he was a slick operator and out only for his own ends.' Roskill considered Marder entirely 'a taker', and he concluded his moaning letter to Sainsbury with a note of self-pity and untruth: '[He] cared not a whit for the trouble and work he was causing me.' Roskill could have declined reading drafts of *From the Dreadnought to Scapa Flow* had he so chosen.

Then Roskill came to the third charge against Marder – the business of use and control of documents:

> The crunch came when I took on the Hankey biography – on condition that the Hankey copyright was leased to me for the term of years for a peppercorn. The 1st Lord Hankey had again and again refused Marder access to his diaries and papers, but as soon as he was dead Marder bounced his son into letting him have access – without telling me, though he knew that I had taken on the biography. The upshot was that I refused Marder permission to publish anything which was Hankey copyright. He was furious and wrote me very rude letters; but I stuck to my guns because I had agreed there would have not been much point in me going on with the biography. Marder then began to lose no opportunity to attack and to slander me. I have no particular quarrel with him over historical matters as history is such a very imprecise art; but consistent misrepresentation and backstairs operations got my goat. So I broke off relations.

Sainsbury told me that Roskill considered the RUSI nomination an object with an ulterior motive – namely, to get back to a state where Marder could again exploit him and his large collection of documents. This was his fourth charge against Marder. Roskill could not see the Chesney as an act of pure and disinterested charity. He felt so strongly on this that he asked Sainsbury whether the award of the medal had resulted from a Marder letter to the council or whether the council had reached its decision independently on the merits of the case. If the former were true, Roskill doubted if he would accept; he did not want to be beholden to Marder and to get himself again into 'awful troubles'. Sainsbury chose his words carefully. No, he replied, the council had not received a letter from Marder – which was entirely true – and the nomination had been dealt with speedily and on its own merits. Marder, as Sainsbury explained, had appeared in the correspondence about the matter only because he had mentioned, 'in a way that I judged perfectly genuine', concern that the Chesney Medal had not come Roskill's way.

'Thank you for your letter of 4 November about the Chesney,' Roskill wrote to Marder, the connection between them not broken (nor, in fact, was it ever). 'A little bird tells me . . . that you had something to do with this idea. If that is so it is very generous of you.'

Meanwhile, the RUSI was making preparations to honour Roskill. Correspondence between Air Vice Marshal S.W.B. Menaul, the RUSI director, and Roskill determined upon 12 March 1975 as the date for presentation of the award, with accompanying lecture by the recipient. Roskill, who decided on 'Hankey – Prince of Secretaries' for his talk, fretted about having to field questions in the RUSI's big auditorium, an impossibility given his growing deafness. He also fidgeted about who was on the invitation list, the number of available offprints of his printed lecture, and lunch details. Had Hankey been awarded the Chesney, he wanted to know, and, if so, when? The answer came back that Hankey was never a recipient. But a list was provided, showing Mahan as the first recipient and Laughton, Corbett, Richmond, and even Arthur Bryant, besides Marder, as the naval historians so honoured. Roskill was in fine company but probably too self-conscious of his own station in life to cast a generous reference to former recipients. Certainly, because of the spat with Marder about the use of Hankey documents, he was not going to mention Marder's name: that would have been too distasteful. This dispute also explains why Roskill attached such importance to having the 2nd Lord Hankey present at the ceremony. The event went smoothly, with Lord and Lady Hankey in attendance as Roskill's special guests. And so Roskill, with no small thanks to Marder and the latter's friends and accomplices, had garnered a great prize, one given to so few.

In Roskill's later years, recognition and awards had come in rapid succession. Besides the Lees Knowles lectures and the Chesney Medal, he was invited to the US Naval Academy, Annapolis, in 1965 as distinguished visiting lecturer. Then, in 1967, he was Richmond Lecturer at Downing College – the occasion being a lecture on Richmond himself. Four years later, Cambridge University awarded him a doctor of letters for published work. That same year he was elected a fellow of the British Academy. He was appointed a commander of the British Empire. Churchill College arranged for a likeness of him to be done by Michael Noakes, and this now hangs in the Roskill Room. In 1975 he was awarded an honorary doctorate by the University of Leeds, nominated by David Dilks, the professor of international history.[10] This was a proud day for Roskill, since Leeds lay not too far distant from Dilke country, and his cousin, Oswald Dilke, was professor of Latin in that university; there were other family connections of note: Stephen's grandfather was Aston Wentworth Dilke, MP and enthusiast for the decimal system. It was a day of celebration for the family, particularly on his mother's side.

Then on 25 June 1980 came an honorary DLitt from the University of Oxford. Roskill looked magnificent, said Howard, who was present on the splendid occasion and a powerful player in these events. At the ceremony, known as Encaenia, a glowing testimony was given about Roskill. In its classical allusions and engaging epithets, it bears compelling and agreeable comparison with that to Marder, made nine years previous.

> Is there anyone who has acquired even a smattering of Greek in his schooldays who has not admired Herodotus, the Father of History, and Thucydides for their brilliant accounts of ancient sea-battles, Herodotus for recording those fought of Cape Artesisium and in the Bay of Salamis (in the Persian War of 480 B.C.) and Thucydides for his description of the disaster suffered by the Athenian fleet in the harbour of Syracuse (in 413 B.C.)? Yet both these writers would, if they were to come to life again, acknowledge a worthy rival, at least so far as nautical matters are concerned, in our honorand, since he lived the life of a professional sailor up to the age of forty-five, and experienced all the hazards of the sea. It was by his skilful seamanship that H.M.N.Z. destroyer [sic] *Leander* was kept afloat after being hit (in the boiler room) by a Japanese torpedo: you might well call him a 'grandson of Nereus' [the Old Man of the Sea in Greek folklore]. He had made important contributions to naval gunnery (more particularly in anti-aircraft weaponry) before his hearing became impaired, as a result of the thunderous crash of heavy naval ordnance. So he reluctantly abandoned 'a life on the ocean wave', but did not fancy a shore posting either. Since, however, his father and his three brothers all got Firsts in Schools here (the father in Classical Honour Moderations, one brother in Chemistry, the other two in History) and thereby gave the first-fruits of high distinction in their several careers later in life, inevitably the fourth brother, when he eventually turned to literary work, proved to be endowed with an outstanding facility for writing. For proof of this there are his dozen books on recent naval history and related matters, of which I mention now his definitive four-volume History of the War at Sea, 1939–1945, but I must not omit the delightful appendix to it entitled *The Secret Capture* (1959). The rest I pass over in the interests of brevity. All, however, who enjoyed reading his Life of Lord Hankey are eagerly awaiting the appearance of his forthcoming Life of Admiral Beatty; both of these distinguished men were given honorary degrees in this building.

It is universally agreed that our present honorand's writings show great clarity of insight, thoroughness in preparation, and a high level of scholarly precision, without, however, lacking the seasoning of a salty wit, as benefits a sailor.

His own University of Cambridge has conferred on him a Doctorate by examination on the evidence of his published works, and he has been elected a Fellow of the British Academy. So it is with the greatest pleasure that we honour him today. I present to you Captain Stephen William [sic] Roskill, Royal Navy, to be admitted to the Degree of Doctor of Letters, *honoris causa*.[11]

His three brothers, all present, must have winced at the mistake with the middle name, for they all bore the family name of their dear mother. But that distastefulness had to be set aside. Tribute had been paid handsomely to the family's connection with Oxford over two generations. The speaker has also noted that Stephen's three brothers, Oxford graduands all, had attained distinction in their professions: Ashton (later Sir Ashton) as chairman of the Monopolies and Mergers Commission; Oliver as an industrial planner and consultant; and Eustace as a judge of the High Court, lord justice of appeal, and lord of appeal in ordinary.

Time there was too for holidays and distant excursions. In fact, since his major illness when a Cabinet Office historian, Stephen had placed great importance on holidays. Beginning in 1947, he and Elizabeth travelled to Paris to visit her French cousins, and thereafter to the countryside so that he and especially Elizabeth could paint. Ireland, Norway, Spain, and France again were all visited despite difficulties of connections and funds. On one occasion, they stayed with old friends Admiral Sir Charles and Lady Madden at their lovely Villa Portelli, Malta, where Sir Charles was flying his flag. Then it was the Dalmatian coast and Venice, always alluring to painters, Padua and Ravenna, and Lake Maggiore. Once, they visited their son Mark, then a professor at Princeton, and on other occasions Corfu and Egypt. By writing the wartime history of Alfred Holt and Company, best known as the owners and operators of the Blue Funnel Line, Roskill gained the right to travel anywhere in their ships, and that brought them to Cairo and Luxor in January sunshine. They also went to the Aegean Islands and to the United States again. Especially lovely were visits to John Ehrman's house in the mountains of northern Corfu and to the travel writer Freya Stark's properties, with brother Oliver, in the Italian countryside. By the time it came to move from Blounce to Cambridge, Stephen was exhausted once again, with his old ulcer problem reasserting itself. Now holidays became mandatory: this brought him and his wife to Morocco, Corfu, and Malta. In 1976 Roskill was a guest scholar of the Rockefeller Foundation at their fabulous Villa Bellagio on Lake Como, there for a glorious month of study and writing, while Elizabeth painted to her heart's content. Connections for Churchill College with the director of the villa, Bill Olsen, and others, were enhanced.[12] All the time there were weddings, christenings of grandchildren, and, before long, in 1980, a fiftieth wedding anniversary. These were full and pleasant years, with travels taken none too soon.

By now, Roskill's deafness seemed almost total. His driving nervous energy was in decline. His sight was fading. And, to make matters even worse, his wife's health was deteriorating too. While he was trying to cope with a second volume on the Naval Air Service for the Navy Records Society, he could hardly concentrate on the slow and tedious work of gathering and collating documents. 'I have felt better since we had the really miraculously report on my wife,' he wrote to his secretary on 14 March 1981. 'She of course is in wonderful form and faces the future whatever it may hold with beautiful calm and exemplary courage.'[13]

Unknown to Roskill at this time was Marder's strong attempt to influence those who counted in such things to recommend him for a knighthood. Although it is thought in some circles that this was a matter of delusion, and that Roskill was not worthy of it, it is also held by some that, if Roskill had not been invalided out of the Navy, he would have reached flag rank. Neither is correct.[14] Roskill had left a trail of difficulty through the Cabinet Office and the civil service, and the memory of his tangle tryst with Churchill never faded in the corridors of power.

Marder was not to be deterred. The story goes as follows. Fresh from the avuncular position taken in procuring Roskill's Chesney Medal from the RUSI on 6 February 1980 (this was Marder's last year), he wrote Sainsbury about a subject that had long been on his mind. He had intended to bring it up with 'Dickie' Mountbatten, as he called him a little too familiarly, had the former admiral of the fleet not been murdered by Provisional Irish Republican terrorists, while he was fishing, in Donegal Bay, County Sligo, on 27 August 1979. Then, at Sainsbury's suggestion, Marder had written to Admiral Sir Terence Lewin soliciting his interest: 'I have never understood why Authority have failed to honor Brother Stephen for his stupendous achievements as a naval historian. A "K" is embarrassingly long overdue.' Marder went on to point how Sir Julian Corbett had won a knighthood, and that Roskill had done more first-class work than Corbett. Marder confided that he could write a long essay on Stephen Roskill and how many people he had offended. A knighthood, however, should be for achievement; besides, advancing age and uncertain health pointed to the need for early action, reasoned Marder. He urged Sainsbury once again to talk it up and keep up the pressure. But he demanded: 'Keep my name out of it!!!'[15]

Sainsbury took up the quest for a knighthood for Roskill. As chairman of the *Naval Review*, he wrote to Admiral Sir James Eberle, commander-in-chief fleet, to get him onside. Meanwhile, Marder had written to Admiral Sir Henry Leach on the same subject, all the while ruing that he had not taken the matter up with Mountbatten. Sainsbury wrote to Lord Carrington, the president of the Navy Records Society, who agreed to do what he could. Sainsbury tried to pacify the demanding Marder: now was the time, he said, to 'desist lest we over-egg the pudding'. Certain other details now made their appearance. Marder confessed that he had made an earlier attempt, in 1977, to obtain the knighthood for Roskill, when he had written solicitous letters to Lewin, Mountbatten, and others. Eberle reported to Sainsbury that in fact Roskill had been put forward for a knighthood in 1977 in a civil recommendation through the Civil Service Department. But now the matter was to determine what Roskill's output had been since he had been made a CBE in 1971. Then Admiral Lewin wrote to Sainsbury to say that he had made a private approach to Sir John ('Jock') Colville, former private secretary to Sir Winston Churchill and a trustee of Churchill College, following Marder's last visit to England in early 1980 when he had raised the issue. Jan Marder, now writing for her bedridden husband, told Sainsbury: 'Arthur says he will never understand the British bureaucratic mind.' Sainsbury asked Marder to write the brief on Roskill's knighthood, but by this time Marder was under such intensive radiation, with no appetite and an inability to sleep, that he had to leave it to others to carry this obligation. He even had to decline doing a letter of recommendation for Roskill's 'K'. He had already written to Leach and Lewin, and it was better, in any event, to have such a statement come from an Englishman, preferably a don with a great reputation. In consequence, Michael Howard's opinion was solicited, and it was agreed that Will Hawthorne, master of Churchill College, be entrusted with the proposal. He agreed, and a letter was sent to Prime Minister Margaret Thatcher's private secretary, Clive Whitmore, on the subject.

There, for the moment, the matter stood, until the ghastly spectre of Roskill being sued by the executors of the 2nd Earl Beatty, for alleged breach of copyright, appeared. A knighthood for Roskill was now unlikely to be successful: the legal charge was 'a nasty threat to an old and distinguished man, both of whose careers have brought distinction to the service'. So wrote Sainsbury. In the event, the Hawthorne nomination came to the attention of Prime Minister Thatcher, via Jock Colville. The private secretary said the matter would be given every attention. Meanwhile, Elizabeth Roskill was dying of cancer, a persuasive argument for awarding the knighthood on top of all others, thought Richard Ollard. Sainsbury became disenchanted. Quality was being denied: 'Where are we failing in this nomination?' he wondered, and expressed the same to Lewin. Lewin shared the frustration, but, as he pointed out, Roskill's name was on the list and nothing more could be done. Not long afterwards, Sainsbury learned from Lord Roskill, Stephen's brother, and also from his son Nicholas, that Stephen Roskill had been put forward for a CBE much earlier than the date of its being awarded, and that the delay had been owing to Harold Macmillan's personal deletion of it because of the criticism of Churchill, however measured, that Roskill had presented in his several works. Nicholas was more direct: he said that his father had a black mark among the civil servants for standing up to Churchill and others. He also said that Stephen Roskill left him instructions about what to do with Arthur Marder – that is, how to deal with him in the future. He wrote Sainsbury that his father had very high moral standards and had 'an ineradicable mistrust of Marder's integrity'.[16]

But it was no doing of Marder's that Roskill did not get a knighthood. Lewin told Sainsbury that he found it difficult to fathom that political interference would put a stop to the nomination, but that was what apparently happened. In fact, it is hinted that academic interest may have had something to do with it, by which is meant the so-called academic committee that advised on honours: and Stephen Roskill had no university degree except honorary ones. Sainsbury, as conscience of the naval-historical fraternity, deeply regretted that Roskill did not get greater public recognition than his CBE for his very considerable academic contribution to naval history, and in the *Naval Review* he made clear that many others held this same view: 'It is not necessary in this context to rehearse Stephen's stupendous performance and output as an historian: members will know the range of his works and their recognition – CBE, Fellowship of the British Academy, honorary degrees from Leeds and Oxford, and the Chesney Medal of the RUSI. *But the disappointment of a far from insignificant group of public figures of some eminence who remain convinced that a further honour would have been appropriate and deserved should be recorded.*' The whole, sad episode, as Sainsbury said, demonstrated the wisdom of the University of Cambridge in giving, for the second time in half a century, a home for a naval officer who had made an outstanding contribution and whose Service career, no matter how distinguished, had failed to reach its promise. He was linking Roskill to Richmond, and indeed this is the first indication of many similar links of Roskill to the legacy of Richmond.

Towards the end of his life, everything seemed to be conspiring against Roskill. The legal tangle with executors and trustees of the Beatty papers was daunting. For someone as meticulous about scholarship as he was, this was a real blow. He felt that the whole unhappy episode had somehow disgraced him and shown him as either careless or less than honest. And then there was the matter of his wife's terminal illness. Suddenly, Roskill became very old and stooped, and the archives staff, on watching his solitary figure make its slow way across the grounds to the porter's lodge, began to wonder how much time he had left.

They did not have to wait long, for some weeks later Marion Stewart received a telephone call from Roskill, who was at Frostlake Cottage, stating that he wanted to see her. He had not been in college for a considerable time. Stewart takes up the story:

> I went round to his house and Mrs Roskill, herself in a dressing gown as she was also ill and confined to bed, let me in and told me to go up to his study, a large, low, airy room next to his bedroom. He was in bed but got up, put on a dressing gown and came through to the study where he propped himself up at his desk, looking very frail. He had had a number of letters from researchers, seeking his advice or information and he wanted me to help him answer them. Most of the answers came from his own vast fund of knowledge but sometimes he would ask me to fetch a certain book to look something up. The opening sentence of each letter he dictated, on the lines of 'I write this letter to you upon a bed of sickness' but the rest he left to me. He had a characteristic way of waving a weary hand at one on such occasions as if to dismiss all the minor detail of a situation. That may sound rude but I always found it amusing and rather endearing – it was so much part of him.

She continues:

> At one stage (this business took us a couple of hours at least), he stooped to retrieve a book himself, staggered and half fell onto a small sofa that was in the room. He looked unutterably weary. He closed his eyes and took up his remarks exactly where he had left off! However, it was plain that the exertion was all becoming too much for him and I decided to end the session, saying I knew now what he wanted and would deal with all other letters that came for him. He gave a big sigh and said 'Yes, dear Marion, please do.' I knew then that he must be dying for he would never otherwise have given up his duty to pass on his experience to

others. As I reached the head of the stairs to leave, he was standing in the doorway of his bedroom so I went back and gave him a hug and we said goodbye. He never rose from his bed again and died three days later.

In these letters that Captain Roskill wrote with me when he was *in extremis* he took just as much trouble and displayed exactly the same courtesy over the ones addressed to unknown undergraduates as over those addressed to an Admiral of the Fleet or a member of Her Majesty's Privy Council. That was the measure of the man. He was a scholar and a gentleman and I count myself privileged to have known him.[17]

Stephen Roskill died on Thursday, 4 November 1982, at home, aged seventy-nine. He had survived Marder by two years. A private funeral, family only, was held at St Andrew's Parish Church, South Warnborough, Hampshire, near to beloved Blounce. His wife passed away in 1983. They had four sons and three daughters.

So ended the life of the sailor-historian. He had come home from the sea, and that home was Cambridge. The written tributes and obituaries paid him suitable and due acclaim.[18] A thanksgiving service was held at Great St Mary's, the University Church, Cambridge, on Friday, 26 November. 'In Cambridge we all loved Roskill,' the Reverend Owen Chadwick, a Cambridge professor, said at the memorial service.

> He was enchanting company. He was widely read, knew fascinating things, was an excellent conversationalist, looked out with a happy twinkle, and above all had nobility of the soul. He himself felt the burdens of deafness to be first the exclusion from the theatre and the music that was important to him, and second the difficulty of talking with friends. This was a difficulty. Many of us had the amusing experience of watching Roskill and someone else talking to each other about different subjects. But the amazing thing was – it was in some ways the most rare thing about the older Roskill – that it did not matter in the least; his conversation was such fun and so illuminating, and so warm-hearted; and he cared very much about the person with whom he talked, even if he could not always be quite sure what was said. You could not know Roskill without being touched in your heart as well as interested at his intelligence.[19]

A Stephen Roskill Memorial Lecture was proposed by Barnett as a fitting tribute and as a major event. The Churchill Archives Centre, embracing the concept, arranged for Lord Carrington, then Secretary General of the North

Atlantic Treaty Organization, to give the inaugural lecture (Carrington had been a sponsor for the elusive knighthood). Since that time, every two years, at the Roskill Memorial Lecture, Stephen Roskill's unique contribution to naval history to the world of learning receives due recognition.

Epilogue

Our Historical Dreadnoughts

THE age in which Marder and Roskill exchanged friendly fire was one of considerable disputation in historical studies. In the post-Second War era, professional historians were, almost for the first time, making challenges to others in public. The tightness of English intellectual circles, the space given in the press to contentious argument, and the new opportunities of radio and television encouraged controversy. By themselves, Marder and Roskill's books received considerable attention in the press as well as in the customary scholarly journals, for military and naval history then as now was of decided significance in the publishing industry. But what made this disputation all the more lively was Marder's unique background as an American historian of the British Navy writing from distant palm-treed lands. That Marder, against odds, had unlocked the Admiralty's documents chest added to the mystique. British radio, television and print media lauded his achievements, and in doing so extended the reach of fresh approaches to British naval history.

A. J. P. Taylor was not the first to disclose Marder's secrets (with appreciative candour) but he was first to advertise them generally. As a journalistic historian in search of fellow talents, he saw Marder as a prize catch. True, before Taylor's media debut, Marder had appeared on a BBC radio programme, hosted by David Woodward, and, equally true, he had been on BBC TV at the time of the Jutland fifty-year anniversary. But, once Taylor as television host had Marder on his programme in 1971, the latter's pre-eminence was ensured. Taylor was slighted by many in the historical profession for being a media presenter, journalist (in the *Daily Express* of all papers!), and a contrarian of note. Marder was not hindered by this, rather the reverse, for Taylor treated him tenderly and appreciatively. Taylor had no quarrel with other historians of the British Navy but he liked Marder's style and zeal and above all his fresh insights. Although Taylor still continues to be seen as contentious on the subject of the origins of the Second World War – critics tend to regard him as blind to Hitler's wickedness and an apologist for appeasement – he left a powerful following. Marder, who knew all about

Taylor's perverseness, was amused by him and had no reason to take issue with him on historical matters as did many others, including Hugh Trevor-Roper and Pieter Geyl. Taylor liked a spare, sharp narrative, fresh perspectives, analytical depth, and, most of all, a strong story line, and all these were present in Marder's books.

The Marder-Roskill quarrel was a strange parallel to the dispute between Trevor-Roper and Taylor. Trevor-Roper entered the lists with a savage attack on Taylor's work in *Encounter* in July 1961. This brought a reply some months later from Taylor under the title 'How to Quote – Exercises for Beginners'. This battle of historical giants is the stuff of legend and has been ably described by Ved Mehta in *Fly and the Fly-Bottle* (1961). Neither Marder nor Roskill made deliberate attempts at historical assassination of the other as did Trevor-Roper of Taylor.

The dispute between Marder and Roskill was both a private and a public affair. The private affair was over the use of the Hankey diaries, with Marder the aggrieved party. The companion event, so to speak, was the quarrel over the Harper Record, with Roskill again out-manoeuvring Marder for the control of hitherto unused documents of great value. The two problems, though distinct in character, merged into a single result – further alienation exhibited by both parties. Only when at last Marder had completed his *From the Dreadnought to Scapa Flow* in 1970 could the contest begin in the public realm. By that time, Roskill had long distanced himself from the Cabinet Office and was a free agent. And, by this time, too, his characteristic assertiveness and willingness to do battle had become a taunting jibe to Marder. Once Roskill began to publish his attacks on Marder's use, selection, and interpretation of evidence – and here the key is the Marder interpretation of Churchill in 'Winston Is Back', published in the *English Historical Review* in 1972 – the feud became a full-fledged battle. Roskill was incensed that Marder printed Sir Eric Seal's letter about Roskill's judgements about the Norway campaign. That Roskill was occasionally denied response to Marder in print – for instance, the editor of the *English Historical Review* declined to print Roskill's riposte about Churchill – only served to further Roskill's cause to attack Marder in other ways. Eventually, Roskill's *Churchill and the Admirals* (1977) provided the place for the full assault. Marder could not let this pass and responded in a letter in the *Times Literary Supplement*.

Beyond the private and public disputation, the rivals continued their individual assaults on each other in correspondence with third parties. They did so in different ways. Marder always dealt with such matters as they arose. He never held a grudge for long. Intensely happy in his work as a historian, he had no desire to undertake the sort of thing that Trevor-Roper undertook against Taylor. Marder showed a tendency to one-upmanship but his main purpose was to reveal that he had made full and accurate use of the extensive sources upon which his history had been constructed. Roskill, by contrast, took the view of principle, and his claims, charges, and responses show a tendency to preach and correct, even to hector. Letters to Marder from close naval historical colleagues about 'our brother Stephen' indicate that Roskill had become typecast as a preaching corrector of the historical record. Roskill undoubtedly wanted to be considered as the authority in British naval matters but Marder had no such aspirations to have the ultimate view from Olympus. Many who knew him marvelled at Marder's insistence, energy, and commitment to task, but they knew too of his boyish inquisitiveness and his continuing modesty: there was something approaching naivety in the way he tackled historical issues. After all, he was an outsider to the Navy, not part of it as was Roskill.

We therefore come to the issue of who was the better historian – the one of the Service or the one from the outside. That, too, will be a historical dispute without end.

In Marder's case, a key part of his method was to employ naval-officer specialists to ensure that what he wrote conformed to correct British naval usage. He was scrupulous in this, and it never failed him, thanks to his committee of quality control which, in the 1960s, when he was writing *From the Dreadnought to Scapa Flow*, included Gretton, Kemp, and Creswell. These three had performed the same role in earlier years, though as part of a much more informal grouping, when Marder was undertaking the book on Admiral Sir Herbert Richmond and compiling the letters of Jacky Fisher; in those years, his helpers also included William Chalmers, A.C. Dewar, Sir Reginald Drax, Sir Frederic Dreyer, and Sir William James. Marder might well have fallen on his face had he not had these luminaries of naval history – all at one time officers in the Royal Navy – to guide and save him from mistakes. They had fought the First World War and survived the Second. Yet, despite their good counsel and documentary offerings, it was Marder who had to ask the questions, undertake the research, write the text, make the necessary changes on the basis of advice received, and get the book contracts.

Roskill, by contrast, was already 'of the Service', and that meant that he was writing from the same side of the ledger as, say, Chalmers or Gretton or Kemp. But Roskill could not write the sort of material they did. His personality and character forbade that. He had too much reforming zeal and was too independent to accept authority duly imposed on him. History was the beneficiary. Roskill was a great historian and he was also a fine biographer. He understood the higher direction of the Second World War at sea better than any of his contemporaries, and he carried the presumption that in nautical matters the Navy was right.

Once freed from the shackles of 'official history', he was a free agent able to range across a wide horizon. His work for the *Sunday Times* and the *Sunday Telegraph* gave him a new position from which to address key and sometimes unsolved questions involving the Navy in the Second World War. The loss of the carrier *Glorious* and two screening destroyers is one such case. This type of approach suited Roskill well. He had strong detective's instincts. His new career afforded a rare opportunity to investigate further certain tantalizing historical subjects that he had written about in *War at Sea*. Though he did not contradict himself, he explored new dimensions of similar topics, fulfilling a public need for more insights into what went wrong, or right, on a certain day in question or in a certain battle or episode of the Second World War. Roskill became a public authority to be reckoned with in consequence of his newspaper work, one that reinforced his already powerful position as 'official historian'. While many consider his life of Beatty to be his best work, the reviews tend to favour his massive three-volume *Hankey*, a truly magisterial study of a central figure in British military and political history. Coupled with his *War at Sea*, the *Hankey* biography anchors Roskill in the historical profession. These two works are his great legacy to historical letters. His outstanding efforts as a collector of documents, his supreme archival effort at Churchill College, Cambridge, give him imperishable position in the history of military affairs, science and warfare, and statecraft. This naval salute of commendation on departure says all: BRAVO ZULU.

Yet one more thing remains to be said about Roskill: it is clear that, apart from the direct path set by his editor, Butler, who was backed by the Cabinet Office subcommittee on the military volumes of the Official War Histories, Roskill liked to take on various subjects if and when they arose. This did not allow him a more systematic agenda of research. His was a fertile mind, one brimming with prospects. Noble Frankland told the author that he had never met a person who had so many bees in his bonnet as Roskill, possibly a harsh judgement. If, however, we take that to be worthy of consideration, it helps explain the scattered, opportunistic approach Roskill took to events or topics as they arose. For instance, when Collins approached him for a cluster of books of his choice, Roskill accepted – even though he had not finished *The War at Sea*. Similarly, when the Hankey authorized biography came his way, he assumed the task immediately, thereby having to delay even further the second volume of his *Naval Policy between the Wars*. He never completed his Navy Records Society series on the Naval Air Service and had to leave it to others. His work on Beatty was sandwiched between other obligations and was again the result of an opportune collection of documents coming his way.

Marder, by contrast, was systematic and linear. From the time he began his studies of the pre-dreadnought Royal Navy right through to the end of his life, when he was toiling on his book on the Royal Navy and the Imperial Japanese Navy, he maintained a progression through time. He never looked back. He did not cover systematically the period from 1919 to 1939 but he did cover essential, hitherto unexamined subjects including the Navy's response to the lessons of the First World War at sea, the Navy and the Ethiopian crisis of 1935, Churchill's return to the Admiralty, the distasteful Oran business, and Operation Menace. His work on the IJN merely continued the behind-the-scenes method that he had patented. At his death, he had completed his task, as defined, from 1880 to 1943. Only in a rare instance would he take issue with a Roskill account as presented in *The War at Sea* – it was not Marder's intent to quarrel with Official History as such. What he sought always to do was to get to the root of the problem, to go behind the scenes, as it were, often to places where Roskill – because of his remit – could not venture. He liked writing the war behind the war. But he had yet another purpose. He despised those who wrote military history from a position of 'if such and such were in command it would have been done differently, or if this had happened then this would have been the result'. After the event, any fool could be wise (he loved to cite Homer on this). Had Marder spoken from Olympus, he would have been savaged by now; but he declined to do so – and this was, indeed, his essential humility. Thus, he will be read for a great many years to come. He would have been the first to say that his words were not final, and that much still needed to be done. He never proclaimed anything he wrote to be inviolate or without contradiction, but he hated positions too easily taken without adequate research. That having been said, he could marshal his own sources to suit his purposes, as his discussion of Churchill and of Pound attests – and Roskill, rightly, had opposing positions on each.

Roskill had put it best, in 1966, about Marder. It bears repetition: fortune had smiled on the Royal Navy when a scholar of Marder's distinctions and abilities had come along to write its history. That is why Marder still commands our attention, for the fine quality of his work and the freshness of the evidence he presents – all brought together in a beautiful, even compelling narrative – is the stuff of the ages. He has and will continue to have his critics. True it was, as Taylor said, that he was soft on the admirals. He may have treated them uncritically, but he did tell their story. He did not write the history of the lower deck, but only a minuscule number of naval historians have. He did not have the advantage of specialist naval-branch histories in signalling, naval intelligence, and gunnery; they were not then written. The business of the Pollen gun-control capability was still known only privately. Economic and fiscal aspects lay largely outside his grasp. But he wrote the story of the Royal Navy against the broad canvas of history. He took naval history out of narrow bounds, giving it a semblance of universality, a rare feat. His great examination of British sea power continued where Mahan had left off and, as with Mahan, he will have his critics – and he would have liked it that way. Some may make it their life's work to bring him down, or to score points at his expense, but to challenge his pre-eminence they will have to develop a better vision of their own. They will have to read his work more carefully. Mere sniping from the wings will not suffice. More, they will have to shed their conceit, even arrogance and become good storytellers. All great historians and practitioners of the historian's craft face critics. But, as is true of Jacky Fisher or Alfred Thayer Mahan or, for that matter, Churchill, Marder's place in history is safe and secure.

Notes

Chapter 1

1 Michael Howard, *Sunday Times*, 21 June 1970. The article is entitled 'Leading seaman', in reference to Marder.
2 *Times Literary Supplement*, 14 August 1970, 905; *Evening Standard*, 31 May 1966, 6.
3 Keegan, 'Why Are Britain's Great Naval Historians Americans?', 10.
4 Although much of this description is drawn from my memory of being with Marder four decades ago, his unusual appearance came to mind recently when I saw the movie *Dr Strangelove*, with Peter Sellers playing the US president. The resemblance to Marder was suggestive. As to the strength of his voice, Marder once told Lady Chatfield, 'Please forgive me if I'm bellowing, but I've been talking to so many old gunnery officers.' 2nd Baron Chatfield to author, 27 April 1998.
5 While this description is based on personal observation, it is confirmed strongly by many the author has interviewed, notably John J. Stephan, Daniel Kwok, and Cedric Cowing.
6 Quoted in Palmer, *Engagement with the Past*, 21.
7 Villa, *Unauthorized Action*, ix–x.
8 Marder Papers, box 3, Marder to Langer, 10 January 1969. This letter was composed for a binder of similar letters from former students and colleagues, given to Langer on the occasion of the publication of a collection of his articles entitled *Explorations in Crisis*. Langer told his own story: *In and Out of the Ivory Tower*.
9 Marder Papers, [Autobiographical sketch], 'I. Fate Knocks Three Times'.
10 MacGregor, *Apostles Extraordinary*, 120.
11 'Arthur Marder's History of the Royal Navy, "From Dreadnought to Scapa Flow", was completed a year ago. He talks here to A.J.P. Taylor', *Listener*, 21 October 1971.
12 The story may be followed in ADM 178/207 (for 1935–46), ADM 1/7264 (1938), ADM 1/28267 (1946–64), and Ministry of Defence Papers 24/96 (1966–67). The fight to get into the Balfour Papers in the British Library (1950) is described in ADM 1/21865/50.
13 As when A.J.P. Taylor exposed Marder's special status and proclaimed him 'the Ali Baba of historical studies', *New Statesman*, 8 September 1961.
14 Years later, in 1970, he wrote 'The Royal Navy and the Ethiopian Crisis of 1935–1936', which was reprinted, with new material, in *From the Dardanelles to Oran: Studies of the Royal Navy in War and Peace 1915–1940*.
15 Langer Papers, HUG (TP), 19.9, box 5, file M, 1936–41, Langer to Marder, 2 December 1935.
16 Information from H.C. Meyer, confirmed by Keith Nelson.
17 Langer Papers, HUG (TP), 19.9, box 5, file M, 1936–41, Marder to Langer, 12 September 1938. The Admiralty's historical guardians disliked the fact that Lord Spencer had given Marder research access to his own papers. The Admiralty could do nothing in the circumstances, or took no action doubtless awkward or embarrassing to themselves. But the matter disclosed the problems of state papers being taken home, as it were, by First Lords.
18 Marder, 'British Naval Policy in 1878'. This appeared in the journal's documents section.
19 Langer Papers, 19.8, box 1, Correspondence 1940, Langer's file letter on Marder's ability, n.d.; also Langer's letters to and from Perkins, June 1940. Marder's correspondence with Langer on the North Dakota misadventure does not survive. Langer had earlier backed Marder's unsuccessful candidacies at Lehigh (Pennsylvania) and Queens College (Flushing, N.Y.). Ibid., Correspondence 1939.
20 Various letters from Marder to Gloria Kaplan, esp. 14 and 24 August, 18 and 22 September, 3 October 1939, and 23 February 1940. Letters in recipient's possession.
21 Marder Papers, G. Steele to Putnam, 18 December 1940, box 3.
22 Ibid., Constant Huntington to Marder, 29 October 1941.
23 On the 1860s and 1870s, see Beeler, *British Naval Policy in the Gladstone-Disraeli Era*.
24 *Naval Review*, 29, 4 (1941): 624–7.

NOTES

25 Gooch and Temperley, eds., *British Documents on the Origins of the War, 1898–1914*.
26 Marder, *Old Friends, New Enemies*, xi–xx.
27 Ibid., 'Arthur Jacob Marder – a Personal Memoir', v.
28 *Naval Review*, July 1964: 341–44. A similar point was made by a reviewer of the first printing: *Times Literary Supplement*, 20 September 1941.
29 Gough, 'Rulers of the Waves', 131–50.
30 Other reviews include *Herald Tribune Books*, 12 January 1941; *New York Times Book Review*, 23 March 1941; *The Scotsman*, 30 October 1941; and *Engineering*, 14 November 1941.
31 See Earle, ed., *The Makers of Modern Strategy*, 440–2.
32 Winks, *Cloak & Gown*, 61.
33 Quoted in ibid., 115. Bundy's correspondence with Sir Stuart Milner Barry of Bletchley Park is in the Milner Barry Papers at Churchill College Archives.
34 Smith, *The Shadow Warriors*, 73.
35 For a partial list, with post-war positions, see Winks, *Cloak & Gown*, 494–6.
36 Copy of review, courtesy Henry Cord Meyer; author's files.
37 Langer Papers, 19.9, box 7, file M, 1941–44, Marder to Langer, 10 October 1942 and 22 June 1943, and replies; Marder Papers, Appendix, 'The Royal Navy and the Imperial Japanese Navy, 1936–1945: Some Early Thoughts', in report to Japan Foundation, 10 August 1976 (being remarks before Japanese naval historians, Kyoto, 1 July 1976), box 26.
38 ADM 178/317, Private secretary to first lord of the Admiralty to Marder, 26 March 1944.
39 Marder made the approach via his fellow Harvard friend and historian Gerald S. Graham, then in the RCN. G.S. Graham Papers (Private), Marder to Graham, 15 November and 12 December 1943.
40 W.H. Cowley to Marder, 9 July, 2 and 25 July 1943; 'Statement [by Cowley] concerning Dr. Arthur J. Marder', 11 January 1944; *ASTP Hamiltonian*, 1944, 29; *Hamilton Alumni Review*, 9, 2 (January 1944): 87–8; Cowley to Marder, 4 April 1944. All in Special Collections, Hamilton College, Clinton, NY.
41 Among others were UCLA, Colorado, and Stanford. These were invariably linked to friends or family. He exchanged assignments with John S. Galbraith. His daughter Toni was an undergraduate at Colorado. His wife, Jan, was a Stanford graduate.
42 Marder was advised 'not to venture beyond the city limits without a guide or chaperone'. University of Hawaii Archives, Presidential Papers, box 455, file 92, Paul Bachman (Graduate Division) to Gregg Sinclair (president), 31 January 1946.
43 MacGregor, *Apostles Extraordinary*, 120.
44 Information from Miriam Emden.

Chapter 2
1 ROSK 24/1, Roskill to Steiner, 27 May 1977.
2 *Who's Who 1980*, 2203.
3 The Nuremberg Laws on Reich Citizenship consisted of the Reich Citizenship Law and the Law for the Protection of German Blood and German Honour, both unanimously enacted by the Reichstag on 15 September 1935. The first protected the subjects of the state; the second, reinforced by the First Regulation to the Citizenship Law, stated that a Jew could not be a Reich citizen, had no vote, and could not occupy a public office.
4 Obituary of J. Roskill, *The Times*, 21 August 1940; see also, for his aggressive courtroom manner in defending Sir Edgar Speyer before the Judicial Committee of the Privy Council, the episode that led to his decline as a practising barrister, Heuston, *Lives of the Lord Chancellors*, 333.
5 Roskill, 'Sailor's Ditty Box', 55.
6 This may be followed in Jenkins, *Sir Charles Dilke*, 215–370; also, Stephen Roskill's introduction to the Dilke-Crawford-Roskill papers (REND) in Churchill College.
7 At this time, two personalities contributed to the intellectual development of the Navy and of the nation in regard to maritime issues (leaving aside the 'navalists' who wrote for the press): the historian, novelist, and proponent of maritime strategy Sir Julian Corbett, and the naval officer Captain (later Admiral Sir) Herbert Richmond. Corbett's work was received with indifference; Richmond was just then completing his first historical works, the influence of which was indeterminate. Today, they are regarded as giants of maritime strategy; in their day, they were voices crying in the wilderness.
8 ROSK 24/1:16, 'Curriculum vitae of Stephen Roskill'.
9 Early and other details on Stephen Roskill come from Ehrman, 'Stephen Wentworth Roskill'.

10 Roskill, 'Sailor's Ditty Box', 7. Boissier was head from 1940 to 1942, a difficult time of low enrolment and house closures, partly due to German bombing.
11 Barnett, 'Stephen Roskill', 5.
12 ROSK 24/1, Roskill to Zara Steiner, 27 May 1977.
13 Roskill, *The Last Naval Hero*, 21–2. A recent study of the cadet system at Osborne and *Britannia* of that time, by Harry Dickinson, states that Roskill's generalizations are unhelpful and misleading. In particular, Dickinson rejects Roskill's view that coerciveness and brutality pervaded Osborne and Dartmouth. The Admiralty disapproved of excessive corporal punishment, says Dickinson, who explains that their lordships were prepared to remove officers who exceeded their authority. Dickinson, 'Ship to Shore.'
14 Ziegler, ed., *The Diaries of Lord Louis Mountbatten*, 278.
15 King-Hall, *My Naval Life*, 202.
16 Quoted in Hall et al., eds., *Cambridge History of Modern Japan*, volume 6, 283.
17 Ehrman, 'Stephen Wentworth Roskill', 580.
18 ROSK 24/1, 'Curriculum Vitae', 75–84.
19 Details from Unilever Archives, 2002, and *Unilever Magazine*, no. 87 (1993).
20 Ibid., 81, 84.
21 ROSK 2/22:2, 'Record of Service'; also, ROSK 24/1, 'Curriculum Vitae', 83, 89.
22 ROSK 2/22, 'Captain S.W. Roskill, D.S.C., R.N., Record of Service and Disability Received through that Service [1948]'.
23 ROSK 24/1, 'Biographical Sketch', 91, 137–8; Roberts, *British Warships of the Second World War*, 42–7.
24 Ibid., 93.
25 Roskill, *HMS Warspite*, xxviii.
26 Quoted in Brodhurst, *Churchill's Anchor*, 101.
27 Roskill, *HMS Warspite*, 21.
28 ROSK 2/22, 'Performance Reviews of S.W. Roskill.'
29 Barnett, 'Stephen Roskill', 6. The story of the Oerlikon – a rapid-firing gun of 20-mm bore spewing out 450 rounds to the minute – may be traced in Pawle, *Secret Weapons of World War II*, 75–89; Terrell, *Admiralty Brief*, 40–1; and Roskill, *War at Sea*, 1:139–40, 'The Adoption of the Oerlikon Gun' and *Naval Policy between the Wars*, 402–4. For a different view, see Ross, 'How the Oerlikon Gun Came to Britain', 19–22, and Ziegler, *Mountbatten*, 98–100.
30 Information from Edward Von der Porten, who interviewed Roskill in 1970.
31 Ehrman, 'Stephen Wentworth Roskill', 581.
32 Ibid. 'Lindemann favoured a project for an anti-aircraft device known as the Naval Wire Barrage (eventually the Un-rotated Projectile), in which a parachute was fired pre-set to open at a given height and trail a long wire to intercept the attacker. Roskill, quite rightly, thought little of the idea, and argued vigorously and persistently against it – his view is reflected in a footnote on p. 406 of the first volume of his *War at Sea*.'
33 'Biographical Sketch', 111.
34 On Bevan, see Marder, *Operation 'Menace'*, 73, 78, and 225.
35 Dennerly, 'The Royal New Zealand Navy', 107–9; Morris, *Cruisers of the Royal and Commonwealth Navies since 1879*, 189–90.
36 ROSK 2/812, R.H. Bevan to Roskill, 28 November 1942; 'Biographical Sketch', 111–13.
37 Morison, *History of United States Naval Operations in World War II, Volume 6*, 160–75.
38 Hughes, Jr, *Fleet Tactics and Coastal Combat*, 123–37.
39 Morison, *Breaking the Bismarck Barrier*, 180–91. Morison used the official New Zealand naval summary of this episode: Waters, *HMNZ Leander*, 21–6. Also, 'Biographical Sketch', 118–23.
40 ROSK 2/812, Roskill to R.T. Jackson, 11 April 1979, and Roskill to N.J. Murphy, 19 June 1975.
41 ADM 199/1236, 201–4, History of the British Admiralty Delegation to USA, 1941–1945.
42 NND 923034, US National Archives, J.M. Reeves to J.W.A. Waller, 4 July 1944, enclosing Waller's interview with Reeves, 14 July 1944. I am obliged to Dr Chris Madsen for this material. See Madsen, 'Limits of Generosity and Trust', as well as Wildenberg, *All the Factors of Victory*. Soybel, *A Necessary Relationship*, discusses similar difficulties in intelligence and administration matters.
43 Best of the Second World War light AA guns, first ordered by the Royal Navy in 1940, they were found in every type of warship. Technical details may be traced in Campbell, *Naval Weapons of World War Two*, 67–71.
44 Roskill, 'Sailor's Ditty Box', 11. From the beginning, the first sea lord, who had served in Washington

NOTES

in 1942–43, had found relations with King exasperating. See Winton, *Cunningham*, 268–9.
45 ROSK 2/812, Roskill to A.W. Clarke, 11 January 1971. Roskill's boastfulness in this letter to Clarke about how he was able to get from the Americans all that he wanted deserves mention, but his actions cannot be confirmed as to their success and fly in the face of other evidence, in particular his report on naval ordnance procurement in 'History of the British Admiralty Delegation' (ADM 199/1236).
46 Date of award: 19 July 1946.
47 Ehrman, 'Stephen Wentworth Roskill', 582; Barnett, 'Stephen Roskill', 7; Churchill Archives Centre, 10l/1/23, 'At the Memorial Service for Stephen Roskill.'
48 'Biographical Sketch', 122–7.
49 'Record of Service', 2; also, 'Biographical Sketch', 130.
50 Quoted in Miller, 'Curiosity at the Crossroads', 18.
51 Hezlet interview, 11 June 2001. Hezlet told the author that Roskill was extremely deaf at this time; Nicholas Roskill advises that his father was then becoming deaf. Whatever the timimg of the affliction, its onslaught was quick.
52 Ballard, *Graveyards of the Pacific*, 237.
53 ROSK 24/2 and 2/20, Report on 1946 Bikini Atomic Bomb Trials.
54 Roskill, 'A Sailor's Ditty Box', chapter 7, 39, 42.
55 ROSK 2/22, J.S. Lang to Roskill, 4 March 1949; also, Roskill to Rear Admiral M.J. Mansergh, 30 December 1947.

Chapter 3

1 Marder Papers, untitled autobiographical sketch, 5; Marder, 'Admiral Sir John Fisher: A Reappraisal'; 'Winston Churchill as First Lord of the Admiralty. Marder's last article in *US Naval Institute Proceedings* was 'Fisher and the Genesis of the *Dreadnought*'. He could not satisfy this journal's hunger for his material, and under the same rationale as that covering the writing of book reviews – not enough time to do them justice or attend to his own professional obligations, including supervising PhD students, teaching a regular load of classes, and writing his books – he was obliged to decline, with regret but insistence, such opportunities. Information from Samuel McCulloch.
2 Details from the dust jacket, as well as preface, to *Portrait of an Admiral*. Diary entries are cited by date not by page, as found in the book.
3 Roskill, 'Richmond in Retrospect', 22.
4 Marder, *Portrait of an Admiral*, 9.
5 Baugh, 'Admiral Sir Herbert Richmond', 19–21.
6 Marder, *Portrait of an Admiral*, 9.
7 Hunt, *Sailor-Scholar*, 233. For Marder on Richmond, see Marder, review of *The Navy as an Instrument of Policy*.
8 Marder, *Portrait of an Admiral*, 9.
9 Hunt, *Sailor-Scholar*, 218.
10 Ibid., 234.
11 Ibid., 45 and 53; Marder, *Portrait of an Admiral*, 10.
12 Marder Papers, 1961 file, W. James to Marder, 28 September 1961.
13 Roskill, review, *The Naval Review*, 339–43. For a similar view, see G.C. Dickens, 'Richmond', ibid., 40 (3) (1952): 335–8; Theodore Ropp, review, *US Naval Institute Proceedings*, 79 (6) (1953): 684–5; John B. Heffernan, review, *American Historical Review*, 58 (3) (1953): 607–8; Burke Wilkinson, review, *New York Times*, 7 December 1952, 7 and 55.
14 Marder Papers, box 3, Marder to Editor, *The Times*, 29 July 1952. Marder's notations on the review proper are found in box 29.
15 Marder Papers, box 3, Arthur Crook to Marder, 12 August 1952.
16 Schurman, *The Education of a Navy*, 110–46; Hoban, 'Admiral Sir Herbert Richmond', 53. Hunt's quote, ibid.
17 Hunt, 'Sir Herbert Richmond and the Naval Review', 61–75 and 92.
18 Marder, *Portrait of an Admiral*, 10.
19 Hunt, 'Richmond and the Education of the Royal Navy', in Goldrick and Hattendorf, *Mahan Is Not Enough*, 67.
20 Goldrick, 'The Irresistible Force and the Immovable Object', 83–102.
21 For an excellent recent example of this, presented to an audience of naval officers, see Rodger, 'Training or Education'.

22 Review, Mackay, *Fisher of Kilverstone*, *Naval Review*, 62 (3) (1974): 267–72.
23 Mackay, *Fisher of Kilverstone*, v–x, discusses various Fisher files and collections. The following sympathetic explanation, by Mackay, is apt here: 'Inevitably, the present writer is much indebted to the works of Professor Arthur J. Marder. However, it should doubtless be mentioned here that some sources important for Fisher and his times were not available when Marder was collecting material for his volumes on the period ending in 1914. Moreover, even so remarkable a researcher as Professor Marder could not be expected to see every document in the collections which he investigated' (ibid., vi).
24 American Philosophical Society, Philadelphia, Marder's first grant application (successful), October 1955.
25 Temperley, *England and the Near East*, 61.
26 This analysis is adopted from Roskill's review of volume I, in *Naval Review*. Roskill thought Marder far more successful than he was with Richmond's diaries. He does not explain why; it was probably a personal preference of Roskill's on grounds that he did not want Richmond's diaries published, or at least published in the way they were.
27 Marder Papers, F2, folder 33, Fisher to Marder, 8 June 1952.
28 Ibid., Fisher to Marder, 18 October 1952.
29 Ibid., James Morris to Marder, 14 and 27 November 1952.
30 Sir John Squire, review in the *Illustrated London News*, 1 November 1952.
31 Ibid. Fisher, like Beresford, exaggerated systematically without fear of consequence.
32 Manchester *Guardian*, 4 November 1952.
33 Glasgow *Herald*, [?] October 1952, copy in Marder Papers, F2–29.
34 *Times Literary Supplement*, 7 November 1952.
35 Review by Hubert Griffith, *Time and Tide*, 25 October 1952. Other reviews: Kenneth Rose in *John O'London's Weekly*, 24 October 1952; *The Times*, 15 October 1952; Admiral Sir William James in *Daily Telegraph*, 17 October 1952; and John B. Heffernan in *American Historical Review*, 59 (1) (1953): 191. None alter the appreciation here given; rather, they reinforce it.
36 King's College, London, Liddell Hart Collection, G.S. Graham Papers, Marder to Gerald S. Graham, 5 October 1953.
37 Marder Papers, F2, box 29, FGDN 2, Gretton to Marder, date indistinct, possibly 1 November 1956.
38 The book was seen in another connection, worthy of notice here. Crane Brinton comments: 'Yet the basic importance of such material as the labours of Professor Marder have made available for all of us is on a rather more serious level. If the historical studies in the decades ahead are going to survive the reaction against such studies already very evident, and yet not simply take refuge in narration (in itself a good thing) or in mere cataloguing and sorting (in itself, for itself, a bad thing), then we shall have to try to put life and reality into our answers to the kind of question the moralist, the literary critic, the intellectual historian, yes, even the sociologist ask: was there a Victorian morality? Was there a Victorian taste, or set of tastes? What were Victorian and Edwardian classes? How far was there social mobility? Or are these and many questions like them as unanswerable, and therefore as silly, as we are often told they are?' From such a book as Marder's, Brinton says, and others like it, historians might hope to build images of Victorian times that were not mere clichés. *Victorian Studies*, September 1957, 88.
39 *Times Literary Supplement*, 30 November 1956.
40 Rowse, while conceding Taylor's 'journalistic insights and abilities', criticized his 'dreadful snap judgements.' A.L. Rowse, *Historians I Have Known* (London: Duckworth, 1995), 128–36.
41 *Observer*, 26 April 1959.
42 Marder Papers, Broadcast text BBC R.P. ref. no. TLO 26057. See also ibid., David Woodward to Marder, 18 November 1960, in which Marder's suggestion that the BBC produce a programme on Lady Hamilton is mentioned.
43 Duchess of Hamilton to Marder, n.d., in Marder, *Fear God and Dread Nought*, 1:11.

Chapter 4
1 The above passage is based on correspondence between Marder and Cumberlege found at Oxford University Press (OUP) Archives, Oxford (PB/ED/009589, box 1301), particularly Marder to Cumberlege, 13 November 1950, 11 October 1951, and 21 February 1952, and replies; also J.R.B. Brett-Jones to Cumberlege, 1 July 1953.
2 He was promoted to professor (from associate professor) on 1 July 1951. He was later made senior professor.

NOTES

3 Information from Daniel Kwok, 2007. For details of the fight in Hawaii against communism, see Daws, *Shoal of Time*.
4 Marder Papers, Marder, 'Fate Knocks Three Times'.
5 OUP Archives, PB/ED/009589, box 1301, G. Wren Howard to Cumberlege 12 July 1956, and Cumberlege to Wren Howard, 17 July 1956.
6 In turn: *From the Dreadnought to Scapa Flow* (5 vols.), *Dardanelles to Oran*, *Operation Menace*, and *Old Friends New Enemies* (2 vols.). A second edition of the third volume of *From the Dreadnought to Scapa Flow* entitled *Jutland and After* was published in 1978. If this is included, the tally of his OUP history volumes comes to ten, perhaps a record for that publishing house for a single historian.
7 OUP Archives, PB/ED/009589, box 1301, Marder to John Brown, 19 May 1959.
8 Information from John J. Stephan, who in turn received it from Marder's University of Hawaii colleague John White.
9 OUP Archives, PB/ED/009589, box 1301, Marder to Gregg Snyder, 26 May 1959, copy.
10 American Philosophical Society, Philadelphia, Willard Wilson to Marder, 16 July 1959, copy.
11 Ibid., Gretton to Marder, 1 June 1959, copy.
12 Ibid., Selkirk to Marder, 24 June 1959, copy.
13 For instance, among recently available materials, Marder used the Edward Carson papers in volume 2 and the Admiral Barry Domville papers in volume 4.
14 Sainsbury review, *Naval Review*, 49 (4) (1961): 402–5.
15 See Schurman, *Julian S. Corbett, 1854–1922*, 193.
16 The Official Secrets Act was born in a spy scare, during the Agadir crisis (1911), and reinforced during the Irish troubles (1920). 'Many authors need to watch its provisions, and its purpose matters to all of us. For the Act has been so applied that the disclosure of any *official* information, whether *secret* or not, may be treated as an offence.' Foot, 'Officials and Secrets', 155–7.
17 'Unfortunately, too, neither the sworn evidence of all the chief actors in this great drama – statesmen, sailors, soldiers, and civilians alike – nor certain important documents on which the reports are based have ever been published in full, and a most dangerous precedent has been thereby established. This is the first occasion in this country on which evidence given before a War Commission has been withheld from the public.' This was the view from 1926 and much later. Ellison, *The Perils of Amateur Strategy*, 34–5.
18 These points of disputation are recounted in Marder's text 'Professor Marder and the Admiralty', OUP Archives, copy.
19 Roskill, 'The U-boat Campaign of 1917 and "Third Ypres".'
20 Marder, 'Jutland: The Human Dimension', unpublished paper, n.d., author's files. The party was hosted by Jellicoe, engineered by OUP, and dubbed 'At Home with Arthur'. Marder drew up a list of invitees, who included Roskill.
21 Marder Papers, box 33, G.M. Bennett to Marder, 23 June 1966.
22 Ibid., J.H. Godfrey to Marder, 17 June 1966.
23 Ibid., Graham Donald to Marder, 31 May 1966. For details on Major Harvey, see Winton, *The Victoria Cross at Sea*, 122.
24 Marder Papers, box 33, W.L. Langer to Marder, 20 September 1966.
25 *Observer Weekend Review*, 29 May 1966.
26 *Mariner's Mirror*, February 1967, 86–7.
27 S.W. Roskill, review, *US Naval Institute Proceedings*, November 1966, 136–8.
28 Author's files, letter from E. Chatfield, 27 December 1999.
29 Frankland, *History at War*, 95.
30 Marder, 'Jellicoe and Beatty as Commanders in Chief, Grand Fleet', 81–90.
31 Ibid., Donald M. Schurman, commentary [on Marder], 91–6; Barnett, *The Swordbearers*.
32 An exception to the general neglect was P.W. Brock (*Mariner's Mirror*, November 1970, 454–5): 'As always, Professor Marder discusses with kindly impartiality the thorny question of the Admiralty's sudden change of front late in April. He accepts Jellicoe's contention that this was due to an independent fresh appraisal by Admiral Duff and not made under duress from Lloyd George. There is likely to remain for some, however, an echo of Dr Johnson's remark about the wonderfully concentrating effect of a death sentence upon a man's faculties.'
33 *History*, June 1971, 299–300.
34 OUP Archives, PB.ED/009590, Richard Brain to Marder, 7 August 1980.
35 Howard, *Sunday Times*, 21 June 1970.

36 The Admiralty Board, formerly the Board of Admiralty, came into existence on 1 April 1964, its full name being the Admiralty Board of the Defence Council. On its returning to the form of a Navy Board, see Rodger, *The Admiralty*, 156.
37 Memories of a previous board's strictures against Corbett may well have come to mind during this meeting: 'The Lords Commissioners of the Admiralty have given the author access to official documents in the preparation of this work, but they are in no way responsible for its production or for the accuracy of its statements. Their Lordships find that some of the principles advocated in the book, especially the tendency to minimize the importance of seeking battle and of forcing it to a conclusion, are directly in conflict with their views.' ADM 116/2067, Admiralty minute, 22 February 1923.
38 *The Times*, 3 August 1970, 6.

Chapter 5
1 ROSK 24/1, 143.
2 4 vols. London: Her Majesty's Stationery Office, 1961.
3 Frankland, *History at War*, 122–4. Further discussion about official history may be followed in Connell, 'Official History and the Unofficial Historian.' Also, Higham, ed., *The Writing of Official Military History*.
4 In later years, Roskill was able to point out how invidious was his position as 'official historian'. He made clear that anyone reviewing Butler's preface to the first volume of his war history would understand that the 'official histories' of the Second World War could not be described correctly as such. Even though they were colloquially known as 'official histories' at the time, both the organization and conditions under which the Military History Series volumes were written, as set forth by Butler in his editor's preface, show that no imprimatur of the state was placed upon the resulting work. Roskill, *Churchill and the Admirals*, 11.
  Marder was kept informed of Roskill's 'title': 'A year or two ago he was twitted in a *Times* leader for doing so [listing himself as "official naval historian"] for there was no such animal. He was the writer of one of the official histories . . . and that was the beginning and the end of his officialness. No harm in his vaunting his remarkable achievement.' Marder Papers, John Creswell to Marder, 15 May 1965. Also, Roskill, 'Some Reasons for Official History'.
5 Attention is drawn particularly to Admiral G.C. Dickens's detailed review of volume 1 in *The Naval Review*, 42 (3) (1954): 353–61, which closes with this: 'It is . . . difficult to do full justice to the author, for the book is a brilliant piece of work and, judging from the reviews I have read in the public press, is widely recognized as such.' His review of volume 2 was even more generous: 'It has been said that genius is an infinite capacity for taking pains – an inadequate definition. Be that as it may, and acknowledging that Captain Roskill has that capacity in full, I feel that better judges than I would agree that real genius is to be found in his handling of this vast and complicated subject.' Ibid., 45 (1) (1957): 82. Consider, too, this accolade: 'Roskill was something of a newcomer to the naval history writers guild in 1954, but by now he is firmly established as a master of his trade . . . his name [is] high on the list of great naval historians of all time.' Robert Langdon, 'Notable Naval Books of 1956', *US Naval Institute Proceedings*, 82 (December 1956): 1333–4.
6 Cambridge University, Emmanuel College, Parkinson Papers, box 10, A. Bryant to C. Northcote Parkinson, 30 September 1945.
7 From dust jacket and preface, Morison, *History of United States Naval Operations in World War II: Volume VI*.
8 Morison, *History of United States Naval Operations in World War II: Volume 1*, 179–92. Hamilton's message at 185–6.
9 This may be followed in ADM 1/20489; Morison, *History of United States Naval Operations in World War II: Volume 1*, 185–6.
10 Inter-service rivalry between the Royal Navy and the Royal Air Force was strong. In regard to historical matters from the recent war, a battle raged about the efficacy of surface naval units versus the RAF's Coastal Command in the protection of shipping and in the sinking of enemy ships and U-boats. Rear Admiral Dick reflected a common naval view that a British history emphasizing the Royal Navy might capsize in favour of the roles and influence of the Royal Air Force and even the United States, for many in that country thought they had won the war at sea.
11 Cabinet Papers (CAB), 103/325, Minutes and discussion, 1 June 1948 (also ADM 1/ 20711 and 20484); ibid., minutes, 17 February 1949.
12 Interview with Alan Pearsall, 4 June 2001.

13 'So, in a sense by chance, this highly fortunate choice was made. It was by no means an obvious one.' Ehrman, 'Stephen Wentworth Roskill, 1903–1982', 583. ROSK 10/5, Roskill, 'Lecture for Canadian Tour, 1969.'
14 ROSK 24/4, chapter 8, 19.
15 Lord Trend, 'Brook, Norman Craven', *Dictionary of National Biography*, 1995; and, on Seal, *Who's Who, 1971–80*, 712. Seal was principal private secretary to Prime Minister Churchill, 1940–41; deputy secretary of the Admiralty (North America), 1941–43; member of British Supply Council, Washington, 1943; and under-secretary of the Admiralty, 1943–45. At the time of his investigations for Churchill, he was deputy minister of the Ministry of Works.
16 Because of a then-raging discussion in the Commons and Lords about Admiral Sir Dudley Pound's responsibility in allowing a French squadron to pass Gibraltar Straits outbound, and his subsequent being relieved of command, Roskill drafted a clarifying letter to *The Times*. He knew that this would 'set a cat among the pigeons' but thought it correct in the circumstances. It was overruled by the Cabinet Office and never sent. CAB 103/327: Draft letter, [10] August 1954, encl. in Roskill to Acheson, 11 August 1954; further memo by Roskill, 20 August 1954; Acheson's memo on same; and Sir John Lang to Norman Brook, 16 February 1955. See also ROSK 6/26, where the quarrel with Churchill may be followed additionally. For discussion of the North affair, see chapter 7.
17 CAB 103/327, Churchill's comments. This became a central question for Marder, who found the relevant cabinet papers still closed to him. Bell, 'Singapore Strategy and the Deterrence of Japan': 'Roskill glossed over the political considerations which motivated the Defence Committee in October 1941 and exaggerated the significance of Churchill's shortcomings as a naval strategist.'
18 CAB 103/327, Allen to Churchill, 24 August 1953.
19 Ibid., Seal to Churchill, 2 June 1954. Edwards was strongly critical of Churchill also in the Dakar expedition, when an Anglo-Free French force, with de Gaulle present, unsuccessfully attempted to detach the French at Dakar, West Africa, from the Vichy government. Marder used Edwards's diary in *Operation Menace*.
20 Reynolds, *In Command of History*, 513 and 619. On brandies, ROSK 4/79, Geoffrey Blake to Roskill, 5 January 1954.
21 Information from John Ehrman, 14 October 2005.
22 Ibid. Also, Roskill to L.P. Pitcairn-Jones, n.d, noted in *Frances Edwards Catalogue 98* (January 2005), 7.
23 Gilbert, *'Never Despair'*, 979. Cf. Roskill, *War at Sea*, 1: 553-9.
24 King's College, London, Liddell Hart Centre for Military Archives, LH 1/610, Basil Liddell Hart to Roskill, 10 July 1957, and Roskill's reply, 12 July 1957.
25 *Naval Review*, 42 (3) (1954): 356.
26 CAB 103/328, Roskill to Acheson, 17 March 1955, and Roskill, 'Mission to America.'
27 Roskill's position bears comparison to the following from a distinguished historian of foreign policy: 'In order to avoid the distortion of "after-knowledge" I have limited myself generally to these archives, that is to say, I have not introduced information about Allied or enemy policy which is now available but was unknown at the time to British ministers or officials.' Woodward, *British Foreign Policy in the Second World War*, v. Clearly, Roskill was introducing historical critique rather than just acting as an annalist or chronicler.
28 Here I follow the correspondence in CAB 103/328, W.M. (42), 101st Conclusions, War Cabinet of 1 August 1942, copy.
29 Ibid., Butler's appreciation.
30 Ibid., Brook to Montague Browne, 25 January 1957, enclosing copies of cabinet discussions, W.M. (42), 101st Conclusions.
31 Stacey was hampered by lack of records, particularly about German foreknowledge: Cook, *Clio's Warriors*, 186–7. Stacey, it seems to me, studiously avoided political controversy. He may well have known much more about this than he led others to believe and certainly his office was not always clear of ministerial complaint or directive. Stacey attributed the shortcomings of the Dieppe raid to bad luck: Villa, *Unauthorized Action*, 25–8.
32 Roskill, *War at Sea*, 2:252. On Mountbatten, see Roberts, *Eminent Churchillians*, 64–72. Beaverbrook's newspapers conducted a vendetta against Mountbatten; Beaverbrook believed that the Dieppe raid was arranged to discredit the case for a Second Front. Taylor, *Beaverbrook*, 538. Roskill, 'The Dieppe Raid: Were the Germans Forewarned' (received by Cabinet Office, 6 May 1964); sanitized essentials appeared as 'The Dieppe Raid and the Question of German Foreknowledge.' The Roskill-Irving dispute is traced in *Daily Telegraph*, 9 September 1963, *Evening Standard*, 1, 2, and 14 October 1963, and *Der*

Spiegel, 6 November 1963. An article Roskill wrote for the *Sunday Telegraph* was not printed (the reason given was lack of space, which seems ludicrous: more likely it was fear of legal tangle); the important points he put in a letter in *Daily Telegraph*, 4 November 1963. Roskill's memo for the Cabinet Office was written after he left its employ. See also ROSK 8/14 and CAB 103/602, containing Roskill's comments of 1964–67 on Dieppe.
33 Information from John Ehrman, 14 October 2005.
34 Roskill to Pitcairn-Jones, 17 January 1957, *Francis Edwards Catalogue No. 98* (January 2005), 7.
35 ROSK 24/4, 27; Hewitt, 'Allied Navies at Salerno'; Roskill, *War at Sea*, 3, part 1, 178–9.
36 ROSK 24/4, 27; cf. Roskill, *War at Sea*, 3, part 1, 214–18.
37 Marc Milner to author, 11 February 2003, based on ROSK 6/47. Milner, *U-Boat Hunters*, 255 and 311n.79. Waters, 'A Study of the Philosophy and Conduct of Maritime War, 1815–1945'.
38 Morison, *Strategy and Compromise*, 33.
39 Information from Edward Von der Porten, who queried Roskill on this point.
40 The 50-year rule (1958) was then in effect.
41 CAB 21/5834, Minute by D. Woods, Historical Section, Ministry of Defence, 25 May 1964, and related correspondence by Sir Percy Faulkner (Stationery Office) and Sir Burke Trend (Cabinet Office) in reply to Roskill's requests. This file contains the secret cabinet document, 'Information and Assistance to Authors of Independent Histories and Other Writings about the War', 8 January 1946.
42 Ewen Montagu surrendered one-third royalties for *The Man Who Never Was* (London: Evans, 1966), Ronald Wheatley 60 per cent for *Operation Sea Lion* (Oxford: Clarendon Press, 1958), and Bernard Fergusson 10 per cent for *Watery Maze: The Story of Combined Operations* (London: Collins, 1961). There may be other cases.
43 CAB 21/5834, Roskill to Trend, 8 April 1965.
44 Ibid., D. Woods, file memo, 27 April 1965.

Chapter 6
1 Galbraith Papers, box 1, Marder to John S. Galbraith, 3 and 22 June and 9 November 1960.
2 For Galbraith's role in these events, see McCulloch, *Instant University*, passim. McCulloch was dean of humanities and a leader in administration and planning besides being an excellent judge of faculty talents and prospects. Clark Kerr's trust in Galbraith is best expressed in his letter to him of 6 March 1963, in Galbraith Papers, box 1.
3 Noted in Marder Papers, Samuel C. McCulloch to Jack Peltason, 27 March 1965.
4 In later years he also taught special seminars on the Roman Empire and on Ireland.
5 Interview with George Akida, 24 January 2007.
6 Marder Papers, Ivan Hinderaker to Gerald Graham, 28 October 1963, and Graham to Hinderaker, 4 November 1963.
7 G.S. Graham Papers, PP43/1/19, Marder to Graham, 7 August 1972.
8 Marder Papers, Charles Moore to Marder, 3 June 1964, Cederic Cowing to Marder, 31 May 1964, and Thomas Hamilton to Marder, 24 May 1964.
9 Marder Papers, Daniel G. Aldrich, Jr, to Marder, 8 October 1964, Edward Steinhaus to Marder, 22 January 1965, and, from the public, Caroline and Torrence Dodds to Marder, 19 November 1964, and Marjorie L. Peffers to Marder, 22 January 1965.
10 Ibid., Gray Boyce to Marder, 22 January 1965, Marder to Boyce, 25 January 1965, Marder to Jack Peltason, 25 January 1965.
11 Interview with Henry Cord Meyer, 5 April 1998. This is one of four such I had with Meyer. Marder's stubborn attitudes and his undeniable great professional abilities was a perplexing combination for Meyer, who nonetheless adored Marder as a friend.
12 Frankland, *History at War*, 150.
13 Marder Papers, Donald E. Walker to Marder, 1 August 1966.
14 Ibid., Meyer to McCulloch, 20 January 1966, McCulloch to Peltason, 20 January 1966, and McCulloch to Meyer, 21 January 1966.
15 Ibid., Marder to Clark Kerr, 1 August 1966; also McCulloch to Marder, 1 August 1966.
16 Ibid., McCulloch to Aldrich, 12 August 1966.
17 Noble Frankland to author, 5 December 2001.
18 Eventually he reached Step VI. Galbraith Papers, box 2, Marder to Galbraith, 21 September 1966; and Marder Papers, McCulloch to Aldrich, 12 August 1966.
19 Arthur Marder, 'The Art of Leadership'.

NOTES

20. MacGregor, *Apostles Extraordinary*, 115–20, quotation at 119. The University of Washington Press attempted without success to lure Marder to write a book on Emma and other women who had influenced the Royal Navy. Marder Papers, Charles Cuningham to Marder, 9 August and 9 September 1966. Marder's essay 'That Hamilton Woman: Clio and Emma Reconciled', 1966, copy in the author's possession.
21. Marder Papers, MS-F3, Kemp to Marder, 3 April 1969. Marder also turned down the family's invitation to write the biography of Admiral of the Fleet Lord Chatfield.
22. *Journal of the Royal United Services Institution*, 113, 651 (August 1968): 188 (photo of Marder), 191–2. Also, Marder Papers, MS-F3, box 3, John White to Marder, 9 May 1968, and John Stephenson to Marder, 24 January 1969; also, Los Angeles *Times*, 21 April 1968, *Daily Telegraph*, 20 April 1968, and *The Bookseller*, 4 May 1968.
23. Marder won Guggenheims in 1941, 1946, and 1958.
24. Arthur Miller was then working on his book *The Air Condition Nightmare* (1942).
25. University of Oxford Archives, UR6/GEV/1, file 9, Moe to Courtney Smith, 21 December 1966; Isaiah Berlin to registrar, 28 December 1966; Marder to Moe, 3 January 1967, encl. in Moe to Berlin, 20 January 1967.
26. Marder Papers, box 17, Marder to Creswell, 25 May and 6 June 1967; also, ibid., old box 26, Moe to Marder, 1 June 1967 and 26 June 1970.
27. Brayer, *George Eastman*, 432, 499–500. Also, Marder Papers, MS-F2, box 33, George Beadle, 'How to be an Eastman Visiting Professor'.
28. Itinerary: McCulloch Papers (in author's possession), Marder to McCulloch, 5 July 1969. Teaching plans: Marder Papers, Marder to Gregg Sinclair, 3 June 1969. University announcement: *The Times*, 20 October 1969.
29. Information from A.B. Sainsbury.
30. Marder Papers, MS-F2, box 2, Balliol College welcome [untitled], 1969. *Times Literary Supplement*, 27 April 1967. The Eastman Professor reception was held on 8 October 1969.
31. Marder Papers, MS-F2, 'A.J.P. Taylor to me —', 3 December 1969. The book they were discussing, *Baldwin: A Biography*, by Keith Middlemas and John Barnes (London: Weidenfeld and Nicolson, 1969), was the first serious academic study of the politician and enjoyed critical acclaim. The labour expended on this massive book (1,149 pages) was one reason why Barnes did not attend to his work on Beatty for the Navy Records Society, as planned.
32. Taylor, ed., *Letters to Eva*, 17–19. On Taylor, see D.C. Watt, 'Taylorian Institute: Review of *The Oxford History of England: English History, 1914–1945*, by A.J.P. Taylor (London: Oxford University Press, 1966)', *History Today*, 16, 5 (May 1966): 359, 361.
33. I owe this reminiscence to Zara Steiner.
34. Marder Papers, MS-F2, box 4, Creswell to Marder, 7 December 1969.
35. Cobb, *People and Places*, 14.
36. Ibid. Marder and Gallagher had much in common. They kept regimented office hours often unsuited to student habits: Marder, 8 to 9 a.m. weekdays, except Tuesdays (golf); Gallagher (when forced to give notice of them on his door), Tuesdays, 2 a.m. Information from R.E. Robinson, 1992.
37. 'Arthur Marder's History of the Royal Navy, *From the Dreadnought to Scapa Flow*, was completed a year ago. He talks here to A.J.P. Taylor', *Listener*, 86, 221 (21 October 1971): 534–7, 542.
38. The only others I know of are William Roger, noted for distinguished contributions to historical literature, especially the multi-volume *Oxford History of the British Empire*, of which he is supreme editor, Thomas Vaughan of the Oregon Historical Society, and Richard Langworth, the Churchill scholar and editor of *Finest Hour*. On Marder's news breaking in California, see *UCI Review*, 2, 5 (February, 1971): 1, 3, and Los Angeles *Times*, 25 January 1971.
39. See chapter 4.
40. *Oxford University Gazette*, 14 January 1971. Marder Papers, 1971 file, Maurice Shock, 14 January 1971.
41. University of Oxford Archives, NW 9/10/45, 'Professor Arthur Jacob Marder, Hon. C.B.E., M.A., Statement in Latin and English for Encaenia, June 1971.

Chapter 7

1. Roskill, *Naval Policy between the Wars, Volume II*, 15–16.
2. Marder Papers, box 33, Roskill to Marder, 9 September 1961.
3. ROSK 24/1, 156.
4. Marder Papers, F2, box 33, Roskill to Marder, 29 September 1961.

HISTORICAL DREADNOUGHTS

5 ROSK, 11/11/3, Roskill, 'Marder v Roskill', 1 May 1975.
6 Marder Papers, box 17, Marder to Creswell, 10 July 1966. This may be followed in various histories, notably by Andrew Gordon, who was not convinced by Roskill's argument that aristocratic connections were hardly enough 'to turn the head of an arrogant young millionaire admiral who was a national celebrity on his own right and who hunted and house-partied easily in the highest circles.' *Rules of the Game*, 384–5.
7 Marder Papers, box 17, Marder to Creswell, 15 March 1967. It will be noted from this that it was not the sharing of the Jutland documents but the issue of the demarcation of dates (1918 or 1919) that was the cause of the subsequent quarrel.
8 Sainsbury Papers (private), Roskill to A.B. Sainsbury, 28 December 1962. Note that Roskill was reading Marder's second volume of *From the Dreadnought to Scapa Flow* at the time of this complaint. Three more volumes lay ahead for Roskill to critique.
9 Marder Papers, box 3, Roskill to Marder, 26 February 1968 and 2 January 1969.
10 ROSK 11/11/3, 'Marder v Roskill', 1 May 1975.
11 Marder Papers, box 17, Roskill to Marder, 10 January 1969, and Roskill's remarks on Marder's vol. 5, part 1, same date.
12 Ibid., box 3, Roskill to Marder, 18 January 1969.
13 Ibid., Marder to Roskill, 23 January 1969.
14 Ibid., Roskill to Marder, 30 January 1969.
15 Ibid., Marder to Roskill, 3 February 1969; ibid., box 3, Welch to Marder, 2 October and 11 November 1970, show the archivist's complete cooperation in releasing documents to the historian when the law permitted, the difficulty of earlier release being the nagging 50-year rule that bound them all.
16 'Marder v Roskill', 1 May 1975, 4.
17 This account draws on a series of 1969 letters in Marder Papers, box 17: Marder to Hankey, 23 January and 3 February, Hankey to Marder, 9 February, Marder to Hankey, 13 February, Hankey telegram of 14 February, Hankey to Marder, 15 February, Marder to Hankey, 19 February, Hankey to Marder, 6 March.
18 Ibid., Gretton to Marder, 6 February 1969.
19 Ibid., Roskill to Marder, 15 November 1969.
20 OUP Archives, PB/ED/009615/305, Marder to Elizabeth Knight, 16 April 1976.
21 NMM, Gretton Papers, GTN/7/4, Marder to Gretton, 3 and 11 February, 3 March 1969.

Chapter 8

1 The statement in question is this: 'Perhaps', says Roskill, 'I could have got it [*Naval Policy between the Wars, I*, which Marder had described as 'badly organized'] better organized had I spent less time reading, checking and criticizing all Marder's typescripts, and in corresponding with him.' *The Times*, 23 June 1971.
2 'Churchill Controversy', *Times Higher Educational Supplement*, undated [June?] 1972; copy in Sainsbury Papers (Private).
3 ROSK 11/11/3, Roskill, 'Marder v Roskill', 1 May 1975.
4 'Winston Churchill at the Admiralty', *US Naval Institute Proceedings* (January 1953).
5 King's College, London, Liddell Hart Centre for Military Archives, LH 1/489, Marder to Basil Liddell Hart, 11 January 1968.
6 Rodger, *The Admiralty*, 153.
7 Brodhurst, *Churchill's Anchor*. Review of same by Lawrence Phillips, *Ships Telegraph*, July 2001. Peter Nailor, 'Great Chiefs of Staff – Admiral of the Fleet Sir Dudley Pound', *RUSI Journal*, 133 (1) (1998): 67–70. Kemp, *Victory at Sea*.
8 Danchev and Daniel, eds., *Alanbrooke War Diaries 1939–1945*, xxiii.
9 Gardner, *Decoding History*, 14. See also, Syrett, 'The Secret War and the Historians'; and, by the same, *The Battle of the Atlantic and Signals Intelligence*, 21–5, which reviews the recent literature.
10 Lindemann was a strong proponent of research into new weapons, the proximity fuse being one, and counter-measures in electronic warfare being another. Besides being Churchill's scientific and technical adviser, Lindemann was in charge of the Admiralty statistical bureau.
11 ROSK 4/79, T.V.C. Phillips to Roskill, 10 February 1962, Roskill to Phillips, 17 February 1962, and Phillips to Roskill, 17 March 1962. The sharp and direct critique of Phillips by Roskill has strengthened in recent years, despite Marder's muting influence. See especially Warren, *Singapore*, 65–78.

NOTES

12 Churchill, *The Gathering Storm*, 654; Winton, *Carrier Glorious*, 218–21; and Slessor, *Ministries of Deception*, vii, 174–227, reissued as *Lying in State* (2004), with an additional chapter on the government's alleged misuse of intelligence in the lead-up to the Iraq War in 2003. For Roskill letters regarding the *Sunday Times* article of 15 June 1980, see ROSK 4/75, 76, 77, and 77A. Analysis of exchange of signals makes for equally compelling study. Barnett, *Engage the Enemy More Closely*, 136–9 and 917n.53, the best study of this subject to date, follows Roskill closely and adds details.
13 Higgins, *Winston Churchill and the Second Front* and *Soft Underbelly*.
14 Taylor, *The War Lords*, 76–7.
15 Gilbert, *Continue to Pester, Nag and Bite*, 55.
16 Sainsbury Papers, Marder to Sainsbury, 2 June 1971.
17 Marder Papers, Creswell to Marder, 16 March 1962.
18 Admiral Sir William Milbourne James (1881–1973). Among his many books, these relate to Churchill's second stint at the Admiralty: *The Portsmouth Letters* (London: Macmillan, 1946) and *The Sky Was Always Blue* (London: Methuen, 1951).
19 When finally captured by the British in 1943, it had been so reduced by bombardment that the only British casualty was, according to Churchill, one man bitten by a mule. On the role of Pantellaria in getting rid of Roger Keyes as director of Combined Operations, see Langdon, 'Too Old or Too Bold?' 80; and Churchill's final letter to Keyes, October 1941, in Gilbert, ed., *The Churchill War Papers, Volume 3*, 1377.
20 The authority on this is Reynolds, *Dog Boats at War*.
21 Marder Papers, box 6, John Litchfield to Marder, 19 December 1971.
22 He was, between these assignments, principal private secretary to Winston Churchill as prime minister, 1940–41; this in no way diminishes the specific Admiralty functions that are at issue here. *Who Was Who* (1996).
23 Marder Papers, box 6, Seal to Marder, 29 July 1971, and subsequent letters. Seal died shortly after this exchange but lived to read Marder's final draft of 'Winston Is Back'.
24 Marder Papers, box 6, J. Michael Wallace-Hadrill to Marder, 16 August and 3 September 1971.
25 Boothby, *Recollections of a Rebel*, 55.
26 Here I follow Roskill's position as stated in 'Marder v Roskill': 'My solicitor remarked that this suggestion was unquestionably libellous and that the defence could only be based either on 'Fair Comment' or 'True in substance or in Fact' and that either would be extremely difficult to prove.'
27 Vol. 4, no. 117.
28 Contained among the Marder letters kept by Peter Kemp, now in the possession of Texas A&M University, Cushing Library, are several from Marder to Kemp, April 1970 to December 1973, regarding Operation 'Menace'.
29 Ibid., Marder to Roskill, 16 August 1972, copy.
30 *From the Dardanelles to Oran*, 173–8.
31 Paul G. Halpern, 'Naval Topics, 1915–40', *Reviews in European History*, 2 (3) (1976): 407–19.
32 Paul Addison, *English Historical Review*, April 1974, 469–70. Also, Theodore Ropp, *American Historical Review*, 81 (1976): 146; and David Hankinson, *US Naval Institute Proceedings*, February 1976, 87. See, too, B.M. Simpson III, *Naval War College Review*, 1976, in which Paul Kennedy's *The Rise and Fall of British Naval Mastery* (New York: Scribner, 1976) is featured in a joint review of *From the Dardanelles to Oran*: Kennedy's large-scale work is set against Marder's detailed, deeper case studies.
33 Made in reference to Marder's chapter on the Navy and the Ethiopian crisis (1935–36) in Terence Lewin, 'The Royal Navy – Its Contribution to National and Western Defence', *RUSI Journal*, September 1976, 4.
34 Bond, *English Historical Review*, 92 (January 1977): 232–3.
35 John Litchfield, *Naval Review*, April 1976, 181–4; A.B. Sainsbury, *Mariner's Mirror*, 62, (1) (1976): 193; A.J.P. Taylor, *Observer*, 8 February 1976; Ronald Lewin, *Listener*, 18 March 1976. See also David Stafford, *American Historical Review*, 82 (February 1977): 110–11; E.J. Grove, *History*, October 1977, 539; Bryan Ranft, *War and Society*, 1976, 186–7; John Terraine, *The Daily Telegraph*, [?] February 1976 (copy, Marder Papers, box 29); David Leitch, *New Statesman*, 9 April 1976; David Woodward, *History Today*, May 1976, 337; Noel Barber, *Spectator*, 14 February 1976; Brian Schofield, *RUSI Journal*, June 1976; *Navy News*, February 1977; *Globe & Laurel* (Royal Marines), May-June 1976, 186; *Economist*, 7 February 1976; Michael Wolff, *The Times*, 5 February 1976; Correlli Barnett, *Eastern Daily Press*, 27 February 1976; C.V. Collinet, *Revue d'hist 2e Guerre*, 111 (1978): 101–4; and J-M d'Hoop, *Revue historique*, 257 (1997): 498–501.

36 Marder Papers, box for 1977, Roskill to Marder, 14 April 1977. It will be noted that, despite the intense public quarrel, the titans maintained their intermittent correspondence. For tactical reasons, enemies must retain contact with each other.
37 Roskill, *Churchill and the Admirals*, 296.
38 Danchev and Todman, *Alanbrooke War Diaries*, 226, 230–1, 356–67; cf. Bryant, ed., *The Turn of the Tide*, 275, 285, and 308.
39 Other reviews include Henry Stanhope, *The Times*, 10 November 1977; Mark Arnold Forster, *Guardian*, 15 December 1977; and (unsigned), *Economist*, 19 November 1977.
40 Ranft, 'Naval Historians at War', 79–80.
41 References as in n.7. Ian McGeoch, review of Brodhurst's *Churchill's Anchor*, in *RUSI Journal*, 146 (3) (2001): 86–8. Subsequent McGeoch-Brodhurst correspondence, Brodhurst collection.

Chapter 9
1 The unhappy affair of the Harper Record and the rewriting of Jutland has been told often. See, most recently, Gordon, *Rules of the Game;* and Yates, *Flawed Victory*, 259–73.
2 Marder Papers, W.S. Chalmers to Marder, 16 June 1966.
3 *Naval Review*, 45 (2) (April 1957): 178–81.
4 Roskill, *The Last Naval Hero*, unpaginated preface.
5 However, it bears repeating that, according to Roskill, Marder's intended book led to a sort of pact or gentlemen's agreement that Marder would end his inquiries at 1918, the end of the war, and that Roskill would begin in 1919: 'The only condition I made was to say to Marder "All right. I will leave the whole of World War I to you but you leave between the wars to me."' And so, even then, Roskill was arguing for strict limits. For his part, Marder had to make clear to his rival that all along he intended to close his series *From the Dreadnought to Scapa Flow* with the internment in November 1918 and scuttling of the High Seas Fleet in 1919 and also with the naval aspects of the treaties ending the conflict, and that Roskill could start where he wanted, at the end of the war or whenever he so chose. ROSK, 11/11/3, Roskill, 'Marder v Roskill', 1 May 1975.
6 Churchill Archives Centre, Shane Leslie-Godfrey Faussett Archive (SLGF), 12/2.
7 The following discussion of the Harper business owes much to Gordon, *The Rules of the Game*, esp. 539–61.
8 Quoted in Roskill, *The Last Naval Hero*, 329.
9 Schurman, *Sir Julian S. Corbett*, 189–90; NMM, Corbett diary, 15 June 1921.
10 Here I rely heavily on Patterson, *Jellicoe Papers, Volume II*, 401–2.
11 Patterson, *Jellicoe*, 109–10.
12 Printed in front matter to Corbett and Newbolt, *Naval Operations*, 3. Original is ADM 116/2067, Admiralty minute, 22 February 1923; Schurman, *Corbett*, 193.
13 Marder, *Jutland and After*, 201; cf. *Jutland and After*, 2nd ed., 248; Marder Papers, box 17, Marder to Creswell, 6 July 1966, 20 April and 1 May 1967. In July 1966, just as Marder was finishing a packed research visit to Britain, the Cabinet Office asked him to examine about one hundred boxes of First World Papers it was readying for shipment to the PRO. It was then that Marder found the Harper statement, 'the A to Z of his experiences with Beatty & Co. . . . the RUSI have a copy they won't show to anybody. Nobody knows I now have the same' (20 April 1967). Marder's copy (from Cabinet Office mss) of Harper's 'Facts dealing with the compilation of the official record of the Battle of Jutland by Captain J.E.T. Harper, R.N., and the reason it was never published' (carbon typescript, 37 pp.), including thirty-six Admiralty documents, is in the Marder Papers, box 27, folder 5.
14 Marder Papers, Gretton to Marder, 12 January 1968. In Marder's to Creswell, 20 April 1967, ibid., he indicated the prospect of publishing the Harper document as an appendix to the intended 2nd edition.
15 I have this observation from A.B. Sainsbury, who is well connected with those reading and writing British naval history. It does not reflect Sainsbury's viewpoint.
16 Roskill, *The Last Naval Hero*, 324. The correspondence is in ROSK 3/10.
17 Bennett, *The Battle of Jutland*, 192–3.
18 Lambert, *Letters and Papers of Professor Sir John Knox Laughton*, 71–3.
19 Information from Donald Schurman.
20 Author's files, Brock to author, 23 April 1968.
21 David (2nd Earl) Beatty recounted this to Paul Halpern sometime between 1968 and 1972, when the Earl died. Author's files, Halpern to author, 30 August 2005.
22 Marder Papers, Roskill to Marder, 10 December 1968.

NOTES

23 Author's files, Lawrence Phillips to author, 2 August 2005.
24 Marder Papers, box 3, Kemp to Marder, 6 January 1969.
25 *Naval Review* 57 (2) (April 1969): 176–7. The review, by A.B. Sainsbury, is signed Brockmill.
26 Marder Papers, MS-F3, Cunninghame Graham to Marder, 13 December 1968.
27 Ibid., Taylor to Marder, 20 December 1968.
28 Ibid., G.N.S. Hunt to Marder, 16 December 1968. In *Jutland and After*, page 201, Marder wrote that the Jutland controversy had surpassed all previous battles royal of British naval annals. He briefly recounted how the controversy had developed, especially with the publication of Jellicoe's *Grand Fleet* in 1919 'and a barrage of anti-Jellicoe books full of factual inaccuracies and false premises . . . The controversy was brought to a boiling-point by the unseemly wrangle in the early 1920's over the preparation and publication of the Official Record (the 'Harper Report') on the battle. And just when the situation was beginning to calm down, the publication in 1927 of Volume iii of Churchill's *The World Crisis* stoked the embers. Reproaches, recriminations, abuse and calumny filled the air and the press through most of the '20's. The Jellicoeites (led by Harper and Bacon) and the Beattyites exchanged violently partisan attacks on the other side's hero, and the two Admirals themselves were drawn into the vortex, though not publicly. The details of this unsavoury affair, including the rights and wrongs, I gladly leave to Captain Roskill and his study of the controversy which is in preparation.'
29 Ibid., David (2nd Earl) Beatty to Marder, 30 December 1968. Beatty was then chairman, Home Oil of Canada. The letter was written from London.
30 Ibid., F3, Roskill to Marder, 2 January 1969.
31 Ibid., Roskill to Marder, 21 December 1968.
32 Author's files, Brock to author, 19 March 1969.
33 Bennett, *Naval Battles of the First World War* [1968], 243.
34 See Admiral Sir William James's letter, in *RUSI Journal*, 653 (March 1969): 68, concerning Harper's statement that Chatfield, flag captain to Beatty, was mainly responsible for the gunnery efficiency of the battlecruisers, and that Chatfield was Beatty's main support in his endeavour to fudge the 'Harper Report.' 'No one who served with Chatfield, and I was his Chief of Staff for five years, will believe this accusation', wrote James. To this, Bennett replied, using Temple Patterson's biography of Jellicoe recently published, that Chatfield and Osmond de B. Brock were party to the first sea lord's attempts to distort the Harper Record. 'Such criticism of Chatfield was, presumably, one reason why this Institution withheld the Harper papers from publication until after his death in 1967' (ibid., 655 [September 1969]: 80). See also *Naval Review*, 57 (4) (1969): 373 – a similar letter from James, also Temple Patterson's reply to Bennett, who, in the review of Temple Patterson's *Jellicoe*, denied Chatfield's encouragement to distort the Harper Record; he had only objected to the tone. Ibid., 58 (1) (1970): 95. History, indeed, is a battle without end.
35 Erskine, 'The Historical Collections of the R.U.S.I.', *RUSI Journal*, 114, 653 (1969): 64–5.
36 Ibid., 81, 82, 84.
37 Beatty, *Our Admiral*, 156–7.
38 NMM, V78/110, Hobson's evaluation and other notations, November 1980 and February 1981.
39 Ibid., Knight to D. Proctor, 21 March 1978.
40 Knight, 'The Beatty Papers at the National Maritime Museum Greenwich', 387–8.
41 ROSK 7/235, Roskill to Peter Carter-Ruck, draft, n.d., in reply to the latter's of 23 April 1982; and other correspondence, notably Roskill to P.R. Davies, 21 August 1982, closing the matter.
42 The continuing project is under the editorship of Dr Eric Grove.
43 Review, *Naval Review*, 67 (1) (1979): 81–2, signed A.B. Sainsbury; Marder's response, ibid., 63 (3) (1979): 234–5; Roskill's reply to Marder, ibid., 63 (4) (1979): 326.
44 Ian McGeoch, *The Times*, 4 December 1980; Michael Howard, *Sunday Times*, 7 December 1980; A.J.P. Taylor, *Observer*, 7 December 1980; Janet Morgan, *Financial Times*, 3 January 1981, and A.B. Sainsbury, *Naval Review*, 69 (1) (1981): 71.
45 On Beatty's anti-Semitism, see Roskill, *The Last Naval Hero*, 24, 88–9.
46 Pollen's designs were repeatedly rejected by the Admiralty despite successful performances. The Navy later incorporated aspects of Pollen's designs into fire-control gear; this led to a retrospective award by the Royal Commission on Awards to Inventors. Sumida, ed., *The Pollen Papers*.
47 Sumida's argument that the Pollen method of fire control was better than that of Dreyer has been challenged. The matter may be followed in Sumida, *In Defence of Naval Supremacy*; Brooks, *Dreadnought Gunnery and the Battle of Jutland*; and Sumida, 'Gunnery, Procurement, and Strategy in the *Dreadnought* Era', 1179–87. The last salvo has yet to be fired.

48 Roskill, *The Last Naval Hero*, 152.
49 Ibid., 339.

Chapter 10
1 Information from Henry Cord Meyer. Robertson's stand against Marder may be followed in the *New University*, 6 and 18 February 1969.
2 Marder Papers, box 5, R. Cobb to Marder, 26 May 1971, encl. 'Times Diary' from *The Times*, 24 May 1971.
3 McCulloch Papers (Private), copy, Cassandra Memo no. 2, 8 November 1972, to the 'Old Goats', McCulloch, Meyer, and G. T. White.
4 Naval Historical Branch, Ministry of Defence files, Marder to J. Lawson, 21 January 1975, Lawson to Marder, 11 July 1975.
5 McCulloch Papers, Arthur Marder, Addendum to Biography, 20 October 1975, McCulloch Papers, copy in author's collection.
6 On this point, Professor Asada's statement is worth repeating here: the documentary holocaust was done by those 'who hastily burned any confidential records that might implicate them in postwar crimes trials. I once stated – to be sure, helplessly – that the act constituted a crime against history.' Asada, *From Mahan to Pearl Harbor*, ix–x.
7 Marder Papers, box 26, Marder's report to Japan Foundation, 10 August 1976 (addressed to Hidemi Kon, president), encl. Sadao Asada to Marder, 4 July 1976.
8 See n.6 above.
9 Author's files, Sadao Asada to author, 29 September 1998.
10 Marder, 'An American Historian's Love Affair with the Royal Navy', 10, 11.
11 London: Croom Helm, 1977.
12 ROSK 8/30, Roskill's 'Essay on the Writings of Arthur Marder'; Jordon to Roskill, 8 July 1976; and ROSK 11/11/3, 'Marder v Roskill', 1 May 1975. The last was headed 'Personal' and was closed to researchers until 2008, when it was released to me courtesy of Nicholas Roskill and Allen Packwood.
13 Information from Zara Steiner.
14 Marder, *Bravery Is Not Enough*.
15 NMM, Lord Fraser of North Cape Papers, Mountbatten to Fraser, 27 July 1979, and enclosures, MS 83/158, file 38/14.
16 Ronald Lewin, review, *The Times*, 3 September 1981.
17 Author's files, Meyer to author, 5 April 1998.
18 This was Admiral Sir John Somerville's term: Marder Collection (Kemp Papers), J.A.F. Somerville to Kemp, 21 February 1983.
19 Marder, *Old Friends, New Enemies*, 2: xii. *Friends of the Library News, University of California, Irvine*, 13 (1) (1990): 3. This tribute contains Meyer's account of how volume 2 was completed. Also, author's interviews with Meyer, 1996 and 1997.
20 An off-colour review – this was Henry Cord Meyer's opinion of it – appeared from the pen of Richard Hough, Marder's old friend (*Daily Telegraph*, 18 August 1990): 'After the few chapters of Marder's magic, when his old pupils take up the narrative it soon becomes evident that they have neither the thrust, economy, balance, powers of expression, nor even the accuracy of their master. Five pages are devoted to the death and replacement of Admiral Sir Dudley Pound, First Sea Lord, as if he were Nelson in the cockpit of the *Victory*.' Hough's judgement seems unfair; the authors coped mightily with a difficult assignment. It is worth making the point that, as good a historian as Hough was, he hardly ever undertook documentary research (and when he did he used Marder's papers on loan) and was never in the same league as Marder, or Horsfield or Jacobsen either. Yes, there probably could never be another Marder, and Hough would have been the first to say it.

Chapter 11
1 This classic interpretation of sea power differs from Corbett's attempt to describe the control of sea communications and from Richmond's trenchant warning to politicians to keep Britain and British trade strong at sea, but equally it credits these founding treatises. Roskill's book became standard reading in British and Commonwealth naval and command colleges, and to this day it is treated with reverence and respect despite its age.
2 This chapter is based principally on Roskill's (still) unpublished memoir, 'A Sailor's Ditty Box', which is found in various states in the Roskill Papers, Churchill Archives Centre, especially ROSK 24/1, 3 and

NOTES

4. See also Zara Steiner's correspondence with Roskill, 1977, in ibid., Zara Steiner Papers, GSNR 9. The Lees Knowles invitation and event is described in ROSK 24/1, 152–6. The chapter also relies on these tributes, written after Roskill's death: Churchill Archives Centre, 101/1/23, Owen Chadwick, memorial address, Great St Mary's Church, Cambridge, 26 November 1982; Barnett, 'Stephen Roskill, 1903–1982', 5–8; Sainsbury, 'Stephen Wentworth Roskill', 3–4, to which is appended 'An Obituary from Australia', by James Goldrick, 5–6; and Ehrman, 'Stephen Wentworth Roskill', 579–94. This last was issued as an offprint, dated 1984.
3. Roskill, 'An Innocent at Cambridge', 3–34. Zara Steiner interview, 12 May 1995. Roskill presents a different account in ROSK 24/1, 152–3.
4. Author's files, Marion M. Stewart to author, 13 February 2002.
5. Barnett, 'Roskill and the Churchill Archives Centre', 17.
6. See n.2 above.
7. Sainsbury Papers (Private), Marder to Sainsbury, 20 August 1974.
8. RUSI Archives, Michael Howard to A.B. Sainsbury, 11 October 1974. Sainsbury told the author that Marder started the nomination process, keen as he was to see Roskill properly recognized for his outstanding historical work in naval history.
9. Sainsbury Papers, B.G.R. Thompson to Sainsbury, 18 October 1974, Marder to Sainsbury, 16 September 1974, Howard to Sainsbury, 29 October 1974, and Marder to Sainsbury, 4 November 1974.
10. Author's files, author's correspondence with University of Leeds librarian Mark Shipway, 25 June 1998, including university correspondence with Roskill, 1974.
11. University of Oxford Archives, NW 9f/10/54. Also, Sainsbury Papers, Howard to Sainsbury, 9 July 1980.
12. ROSK 24/1, 161–6, recounting foreign travel.
13. ROSK 14/16, Roskill to E.V. Eales, 14 March, 28 July and October 1981.
14. Author's files, Noble Frankland to the author, 5 December 2001.
15. Sainsbury Papers, Marder to Sainsbury, 6 February 1980.
16. This unhappy story may be traced in the Sainsbury Papers, especially James Erbele to Sainsbury, 12 March 1980, Marder to Sainsbury, 15 March 1980, Lewin to Sainsbury, 27 March 1980, Carrington to Sainsbury, 2 April 1980, Jan Marder to Sainsbury, 18 April 1980, Sainsbury to W. Hawthorne, 29 July 1980, Sainsbury to Lewin, 21 October 1981, Lewin to Sainsbury, 21 March 1982, Lord Roskill's phone call to Sainsbury (notes), 2 February 1983, and Nicholas Roskill to Sainsbury, 10 February 1983.
17. Author's files, Stewart to author, 13 February 2002.
18. These are listed in n.3 above. Also, *The Times*, 6 November 1982.
19. Churchill Archives Centre, 101/1/23.

Bibliography

WHEREVER possible, this book relies on original correspondence, memoranda, and other materials collected by Arthur Marder and Stephen Roskill. The lion's share of Marder materials is to be found in the University of California, Irvine (UCI), Special Collections and Archives, and consists of about 21,000 letters. An estimated 70 per cent of these are in-letters, for Marder did not always keep carbon copies or photocopies of his outgoing letters. Those that are not found in the form of a copy may invariably be located in the recipient's files (for example, the Kemp Collection of Marder materials at Texas A&M University, the archive files of Oxford University Press, and private collections such as that of A.B. Sainsbury). The Marder Papers at UCI are mainly arranged chronologically, and, apart from a few retrospective items dating to *c.*1940, consist mainly of materials collected by Marder and archived by R. Berry. Marder's only autobiographical work is 'Fate Knocks Three Times', various forms of which are found in the collection. Of related interest is his 'An American Historian's Love Affair with the Royal Navy: Reflections on Forty-Seven Years of Marital Bliss'. Key Marder correspondence, that is, in- and out-letters, is also in the Marder Collection of Peter Kemp at Texas A&M University. Note that these are classified as Marder papers in that collection; accordingly, and for the sake of clarity, they are here referred to as Marder Collection (Kemp Papers).

The Stephen Roskill Papers (ROSK) are lodged in the Churchill Archives Centre, Churchill College, Cambridge, and arranged by topic, the work of sorting having been essentially undertaken by Roskill himself. A general inventory may be found on the centre's website (http://www.chu.cam.ac.uk/archives/) and is not reproduced here. Roskill's papers are of similar size to Marder's but mainly topical and autobiographical in character. Roskill was conscious of his own place in the history of the Royal Navy and of historical writing: his unpublished autobiography (printed for private circulation), 'A Sailor's Ditty Box: An Account of Naval and Academic Life in the 20th Century', is found in various states of development in ROSK 24/1–4. Roskill's outgoing correspondence may also be traced in the files of recipients, notably Marder, Chatfield, and Sainsbury.

Published Writings of Arthur Jacob Marder

'The English Armament Industry and Navalism in the Nineties'. *Pacific Historical Review*, 7 (3) (1938): 241–53.

'British Naval Policy in 1878'. *Journal of Modern History*, 12 (3) (1940): 367–73.

The Anatomy of British Sea Power: A History of British Naval Policy in the Pre-Dreadnought Era, 1880–1905. New York: Alfred A. Knopf, 1940; published in Britain as *British Naval Policy, 1880–1905: The Anatomy of British Sea Power*. London: Putnam, 1941; reprinted, with original title, by both Hampden, Conn.: Archon Books, and London: Frank Cass, 1964.

'Admiral Sir John Fisher: A Reappraisal'. *US Naval Institute Proceedings*, 68 (March 1942): 317–26.

'From Jimmu Tenno to Perry: Sea Power in Early Japanese History'. *American Historical Review*, 51 (1) (1945): 1–34.

Portrait of an Admiral: The Life and Papers of Sir Herbert Richmond. London: Jonathan Cape, and Cambridge, Mass.: Harvard University Press, 1952.

Fear God and Dread Nought: The Correspondence of Admiral of the Fleet Lord Fisher of Kilverstone, 3 vols. London: Jonathan Cape, and Cambridge, Mass.: Harvard University Press, 1952–59.

'Winston Churchill as First Lord of the Admiralty, 1911–1915'. *US Naval Institute Proceedings*, 79 (1) (1953): 19–27.

'Fisher and the Genesis of the Dreadnought'. *US Naval Institute Proceedings*, 82 (December 1956): 1309–15.

'The Channel Tunnel in pre-World War I Strategy'. *Naval Review*, 48 (July 1960): 337–40.

'The Art of Leadership: Nelson, a Case Study'. *Naval Review*, 49 (October 1961): 124–32.

From the Dreadnought to Scapa Flow: The Royal Navy in the Fisher Era, 1904–1919. Vol. I, *The Road to War (1904–1914)* (London: Oxford University Press, 1961); vol. II, *The War Years: To the Eve of Jutland (1914–1916)* (London: Oxford University Press, 1965); vol. III, *Jutland and After (May 1916–December 1916)* (London: Oxford University Press, 1966); vol. IV, *1917: Year of Crisis* (London: Oxford University Press, 1969); vol. V, *Victory and Aftermath (January 1918–June 1919)* (London: Oxford University Press, 1970).

'Jellicoe and Beatty as Commanders in Chief, Grand Fleet'. In William Geffen, ed., *Command and Commanders in Modern Warfare: The Proceedings of the Second Military History Symposium, US Air Force Academy, 2–3 May*

1968. 2nd ed.: Office of Air Force History, Headquarters USAF and United States Air Force Academy, 1971, 81–90, with commentary by Donald M. Schurman, 91–6, and Admiral Sir William James, Rear Admiral S.A. Pears, Rear Admiral C.M. Blackman, Captain G.E. Bannister, and Admiral Sir Angus Cunninghame-Graham (jointly), and Captain R.H.F. de Salis, 'The Military View: Comments by Members of the Royal Navy', 97–115.

'The Royal Navy and the Ethiopian Crisis of 1935–1936'. *American Historical Review*, 75 (5) (1970): 1327–56; republished, with added material, in *From the Dardanelles to Oran*.

'The First World War at Sea', in Robin Higham, ed., *A Guide to the Sources of British Military History*, London: Routledge & Paul, Berkeley: University of California Press, 1971, 365–95.

'"Winston Is Back": Churchill at the Admiralty, 1939–1940'. *English Historical Review*, Supplement 5, London: Longman, 1972; revised and republished in *From the Dardanelles to Oran*.

'The Influence of History on Sea Power: The Royal Navy and the Lessons of 1914–1918'. *Pacific Historical Review*, 46 (November 1972): 413–43. [Presidential address, Pacific Coast Branch, American Historical Association. Reworked and expanded in *From the Dardanelles to Oran*.]

'The Dardanelles Revisited: Further Thoughts on the Naval Prelude'. In A.M.J. Hyatt, ed., *Dreadnought to Polaris: Maritime Strategy since Mahan* (Annapolis, Md.: Naval Institute Press, Toronto: Copp Clark, 1973), 30–46.

From the Dardanelles to Oran: Studies of the Royal Navy in War and Peace, 1915–1940. London and New York: Oxford University Press, 1974.

'An American Historian's Love Affair with the Royal Navy: Reflections on Forty-Seven Years of Marital Bliss'. *Doshisha Hogaku* (Doshisha Law Review), 143 (November 1976): 1–15.

'Lord Fisher, John Arbuthnot'. In Peter Kemp, ed., *Oxford Companion to Ships and the Sea* (New York and London: Oxford University Press, 1976).

Operation 'Menace': The Dakar Expedition and the Dudley North Affair. London and New York: Oxford University Press, 1976.

Bravery Is Not Enough: The Rise and Fall of the Imperial Japanese Navy. Irvine: University of California, Irvine, 1978.

Jutland and After (May 1916–December 1916), volume III of From the Dreadnought to Scapa Flow. Revised and enlarged ed. of 1966 original; London: Oxford University Press, 1978.

Old Friends, New Enemies: The Royal Navy and the Imperial Japanese Navy, vol. I: Strategic Illusions, 1936–1941. Oxford: Clarendon Press, 1981.

— and Mark Jacobsen and John Horsfield. *Old Friends, New Enemies: The Royal Navy and the Imperial Japanese Navy, vol. II: The Pacific War, 1942–1945*. Oxford: Clarendon Press, 1990.

Published Writings of Stephen Wentworth Roskill

History of the Second World War. The War at Sea, 3 vols. in 4. London: HMSO, 1954–61. *Volume I: The Defensive*, 1954; *volume II: The Period of Balance*, 1956; *volume III, part 1: The Offensive, 1st June 1943 – 31st May 1944*, 1960; and *volume III, part 2: The Offensive, 1st June 1944 to 14th August 1945*, 1961. [These volumes were reprinted many times by HMSO, and references were added in 1972; since that time, commercial reprints have appeared, including one from the Imperial War Museum. No attempt is made here to give the various dates of these serial reprints. Roskill's book is readily available more than sixty years after its initial volume appeared. Marder has been less fortunate in this regard.]

Foreword to D.A. Rayner, *Escort: The Battle of the Atlantic*. London: William Kimber, 1955.

'*CAPROS* not *CONVOY*: Counterattack and Destroy'. *US Naval Institute Proceedings*, 82 (October 1956): 1046–53.

HMS 'Warspite': The Story of a Famous Battleship. London, Collins, 1957. Original ed. republished, with introduction by H.P. Willmott, Annapolis, Md.: Naval Institute Press, 1997.

'Truth and Criticism in History – and Jutland'. *Naval Review*, 45 (2) (1957): 178–81.

The Secret Capture. London: Collins, 1959.

'The U-boat Campaign of 1917 and "Third Ypres".' *RUSI Journal*, 54 (616) (1959): 440–2.

White Ensign: The British Navy at War, 1939–1945. Annapolis: Naval Institute Press, 1960. Subsequently published in the United Kingdom as *The Navy at War, 1939–1945*. London: Collins, 1960; reprinted, Ware, UK: Wordsworth, 1998.

'The Destruction of Zeppelin L.53'. *US Naval Institute Proceedings*, 86 (August 1960): 70–8.

A Merchant Fleet at War: Alfred Holt and Co., 1939–1945. London: Collins, 1962.

The Strategy of Sea Power: Its Development and Application. London: Collins, 1962.

'The Navy at Cambridge'. *Mariner's Mirror*, 49 (August 1963): 178–93.

'Richmond in Retrospect'. *Naval Review* 51 (1) (1963): 22.

The Art of Leadership. London: Collins, 1964.

'The Dieppe Raid and the Question of German Foreknowledge: A Study in

Historical Responsibility'. *RUSI Journal*, 109 (February–November 1964): 27–31.
'The Dismissal of Admiral Jellicoe'. *Journal of Contemporary History*, 1, (4) (1966): 69–93.
'History – Dust Heap or Cornerstone?'. *US Naval Institute Proceedings*, 92 (January 1966): 68–75.
Naval Policy between the Wars. Vol. I: The Period of Anglo-American Antagonism, 1919–1929. London: Collins, and Annapolis, Md.: Naval Institute Press, 1968; vol. II: *The Period of Reluctant Rearmament, 1930–1939*. London: Collins, and Annapolis: Naval Institute Press, 1976.
Documents Relating to the Naval Air Service. Vol. I, 1908–1918. London: Navy Records Society, 1969.
Hankey: Man of Secrets. Vol. I, 1877–1918, London: Collins, 1970; vol. II, *1919–1931*, London: Collins, 1972; vol. III, *1931–1963*. London: Collins, 1974.
'An Innocent at Cambridge'. *Churchill Review*, 1970, 3–34.
'Some Reasons for Official History'. In Robin Higham, *Official Histories: Essays and Bibliographies from around the World* (Manhattan: Kansas State University Library, 1970), 10–19.
'The Ten Year Rule: The Historical Facts.' *RUSI Journal*, 117 (March 1972): 69–71.
'Marder, Churchill and the Admiralty'. *RUSI Journal*, 117 (December 1972): 49–53.
'The Churchill College Archives Centre'. *Churchill Review*, 1973, 4–7.
'The Churchill Centenary'. *Churchill Review*, 1974, 5–10.
'Lord Hankey: The Creation of the Machinery of Government'. *RUSI Journal*, 120 (September 1975): 10–18.
Introduction to John Barrow, *The Eventful History of the Mutiny and Piratical Seizure of HMS Bounty: Its Causes and Consequences*. London: Folio Society, 1976.
Churchill and the Admirals. London: Collins, and New York: Morrow, 1977.
Admiral of the Fleet Earl Beatty: The Last Naval Hero, an Intimate Biography. London: Collins, and New York: Athenaeum, 1980.
'The Adoption of the Oerlikon Gun – 1939–40'. *Naval Review*, 68 (2) (1980): 151–4.
'Lord Cecil and the Historians'. *Historical Journal*, 25 (4) (1982): 953–4 [reply and counter-reply to J.A. Thompson, 'Lord Cecil and the Historians' and 'Lord Cecil and Stephen Roskill', *Historical Journal*, 24 (3) (1981): 709–15, and 24 (4) (1982): 955–6].

Assorted Archival Materials
Admiralty Papers (ADM) (National Archives, Kew, Surrey)
American Philosophical Society (Philadelphia)
Balliol College Archives (Oxford)
Beatty, Earl (National Maritime Museum [NMM] Greenwich)
Bodhurst, Robin (Private)
Cabinet Papers (National Archives)
Chatfield, 2nd Lord (Author's files)
Churchill Archives Centre (Cambridge)
Churchill College Registrar Files (Cambridge)
Defence, Ministry of, Papers (National Archives)
English High School (Boston)
Fraser, Lord, of North Cape (NMM)
Galbraith, John S. (University of California, San Diego)
Graham, G.S. (King's College, London)
Graham, G.S. (Private)
Gretton, Vice Admiral Sir Peter (NMM)
Hamilton College (Clinton, NY)
Jordan, Gerald (Private)
Kaplan, Gloria (Private)
Langer Papers (Harvard University)
Leeds University Archives
Liddell Hart, Basil, Papers (Liddell Hart Centre for Military Archives, King's College, London)
McCulloch, Samuel C. (Author's files)
Meyer, Henry Cord (Author's files)
National Maritime Museum, Marder files (Greenwich)
Naval Historical Branch, Ministry of Defence (Navy), files (Portsmouth)
Oxford University Press Archives, Marder files (Oxford)
Parkinson, C. Northcote (Emmanuel College, Cambridge)
Pearsall, A.W.H. (NMM)
Rose, Kenneth (Private)
Royal United Services Institute for Defence Studies, medal files (London)
Sainsbury, A.P. (Private)
University of Hawaii Archives, Presidential Papers: Sinclair
University of Oxford Archives (Eastman professorship)
Waters, D.W. (NMM)

Interviews
Alvin Coox

John Ehrman
John S. Galbraith
Rear Admiral James Goldrick
Mrs Mary Graham
Admiral Sir Arthur Hezlett
Norman Hillmer
John Horsfield
Mrs. Jane Hough
Roger Knight
Alan Kucia
Andrew Lambert
Nicholas Lambert
Samuel Clyde and Sally McCulloch
Kevin Marder
Henry Cord Meyer
Keith Nelson
Axel Ornelles
Mary Z. Pain
Alan Pearsall
Lawrence Phillips
Clark Reynolds
Geoffrey Plowden
N.A.M. Rodger
Kenneth Rose
Anthony B. Sainsbury
Donald M. Schurman
Zara Steiner
John Stephan
Edward Von der Porten

Books, Chapters in Books, Articles, and Ephemera
'Arthur Marder's History of the Royal Navy, *From the Dreadnought to Scapa Flow*, Was Completed a Year Ago: He Talks Here to A.J.P. Taylor'. *Listener*, 86, 221 (21 October 1971): 534–37, 542.
Asada, Sadao. *From Mahan to Pearl Harbor: The Imperial Japanese Navy and the United States Navy*. Annapolis, Md.: Naval Institute Press, 2006.
—— *Culture Shock and Japanese-American Relations: Historical Essays*. Columbia: University of Missouri Press, 2007.
Ashley, Maurice. *Churchill as Historian*. New York: Charles Scribner's Sons, 1968.
Aspinall-Oglander, Cecil. *Roger Keyes: Being the Biography of Admiral of the*

Fleet Lord Keyes of Zeebrugge and Dover. London: Hogarth Press, 1951.
Ballard, Robert D. *Graveyards of the Pacific: From Pearl Harbor to Bikini Atoll*. Washington: National Geographic, 2001.
Barnett, Correlli. *The Swordbearers*. London: Eyre and Spottiswoode, 1963.
—— 'Roskill and the Churchill Archives Centre'. *Churchill Review*, 1981, 17.
—— 'Stephen Roskill, 1903–1982'. *Churchill Review*, 1982, 5–8.
—— *Engage the Enemy More Closely: The Royal Navy in the Second World War*. London and New York: W.W. Norton, 1991.
—— 'Stephen Wentworth Roskill, 1903–1982'. *Oxford Dictionary of National Biography*. Oxford University Press, 2004.
Baugh, Daniel. 'Admiral Sir Herbert Richmond and the Objects of Sea Power'. In James Goldrick and John B. Hattendorf, eds., *Mahan Is Not Enough: The Proceedings of a Conference on the Works of Sir Julian Corbett and Admiral Sir Herbert Richmond*. Newport, RI: Naval War College Press, 1993), 13–48.
Beatty, Charles. *Our Admiral: A Biography of Admiral of the Fleet Earl Beatty*. London: W.H. Allen, 1980.
Beeler, John F. *British Naval Policy in the Gladstone-Disraeli Era, 1866–1880*. Stanford, Calif.: Stanford University Press, 1997.
Beesley, Patrick. *Very Special Intelligence: The Story of the Admiralty's Operational Intelligence Centre, 1939–1945*. London: Hamish Hamilton, 1977.
—— *Very Special Admiral: The Life of Admiral William J.H. Godfrey*. London: Hamish Hamilton, 1980.
—— *Room 40: British Naval Intelligence, 1914–1918*. London: Hamish Hamilton, 1982. Paperback ed., London: Oxford University Press, 1984.
Bell, Christopher. 'Singapore Strategy and the Deterrence of Japan'. *English Historical Review*, 116, 467 (2001): 604–34.
Bennett, Geoffrey M. *The Battle of Jutland*. London: B.T. Batsford, 1964.
—— *Naval Battles of the First World War* [1968]. Rev. ed., London: Pan Books, 1983.
Boothby, Robert J.G. *Recollections of a Rebel*. London: Hutchinson, 1978.
Brayer, Elizabeth. *George Eastman, a Biography*. Baltimore and London: Johns Hopkins University Press, 1996.
Brodhurst, Robin. *Churchill's Anchor: The Biography of Admiral of the Fleet Sir Dudley Pound*. Barnsley: Leo Cooper, 2000.
Brooks, John. *Dreadnought Gunnery and the Battle of Jutland: The Question of Fire Control*. London and New York: Routledge, 2005.
Brown, David. 'Mountbatten as First Sea Lord'. *RUSI Journal*, 131 (June 1986): 63–8.
Bryant, Arthur, ed. *The Turn of the Tide, 1939–43* [*The Alanbrooke Diaries*].

London: Collins, 1957.

Butler, James R.M. 'The British Official Military History of the Second World War'. *Military Affairs*, 22 (3) (1958): 149-51.

Campbell, John. *Naval Weapons of World War Two*. Annapolis, Md.: Naval Institute Press, 1985.

Chalmers, William S. *The Life and Letters of David, Earl Beatty, Admiral of the Fleet*. London: Hodder and Stoughton, 1951.

—— *Max Horton and the Western Approaches*. London: Hodder and Stoughton, 1954.

Churchill, Winston S. *The Gathering Storm*. Boston: Houghton Mifflin, 1948.

Cobb, Richard. *People and Places*. Oxford and New York: Oxford University Press, 1985.

Connell, John. 'Official History and the Unofficial Historian'. *RUSI Journal*, 110-640 (1965): 329-34.

Cook, Tim. *Clio's Warriors: Canadian Historians and the Writing of the World Wars*. Vancouver: University of British Columbia Press, 2006.

Corbett, Julian S., and Henry Newbolt. *History of the Great War Based on Official Documents: Naval Operations*. 5 vols. London: Longmans, 1920-31.

Danchev, Alex, and Daniel Todman, eds. *War Diaries 1939-1945: Field Marshal Lord Alanbrooke*. London: Weidenfeld and Nicolson, 2001.

Davis, John H. *The Guggenheims: An American Epic*. New York: William Morrow, 1978.

Davison, Robert L. '"The Half-Armed Athene": The Royal Navy 1914'. Unpublished paper, Memorial University of Newfoundland, 2000.

Daws, Gavan. *Shoal of Time: A History of the Hawaiian Islands*. Honolulu: University of Hawaii Press, 1979.

Dennerly, Peter. 'The Royal New Zealand Navy'. In John Crawford, ed., *Kia Kaha: New Zealand in the Second World War* (Auckland: Oxford University Press, 2000).

Derry, Thomas K. *The Campaign in Norway*. London: HMSO, 1953.

Dickinson, Harry. 'Ship to Shore: Young Officer Training in the Royal Navy, 1870-1902'. Unpublished paper, 2001.

D'Ombrain, Nicholas J. *War Machinery and High Policy: Defence Administration in Peacetime Britain, 1902-1914*. London: Oxford University Press, 1973.

Earle, Edward Mead, ed. *The Makers of Modern Strategy: Military Thought from Machiavelli to Hitler*. Princeton, NJ: Princeton University Press, 1943.

Ehrman, John. 'Stephen Wentworth Roskill, 1903-1982'. *Proceedings of the British Academy*, 69 (1983): 579-94.

Ellison, Gerald. *The Perils of Amateur Strategy as Exemplified by the Attack on the*

Dardanelles Fortress in 1915. London: Longmans Green, 1926.

Erskine, David. 'The Historical Collections of the R.USI.' *Royal United Service Institute Journal*, 114, 653 (1969): 64–5.

Fergusson, Bernard E. *The Watery Maze: The Story of Combined Operations*. London: Collins, 1961.

Foot, M.R.D. 'Officials and Secrets'. *The Author*, 81 (4) (1971): 155–7.

Frankland, Noble. *History at War: The Campaigns of an Historian*. London: Giles de la Mare, 1998.

Gardiner, Leslie. *The British Admiralty*. London: Blackwood, 1968.

Gardner, W.J.R. *Decoding History: The Battle of the Atlantic and Ultra*. London: Macmillan, 1999.

Gilbert, Martin. *'Never Despair': Winston S. Churchill 1945–1965*. London: Heinemann, 1988.

—— *The Churchill War Papers, Volume 3: The Ever Widening War*. New York and London: W.E. Norton, 2000.

—— *Continue to Pester, Nag and Bite: Churchill's War Leadership*. Toronto: Vintage Canada, Random House, 2004.

Goldrick, James. *The King's Ships Were at Sea: The War in the North Sea, August 1914–February 1915*. Annapolis, Md.: Naval Institute Press, 1984.

—— 'The Irresistible Force and the Immovable Object: *The Naval Review*, the Young Turks, and the Royal Navy, 1911–1931'. In Goldrick and John B. Hattendorf, eds., *Mahan Is Not Enough: The Proceedings of a Conference on the Works of Sir Julian Corbett and Admiral Sir Herbert Richmond* (Newport, RI: Naval War College Press, 1993), 83–102.

—— 'Admiral Sir Rosslyn Wemyss (1917–1919)'. In Malcolm Murfett, ed., *The First Sea Lords: From Fisher to Mountbatten* (Westport, Conn.: Praeger, 1995), 113–25.

Gooch, G.P., and Harold Temperley, eds. *British Documents on the Origins of the War, 1898–1914*. 11 vols. London: HMSO, 1926–38.

Gordon, Andrew. *The Rules of the Game: Jutland and British Naval Command*. London: John Murray, 1996.

Gough, Barry. 'Rulers of the Waves: British Naval Memoirs'. In George Egerton, ed., *Political Memoir: Essays on the Politics of Memory* (London: Frank Cass, 1994), 131–50.

Gretton, Peter. *Convoy Escort Commander*. London: Cassell, 1964.

—— *Winston Churchill and the Royal Navy*. London: Cassell, 1968.

Grove, Eric J. *Vanguard to Trident: British Naval Policy since World War Two*. Annapolis, Md.: Naval Institute Press, 1987.

—— ed., *Great Sea Battles of the Royal Navy as Commemorated in the Gunroom, Britannia Royal Naval College, Dartmouth*. Annapolis, Md.: Naval Institute

Press, 1994.

Guinn, Paul S. *British Strategy and Politics, 1914 to 1918*. Oxford: Clarendon Press, 1965.

Hall, J.W., et al. *Cambridge History of Modern Japan*. 6 vols. Cambridge: Cambridge University Press, 1988.

Halpern, Paul, ed. *The Keyes Papers: Selections from the Private and Official Correspondence*. 3 vols. London: Navy Records Society, 1972–81.

—— 'Naval Topics, 1915–40'. *Reviews in European History*, 2 (3) (1976): 407–19.

—— *A Naval History of World War I*. Annapolis, Md.: Naval Institute Press, 1994.

Hankey, Maurice P.A. *The Supreme Command, 1914–1918*. 2 vols. London: Allen and Unwin, 1961.

Harper, J.E.T. *The Truth about Jutland*. London: John Murray, 1927.

Hattendorf, John B. 'Sir Julian Corbett on the Significance of Naval History'. *American Neptune*, 31 (October 1971): 275–85.

Heuston, R.F.V. *Lives of the Lord Chancellors, 1885–1940*. Oxford: Clarendon Press, 1964.

Hewitt, H.K. 'Allied Navies at Salerno'. *US Naval Institute Proceedings*, September 1953.

Hezlet, Arthur R. *The Submarine and Sea Power*. London: P. Davies, 1967.

Higgins, Trumbull. *Winston Churchill and the Second Front, 1940–1943*. New York: Oxford University Press, 1957.

—— *Soft Underbelly: The Anglo-American Controversy over the Italian Campaign 1939–1945*. New York: Macmillan, 1968.

Higham, Robin, ed. *The Writing of Official Military History*. Westport, Conn.: Greenwood, 1999.

Hoban, Mac. 'Admiral Sir Herbert Richmond'. *Naval Review*, 85 (1) (1997): 53.

Horsfield, John. *The Art of Leadership in War: The Royal Navy from the Age of Nelson to the End of World War II*. Westport, Conn.: Greenwood, 1980.

—— 'Arthur Marder'. *Oxford Dictionary of National Biography*. Oxford University Press, 2004.

Hough, Richard. *The Great War at Sea, 1914–1918*. New York: Oxford University Press, 1983.

Hughes, Edward A. *The Royal Naval College, Dartmouth*. London: Winchester, 1950.

Hughes, Wayne P., Jr. *Fleet Tactics and Coastal Combat*. 2nd ed. Annapolis, Md.: Naval Institute Press, 2000.

Hunt, Barry D. 'Sir Herbert Richmond and the Naval Review'. In Clark

Reynolds and William McAndrew, eds., *Proceedings University of Maine 1971 Seminar in Maritime and Regional Studies* (Orono: University of Maine, 1972), 61–75.
—— *Sailor-Scholar: Admiral Sir Herbert Richmond, 1871–1946.* Waterloo, Ont.: Wilfrid Laurier University Press, 1982.
—— 'Richmond and the Education of the Royal Navy'. In James Goldrick and John B. Hattendorf, eds., *Mahan Is Not Enough: The Proceedings of a Conference on the Works of Sir Julian Corbett and Admiral Sir Herbert Richmond* (Newport, RI: Naval War College Press, 1993), 65–81.
Hyatt, A.M.J., ed. *Dreadnought to Polaris: Maritime Strategy since Mahan.* Toronto: Copp Clark, 1973.
Irving, David J.C. *The Destruction of Convoy PQ.17.* London: Cassell 1968.
Irving, John J. *The Smoke Screen of Jutland.* London: Kimber, 1966.
James, William Milbourne. *The Portsmouth Letters.* London: Macmillan, 1946.
—— *The Sky Was Always Blue.* London: Methuen, 1951.
Jenkins, Roy. *Sir Charles Dilke: A Victorian Tragedy.* London: Collins, 1958.
—— *Victorian Scandal: A Biography of the Right Honourable Gentleman Sir Charles Dilke.* New York: Chilmark, 1965.
Jordan, Gerald, ed. *Naval Warfare in the Twentieth Century, 1900–1945: Essays in Honour of Arthur Marder.* London: Croom Helm, New York: Crane Russak, 1977.
Keegan, John. 'Why Are Britain's Great Naval Historians Americans?'. *Naval History,* April 1987, 7–11.
Keen, Maurice. 'Richard Cobb'. *Balliol College Record,* 1996, 17–19.
Kemp, Peter. *Victory at Sea, 1939–1945.* London: Frederick Muller, 1947.
—— 'Marder on Jutland'. *Navy,* June 1966, 191, 207.
Kennedy, Paul. *The Rise and Fall of British Naval Mastery.* New York: Scribner, 1976 (and subsequent eds.).
—— *The Rise of Anglo-German Antagonism, 1860–1914.* London and Boston: George Allen and Unwin, 1980.
—— *The Rise and Fall of the Great Powers: Economic Change and Military Conflict from 1500 to 2000.* New York: Random House, 1987.
King-Hall, Stephen. *My Naval Life 1906–1929.* London: Faber and Faber, 1962.
Knight, R.J.B. 'The Beatty Papers at the National Maritime Museum Greenwich'. *Mariner's Mirror,* 67 (4) (1981): 387–8.
Lambert, Andrew, ed. *Letters and Papers of Professor Sir John Knox Laughton, 1830–1915.* Aldershot, UK: Ashgate for the Navy Records Society, 2002.
Lambert, Nicholas A. *Sir John Fisher's Naval Revolution.* Columbia: University of South Carolina Press, 1999.
—— 'Strategic Command and Control for Maneuver Warfare: Creation of

the Royal Navy's War Room System, 1905—1915'. *Journal of Military History*, 69 (2) (2005): 361—410.

Langdon, Jeremy. 'Too Old or Too Bold? The Removal of Sir Roger Keys as Churchill's First Director of Combined Operations'. *Imperial War Museum Review*, 8 (1993).

Langer, William L. *The Diplomacy of Imperialism, 1890—1902.* 2nd ed., New York: Alfred A. Knopf, 1960.

——— *In and Out of the Ivory Tower.* New York: Watson Academic Publications, 1977.

Lewin, Terence. 'The Royal Navy — Its Contribution to National and Western Defence'. *RUSI Journal*, September 1976.

Liddell Hart, Basil. 'The Military Strategist'. In A.J.P. Taylor et al., *Churchill Revised: A Critical Assessment* (New York: Dial Press, 1969).

McCulloch, Samuel Clyde. *Instant University: The History of the University of California, Irvine.* Irvine: University of California, 1996.

McGeoch, Ian. *The Princely Sailor: Mountbatten of Burma.* London and Washington: Brassey's, 1996.

MacGregor, Geddes. *Apostles Extraordinary: A Celebration of Saints and Sinners.* San Francisco: Strawberry Hill Press, 1986.

Mackay, Ruddock F. *Fisher of Kilverstone.* Oxford: Clarendon Press, 1973.

McLachlan, Donald. *Room 39: Naval Intelligence in Action, 1939—45.* London: Weidenfeld and Nicolson, 1968.

Madsen, Chris. 'Limits of Generosity and Trust: The Naval Side of the Combined Munitions Assignment Board'. *War & Society*, 21 (2) (2003): 77—108.

Mehta, Ved. *Fly and the Fly-Bottle: Encounters with British Intellectuals* [1961]. Boston: Little Brown, 1962.

——— *Up at Oxford.* New York: Norton, 1993.

Meyer, Henry Cord. 'Arthur J. Marder, 1910—1980'. *Military Affairs*, 45 (2) (1981): 87.

Miller, Jerry. 'Curiosity at the Crossroads'. *Naval History*, 20 (4) (2006): 16—23 [which includes the segment by James P. Delgado, 'Diving at the Crossroads'].

Milner, Marc. *U-Boat Hunters: The Royal Canadian Navy and the Offensive against Germany's Submarines.* Toronto: University of Toronto Press, 1994.

Moran, Lord. *Churchill: Taken from the Diaries of Lord Moran.* Boston: Houghlin Mifflin, 1966.

Morison, Samuel Eliot. *History of United States Naval Operations in World War II. Volume 1: The Battle of the Atlantic, September 1939—May 1943* [1947]. Champaign: University of Illinois Press, 2001.

—— *History of United States Naval Operations in World War II. Volume 6: Breaking the Bismarck Barrier, 22 July 1942–1 May 1944* [1950]. Champaign: University of Illinois Press, 2001.
—— *Strategy and Compromise.* Boston: Little, Brown, 1958.
Morris, Douglas. *Cruisers of the Royal and Commonwealth Navies since 1879.* Liskeard, UK: Maritime Books, 1987.
Morris, Jan. *Fisher's Face.* London: Viking, 1995.
Murray, Jerry. 'Curiosity at the Crossroads [Operation Crossroads]'. *Naval History*, 20 (4) (2006): 16–23.
Nailor, Peter. 'Great Chiefs of Staff – Admiral of the Fleet Sir Dudley Pound'. *RUSI Journal*, 133 (1) (1988): 67–70.
Palmer, William. *Engagement with the Past: The Lives and Works of the World War II Generation of Historians.* Lexington: University Press of Kentucky, 2001.
Pawle, Gerald. *Secret Weapons of World War (formerly The Secret War).* New York: Ballantyne, 1957.
Ranft, Bryan M. 'Naval Historians at War'. *Journal Royal United Services Institution for Defence Studies*, 120 (March 1975): 79–80.
——, ed. *The Beatty Papers: Selections from the Private and Official Correspondence of Admiral of the Fleet Earl Beatty.* 2 vols. London: Navy Records Society, 1989, 1993.
Rasor, Eugene L. *The Battle of Jutland, a Bibliography.* New York: Greenwood, 1992.
Reischauer, Edwin O. *My Life between Japan and America.* New York: Harper and Row, 1978.
Reynolds, David. *In Command of History: Churchill Fighting and Writing the Second World War.* London: Allen Lane, 2004.
Reynolds, Leonard C. *Dog Boats at War.* Stroud, UK: A. Sutton, 1998.
Roberts, Andrew. *Eminent Churchillians.* London: Weidenfeld and Nicolson, 1994.
Roberts, John. *British Warships of the Second World War.* Annapolis, Md.: Naval Institute Press, 2000.
Rodger, N.A.M. *The Admiralty.* Lavenham: Terence Dalton, 1979.
—— 'Training or Education: A Naval Dilemma over Three Centuries'. In Peter Hore, ed., *Hudson Papers Volume 1* (London: Royal Navy Defence Studies, 2001), 1–34.
Ross, George. 'How the Oerlikon Gun Came to Britain'. *Naval Review*, 69 (1) (1954): 19–22.
Rowse, A.L. *Historians I Have Known.* London: Duckworth, 1995.
Sainsbury, Anthony B. 'Stephen Wentworth Roskill, CBE, DSC, LITT.D, FBA, Captain, Royal Navy, 1903–1982'. *Naval Review*, 71 (1) (1983): 3–4, to

which is appended, 'An obituary from Australia', by James Goldrick, 5–6.

Schorske, Carl and Elizabeth, eds. *Explorations in Crisis: Papers on International History by William Langer*. Cambridge, Mass.: Belknap Press of Harvard University Press, 1969.

Schurman, Donald M. *The Education of a Navy: The Development of British Naval Strategic Thought, 1867–1914*. London: Cassell, 1965.

—— *Sir Julian Corbett, 1854–1922: Historian of British Maritime Policy from Drake to Jellicoe*. London: Royal Historical Society, 1981.

Simpson, Michael, and Robin Brodhurst, 'The Relief of Admiral North from Gibraltar in 1940'. In Susan Rose, ed., *Naval Miscellany, Vol. VII*. Aldershot, UK: Ashgate for Navy Records Society, 2008.

Sisman, Alan. *A.J.P. Taylor: A Biography*. London: Mandarin, 1994.

Slessor, Tim. *Ministries of Deception*. London: Aurum, 2002. Reissued as *Lying in State* (London: Aurum, 2004).

Smith, Bradley F. *The Shadow Warriors: OSS and the Origins of the CIA*. New York: Basic Books, 1983.

Soybel, Phyllis L. *A Necessary Relationship: The Development of Anglo-American Cooperation in Naval Intelligence*. Westport, Conn.: Praeger, 2005.

Sumida, Jon Tetsuro. *In Defence of Naval Supremacy: Finance, Technology and British Naval Policy, 1889–1914*. Boston: Unwin Hyman, 1989.

—— 'A Matter of Timing: The Royal Navy and the Tactics of Decisive Battle, 1912–1916'. *Journal of Military History*, 67 (January 2003): 85–136.

'Gunnery, Procurement, and Strategy in the *Dreadnought* Era'. *Journal of Military History*, 69 (October 2005): 1179–87.

—— ed. *The Pollen Papers: The Privately Circulated Printed Works of Arthur Hungerford Pollen, 1901–1916*. London: George Allen and Unwin for Navy Records Society, 1984.

Syrett, David. 'The Secret War and the Historians'. *Armed Forces and Society*, 9 (winter 1983): 293–328.

—— ed. *The Battle of the Atlantic and Signals Intelligence: U-Boat Tracking Papers, 1941–1947*. Aldershot, UK: Navy Records Society, 2002.

Taylor, A.J.P. *Beaverbrook*. London: Hamish Hamilton, 1972.

—— *The War Lords*. New York: Athenaeum, 1978.

—— *A Personal History*. New York: Athenaeum, 1983.

—— et al. *Churchill Revised: A Critical Assessment*. New York: Dial Press, 1969.

Taylor, Eva Haraszti, ed. *Letters to Eva, 1969–1983* [by A.J.P. Taylor]. London: Century, 1991.

Temperley, Harold. *England and the Near East: The Crimea* [1936]. London: Frank Cass, 1964.

Temple Pattterson, A. *Jellicoe: A Biography*. London: Macmillan, 1969.
—— ed. *The Jellicoe Papers*. 2 vols. London: Navy Records Society, 1966, 1968.
Terrell, Edward. *Admiralty Brief: The Story of Inventions That Contributed to Victory in the Battle of the Atlantic*. George G. Harrap, 1958.
Villa, Brian Loring. *Unauthorized Action: Mountbatten and the Dieppe Raid*. Rev. ed., Toronto: Oxford University Press, 1994.
Warren, Alan. *Singapore: Britain's Greatest Defeat*. London: Hambledon and London, 2002.
Waters, David W. 'A Study of the Philosophy and Conduct of Maritime War, 1815–1945'. Typescript 1954, rev. 1957.
Waters, Sydney. HMNZ *Leander*. Wellington, New Zealand: War History Branch, 1950.
Watt, Donald C. 'Restrictions on Research: The Fifty-Year Rule and British Policy'. *International Affairs*, 41 (January 1965): 89–95.
Wemyss, Lady W. Rosslyn. *Life and Letters of Lord Wester Wemyss*. London: Eyre and Spottiswoode, 1935.
Wheeler-Bennett, John, ed. *Action This Day: Working with Churchill: Memoirs by Lord Normanbrook, John Colville, Sir John Martin, Sir Ian Jacob, Lord Bridges and Sir Leslie Rowan*. London: Macmillan, 1968.
Wildenberg, Thomas. *All the Factors of Victory: Admiral Joseph Mason Reeves and the Origins of Carrier Airpower*. Dulles, Va.: Brassey's, 2003.
Williams, John. *The Guns of Dakar: Operation Menace, September 1940*. London: Heinemann, 1976.
Williams, Rhodri. *Defending the Empire: The Conservative Party and British Defence Policy, 1899–1915*. New Haven, Conn.: Yale University Press, 1991.
Wilson, Tom. *Churchill and the Prof*. London: Cassell, 1995.
Winks, Robin W. *Cloak & Gown: Scholars in the Secret War, 1939–1961*. New York: William Morrow, 1987.
Winton, John. *The Victoria Cross at Sea*. London: Michael Joseph, 1978.
—— *Cunningham: The Greatest Admiral since Nelson*. London: John Murray, 1998.
—— *Carrier Glorious: The Life and Death of an Aircraft Carrier*. London: Cassell Military, 1999.
Woodward, E. Llewellyn. *Great Britain and the German Navy*. London: Oxford University Press, 1935.
—— *British Foreign Policy in the Second World War*. London: HMSO, 1962.
Yates, Keith. *Flawed Victory: Jutland, 1916*. Annapolis, Md.: Naval Institute Press, 2000.

Ziegler, Philip. *Mountbatten: The Official Biography*. London: Collins, 1985.
—— ed. *The Diaries of Lord Louis Mountbatten 1920–1922: Tours with the Prince of Wales*. London: Collins, 1987.

Index

Acasta, HMS 224–5
Acheson, A.H. 144, 149, 152
Achilles, HMNZS 54
Adams, Dr Hazard 280
Addison, Paul 241
Admiralty
  censorship and secrecy 10–11, 116–17, 130, 139–44, 155, 226
  assistance to Marder 9–12, 68, 74–5, 104–5, 105, 112–14, 126, 132–3, 172, 190–1, 259
    lack of assistance 68–9, 87–8, 113, 116–19
    Marder's criticisms of *see under* Marder
  assistance to Roskill 166, 169, 199
    appointment of Roskill 134, 140–3
    invites Roskill to write *The Art of Leadership* 300
    lack of assistance 143–5, 147, 154–5, 158–60, 163–4, 169–70
    Roskill's criticisms of *see under* Roskill
  and Dakar signals delay 242, 244–5
  at Jutland
    failure to pass on German deciphers 120–4, 159, 254, 258–9, 275
    tampers with Jutland announcements 255–7, 259
  and PQ.17 136–7, 139–40, 158–61
  'Winston is Back' signal 236–7
Ainsworth, R/A Walden L 55–6, 59
Akita, George 35
Alanbrooke, Lord 218, 228, 248
  War Diaries 221, 251
Albion, Robert 112
Aldrich, Professor Daniel G. Jr 176
Alexandra, HMS 24–5
Allan, Captain Gordon 225
Allardyce, Sir William 47
Allen, Captain Gordon 149–50, 152
Altman, Jan North 39

Altmark (Ger) 230
Ambrose, Stephen 181
American Historical Association 25, 283
American Historical Review 25, 35, 187, 216
American Philosophical Society 112, 191, 198, 203
Anglo-Japanese alliance ship ratio 46
Annapolis Naval Academy 157
Annenberg, Walter 301
Anzio landings 156
Ardent, HMS 224–5
Arkansas, USS 64
Ark Royal, HMS 225–6, 244
Arnold-Foster, Mark 77–8, 93
Asada, Professor Sadao 286
Asquith, H.H. 41, 70, 98, 114–15
Atherton, Noel 233
Attlee, Earl, papers of 301
Aubrey, Cdr Robert 142
Auden, W.H. 191
Australia 286, 291, 293

Bacon, Admiral Sir Reginald 11, 98
  Jutland Scandal 258
  The Life of Lord Fisher of Kilverstone 86–7, 91
Balfour, A.J. 119, 255
Balfour, Stephen 48–9
Ballard, Robert 64
Barley, Cdr Fred 166
Barnard, V/A Sir Geoffrey, RN 50, 104, 156
Barnes, John 261, 264, 267–8, 270
  a vol of Beatty papers 267
Barnett, Corelli 44, 53, 61, 301–2, 314
  Engage the Enemy More Closely 226
  The Swordbearers 128
Barraclough, Geoffrey 178
Battenburg, Admiral of the Fleet Prince Louis of 284
Baugh, Daniel 85, 262

355

Baxter, Dr James Phinney III 27
Beach, Cdr Ned 157
Beatty, Admiral of the Fleet Earl 11, 76, 78, 98, 111, 120, 123–5, 127, 141, 167, 201–2, 252–3, 253, 257, 267–8
  Beatty papers 262, 264, 268–76, 311
  at Jutland 126, 128, 130, 252–3, 255–8, 275
    falsifying Jutland signals record 256–7, 259, 262–6, 268
  private life 253–5, 269–71, 275–6
Beatty, Charles 268–70
Beatty, David (2nd Earl, Viscount Borodale) 127, 255, 260, 262, 264–70, 272–5
Beaverbrook, Lord 163
Bellairs, Carlyon
  The Battle of Jutland: Sowing and Reaping 258
Bellairs, R/A R.M. 142
Beloff, Max 188
Bennett, Captain Geoffrey 123, 260, 262, 268
Beresford, Admiral Lord Charles 92–3, 98, 114
Berkeley University 12
Berlin, Sir Isaiah 184
Bevan, Captain Robert 54–5
Bikini Atoll 62–5, 67, 262
Birmingham Mail 20
Bismarck (Ger) 53, 120, 147
Blackman, Admiral C.M. 128–9
Blake, Admiral Sir Geoffrey 141–2, 144, 154, 202
Blandy, Admiral William 63, 65
Blue Ridge (US auxiliary) 63
Boissier, A.P. 44
Bond, Professor Brian 242–3
Boothby, Robert 237–8
Brain, Richard 132
Breslau (Ger) 116–17
Brett-Smith, John 102–3, 106
Bridge, Admiral Sir Cyprian 261
Brinton, Crane 112
British Naval Policy, 1880-1903 see *Anatomy of British Sea Power*
Brock, R/A P.W. 126, 257, 262, 267
Brockman, V/A Sir Ronald 218–19
Brodhurst, Robin
  Churchill's Anchor 218–19, 251
Bromley, Professor John 262
Brook, Sir Norman 148–9, 152–5, 160–1, 163, 169, 220–2, 227, 233

Broome, Cdr John E. 139
Brown, David 226
Brown, John (publisher, OUP) 105–6, 285
Browne, Sir Anthony Montague 161, 301
Bryant, Arthur 136, 307
  Triumph in the West 221
  The Turn of the Tide 221
Bulldog, HMS 168
Butler, Sir James 134, 137, 141, 143–4, 146–7, 151–2, 154, 159–60, 163, 182, 203, 220, 297–8, 319
Butterfield, Herbert 170

Campania, HMS 125
Campbell, John 275
Capper, D.P. 20–1
Carlyle, Thomas
  The French Revolution 108
Carrington, Lord 262, 270, 274, 311, 314–15
Carson, Edward 203
Cary, Sir Michael 262
Chadwick, Rev Owen 314
Chalmers, R/A W.S. 253, 318
  The Life and Letters of David Earl Beatty 76, 254–5, 271
Chatfield, Admiral of the Fleet Lord 126–7, 259, 266
  papers 286
Chatfield, Ernle, 2nd Baron (son) 127, 167, 256
Christian Science Monitor 19–20
Churchill, Sir Winston 13, 54, 69, 72, 95, 113, 119, 135, 146, 153, 160–1, 182, 186, 188, 220, 228, 231, 236–7, 240–1, 255, 270, 298, 300–1, 320
  character 115, 235, 237–8, 240–1, 249, 321
  criticisms of Roskill's *War at Sea* 148–56, 171, 219, 221, 234
  and Dakar 242–5
  and Dardanelles campaign 76–7, 84, 118–19
  and Dieppe raid 163
  and Fisher 87, 95–8, 108, 120, 192, 228, 235
  interference with Admirals 147, 152, 224, 236–41
  and Pound 160–1, 214, 217, 219–20, 224, 238, 240, 248–51, 292–3, 304, 320
  and Narvik 152, 249

INDEX

papers 95, 270, 301–3
works
   The Gathering Storm 225
   Great Contemporaries 87
   The Second World War 147, 149, 159–61, 195, 257–8
Clarke, Edward 254
Cobb, Richard 189, 280–1
Collins (publishers) 168, 195, 201, 210, 248, 252, 269, 272–3, 300, 303, 319
Colomb, V/A Sir Philip 85
Colville, Sir John ('Jock') 227, 311
Connolly, Admiral R.I. 66
Connors, James 35
convoys 87, 121, 129, 155, 188, 192, 204
  see also PQ.17
Cooper, Duff 24
Coox, Alvin 284, 286, 293–4
Corbett, Sir Julian 72–3, 85, 98, 116, 126, 143–4, 146, 155, 182, 257, 261, 276, 310
  Naval Operations 147, 159, 257–8, 268, 290
  Some Principles of Maritime Strategy 146
Cork and Orrery, Admiral of the Fleet the Earl of 152, 231, 249
Coromandel, battle of 116
Coronel, battle of 71, 119
Cowing, Cedric 175
Cowley, Professor W.H. 32–3
Cradock, R/A Sir Christopher 71, 116
Craig, Gordon 28
Creasy, Admiral of the Fleet Sir George 237
Creswell, Captain John 141–2, 144, 188, 197, 201–2, 229, 318
  Sea Warfare 1939-1945: A Short History 197
Crook, Arthur 82
Crossley, Edward 77
Crutchley, Captain Victor 52
Cumberlege, Geoffrey 101–3, 105–6
Cunningham, Admiral of the Fleet Sir Andrew Browne 47, 60, 167–8, 224, 230–1, 235
Cunninghame-Graham, Admiral Sir Angus 128–9, 266

Daily Express 163
Daily Telegraph 160, 163, 182, 248
Dakar 54, 147, 242–6
Danchey, Alex 219
Daniel, Charles 229–30

Dardanelles campaign 76, 80, 84, 87, 96–7, 116, 118–19, 192, 228, 234, 243, 283, 301
Davis, Admiral Sir William 224
Daws, Gavin 35
Day, Professor A. Grove 35
Deakin, William 154
Dean, Sir Maurice 199
de Gaulle, General Charles 147, 242
de Robeck, Admiral of the Fleet Sir John 97, 301
Der Spiegel 163
Devonshire, HMS 225
Dewar, Captain A.C. 31, 69, 257, 318
Dewar, Captain K.G.B. 71, 257
De Wolf, V/A Harry 157
Diana, HMS 226
Dick, R/A Rover 140–1
Dickens, Admiral G.C. 155–6
Dickson, R.K. 140–1
Dieppe raid 149, 157–8, 162–3
d'Ombrain, Nicholas
  War Machinery and High Policy 212
Donald, Captain Graham 124–5
Donovan, Colonel William 'Wild Bill' 26–7
Dorling, Taprell 262
Dorn, Walter 27–8
D'Oyly-Hughes, Captain Guy 225–6
Drax, Sir Reginald 318
Dreadnought, HMS 17–18, 71
Dreyer, Admiral Sir Frederick 85, 318
  The Sea Heritage: a Study of Marime Warfare 85
Duff, Admiral Sir Alexander 205
Duke of York, HMS 139
Duke University 173, 175
Dunkirk evacuation 147
Durban, HMS 45–7

Eagle, HMS 47–9, 66, 226
Eaker, General Ira 127–8
Eales, Mrs E.V. (secretary to Roskill) 145, 199, 303
Earle, Edward Mead 25
Eberle, Admiral Sir James 311
Economist, The 79, 283
Edwards, Admiral Sir Ralph 153, 224, 234, 246
Edward VII, King 90, 95, 289
Ehrman, John 53–4, 61, 141, 154, 163, 202, 262, 309
Eisenhower, President Dwight D. 157

357

Eller, R/A Ernest M. 138
Ellmers, H.H. 74
Elton, Geoffrey 99, 214
Empress of Britain, RMS 223
Engadine, HMS 124–5
English Historical Review 186, 232, 234, 236, 238, 317
  see also Winston is Back under Marder
Enigma machine, capture of 253
Erskine, David 202, 260, 262, 265, 268
Esher, Lord 89–90, 95, 301
Ethiopia 11, 49, 216
Ethiopian crisis and Marder's book on it 320
Evan-Thomas, R/A Sir Hugh 257
Evening Standard 3, 122–3, 163
Everett, Cdr D.H. 51
Excellent, HMS 47, 49

Fairbank, John K. 28
Falkland Islands, battle of (1914) 119
Fay, Professor Sidney 101–2
Firth, Sir Charles 196–7
Fischer, Professor Fritz 185–6
Fisher, Admiral of the Fleet John Arbuthnot, 1st Baron Kilverstone 20, 23, 25, 30, 39, 45, 69–70, 72, 86–100, 113–15, 192, 217, 256, 283, 321
  and Dardanelles campaign 76–7, 86–7, 96–7
  introduction of dreadnoughts 78, 94, 113
  letters and papers 12, 19, 88–9, 91–2, 94–5, 253, 270, 301, 318
  relations with Churchill 67, 96–8, 113, 120, 228, 235
  and underwater weapons 89–90, 96–8, 271–2, 289
  resignation 96–7, 107, 119–20, 228
Fisher of Kilverstone, 2nd Lord 70, 90–1, 289
Forbes, Admiral Sir Charles 223–4
Force Z see *Prince of Wales, Repulse*
Forester, C.S. 255
Franconia, SS 65
Fraser of North Cape, Admiral of the Fleet Lord 167, 292–3, 218–19, 292–3

Galbraith, Professor John S. 172–3, 175–6, 178, 180, 295
Gallagher, Jack 190
Gardner, W.J.R. 220
Garrod, Air Chief Marshal Sir Guy 146

Garvin, H. 95
Geyl, Pieter 317
Ghormley, Admiral Robert 59
Gibbs, Professor Norman 184
Gibraltar 147, 244–6
  see also North, Admiral Sir Dudley
Gilbert, Felix 28
Gilbert, Sir Martin 97, 227, 250
  Winston S. Churchill 188, 207, 228, 241
Glasgow Herald 21, 93–4
Glorious, HMS 224–6, 319
Gneisenau (Ger) 224–5
Godfrey, R/A John H. 124, 219
Goeben (Ger) 10, 116–18
Goldrick, James 85–6, 262, 299, 302
  The King's Ships Were At Sea 275
Gooch, Dr G.P. 9
  and Temperley, *Origins of the War* 22
Graf Spee (Ger) 54
Graham, Professor Gerald 112, 262
Gretton, V/A Sir Peter 70, 95, 106, 111, 156, 167, 179, 182, 197, 210–11, 213–14, 215, 245, 249–50, 259–60, 318
  Former Naval Person: Churchill and the Royal Navy 227
Gringell, Basil 264, 266
Guardian, The 266
Guggenheim Foundation 69, 112, 183

Haffernan, Admiral John, USN 156
Halpern, Professor Paul 241, 262
Halsey, Admiral William ('Bull'), USN 55–6, 286
Hamilton, Lady Emma 3, 91, 122, 181, 254
Hamilton, Professor Thomas 175–6
Hamilton, R/A L.H.K. 'Turtle' 138–40, 158–9
Hamilton College, Clinton 32–3, 172
Hanke, Lewis 178
Hankey, Maurice (1st Baron) 88, 307
  criticism of Admiralty 204–5
  diaries and papers 204–16, 239, 247, 251–2, 290, 301, 306, 317
    see also under Roskill; quarrels with Marder
  The Supreme Command 205
Hankey, Robin (2nd Baron) 109, 204–6, 209–12, 306
Hare, Cdr Geoffrey 145, 199
Harper, V/A J.E.T. 256, 263
  Harper papers 123, 126–7, 252–69, 274–6

INDEX

published by NRS in *Jellicoe II* 123, 204, 210, 261–3, 266
   Roskill and Marder's battle over 253 and on
The Official Record of the Battle of Jutland 256–7, 263
The Truth about Jutland 258
Harris, Sir Arthur 'Bomber' 127
Harvey, Major F.J.W., RM 125
Heath, Cdr J.B. 225–6
Hefferman, R/A John B. 80, 138, 140
Helena, USS 55
Henderson, William 71
Hercules, HMS 256
Hexter, Jack (historian) 214
Hezlet, V/A Sir Arthur 62, 64–5, 262
Hideyoshi 35–6
Higgins, Trumbull 227
Higham, Professor Robin 127
Hill, A.V. 64
   papers 301
Hill, Christopher 186
Hindereker, Ivan 175
Hinsley, F.H. 131
Hipper, Admiral Franz von 120, 124
Hitler, Adolf 13, 219, 242, 316
Hobson, Anthony R.A. 271–2
Hong Kong 48–9
Honolulu, USS 56
Hood, HMS 53, 120
Hornet, HMS 231
Horsfield, John 296
Horton, Admiral Sir Max 51
Hoskin, Dr Michael 301
Hough, Richard 132, 186–7, 266
Howard, Professor Sir Michael 132, 134, 180, 188, 281, 305, 308–9, 311
Hunt, Barry 84–5
Hunt, Geoffrey (editor, OUP) 131, 266, 283
Hunter, Professor Charles 34, 36
Hurd, Archibald 130
Hussey, Admiral G.F. 61

Indefatigable, HMS 120, 124
Indomitable, HMS 150
Inflexible, HMS 89
Inquirer (Philadelphia) 20
Invincible, HMS 120
Iron Duke, HMS 122, 256
Irvine Smith, Joan 176
Irving, David 163

Jackson, Admiral Sir Henry 71
   replaces Fisher 119
Jackson, Captain Thomas 258
Jackson, Cdr R.T., RNZN 57
Jacob, Lt-General Sir Ian 146, 218–19, 227, 240
Jacobsen, Mark 296
James, Admiral Sir William 78–9, 128–32, 264, 268, 318
Jarrett, Sir Clifford 221–2
Jellicoe, Admiral Sir John, 1st Earl 11, 69, 94, 97–8, 114, 117, 119–23, 127, 141, 167, 180, 188, 197, 201, 205, 253–4, 257–8, 268
   at Jutland 120–1, 125–6, 128, 255–6, 258
   papers 260–70
Jenkins, USS 56–7
Jintsu (Japan) 56–7
Jonathan Cape (publishers) 86, 101–2, 105, 195–6
Jordan, Gerald 283
   Naval Warfare in the Twentieth Century, 1900 - 1954 (the Marder *Festschrift*) 289–90
Journal of Modern History 15, 25
Jun, Professor Tsunoda 287
Jutland, battle of 3, 11, 76, 113, 116, 120–5, 130, 143, 188, 192, 202, 212, 252–3, 255–8, 275–6, 283
   Narrative of Jutland 258
   Naval Staff Appreciation 254, 257–8
   see also Harper papers *and under* Admiralty

Keegan, Sir John 3
Kemp, Lt-Cdr Peter 24, 182, 197, 239–40, 259–60, 262, 265, 294–6, 295–6, 318
   Oxford Companion to Ships and the Sea 87
   Victory at Sea, 1939-1945 136–7, 169, 219
Kennedy, Paul 188, 302
   The Rise and Fall of British Naval Mastery 272
   Rise and Fall of Great Powers 20
Kent, Dr Sherman 28–9, 178
Kent, George 280
Kenworthy, Cdr Joseph (later Baron Strabolgi) 85
Kenya, HMS 262
Keppel, HMS 139
Kerr, Clark 173, 180, 279
Keyes, Admiral of the Fleet Sir Roger 120, 212, 230–2
   papers 207–8, 262, 301

359

King, Admiral Ernest, USN 60–1, 166, 235, 286, 293
King-Hall, Stephen 46, 198
  The China of Today 46
  My Naval Life 46, 77–8
  Western Civilisation and the Far East 46
Kiralfy, Alexander 36
Kitts, R/A Willard F 61
Knopf, Alfred A. 15–16, 25, 31, 106
Knox, Frank 58
Kobe Chronicle 46
Kolombangara, battle of 56–7
Korea 36, 262
Kuchia, Alan 302
Kula Gulf, battle of 55
Kuykendall, Ralph 35

Lang, Sir John 63, 66–7, 141, 147, 158–9, 199, 262
Langer, William Leonard 6–8, 11–16, 26–9, 37, 112, 125–6, 190, 293
  step incident 7–8, 191
Latham, General Harry 162
Laughton, Professor Sir John Knox 261, 307
Lawes, CPO George 55
Lawrence, T.E. 108
Lawson, Alan 178
Lawson, John 285
Leach, Admiral Sir Henry 311
Leander, HMNZS 40, 54–8, 308
Leslie, Sir Shane 255, 269, 271
Lewin, Admiral Sir Terence 241, 310–12
Lewin, Ronald 243–4, 295
Lewis, Professor Michael 18, 44, 114, 262
Liddell Hart, Sir Basil 155, 182, 212, 217, 227, 281, 292
Lindemann, Professor Frederick 53, 222
Lion, HMS 125, 253, 256
Listener, The 114, 190
Litchfield, Captain John 232–3, 243
Lloyd George, David 41, 85, 97, 111, 188
  and adoption of convoys 87, 129, 188, 204
  assessment of Richmond 71, 85
London, HMS 138
Long, Walter 257
Lopez, Robert 184
Lutzow (Ger) 121

MacArthur, General Douglas 286
Mackesy, Piers 262, 267

Macksey, Kenneth 182
Macmillan, Harold 244, 312
Madden, Admiral Sir Charles and Lady 257, 309
Magnus, Sir Philip 207
Mahan, Admiral Alfred Thayer 3, 72, 85, 98, 143, 186, 192, 295, 307, 321
  The Life of Nelson 182
Malkin, Sir Roger 156
Malta 52, 167–8
Manchester Guardian 47, 77–8, 93
Mansergh, Captain C. Aubrey L. 55, 57
Mansergh, V/A Sir Maurice 141
Marcuse, Herbert 28
Marder, (Jacob) Arthur 3–39, 68–133, 141, 167, 172–92, 279–96, 300, 312
  birth and family 4, 13–14, 38–9, 129, 184–5
    see also Marder, Jan below
  character 3–5, 9, 11–15, 28, 31–3, 37, 68, 88–9, 102–4, 122–3, 169, 178, 181–2, 189–90, 203, 295–6, 306, 317–18, 320–1
  education 4–7, 11–12, 198
  works with COI and applies for Naval career 26–32, 196
  academic career 25
    at Harvard 5–9, 12–14, 30, 38, 102, 191, 196
    interest in British naval history starts 7–9, 191
    assistant professorship at Eugene, Oregon 12
    offered post at North Dakota University 14–15
    at Hamilton College 32–3, 172
    at Hawaii University 33–9, 91, 94, 96, 103, 172–6, 185–6
    at University of California 3, 233, 290
    Irvine 109, 175–80, 182, 279, 290–5, 304
    Santa Barbara 293–4
    at Oxford (Balliol) 180, 183–90, 213, 280
    retirement 289–90
  criticisms of Admiralty 116–17, 122–3, 122–4, 130, 219, 244–5
  honours 190–1
    CBE 190, 213
    Chesney Memorial Gold Medal (RUSI) 182–3, 305, 307
    D Litt at Cambridge 213
    honorary Oxford degree 216, 241–2

INDEX

ill-health 31, 39, 293, 311
languages 17, 30–3, 36, 174, 284
relations with Roskill 171, 214–15
  good relations, influence and assistance 121, 171, 202–3, 248, 253–4, 266
  nominates Roskill for RUSI's Chesney Medal 304–7
  tries to recommend Roskill for a knighthood 310–11
  quarrels with Roskill *see under* Roskill
views on history 18–19, 23–4, 182–3, 187, 192, 195–7, 195–8, 198, 206, 281–2, 296, 317–18, 320
works
  articles, lectures and papers 69, 127–8, 181–2, 186, 217
    Admiral Sir John Fisher: A Reappraisal 69, 87
    The Battle of the Atlantic 26
    Bravery Is Not Enough 290
    The Censors and I 116–17
    Churchill as First Lord of the Admiralty 69
    From Jimmu Tennu to Perry: Sea Power in Early Japanese History 35–6
    Naval Balance of Power 26
    The Royal Navy and the Ethiopian Crisis of 1935-6 186, 216–17
    The Struggle for Power in the Mediterranean 25
  books 116
    Anatomy of British Sea Power 9–25, 39, 72–3, 80, 106, 115, 183
    autobiography (unpublished) 7–8
    From the Dardanelles to Oran: Studies of the Royal Navy in War and Peace 214, 239–40, 246, 249–50, 283, 303, 320
    The End of the Japanese Navy 283–92
    Fear God and Dread Nought: The Correspondence of Admiral of the Fleet Lord Fisher of Kilverstone 70, 76, 83, 86–102, 104, 172 183, 186–7, 289
      Vol 1: *The Making of an Admiral* 86, 89–94
      Vol 2: *The Years of Power, 1904-1910* 94–6
      Vol 3: *Restoration, Abdication and Last Years* 96
    From the Dreadnought to Scapa Flow 3, 8, 12–14, 68–9, 99, 101–33, 179–80, 183, 188, 191, 198, 201, 217, 229, 232–3, 240, 262–3, 290, 295, 317–18

    loss of research documents 107–14
    Vol 1: *The Road to War, 1904-1914* 108–9, 113–19, 199
    Vol 2: *The War Years: To the Eve of Jutland (1914-1916)* 108–9, 117, 119–20, 226–7, 274–5
    Vol 3: *Jutland and After (May 1916 - December 1916)* 109, 120–2, 132, 179, 182, 184, 190, 192, 198, 201, 253–4, 259, 266–7, 283
    Vol 4: *1917: Year of Crisis* 109, 113, 182, 184, 211–12, 246–7
    Vol 5: *Victory and Aftermath (January 1918 - June 1919)* 109, 115, 129–31, 186, 190, 205–6 and on (use of Hankey papers), 210–12, 216–17, 246–7, 267
    review by Roskill 198, 200, 203–4
    use of Hankey's diary 204
  The Influence of Sea Power upon History 289
  Old Friends, New Enemies: The Royal Navy and the Imperial Japanese Navy 29, 35, 68, 178, 320
    Vol 1: *Strategic Illusions 1936-1941* 23, 132, 186, 214, 228, 284–95
    Vol 2: *The Pacific War 1942-1943* 283, 295–6
  Operation Menace: The Dakar Expedition and the Dudley North Affair 142, 186, 243–6, 249, 283, 320
  Portrait of an Admiral: The Life and Papers of Sir Herbert Richmond 74–86, 92, 101–3, 172, 183, 318
  Winston is Back: Churchill at the Admiralty, 1939-40 217, 228, 237, 241, 317, 320
  reviews and reception 248
  dissertation 'English Navalism in the Nineties' 11
  radio broadcasts 103, 114, 116–17, 123–4, 190, 316
    on Fisher 98–9
  sermon '*Theodor Herzl: A Study in Practical Idealism*' 38
  thesis on Haldane Mission 8, 191
  TV interview by A.J.P. Taylor 9, 316
death of and memorial service 3, 132, 294–5
reputation 3, 25, 70–3. 26, 112–13, 128, 131, 171–2, 180–1, 183, 189–90, 192, 281, 292–6, 316, 320–1

Marder, Jan (wife) 39, 175, 184–5, 293, 295–6, 311
Mariner's Mirror 126, 262, 272
Marshall, General George 166
Matapan, Battle of Cape 168
Mattingly, Garrett 184
Mauritius, HMS 141
May, Admiral Sir William 81
McCarthy, Senator Joseph 103
McCulloch, Samuel 175, 178–9, 189, 293, 295
McGeoch, V/A Ian 251
McKay, Dr Donald Cope 12, 25, 30–1, 284
McKenna, Reginald 88, 95
  papers 301
  replaced by Churchill 114–15
McLachlan, Donald 219–20
  Room 39: Naval Intelligence 220
Menaul, AVM S.W.B. 307
Meyer, Henry Cord 27–30, 178, 293, 295–6
Miller, Arthur 183
Milner, Marc 165–6
Mochihizuki Kotaro 46
Moe, Henry Allen 183–4
Moore, Admiral Sir Henry 262
Moran, Lord 227
Morison, R/A Samuel Eliot, USNR 8, 55–7, 80, 138, 142, 157, 166, 186, 203, 286, 298–9
  History of the United States Naval Operation in World War II 137–40, 156–7
Morris, James (Jan) 95–6
  Fisher's Face 86, 91
Morrison, John 297–8
Mountbatten of Burma, Admiral of the Fleet Lord Louis 7, 45–6, 157, 162–3, 182, 219, 229–30, 283–4, 286, 290, 292, 310–11
  quarrels with Roskill 135
Murray, Sir Oswyn 11

Nagato (Japan) 64
Nagumo, Chuchi 290
Naish, George 262
Namier, Sir Lewis 196–7
Naokes, Michael 307
Naval Review 21–2, 55, 67, 71, 84, 115, 142, 155–6, 181, 202, 216, 253, 262, 265, 268, 300, 311–12
Navy News 237
Navy Records Society 40, 123, 202, 204, 252, 260–5, 310–11, 319
  Council 261–2
  and Jellicoe II 273
Nelson, Keith 178
Nelson, V/A Horatio Lord 3, 69, 87, 91, 94, 96, 124, 162, 167, 181, 254, 262, 268, 283, 289–90
Nevada, USS 64
Newbolt, Sir Henry 116, 126, 257
New Mexico, University of 33
New Republic 18
News Chronicle 76
New Statesman 96, 114, 283
New York Times 36
New Zealand 40, 54, 291
Nichols, Admiral C. 32
Nicholson, Admiral Sir Douglas 14
Nicolas, Sir Harry 94
Nimitz, Admiral Chester, USN 156
Nina, Duchess of Hamilton 87–8, 99–100
Noble Frankland, Anthony 127–8, 134, 177, 180
Norfolk, HMS 141
North, Admiral Sir Dudley 147, 149, 239, 244–6, 250, 290
Norwegian campaign and Narvik battle 137, 139, 149, 152, 155, 217, 219, 224–6, 228, 231–5, 239, 246, 249, 304, 317
Notestein, Wallace 184
Nutting, Sir John and Lady 270–1, 273

Olin, Spencer C., Jr 178
Oliver, Admiral Sir Geoffrey 142, 167
Ollard, Richard 269, 274, 303–4, 312
Onslow, Admiral Sir Richard 142, 167
Oran 214, 244
Oxford University Press (OUP) 101–2, 105–6, 109, 112, 122, 131–2, 190, 195–6, 233, 239, 246, 266, 283, 285, 296
Owen, Captain John, RN 136, 262
Owen, David 112–13
Oxford Companion to Ships and the Sea 182

Pantellaria scheme 231
Parkinson, C. Northcote 136
Parmiter, Charles 5, 39
Parry, R/A Edward 66
Patterson, Professor A Temple 262–3, 265, 268
  The Jellicoe Papers 260
Pearl Harbor 104
  Japanese attack on 26, 138, 290

INDEX

Pearsall, Alan 142, 262, 270
Peltason, Professor Jack 177, 179
Perkins, Clarence 14–15
Perry, Cdre Matthew 36
Phillips, Admiral Tom 150, 222–4, 234, 294, 296
Phillips, R/A A.J.J. 141
Pincher, Chapman 116
Pineau, Roger 157
Pitcairn-Jones, Cdr L.J. 163–4
Pocock, Guy 44, 300
Pollen, Arthur 275, 321
Pommern (Ger) 121
Pool, Bernard 262
Pope, Dudley 262
Portsmouth 231–2
Possony, Stefan 36
Postgate, Raymond 31
Potter, Admiral E.B. 127
Pound, Admiral Sir Dudley 51–2, 137, 139, 149, 158–61, 214, 217–20, 222, 228, 234–6, 239–41, 244–6, 248, 250–1, 292–3
  see also under Roskill
Powell, Rev J.P. 262
PQ.17 convoy disaster 136–40, 149, 158–61, 218–19
Prince of Wales, HMS 53, 149–51, 154, 214, 218, 222–3, 228, 249, 285, 290–1, 292–4
Princeton University 18, 25
Prinz Eugen (Ger) 53, 120
Purvis, Sir Charles Kennedy 62

Queen Elizabeth, RMS 157
Queen Mary, HMS 121, 124

Radford, USS 56–7
Ramillies, HMS 47
Ranft, Professor Bryan 250, 262, 270
Ranke, Leopold von 6
Rawson, Geoffrey 254
Read, Conyers 27–8
Reagan, Governor Ronald 279
Redman, Sidney 133
Reeves, Admiral Joseph M 58–60
Reischauer, Edwin O. 5, 30–1
Renown, HMS 45–6
Repulse, HMS 149–51, 154, 214, 218, 222, 228, 249, 285, 290–1, 292–4
Reviews in European History 241
Richards, Admiral Sir Frederick (1SL) 22
Richmond, Admiral Sir Herbert William 9, 20, 22–3, 38, 69–79, 81–2, 143–4, 155, 182, 218, 307, 312
  diaries 72–7, 80–1, 84–5
  proposes a Naval General Staff 74, 78
  The Navy in the War of 1739-48 70
  review of *Dreanought to Scapa Flow* 115
  Statesmen and Sea Power 72–3, 297
  works 85
River Plate, battle of 54
Riviere, Mrs Michael 226
Robertson, Rich 280–1
Rockefeller Foundation 198, 293–4, 310
Rodger, Nicholas 218, 275
Roosevelt, President F.D. 26, 58, 61, 138
Ropp, Theodore 25, 79–80
Rose, Kenneth 186, 237, 273
Roskill, Elizabeth Charlotte (second wife) 48–50, 146, 156–7, 202, 298, 309–10, 312
Roskill, Stephen Wentworth 8–9, 40–67, 70, 134–71, 140, 163, 167, 202, 217, 234, 262, 264, 281
  birth and family 33, 40–4, 48–50, 272, 299–300, 307–9, 312–14
    see also Roskill, Elizabeth
  character 40, 44, 46–7, 51, 54, 57, 59–61, 63, 67, 136, 201, 207, 239, 299, 302, 310, 314, 318–19
  education 192, 198, 312
  naval career 42–67, 198, 308, 310, 318
    gunnery specialisation 47–9, 52–3, 59, 223, 275, 303
    Bikini Atoll report 62–5, 67, 142, 262
  academic career 47, 308
    appointed to Cabinet Office 134–5, 142–5, 196–9, 303, 309–10, 317
    see also The War at Sea under works *below*
    to Churchill College 171, 200–1, 297–8, 307
    Lees Knowles lecturer at Cambridge 297
    visiting lecturer at Annapolis 307
  and Beatty papers 252, 262, 269, 272–6, 313
  and Churchill 152, 219–22, 235–6, 312
  criticisms of Admiralty 54, 149, 158, 162, 226, 275–6
  and Harper papers 274–5
  honours 213, 307–9, 312
    CBE 213, 311–12
    Chesney Medal (RUSI) 304–7, 310
    Fellow of British Academy 307, 309
    Legion of Merit 61

proposed for knighthood 310–12, 315
ill-health 49, 56–7, 65, 142, 144, 150, 154, 156, 263, 265, 299, 305, 309–10, 313–14
relations with Marder 168, 171, 213–14, 267, 276, 290
   good relations and assistance 121, 133, 198–9, 201–2, 207–8, 212–13, 246–7, 254, 262, 267, 275, 303–4, 306–7
      Festschrift 289–90
   criticisms and reviews of Marder 126, 198–200, 245–6, 290, 305–6, 312
   quarrels with Marder 84, 171, 186, 212–51, 216–51, 266 10–11, 276, 303–5, 304, 317–18, 320
      about post-Armistice deadline 199–202, 205, 216, 290
      over Churchill 235–41, 247–50, 252, 304, 317
         interference with Admirals and naval affairs 150, 217, 219–22, 234–8, 249–50
         and Pound 214, 218–19, 239–41, 247–52
      over Dakar 245
      over Ethiopian Crisis article 216–17
      over Hankey papers 204–12, 204–16, 216, 239, 247, 251–2, 290, 306–7, 317
      over Harper papers, Jutland and Beatty 126–7, 202, 252–3, 259–68, 274–6, 303–4, 317
      over his assistance to Marder 216–17
      over Pound, Dakar and Gibraltar 245–6, 248–50, 252, 292–3
      over sources 240
views on history 195–8
works
   articles, lectures and papers 67, 84–5, 142, 222, 299
   Churchill and the Admirals 221–2, 224
   review of Marder's *Portrait of an Admiral* 79
   Sir Dudley Pound: a Balanced View 221–2
   The Strategy of Sea Power: Its Development and Application 297
   Thoughts on Leadership 300
   Truth and Criticism in History - and Jutland 143, 253
   books
      Admiral of the Fleet Earl Beatty, The Last Naval Hero: an Intimate

Biography 45, 127, 252, 254–5, 268–9, 270–3, 275–6, 308, 319–20
The Art of Leadership 199, 300
autobiography *'A Sailor's Ditty Box'* (unpublished) 303. 298, 304
Churchill and the Admirals 214, 226, 247–50, 292, 317
reviews
   Marder's letter 249–50
From the Dreadnought to Scapa Flow 306
Hankey, Man of Secrets 204 and on, 211–13, 247, 305, 308, 319
History of The War at Sea, 1939-1945 135–6, 143–5, 157, 170, 195, 198–9, 199, 202, 219–22, 225–6, 233, 235, 240, 243, 253, 290, 305, 308, 319–20
   Vol 1: *The Defensive* 135, 146–56, 219
      appendix *The Secret Capture* 168, 199, 308
   Vol 2: *The Period of Balance* 135, 146–7, 156–64, 219
   Vol 3: *The Offensive* 164–6, 199
HMS *Warspite* 50, 168, 199, 253
Jellicoe Papers Vol II (ed) 260–9
A Merchant Fleet in War: Alfred Holt and Company 309
Naval Air Documents 262, 274, 303, 310, 319
Naval Policy Between The Wars, 1919-1929 168–70, 199, 202, 214, 217, 271–2
   Vol 1 199, 212
   Vol 2 203, 319
The Navy at War (summary of *War At Sea*) 169
The Strategy of Sea Power: Its Development and Application (lectures) 199, 201
White Ensign: The British Navy at War, 1929-1945 199
talks
   talk to RUSI *Hankey - Prince of Secretaries* 307
TV series 'The Admirals' 303
death, funeral and memorial service 61, 314–15
reputation 65, 169, 171, 262, 295, 302, 305, 308–9, 315–16, 154
Rowan, Sir Leslie 227

INDEX

Rowse, A.L. 96, 99
Royal Historical Society 190
Royal Oak, HMS 217
Royal Sovereign, HMS 47–8
RUSI 178, 182, 190, 197, 241, 252, 259–60, 263–4, 267–8
 Chesney Medal for Roskill 304–7, 310
 RUSI Journal 238–9, 248, 251, 259–60, 262, 265, 267–8
Ryan, Anthony 262

Sainsbury, Captain A.B. 24, 115–16, 186, 202, 216, 243, 250, 262, 265, 272, 274, 276, 304–6, 310–12
Saratoga, USS 64
Scapa Flow 80, 97, 125, 217, 225–6, 230
 scuttling of German fleet at 130, 184
Scharnhorst (Ger) 224–5
Scheer, Admiral Reinhard 120–3, 268, 274
Schofield, Admiral B.B. 166
Schurman, Donald 128, 233, 262, 302
 The Education of a Navy 84
Seal, Sir Eric 148, 153, 233–6, 238–9, 248, 251
 comments on Roskill 233, 238, 303–4, 317
Selborne, Earl 89–90
Selkirk, Earl of 112
Seymour, Captain Sir Ralph 202
Shimada, Professor Shigetar 286
Shunzi Izaki, R/A 56
Sims, Admiral W.S., USN 80
Sinclair, Andrew 299
Sinclair, Dr Gregg 104
Slavin, Arthur Joe 178
Slessor, Jack 229
Slessor, Tim
 Ministries of Deception 226
Smith, Courtney 183
Smuts, General Jan 150
Snyder, Professor Lawrence 109–11
Society for the Propagation of Sea-Military Knowledge, The 71
Solomon Islands campaign 55–6
Somerville, Admiral of the Fleet Sir James 167, 245, 286
Spaatz, General Carl A. 62, 127–8
Spectator, The 20, 73, 78, 283
Spee, V/A Count Maximilian Graf von 71, 119
Spencer, Lord 12, 89, 92–3, 262
Stacey, Colonel Charles 163

Stalin, Joseph 13
Star-Bulletin 34
Stark, Freya 309
Stavanger, bombardment of 224
Stead, W.T. 95
Steele, Cdr Gordon 16
Steinberg, Jonathan 262
Steiner, George and Zara 41, 44, 62, 299, 303
Stephenson, Brigadier John 182
Stewart, Marion 302, 313–14
St Louis, USS 56
Strong, USS 55
Subiyaki (Japan) 30
Suffolk, HMS 224
Sumida, Jon 275, 302
Sunday Telegraph, The 170, 200, 219, 223, 273, 300, 319
Sunday Times, The 170, 226, 300, 319

Tahiti 296
Talbot, V/A A.G. 237
Taylor, A.J.P. 36, 96, 99, 114, 126, 184, 187–8, 192, 206, 214, 227–8, 243, 266, 286, 293, 316–17, 320
 interview with Marder 9, 316
Tedder, Lord 298
Terraine, John 244
Thatcher, Margaret 311
Thursfield, R/A H.G. 74, 80–3, 88, 94
'Tiger' convoy to Egypt 155
Time and Tide 20–1
Times, The 8, 23, 74, 91, 94, 99, 133, 149, 185, 211, 213, 216, 239, 263, 266, 268, 280
Times Higher Educational Supplement 216, 238
Times Literary Supplement, The 3, 80, 82–4, 95–6, 134, 186, 214, 245, 247, 249–50, 283, 290, 317
Tirpitz, Grossadmiral Alfred von 17, 98
Tirpitz (Ger) 139
Todman, Daniel 219
Togo, Admiral Heihachiro 289
Toland, John 292
torpedoes 88–9
Tovey, Admiral Sir John 139, 158–9
Toyuda, Admiral Soemu 291
Trafalgar, battle of 120
Tree, Edith 254
Trend, Sir Burke 169–70, 199
Trevelyan, G.M. 74, 286

Trevelyan, Sir Charles 43
Trevor-Roper, Hugh 99, 214, 317
Trondheim 231, 235–6
Troubridge, Admiral Sir Ernest 10
Tsushima, battle of 291
Tuscaloosa, USS 138, 140

'Ultra' project 66, 145, 168, 220
United States Naval Institute Proceedings 69, 87
Usborne, Admiral C.V. 121

Vagts, Dr Alfred 18–19
van den Bergh, Henry 48
Vansittart, Baron 301
Vereker, Lt Charles 54
Vernon, HMS 89
Vian, Admiral Philip 167
Victory, HMS 89
Villa, Brian Loring 6
Vogt, Alfred 80
von Ranke, Leopold 196

Walker, Donald 179
Waller, Admiral James W.A. 58–61, 240
Warner, Oliver 262
Warspite, HMS 47, 50–3
Washington, Captain Basil 45
Washington, USS 139
Waters, Lt-Cdr D.W. 166
Watt, D.C. 170
Waugh, Evelyn 243–4
Webster, Sir Charles 127
  The Strategic Air Offensive Against Germany, 1939-1945 134
Wedgwood, Dame Veronica 262
Welsh, Dr Edwin 208
Welsh, Robert 187
Wemyss, Admiral Sir Rosslyn 254, 256, 270
Westcott, Professor Alan 25
Wheeler-Bennett, Sir John
  Action This Day: Working with Churchill 227
White, Arnold 95
White, Gerald T. 178
White, John Albert 34, 107
Whitmore, Clive 311–12
Wichita, USS 138
Wilhelm II, Kaiser 11, 17, 130
Wilhelmshaven 120, 122
Wilkinson, Burke 80

Wilkinson, Spencer 11
Williams, Brigadier E.T. 183
Williams, Glyndwr 262
Williams, John
  The Guns of Dakar 243
Wilson, Harold 11, 116, 170
Wilson, President Woodrow 23
Wilson, Provost William 111
Winterbotham, F.W.
  The Ultra Secret 220
Winton, John 225–6
Wistaria, HMS 47
Woods, D. 170
Woodward, David 99. 98, 123–4, 316
Woodward, Sir Llewellyn
  Great Britain and the German Navy 23
Wright, Louis B. 282
Wylie, Captain F.J. 141

Yamamoto, Admiral Isoroku 286–7
Yexley, Lionel 24–5
Yorkshire Post 77

Zeebrugge 130, 231
Zeppelin airships 122
Ziegler, Philip 286